BLOOD IN THE FIELDS

MATTHEW PHILIPP WHELAN

BLOOD IN THE FIELDS

Óscar Romero, Catholic Social Teaching,
and Land Reform

The Catholic University of America Press

Washington, D.C.

Thanks to Carolyn Forché for permission to publish lines from
her poem "Ourselves or Nothing" from the collection *The Country
Between Us*.

Library of Congress Cataloging-in-Publication Data
Names: Whelan, Matthew Philipp, author.
Title: Blood in the fields : Óscar Romero, Catholic social teaching,
and land reform / Matthew Philipp Whelan.
Description: Washington, D.C.: The Catholic University of America
Press, 2020. | Includes bibliographical references and index. |
Summary: "Examines the life and martyrdom of Archbishop Oscar
Romero in El Salvador through the lens of agrarian reform, arguing
that his advocacy for the just distribution of land drew heavily on
Catholic Social Doctrine and its conviction that creation
is a common gift"— Provided by publisher.
Identifiers: LCCN 2019048962 | ISBN 9780813232522 (cloth) |
ISBN 9780813232539 (ebook)
Subjects: LCSH: Romero, Óscar A. (Óscar Arnulfo), Saint, 1917–1980.
Classification: LCC BX4705.R669 W43 2020 | DDC 282.092 [B]—dc23
LC record available at https://lccn.loc.gov/2019048962

For Natalie

CONTENTS

The seeds of this book were first sown during my time as a volunteer with Peace Corps Honduras's Hillside Family Farming project from 2000 to 2002. In Honduras, I lived in a small hamlet in that country's central highlands and worked with farmers growing maize, beans, and squash for subsistence as well as coffee for cash income. While there, I often heard stories about the Jesuits of the Aguán valley of Northern Honduras, who supported agricultural cooperatives and worked with their neighbors to help secure access to land to farm—similar to Óscar Romero's friend, Blessed Rutilio Grande, SJ, who was slain at the outset of Romero's ministry as archbishop of San Salvador.

Where I lived in Honduras, like in the Aguán—and like in Romero's El Salvador—there existed a tension between the valley and the hills: between the extensive agricultural plantations, owned by few people, and dedicated to export agricultural production, on the one hand, and the smallholdings of the countless families struggling—or *luchando* (fighting), as they put it—to secure a livelihood on that nation's denuded and eroded hillsides, on the other. As I worked with my friends and neighbors or walked the hamlet's paths, the vast fields of *caña* (sugar cane) below were often perceptible through the pine trees. The contrast between the valley and the hills seared itself into my mind along with the question, how to hold the tension between these spaces together? It was during this time that I first traveled to El Salvador, to the sites associated with Romero's life and death, and it first began to dawn on me how

Romero faced a similar question, to which his life became an answer.

It is fitting for a work centering upon gifts to begin by acknowledging what others have contributed to it. I must give thanks first to my Honduran friends from Las Joyas del Carballo and from San Marcos, especially Juan Antonio, Delmy, Alex, Javier, Mila, Pedro, Tina, Ronny, Lady, Samuel, Hector, Rosa, and Beatriz. They taught me most of what I know about agriculture—and a great deal about the gospel in the process. *Gracias.*

This book began at Duke University under the guidance of Stanley Hauerwas. I first started writing to Stanley while I was living in Central America. His correspondence during that time—and his belief that I had something to say about "dirt"—has been life-giving. Paul Griffiths has also been unfailing in his support of this project and of me. Edgardo Colón-Emeric invited me to participate in a Romero reading group he led, and later in Duke Divinity School's Course of Study program in Ahuachapán, El Salvador. I am grateful that he shared his love of San Romero de las Américas and of El Salvador with me. Warren Smith was part of one of those trips to El Salvador, and conversations with him about Gregory of Nyssa and Ambrose, and about connections between them and Romero, were immensely beneficial. Reinhard Hütter was a champion of this project from beginning to end, and he offered much-needed advice and assistance at some particularly critical points. And although they might find it difficult to discern, Willie Jennings and David Aers's influence upon what follows runs deep. Finally, Susan Keefe passed away just before I began writing, and I have missed her friendship and felt her absence ever since. However, the fruit of several independent studies with her and insights from countless conversations found their way into these pages.

Generous funding from Duke's Graduate Program in Religion and Graduate School facilitated several research trips to San Salvador: to La Biblioteca de Teología Juan Ramón Moreno at the Universidad Centroamericana (UCA) and to the Archivo Histórico del Archidiócesis de San Salvador. María Ester Cerón and her staff at La Biblioteca de Teología Juan Ramón Moreno were extraordinarily helpful, as were Rafael Flores and Rubén Ortiz at the Archivo Histórico del Archidiócesis. Thanks also to Morgen MacIntosh Hodgetts, the Special Collections Instruction

Librarian/Archivist at the John T. Richardson Library at DePaul University, for assisting me in navigating the papers of Rev. James Brockman, SJ.

A week-long Lumen Christi Institute summer seminar with Russell Hittinger renewed my interest in Catholic social teaching and helped me see its significance for approaching Romero.

It has been a great joy to have written on a figure who, even in death, continues to be surrounded by those who love and remember him—and who go out of their way to help others do the same. Among the many who offered help were Denise Wright and Rev. Robert Pelton, CSC, at the Kellogg Institute for International Studies at Notre Dame; Luisiana de Beltrán and Mons. Ricardo Urioste (of blessed memory) at the Fundación Monseñor Óscar Arnulfo Romero; Julian Filochowski at the Romero Trust; and Roberto Cuéllar of the Instituto Interamericano de Derechos Humanos. Whenever I was in El Salvador, José Jorge Simán fed me, made introductions, and shared stories. Rodrigo Guerra y Guerra did the same. Conversations with Rene Aquliz Ventura, Carlos Gregorio López Bernal, Adolfo Bonilla Bonilla, Jorge Zablah, and above all Claudia Marlene Rivera Navarrete were illuminating. For over a decade, Carlos Colorado has run *Super Martyrio*, a blog dedicated to the life, death, and legacy of Romero and to chronicling his cause for beatification and canonization. Now, Carlos is following his cause for Doctor of the Church at *Eminens Doctrina*. Carlos knows more about Romero than just about anyone I know, and we are all fortunate that he devotes himself to sharing it with others.

It is often said that writing is a lonely process. But I have found the opposite to be the case, and it is a privilege to acknowledge my many companions. Over the course of bringing this book to completion, I participated in two writing groups. The first—with Pete Jordan and Joseph Wolyniak—spanned continents. The second—with David Cramer, Jordan Rowan Fannin, and Jenny Howell—took place in Waco, Texas. I am grateful for conversations with them, for their feedback and encouragement, and, above all, for their friendship. This book is better because of each of them.

Along the way, I also benefited greatly from conversations with Fr. Ashley Beck, Carole Baker, Jorge Burmicky, Tom Bushlack, Peter Casarella, Karla Coleman, Damian Costello, Sarah and Joel Decker, Emily Edmundson, Tommy Givens, Ben Haworth, Barry Harvey, Theodora Hawksley, Karen Kilby, Nicholas Krause, David Lantigua, Paul Martens, Tom McLaughlin, Rob Minor, Maria and Jeff Morrow, Sheryl Overmyer, Bharat Ranganathan, Mandy Rodgers-Gates, Emmanuel Roldan, Miguel Romero, Alessandro Rovati, Ismael Ruiz-Millán, Francisco Solorzano, Debbie Thompson, Luis Vera, Todd Walatka, Norman Wirzba, and Jessica Wong. Various friends and colleagues read the manuscript—or parts of it—and offered insightful and indispensable feedback: Ben Dillon, Nathan Eubank, Willis Jenkins, John Kiess, Travis Knoll, T. J. Lang, Sean Larsen, and Greg Lee. In addition to reading the manuscript, Victor Hinojosa offered his expertise on Latin American politics, and his encouragement helped keep me and this work grounded. Stephen Pluháček reminded me of what lay beyond the field's edge. And as always, Jonathan Tran gave more than he knows.

I am fortunate to have had the opportunity to present my research on Romero at various venues, among them the New Wine New Wineskins Symposium at Notre Dame in 2012 and 2014, the Catholic Theological Association of Great Britain in 2014, the Society of Christian Ethics in 2016, and the annual Romero Days conference at Notre Dame in 2018. The questions I received during those sessions helped clarify the project and hopefully improved it as well.

Thanks are due to the good people at the Catholic University of America Press, especially John Martino, Brian Roach, Theresa Walker, and Aldene Fredenburg. Thanks are also due to Baylor University's Department of Religion, above all to the chair, Bill Bellinger, whose support meant the very adept Maggi Jones was able to assist me in various tasks to bring this book (finally) to completion.

I am blessed beyond measure by my family—my parents, Will and Pam; my parents-in-law, Suzi and Mike; and my siblings and siblings-in-law: Kate, Joseph, Elizabeth, Kevin, Kiraz, Rosalind, Victoria, and Mathew. My parents deserve a special word of thanks. My father retired from work in hunger relief just as this project was getting off the ground. Since then, he has devoted weeks to my children so that I could write; he read multiple drafts of the manuscript and offered detailed commentary; he passed along articles and reading suggestions; and he was always ready and eager to converse about the project. But above all, so many of the questions and concerns that animate it were given to me by him, as well as by my mother. Both of them beautifully model, in different ways, how love takes root and bears fruit in the world.

My first daughter, Chora, was born right as I began doctoral studies at Duke, and my other two daughters, Edith and Simone, were born during its middle and end, respectively. Without them, I would have been much more productive and this book would have been written much faster. A very meager price to pay for their company. Learning to receive and love my girls alongside my wife, Natalie, has been the most wonderful gift of all. Her daily goodness and love help our center hold. Her fingerprints are on every page of what follows, and her words and thoughts have steadily interwoven with my words and thoughts. Though what follows bears my name, in the most important ways, it is really ours.

NOVEMBER 1, 2018
SOLEMNITY OF ALL SAINTS

ABBREVIATIONS AND ACRONYMS

ABBREVIATIONS

Diario	Monseñor Óscar Arnulfo Romero, *Su Diario* (San Salvador: Imprenta Criterio, 2000)
Diario Official	Archivo digital del Diario Oficial de la República de El Salvador (https://imprentanacional.gob.sv/archivo-digital-del-diario-oficial/)
Cartas	*Monseñor Romero, Sus cartas personales, pensamientos, y consejos* (San Salvador: Imprenta Criterio, 2004)
Evangelii Nuntiandi	Paul VI, Apostolic Exhortation *Evangelii Nuntiandi*, December 8, 1975 (http://w2.vatican.va/content/paul-vi/en/apost_exhortations/documents/hf_p-vi_exh_19751208_evangelii-nuntiandi.html)
Gaudium et Spes	Vatican Council II, Pastoral Constitution on the Church in the Modern World, *Gaudium et Spes*, December 7, 1965 (http://www.vatican.va/archive/hist_councils/ii_vatican_council/documents/vat-ii_const_19651207_gaudium-et-spes_en.html)
Homilías	Óscar Romero, *Homilías Monseñor Óscar A. Romero*, ed. Miguel Cavada Diez, 6 vols. (San Salvador: UCA Editores, 2005–9)
Lumen Gentium	Vatican Council II, Dogmatic Constitution on the Church, *Lumen Gentium*, November 21, 1964 (http://www.vatican.va/archive/hist_councils/ii_vatican_council/documents/vat-ii_const_19641121_lumen-gentium_en.html)

<table>
<tr><td>Medellín</td><td>Episcopado Latinoamericano, Conferencias Generales: Río de Janeiro, Medellín, Puebla, Santo Domingo (Santiago de Chile: Ediciones San Pablo, 1993)</td></tr>
<tr><td>Populorum Progressio</td><td>Paul VI, Encyclical Letter Populorum Progressio, March, 26, 1967 (http://w2.vatican.va/content/paul-vi/en/encyclicals/documents/hf_p-vi_enc_26031967_populorum.html)</td></tr>
<tr><td>Puebla</td><td>Episcopado Latinoamericano, Conferencias Generales: Río de Janeiro, Medellín, Puebla, Santo Domingo (Santiago de Chile: Ediciones San Pablo, 1993)</td></tr>
<tr><td>Quadragesimo Anno</td><td>Pius XI, Encyclical Letter Quadragesimo Anno, May 15, 1931 (http://w2.vatican.va/content/pius-xi/en/encyclicals/documents/hf_p-xi_enc_19310515_quadragesimo-anno.html)</td></tr>
<tr><td>Rerum Novarum</td><td>Leo XIII, Encyclical Letter Rerum novarum, May 15, 1891 (http://w2.vatican.va/content/leo-xiii/en/encyclicals/documents/hf_l-xiii_enc_15051891_rerum-novarum.html)</td></tr>
<tr><td>Sertum Laetitiae</td><td>Pius XII, Encyclical Letter Sertum Laetitiae, November 1, 1939 (http://w2.vatican.va/content/pius-xii/en/encyclicals/documents/hf_p-xii_enc_01111939_sertum-laetitiae.html)</td></tr>
<tr><td>ST</td><td>Thomas Aquinas, Summa Theologiae, 61 vols., Blackfriars (Cambridge: Cambridge University Press, 2006)</td></tr>
<tr><td>La voz de los sin voz</td><td>La voz de los sin voz: La palabra viva de Monseñor Romero, ed. Rodolfo Cardenal, Ignacio Martín-Baro, and Jon Sobrino (San Salvador: UCA Editores, 1980)</td></tr>
</table>

ACRONYMS

<table>
<tr><td>ANEP</td><td>Asociación Nacional de la Empresa Privada (National Association of Private Enterprise)</td></tr>
<tr><td>ARENA</td><td>Alianza Republicana Nacionalista (National Republican Alliance)</td></tr>
<tr><td>CEDES</td><td>Conferencia Episcopal de El Salvador (Episcopal Conference of El Salvador)</td></tr>
<tr><td>CELAM</td><td>Consejo Episcopal Latinoamericano (Latin American Episcopal Council)</td></tr>
</table>

FARO	Frente Agrario de la Región Oriental (Agrarian Front of the Eastern Region)
FECCAS	Federación Cristiana de Campesinos Salvadoreños (Christian Federation of Salvadoran Peasants)
FMLN	Frente Farabundo Martí para la Liberación Nacional (Farabundo Martí National Liberation Front)
FUNPROCOOP	Fundación Promotora de Cooperativas (Foundation for the Promotion of Cooperatives)
ISTA	Instituto Salvadoreño de Transformación Agraria (Salvadoran Institute of Agrarian Transformation)
JRG	Junta Revolucionaria de Gobierno (Revolutionary Government Junta)
ORDEN	Organización Democrática Nacionalista (National Democratic Organization)
PCS	Partido Comunista Salvadoreño (Communist Party of El Salvador)
SEDAC	Secretariado Episcopal de América Central (Episcopal Secretariat of Central America)
SSI	Secretariado Social Interdiocesano (Inter-Diocesan Social Secretariat)
UCA	Universidad Centroamericana (University of Central America)
UGB	Unión de Guerrera Blanca (White Warriors Union)
UTC	Unión de Trabajadores del Campo (Farm Workers' Union)
YSAX	Radio station of the Archdiocese of San Salvador
WMPM	World Meeting of Popular Movements

... in Salvador

where the blood will never soak

into the ground ...

> —Carolyn Forché,
> "Ourselves or
> Nothing"

INTRODUCTION

—Óscar Romero, *La dimensión política de la fe desde la opción por los pobres*

On the morning of February 18, 1979—the seventh Sunday of ordinary
time—Archbishop Óscar Romero ascended the pulpit of the Metropolitan Cathedral of San Salvador to deliver his homily, "Christ, the Church's
Perpetually New Word." He was not only addressing the crowd thronging
the cathedral that morning, but also the tens of thousands listening in
El Salvador and beyond through the transmission of the archdiocesan
radio station YSAX.[1] It had been about a month since he last said mass

Unless otherwise indicated, all translations from Spanish, French, Italian, and Portu-
guese are my own. While I have tried to be sensitive to gender inclusivity in my own render-
ings, I have left other material, such as official translations of magisterial documents, as they
are. Biblical citations in nonquoted material are from the New Revised Standard Version.

1. Romero's homilies were enormously popular, and most people in El Salvador listened
to them. As Romero's renown grew, the homilies were broadcast to an international audi-
ence; James R. Brockman, *Romero: A Life* (Maryknoll, N.Y.: Orbis, 2005), 64; Scott Wright,

there because of his participation in the Third General Assembly of the Consejo Episcopal Latinoamericano (Latin American Episcopal Council, CELAM) in Puebla de los Ángeles, Mexico. The homily that Sunday morning was, among other things, a reflection upon his time in Puebla in the light of the scripture readings for the day.

By this point in his tenure as archbishop, there had been a notable shift in Romero's homilies. They had become longer, often lasting for well over an hour. Moreover, like the work of the archdiocese more generally, they increasingly assumed the burden of truth-maintenance in the midst of the disinformation campaign of the military regime and official media outlets.[2] Romero typically concluded his homilies with lengthy discussions of church life and the week's events, offering insights into what was actually happening in El Salvador. For this reason, Roberto Morozzo della Rocca refers to Romero's cathedral as "a living school of journalism," where reporters could learn what media outlets either ignored or falsified.[3] "It is no accident," he writes, "that many defined the homilies of Romero with a single word: truth."[4]

Just days prior to Romero's departure for Puebla, he received news of the death of a priest and a nun. Father Octavio Ortiz and Sister Chepita were offering a retreat in the parish of San Antonio Abad when, early one morning, security forces battered the gate with an armored car and entered with guns drawn. Father Octavio was later found in the courtyard, his head and face crushed by the vehicle. The corpses of four armed young men were on the roof. While the national press ran stories of a fierce gunfight, Romero cast doubt on the official narrative. It was discovered not long after that the dead men were dragged to the roof and pistols then placed in their hands.[5]

Óscar Romero and the Communion of the Saints: A Biography (Maryknoll, N.Y.: Orbis, 2009), 18–20, 56–57, 120–21.

2. Roberto Morozzo della Rocca, *Primero Dios: Vida de Monseñor Romero* (Buenos Aires: Edhasa, 2010), 15; see also Brockman, *Romero*, 6.

3. Morozzo della Rocca, *Primero Dios*, 15.

4. Morozzo della Rocca, *Primero Dios*, 286.

5. Brockman, *Romero*, 154–55. See also Secretaria de Comunicación Social del Arzobispado, "Boletín Informativo Internacional No. 55" (San Salvador, January 1979); Secretaria de Comunicación Social del Arzobispado, "Boletín Informativo Internacional No. 56" (San Salvador, January 1979).

Ortiz and Chepita were respectively the fourth priest and the first nun to be murdered since Romero assumed the archbishopric in 1977, further confirming that, in the words of the Jesuit Rutilio Grande, "It is dangerous to be a Christian in this place," where "the mere proclamation of the Gospel is considered subversive."[6] Approximately a month after he preached these words, Grande was gunned down with Manuel Solorzano and Miguel Lemus in the sugar cane fields outside of Aguilares on his way to celebrate mass. The killings of this period lent reality to the infamous slogan scrawled on walls and distributed in leaflets in El Salvador: "Be a patriot, kill a priest."[7] In this predominantly Catholic country, the military regime and its allies saw large segments of the church as a foreign organism that they were moving to surround and expel.

One of Romero's purposes in his February 18, 1979, homily is to relate what is happening in El Salvador to the gathering at Puebla and to remind his flock of the wider communion of which they are a part. "I want to place my words today," Romero says, in relation to the Word of God "and the concrete message that the bishops gathered at Puebla directed to all the people of Latin America."[8] For the message of Puebla, Romero believes, shows the church in Latin America to be a "living Church," which has something to say "to the whole world."[9]

Romero draws attention to a passage in which the bishops frame their examination of the Latin American reality: "If we focus our gaze on our Latin American world, what do we see? No deep scrutiny is necessary. The truth is that there is an ever-increasing distance between the many who have little and the few who have much."[10] Romero then comments:

6. Salvador Carranza, Miguel Cavada Diez, and Jon Sobrino, *XXV Aniversario de Rutilio Grande: Sus homilías* (San Salvador: Centro Monseñor Romero, UCA, 2002), 79.

7. Morozzo della Rocca, *Primero Dios*, 35.

8. Óscar Romero, *Homilías Monseñor Óscar A. Romero*, ed. Miguel Cavada Diez, 6 vols. (San Salvador: UCA Editores, 2005–9), 4:206. In what follows, I use this edition for the homilies Romero preached as archbishop, citing volume and page number.

9. Romero, *Homilías*, 4:206.

10. Romero, *Homilías*, 4:214–15, quoting from Puebla's "Mensaje a los pueblos de América Latina," in Episcopado Latinoamericano, *Conferencias Generales: Río de Janeiro, Medellín, Puebla, Santo Domingo* (Santiago de Chile: Ediciones San Pablo, 1993).

> These words … perfectly describe our Salvadoran reality … except that
> in El Salvador we must speak of the distance between the many who
> have nothing and the few who have everything. This is not communism.
> This is the message of Puebla, the message of the popes, the message
> John Paul II proclaimed in Santo Domingo, in Oaxaca, in Monterrey, and
> in Guadalajara: that the Church must serve human beings and guard
> their rights. And as the Holy Father stated in Santo Domingo, by "rights"
> we mean that *campesinos*[11] should have land, and that workers must be
> able to organize and to be paid just salaries.[12]

In this programmatic passage, Romero names two of the central pre-occupations that by 1979 had come to dominate his ministry as archbishop and the life of the church in El Salvador. The first is the problem of pervasive landlessness and the pressing need for the reform of agriculture. The second is the closely related problem of the persecution of workers' associations and organizations—particularly of rural and agricultural workers—as they sought to secure access to land, increase wages, and improve working conditions.

Romero also implies that broaching such problems courted the accusation of communism, which in El Salvador, like elsewhere in Latin America during this time, was often deadly. As Lesley Gill observes, "Fighting 'communists'" was "an enormously elastic category that could accommodate almost any critic of the status quo."[13] Indeed, it was so elastic that it included those like Romero who were not arguing for the abolition of private property, as communism did,[14] but rather for justice in the distribution of land.[15]

Yet Romero insists that facilitating access to land and protecting the ability to organize is not communism but church teaching—a teaching

---

11. *Campesino/a* refers to smallholders who subsist (or aspire to) by growing their own food, especially maize, beans, and other subsistence crops. They can be tenants, share-croppers, smallholders, squatters, claimants to untitled land, and so on. *Campesinado* refers to *campesinos* as a group.

12. Romero, *Homilías*, 4:214–15.

13. Lesley Gill, *The School of the Americas: Military Training and Political Violence in the Americas* (Durham, N.C.: Duke University Press, 2004), 10.

14. See Karl Marx and Friedrich Engels, *The Communist Manifesto* (New York: Penguin, 2004).

15. Brockman, *Romero*, 3.

founded on the theological claim that creation is a common gift to which all people have access. These are the preoccupations of Puebla, he says. Pope John Paul II spoke of them repeatedly throughout his journey to the Dominican Republic and Mexico in 1979.[16] Elsewhere in the homily, Romero describes the plan of the Instituto Salvadoreño de Transformación Agraria (Salvadoran Institute of Agrarian Transformation, ISTA) to distribute 26,293 hectares of land to 356 *campesino* households as an attempt to implement "the social doctrine of the Church."[17]

As the homily continues, Romero acknowledges that these preoccupations regarding land and work also intimately relate to the church's so-called preferential option for the poor.[18] Romero's point can be posed as a question: If God in Christ spanned the infinite distance between Creator and creation to heal sin and to share God's life with humankind, why would participants in this life accept the distances that wealth and property establish between one another? This is "the perpetually new Word" to which the title of Romero's homily alludes. Rightly understood, Romero claims, the preferential option for the poor is "an invitation to all people, across the lines of class" to assume these preoccupations—for land to farm, for living wages, for the ability to gather without suffering repression—as if they were *su propia causa* (their own cause), as if they held these preoccupations in common with the impoverished.[19]

This has important implications for property. According to Romero, commonplace understandings of property, in which property is regarded as essentially private and exclusionary, only exacerbate injustice. This is because people cannot learn to share the preoccupations of the impoverished if they understand their property to be exclusively their

16. See especially John Paul II's addresses in Santo Domingo and Oaxaca, which can be found in *Puebla: A Pilgrimage of Faith* (Boston: St. Paul Editions, 1979).

17. Romero, *Homilías*, 4:212–13, 280. See also *La Prensa Gráfica*, February 14, 1979; *El Diario de Hoy*, February 10, 1979. At the time, seven people held the targeted land.

18. Romero, *Homilías*, 4:216. As Gustavo Gutiérrez writes, the preferential option for the poor and its underlying Christology is "the most substantial part of the contribution from the life and theological reflection of the church in Latin America to the universal church"; Gutiérrez, "The Option for the Poor Arises from Faith in Christ," *Theological Studies* 70, no. 2 (2009): 318. See also Maria Clara Bingemer, *Latin American Theology: Roots and Branches* (Maryknoll, N.Y.: Orbis, 2016), 42.

19. Romero, *Homilías*, 4:216.

own, protecting it—by force if necessary—from the claims of those in need.[20] Instead, Romero continues, people must rediscover what he calls the "true social sense" of property, quoting from John Paul's opening address at Puebla: "When the growing wealth of a few parallels the growing poverty of the masses … the Church's teaching, according to which all private property bears a social mortgage (*hipoteca social*), acquires an urgent character."[21] Romero concludes this part of his homily with these words: "It is on this point that the message of Puebla is the history of our peoples (*la historia de nuestros pueblos*)."[22]

When Romero delivered this homily in 1979, the urgency about which John Paul spoke at Puebla was clear. In El Salvador, this teaching had become a flashpoint in a long-simmering societal and ecclesial conflict over land reform. By defending church teaching on property's social mortgage, Romero and many others were risking their lives.

Óscar Arnulfo Romero y Galdámez was born in 1917 in Ciudad Barrios, a small town in the province of San Miguel in the mountains of eastern El Salvador.[23] He was one of seven children born to Santos Romero, a local telegraph operator, and his wife, Guadalupe de Jesús Galdámez, a primary school teacher. In addition to Santos's work as a telegraph operator, he farmed 104 acres of land that he inherited from his father-in-law. He planted coffee, cacao, coconut palms, and nance. Óscar and his bothers assisted their father not only by delivering telegrams, but also by working on El Pulgo, as the farm was known.[24]

Although his father apprenticed him to a local carpenter, Óscar's sights were set on the priesthood from a very young age. In 1931, at the age of thirteen, he entered the Claretians minor seminary in San Miguel. After completing his studies in 1937, he briefly entered the Jesuit semi-

---

20. Romero, *Homilías*, 4:216.

21. Romero, *Homilías*, 4:216.

22. Romero, *Homilías*, 4:216.

23. This biographical sketch of Romero draws especially upon Jesús Delgado, *Óscar A. Romero* (San Salvador: UCA Editores, 1990); Brockman, *Romero*; Morozzo della Rocca, *Primero Dios.*

24. Emily Wade Will, *Archbishop Óscar Romero: The Making of a Martyr* (Eugene, Ore.: Resource, 2016), 13.

nary, San José de la Montaña, in San Salvador, where he was selected by the bishop of San Miguel, Juan Antonio Dueñas, to study in Rome.

Around this time, the family lost El Pulgo because of financial difficulties and plummeting coffee prices in the wake of the Great Depression. This story of land loss was not unique to Romero's family. It fueled social unrest across El Salvador, which culminated in the 1932 *campesino* uprising remembered simply as *La Matanza* (The Massacre) because of how it was crushed by the military, leaving thousands—perhaps tens of thousands—dead.[25] State control of the country by the military, which began the previous year, lasted for most of the following five decades, officially ending in the final year of Romero's tenure as archbishop in 1979. It was the longest period of uninterrupted military rule in Latin American history.

While in Rome, Romero studied at the Jesuit-run Gregorian University and resided at their Colegio Pío Latino Americano. He imbibed Jesuit spirituality and participated in the Spiritual Exercises of Ignatius of Loyola. These years were decisive ones for Romero's formation. They led to a lifelong admiration for Pope Pius XI and his resistance to fascism in Italy and Nazism in Germany, which Romero emulated as archbishop when he faced the repression of the Salvadoran state.[26] The Rome years also offered Romero an encounter with the church as a truly worldwide communion. Until the very end of his life, Romero placed great emphasis upon this communion and the church in El Salvador's participation in it. As archbishop, for instance, he frequently spoke about the martyrs being produced by the persecution in El Salvador as a gift to the church in all lands.

Romero was ordained a priest in 1942. After a brief period in the parish of Anamorós in La Unión province near the Honduran border, Romero went to San Miguel to serve as Bishop Miguel Angel Machado's personal secretary. For the next twenty years, Romero lived and worked in San

25. It still remains unclear how many died. General Calderón said that his troops had killed 4,800 communists, but others have claimed the toll is as high as 25,000–30,000; Jeffrey L. Gould and Aldo Lauria-Santiago, *To Rise in Darkness: Revolution, Repression, and Memory in El Salvador, 1920–1932* (Durham, N.C.: Duke University Press, 2008), 233–34.

26. See Pius XI, Encyclical Letter *Non Abbiamo Bisogno* (June 29, 1931); Pius XI, Encyclical Letter *Mit Brennender Sorge* (March 14, 1937). Unless otherwise indicated, all magisterial documents are from http://www.vatican.va.

Miguel, his responsibilities increasing considerably. He was assigned as a priest of the cathedral parish. He collaborated closely with the diocesan radio station and regularly wrote for and eventually became editor of the weekly diocesan newspaper, *El Chaparratique*. During this time, he also served as the rector of the minor seminary and actively assisted the numerous Catholic associations and organizations of the diocese, among other tasks. He even helped found a workers' association of shoe shiners for children, opening parish property in order to provide them food and shelter.

Romero was summoned to San Salvador in 1967 to become secretary of the Conferencia Episcopal de El Salvador (Episcopal Conference of El Salvador, CEDES), and he resided in the San José de la Montaña seminary. Soon Romero was also named executive secretary of the Secretariado Episcopal de América Central (Episcopal Secretariat of Central America, SEDAC). This was a tumultuous time for El Salvador, which briefly went to war with neighboring Honduras in 1969. The war was the result of land reform legislation enacted by the Honduran government, which expelled hundreds of thousands of undocumented Salvadorans who had settled on land in Honduras targeted for reform.

In 1970, at the age of fifty-three, Romero became auxiliary bishop for the Archdiocese of San Salvador. This was the year of the Congress on Land Reform, organized by the Legislative Assembly in response to those forced to return to El Salvador from Honduras. As bishop, Romero chose as his motto *Sentir con la Iglesia* (from the Latin *sentire cum Ecclesia*), which means "to think or feel with the Church." It was a phrase that had long been important to him, one with roots in the Spiritual Exercises.

In 1974, Romero became the second bishop of Santiago de María, the newest, smallest, and poorest of El Salvador's five dioceses, whose boundaries stretched from the Pacific coast to the mountainous border with Honduras. Santiago de María was mostly rural, without a large urban center. Many of its inhabitants worked as day laborers on large plantations. During harvest season, migrants from all over the country streamed into Santiago de María. The misery and impoverishment of those Romero encountered moved him tremendously.[27] This was a time in which the re-

27. On this point, see Zacarías Díez and Juan Macho, *"En Santiago de Maria me topé con la miseria": Dos años de la vida de Mons. Romero (1975–1976)* (Costa Rica, 1994).

pression of the Salvadoran state was beginning to mount, with four separate massacres between 1974 and 1975. One occurred in Santiago de María itself in the hamlet Tres Calles, where National Guardsmen shot and subsequently dismembered five *campesinos* after having dragged them from their homes in the middle of the night. In an attempt to quell the growing unrest in the countryside, the regime of Colonel Arturo Armando Molina moved forward with a land reform initiative, one that targeted Romero's diocese.

On February 22, 1977, Romero became archbishop of the metropolitan see of San Salvador.[28] Tensions had continued to rise in the country, largely the result of the fallout over President Molina's attempted land reform in 1975–76 and retaliation for the church's support of it under Romero's predecessor, Archbishop Luis Chávez y González. In 1976 alone, the Jesuit-run Universidad Centroamericana (University of Central America, UCA) was bombed six times and the archdiocesan publishing house once. In the days immediately surrounding Archbishop Romero's installation, security forces captured and expelled three priests from San Salvador, torturing two of them. Moreover, massive demonstrations filled

28. According to Jesús Delgado, in the run-up to the selection of the new archbishop, Emanuele Gerada, the papal nuncio, polled forty members of the "influential class" of El Salvador, and Romero was the unanimous choice; see Delgado, *Óscar A. Romero*, 69. Cardinal Sebastiano Baggio, prefect of the Congregation for the Bishops, apparently told Arturo Rivera y Damas, then auxiliary bishop of the archdiocese and widely regarded as the natural successor to Chávez y González, that he wanted an archbishop who would be less critical of the government and that could ease tensions. Most of the archdiocesan clergy were deeply disappointed with the selection of Romero. As auxiliary of San Salvador in the early 1970s, Romero repeatedly clashed with the clergy over the interpretation of the Second Vatican Council and Medellín, as well as over what Romero regarded as the "politicization" of the faith and tendencies toward "immanentism" prevalent among them; see Morozzo della Rocca, *Primero Dios*, 106–33, 165. For instance, in a notorious 1973 episode regarding the Externado San José, a local Jesuit high school, Romero published an article in which he follows Medellín in calling for a "liberating education [*educación liberadora*], capable of freeing our people from cultural, social, economic, and political servitude." But he opposes an understanding of such education that "only stays on the surface of sociopolitical considerations," linking it to literature "of known red origin" being distributed at the high school. At issue here were hermeneutical questions about what liberation entails and how true liberation, in Romero's words, "reaches the depths of the freedom the Redeemer," which liberates from the slavery "whose root is sin" and death. However, in a context in which fighting communism was such an elastic category, Romero's reckless words infuriated the Jesuits, won him few friends among the clergy, and generated a maelstrom of controversy; Romero, "Educación liberadora," *Diario de Oriente*, May 30, 1973.

the streets of the capital over the fraudulent presidential election of General Carlos Humberto Romero (no relation to Óscar Romero) and government troops fired on protesters at several points, leaving scores dead. One of the expelled priests, the Belgian Willibrord Denaux—or Padre Guillermo to his parishioners—wrote to the outgoing Archbishop Luis Chávez y González from prison in Guatemala, "The moment of trials, of the desert, has come for the Salvadoran Church."[29]

From 1977 to 1980, Archbishop Romero shepherded the church through the trials and the desert about which Denaux wrote. It is the time for which Romero is best known, especially for allegedly having undergone a sudden and dramatic conversion, similar to Paul the Apostle's on the road to Damascus, upon becoming archbishop following the death of his friend Rutilio Grande. During Romero's days as archbishop, the government repeatedly called states of siege in response to unrest, as El Salvador steadily descended into civil war. In a 1979 funeral homily for Father Rafael Palacios, Romero memorably spoke about how "the voice of blood" had become an "ordinary" one, which could be heard crying out everywhere in El Salvador—from its fields, its city streets, its highways, its beaches, and even its churches.[30]

During his tenure as archbishop, Romero rose rapidly to international prominence for his relentless pursuit of justice, truth, and peace and for his steadfast defense of his terrorized flock. He thought such a stance was simply the outworking of the gospel. "This is not the hour to show who is the strongest" by the display of brute power, Romero wrote in his diary in 1979, "but who is the most human and willing to yield and to forgive."[31] Romero's ministry was marked by special sensitivity to human misery, especially for those suffering from lack of access to farmland, as well as for workers and other victims of government repression. Like a good shepherd, he sought to protect his flock when the wolves descended, willingly laying down his life for his sheep. On March 24, 1980, he was shot by a

29. Guillermo Denaux, "Desde Guatemala: Carta de Padre Denaux y Bernardo Survil," *Orientación*, March 27, 1977.

30. Romero, *Homilías*, 5:25.

31. Romero, *Diario* (San Salvador: Imprenta Criterio, 2000), 181.

sniper connected to one of the *escuadrónes de la muerte* (death squads) operating with impunity in El Salvador.[32] At the time of his death, Romero was celebrating mass, just beginning the liturgy of the Eucharist.

News of the archbishop's death reverberated far beyond Central America's *pulgarcito* (little thumb), as the Chilean poet Gabriela Mistral affectionately dubbed El Salvador. "This death," Gustavo Gutiérrez, one of the founders of liberation theology, declared, "divides the recent history of the Church in Latin America into a 'before' and an 'after.'"[33]

Most immediately, it meant civil war. Morozzo della Rocca observes that Romero's murder silenced the principal voice of opposition to the mounting violence. It eliminated the person who best represented the possibility of a peaceful solution to the country's crisis, who demonstrated on a daily basis a willingness for "mediation, encounter, and dialogue."[34] During the 1970s, the continual killing of peacemakers like Romero polarized the country, leaving little space for the politics of the church Romero advocated and embodied. State repression not only left victims in its wake, but also gradually produced an armed resistance, which swelled in the aftermath of Romero's death.[35] Romero's existence, Morozzo della Rocca writes, stood as a "barrier" to the spread of the violence. With his slaying, the "retaining walls" that had been holding back war finally broke.[36]

32. The death squads operating in El Salvador were typically heavily armed men who dressed in civilian clothing and who drove unmarked vehicles. With the acquiescence of the Salvadoran state, these groups conducted extrajudicial killings and forced disappearances, the purpose of which was to eliminate the opposition and terrorize the population.

33. Quoted in Manuel Useros and María López Vigil, *La vida por el pueblo: Cristianos de comunidades populares en América Latina* (Madrid: Editorial Popular, 1981), 21; Wright, *Óscar Romero and the Communion of the Saints*, 3; *La Iglesia en El Salvador* (San Salvador: UCA Editores, 1982), 103.

34. Morozzo della Rocca, *Primero Dios*, 11, 21.

35. Morozzo della Rocca, *Primero Dios*, 26.

36. Morozzo della Rocca, *Primero Dios*, 30. Former guerilla leader Gerson Martínez concurs, saying, "This assassination was the consecration of the civil war"; quoted in Russell Crandall, *The Salvador Option: The United States in El Salvador, 1977–1992* (New York: Cambridge University Press, 2016), 145.

What does it mean to think of Romero's life as a bulwark against the mounting pressure of war? To what do his life and death bear witness? Or to put it another way, to what does the voice of his blood speak? This book offers an extended response to these questions. In addition to generating revolutionaries, *la locura* (the madness) that consumed El Salvador like a fire during this time also produced those the church is now beginning to name martyrs—witnesses—and, in Romero's case, saints. Romero was beatified a martyr in downtown San Salvador on May 23, 2015, and then canonized in Rome on October 14, 2018. But popular traditions recognizing his martyrdom arose immediately after his death, since which time Romero's renown has only continued to increase.[37]

Nevertheless, the question of Romero's witness has always been a complex and contested one. The Frente Farabundo Martí para la Liberación Nacional (Farabundo Martí National Liberation Front, FMLN), which fought the Salvadoran government to a stalemate during a twelve-year civil war, glorified Romero as a martyr of the people.[38] Carlos Mauricio Funes Cartagena, the first FMLN candidate elected president, ran on a platform directly inspired by Romero.[39] After his election, Funes issued a public apology for the Salvadoran state's complicity in Romero's death—a remarkable act for the new commander in chief.[40] Others like Luis López Portillo criticize this appeal to Romero, accusing Funes and the FMLN of effectively saying, "This is *our* saint, ... the left's saint."[41] To this day in El Salvador and throughout Latin America, one frequently finds Romero's

37. As Casas Andrés reminds us, "To speak in public about Romero was extremely dangerous, and one could not trust anyone in this regard; the consequences of showing esteem for Romero could be deadly"; Roberto Casas Andrés, *Dios pasó por El Salvador: La relevancia teológica de las tradiciones marrativas de los mártires Salvadoreños* (Bilbao: Desclée de Brouwer, 2009), 193, 179–244.

38. Morozzo della Rocca, *Primero Dios*, 485.

39. "I will govern like Monseñor Romero," Funes said, with "courage" and "prophetic vision," listening "to the cry of justice from the Salvadoran people"; quoted in Kevin Clarke, *Óscar Romero: Love Must Win Out* (Collegeville, Minn.: Liturgical Press, 2014), 136.

40. "I am seeking pardon in the name of the state," Funes said. The right-wing death squads that killed Romero and terrorized the Salvadoran people "acted with the protection, collaboration or participation of state agents"; quoted in "Official El Salvador Apology for Romero's Murder," BBC, March 25, 2010.

41. Luis López Portillo, "El Salvador, Divided by Its First Saint," Public Radio International, *The World*, May 22, 2015.

image emblazoned together with that of Ernesto "Che" Guevara.[42] Many in El Salvador were reared on stories of Romero the *guerrillero* disguised as an archbishop, who sympathized with kidnappers, allowed criminals to take shelter in his churches, and permitted the poor to steal from the hard-earned wealth of the rich.[43]

Yet in the initial years after Romero's death, John Paul II visited a war-torn El Salvador and, against the opposition of his advisors, went to pray at Romero's tomb, justifying his actions with the words, "Romero is ours."[44] It is a fascinating statement, because it implies that Romero had been wrested away from the church and that it was necessary to reclaim him. John Paul repeatedly referred to Romero as a martyr, even insisting that he be included in the Jubilee Year's commemoration of the martyrs of the twentieth century.[45] Pope Benedict XVI spoke in similar terms, calling Romero's death "truly 'credible,' a witness of faith."[46]

Scholarly and popular literature is similarly a site of contestation about the meaning of Romero's witness. Some have hailed him as a martyr of liberation,[47] of the *Iglesia popular* (popular church),[48] and of solidarity,[49] while others regard him as martyr of the Eucharist,[50] the magisterium of the Catholic Church,[51] and even how the Cold War rendered

42. Vidales explicitly calls Romero a revolutionary and explicitly compares him to Che Guevara in R. Vidales, "La muerte del obispo Romero: Juicio del pastor," *Servir*, May 1980, 398.

43. López Portillo, "El Salvador, Divided by Its First Saint."

44. Carlos Colorado, "Romero: Whose Beatification Is It, Anyway?" *Super Martyrio*, May 11, 2015.

45. Kenneth L. Woodward, *Making Saints: How the Catholic Church Determines Who Becomes a Saint, Who Doesn't, and Why* (New York: Simon and Schuster, 1996), 44.

46. Pope Benedict XVI, *Interview of His Holiness Benedict XVI during the Flight to Brazil,* May 9, 2007. In fact, it was Benedict, and not Pope Francis (as it is often reported), who "unblocked" Romero's cause for sainthood in 2012: "Pope Benedict, Not Francis, Unblocked Romero Sainthood Case," Associated Press, February 4, 2015.

47. Jon Sobrino, *Romero: Martyr for Liberation* (London: Catholic Institute for International Relations, 1986).

48. Plácido Erdozaín, *Monseñor Romero, mártir de la Iglesia popular* (San José, Costa Rica: Departamento Ecuménico de Investigaciones, 1980).

49. Michael Lee, *Revolutionary Saint: The Theological Legacy of Óscar Romero* (Maryknoll, N.Y.: Orbis, 2018), 135.

50. William Cavanaugh, "Dying for the Eucharist or Being Killed by It? Romero's Challenge to First-World Christians," *Theology Today* 58, no. 2 (2001).

51. Ricardo Urioste, *Monseñor Romero mártir por el magisterio eclesiástico* (San Salvador: Fundación Monseñor Romero, 2012).

the church's politics incomprehensible.[52] Romero's death has been understood in terms of the hatred of justice[53] as well as of the gospel.[54]

These disagreements, in turn, closely relate to ongoing debates about whether Romero was a liberation theologian or how best to characterize his relationship to that theological movement. It is commonplace for Romero to be characterized as a liberation theologian.[55] However, as Morozzo della Rocca has argued, this is a misreading of Romero, one that mainly relates to the post-mortem reception of a figure who in his own lifetime adhered to church teaching, rejected any perceived heterodoxy (such as liberation theology), and who understood himself above all to be a pastor rather than a member of this (or any other) theological movement.[56] Those who offer critical assessments of Romero's relationship to liberation theology also tend to speak of liberation theology in the singular and then proceed to argue for or against Romero's identification with it. But as Edgardo Colón-Emeric and Michael Lee have each demonstrated, deeper insight comes when Romero is situated in relationship to the liberation theolog*ies* present in El Salvador and throughout the continent.[57] We will return to this topic at greater length in chapters 1 and 4.

52. Roberto Blancarte, "Romero, mártir de la guerra fria," in *Óscar Romero: Un obispo entre guerra fría y revolución* (Madrid: Editorial San Pablo España, 2013).

53. Karl Rahner, "Dimensions of Martyrdom: A Plea for Broadening a Classical Concept," *Concilium* 3, no. 163 (1983): 9.

54. See the preface of the French edition of Morozzo della Rocca, *Msr Óscar Romero*, trans. Chrystèle Francillon (Paris: Éditions Desclée de Brouwer, 2015), 6.

55. Alfred T. Hennelly, ed., *Liberation Theology: A Documentary History* (Maryknoll, N.Y.: Orbis, 1990), 264, 266, 268, 292–306, 314, 340, 389, 535.

56. See Morozzo della Rocca, *Primero Dios*, 320–35. In his study on the influences upon Romero's thought, Delgado reports that the books given to Romero by prominent liberation theologians appear to have remained unread on Romero's bookshelf; Jesús Delgado, "La cultura de Romero," in *Óscar Romero: Un obispo entre guerra fría y revolución* (Madrid: Editorial San Pablo España, 2013), 58.

57. Lee, *Revolutionary Saint*, 188–99; Edgardo Colón-Emeric, *Óscar Romero's Theological Vision: Liberation and the Transfiguration of the Poor* (South Bend, Ind.: University of Notre Dame Press, 2018), 16–17. Colón-Emeric relies upon the Argentinian Jesuit Juan Carlos Scannone, who distinguishes four distinct streams of liberation theology. Gustavo Gutiérrez famously defines theology as a critical reflection on *praxis* or action, which all the streams emphasize. Where the streams diverge, according to Scanonne, is in the priority they place upon the agent of the *praxis*.

The first of the four streams focuses on the pastoral work of the church as a social body, especially the application of the conciliar renewal to Latin America and the work of the Holy Spirit in the CELAM gatherings at Medellín and Puebla. This stream stresses the integral

Contestation about the meaning of Romero's witness and his relationship to the diverse theologies of liberation is also visible in the divergent assessments of Romero's life, especially whether or not Romero experienced a dramatic, Pauline-like conversion upon becoming archbishop.[58] Those who think he did tend to see the catalyst not as a blinding light or a

and evangelical character of liberation, insisting upon, in Cardinal Eduardo Pironio's words, "its biblical and spiritual foundations, without direct reflection upon its political aspects." As for the other streams, the second focuses on the *praxis* of revolutionary groups and relies heavily on Marxist social analysis. Scannone names Hugo Assman and the group Christians for Socialism as representatives. The third stream focuses on what Scannone calls "historical *praxis*" and the various efforts by conscientized Christians to transform society. This stream, which Scannone associates especially with the early work of Gustavo Gutiérrez, regards ecclesial base communities as the subject of theological reflection and the principal agent of historical *praxis*. It construes *el pueblo* (the people) primarily in economic terms, revealing the influence of Marxist social analysis. Scannone specifies the fourth and final stream in terms of the *praxis* of the Latin American peoples. What differentiates it from the third stream is its understanding of what constitutes *el pueblo*. The third stream, like the second one, understands *el pueblo* as an impoverished and oppressed class engaged in conflict with other classes. While the fourth stream certainly recognizes the realities of impoverishment and oppression, it understands the people in question primarily from a historical-cultural perspective as both recipients and agents of a history. Consequently, it attends much more than the other streams to the particularities of history and culture in interpreting reality, and it esteems popular religiosity. The Argentinian priests Lucio Gera and Rafael Tello are often cited as proponents of this fourth stream.

Scannone's typology is by no means exhaustive, but it begins to capture the diversity of what is often represented monolithically and to convey the complexity of Romero's relationship to that diversity. Although Romero does not fit perfectly into any of these streams, his thought has important affinities with the first and fourth streams especially; Juan Carlos Scannone, "La teología de la liberación: Caracterización, corrientes, etapas," *Stromata* 38 (1982): 20; Gutiérrez, *Teología de la liberación: Perspectivas* (Salamanca: Ediciones Sígueme, 2004), 61.

58. For a discussion of divergent assessments of Romero's life and conversion, see Morozzo della Rocca, *Primero Dios*, 185–95. Grande's death brought important changes. The murder led to a rapid deterioration of relations between the church and the government. Grande's death helped to reconcile Romero's previously tense relationship with the diocesan clergy and with Jesuits like Jon Sobrino and Ignacio Ellacuría. After Grande's death, whatever theological differences remained between Romero and those he previously opposed grew increasingly insignificant in a context of mounting violence, in which any construal of liberation theology was under attack. Sobrino became a close advisor to Romero, collaborating on the third and fourth pastoral letters, and even drafting the second one, as well as working with him on the Louvain address. Ellacuría, an expert on land reform who represented the UCA at a historic gathering on land reform in 1970 and who taught classes on the subject throughout the 1970s, advised Romero as well; see Lee, *Revolutionary Saint*, 30–42, 44–85. For an indication of Romero's extensive collaborations with Sobrino and Ignacio Ellacuría, see Romero, *Diario*. The notes for Ellacuría's classes can be found in the Ignacio Ellacuría Archives, Universidad Centroamericana, San Salvador, El Salvador. See "Seminario de reforma agraria" (1973) in box 5, folder 6.

voice from heaven, but as the death of his friend, Rutilio Grande. Perhaps the most famous version is Jon Sobrino's, according to which "scales fell from [Romero's] eyes" as he stood before Grande's corpse.[59] The phrase implies Romero, who was once morally blind, could now see. What did this restoration of vision involve? Sobrino writes that the day of Grande's death, Romero was surrounded by terrorized *campesinos* who "were asking him to defend them," and Romero's response was "to be converted and transformed into their defender."[60] According to Sobrino, Romero had previously opposed Grande's organizing work with *campesinos* in Aguilares, which he considered "too political ... too 'horizontal,' ... and dangerously close to revolutionary ideas."[61] Therefore, at least on Sobrino's narration, Romero now saw Grande was right, whereas previously Romero had disagreed with him.

There are various iterations of this narrative, but the basic story is largely the same: with Romero's conversion, there is a radical rupture with the past, and Romero embraces, in a way he had not previously, the cause of Salvadoran *campesinos*, progressive politics, and the church emerging out of the Second Vatican Council and Medellín. Yet as Morozzo della Rocca observes, skeptically, "The thesis of the conversion of Romero requires ... the schema of a conservative, reactionary, theologically retrograde Romero, which could be opposed to the new Romero, the Romero of the option for the poor, the popular pastoral, etc."[62] This view of radical rupture, he maintains, presses Romero's life into an ill-fitting framework, in which Romero transforms from a timid, conservative cleric, blindly obedient to the church and its teaching office, into a bold, progressive fighter for social justice and an advocate of the popular church.[63]

---

59. Sobrino, *Monseñor Romero*, 19.

60. Sobrino, *Monseñor Romero*, 16–17.

61. Sobrino, *Monseñor Romero*, 19.

62. Morozzo della Rocca, *Primero Dios*, 154–55.

63. Morozzo della Rocca, *Primero Dios*, 185–95. Romero himself also challenged this narrative while he was still alive. In a letter to Cardinal Baggio, he wrote, "What happened in my priestly life, I have tried to explain to myself, is an evolution of the same desire I have always had to be faithful to what God asks from me." Elsewhere, Romero also resisted the description that he had undergone a radical conversion, suggesting that he had always been preoccupied about the impoverishment of his people, but that he became archbishop at a time of drastically deteriorating conditions, which required a different exercise of

Battles over Romero and his legacy continue to this day. In the weeks before Romero's beatification ceremony in 2015, media outlets were abuzz with controversy about the church's handling of the preparations. Were the pomp and circumstance of the event, the marketing campaign promoting it, and the exclusive broadcast rights given to the Telecorporación Salvadoreña a betrayal of Romero and what he stood for? Why were those artists who had long been devotees of Romero and committed to maintenance of his memory not performing during the ceremony? Did the official motto for the beatification, *Romero, mártir por amor* (Romero, martyr for love) obscure the fact that Romero was killed *in odium fidei* (in hatred of the faith)—a hatred still very much alive and well among the church's detractors as well as its own members? As Carlos Colorado observes, the beatification was "the climax of an epic battle" over "who owns the legacy of Romero" and "who really has the right to claim Romero and speak for him," which began the day he was buried.[64]

These battles over Romero's legacy indicate the complexity of his witness, as well as the ongoing disputes into which this study intervenes. However, especially given the central role of gifts to this study, as we will soon see, Jon Sobrino's admonition is particularly fitting: "The greatest danger is to declare [Romero] an object of private property ... as if grace and truth had an owner and did not belong to everyone."[65]

responsibility. Many figures who were close to him, such as Jesús Delgado, Arturo Rivera Damas, Ricardo Urioste, and Gregorio Rosa Chávez, similarly support this alternative view. They do not reject the language of conversion—which is, after all, constitutive to the Christian life—only that in Romero's case it can be distilled into a single, dramatic moment of radical rupture with the past. Bolstering this alternative view is the fact that Romero denounced social inequality and the maldistribution of wealth long before he became archbishop. Also bolstering it is the fact that his understanding of the liberation announced by Catholic social teaching clearly preceded Grande's death, as did his respect for Grande's work. The Romero-Baggio correspondence can be found in Series 5, Boxes 25 and 27, Brockman-Romero Papers, Special Collections and Archives, DePaul University, Chicago, Illinois. See also René Antonio Chanta Martínez, "Antimasonería y antiliberalismo en el pensamiento de Óscar Arnulfo Romero 1962–1965," REHMLAC 3, no. 1 (2001): 127; Óscar Romero, "Con los que sufren: Mons. Óscar Romero," *Amigos Del Hogar*, March 1979; Arturo Rivera y Damas, "Homília de 24 marzo de 1986," *Orientación*, April 6, 1986; Delgado, *Óscar A. Romero*. For additional passages, see Morozzo della Rocca, *Primero Dios*, 186–87.

64. Colorado, "Romero: Whose Beatification Is It, Anyway?"

65. Sobrino, *Witnesses to the Kingdom: The Martyrs of El Salvador and the Crucified Peoples* (Maryknoll, N.Y.: Orbis, 2003), 187.

What follows approaches Romero from a different angle than much of the existing English-language scholarship on him. It focuses on his involvement in the reform of Salvadoran agriculture, particularly the vision of property and work underlying that reform. In much scholarship on Romero, the agrarian crisis El Salvador experienced in the 1960s and 1970s, along with the church's efforts to resolve the crisis by calling for land reform,[66] often remains in the background. Similarly, while it is often observed that Romero's ministry was characterized by sensitivity to the impoverished and victims of state-sponsored violence, the specifically agricultural face of this impoverishment has yet to be explored at length in relation to Romero.[67] There are excellent short discussions of these matters in leading works on Romero,[68] but there remains no substantive exploration of Romero's support for land reform and its underlying theological rationale. This is the central subject of the present study.

Drawing extensively on historical and archival sources, this book situates Romero in relation to the concentration of landholding and the production of landlessness in El Salvador over the course of the twentieth century, and focuses on Romero's participation in the longstanding societal and ecclesial debate about land reform provoked by these realities. Its aim is to show how Romero's advocacy for land reform and its theological basis illuminate the particular conflicts that occasioned his

66. While I use the phrases "land reform" and "agrarian reform" interchangeably as translations for the Spanish *reforma agraria*, I favor "land reform" because of its familiarity in English. When a distinction is made in the literature, land reform typically refers to state-led redistribution (government expropriation and redistribution of land) while agrarian reform refers to redistribution of land and to broader measures to transform rural living conditions (access to credit, provision of tools and other farming equipment, establishment of cooperatives, training and education for farmers, etc.). Romero means something much more like the latter when he speaks of *reforma agraria*.

67. For a good, general overview of this problematic in Latin America, see Alain de Janvry, Elizabeth Sadoulet, and Linda Wilcox Young, "Land and Labour in Latin American Agriculture from the 1950s to the 1980s," *Journal of Peasant Studies* 16, no. 3 (1989): 396–424.

68. See Brockman, *Romero*, 2–3, 214–15, 237; Wright, *Óscar Romero and the Communion of the Saints*, 109, 125; Robert S. Pelton, CSC, ed., *Archbishop Romero: Martyr and Prophet for the New Millennium* (Scranton, Pa.: University of Scranton Press, 2006), 2; Robert S. Pelton, CSC, ed., *Monsignor Romero: A Bishop for the Third Millennium* (Notre Dame, Ind.: University of Notre Dame Press, 2004), 89; Pelton, *Archbishop Romero and Spiritual Leadership in the Modern World* (Lanham, Md.: Lexington, 2015), 56, 76, 117.

martyrdom, while also shedding considerable light on the meaning of his witness for us today, the role he plays in the drama of salvation.

To grasp Romero's reasons for supporting land reform, it is necessary to examine a specific tradition he frequently invokes, one that he variously calls the "social doctrine" (*doctrina social*) or the "social teaching" (*enseñanza social*) of the church.[69] As we will see, in seeking a path through the agrarian crisis, Romero relies heavily upon this tradition, especially its distinctive account of property and possession. "What does the Church contribute to this universal struggle for liberation from so much misery?" Romero asks in his funeral homily for Rutilio Grande. Drawing especially on Pope Paul VI's 1975 apostolic exhortation *Evangelii Nuntiandi*, Romero's response is that the church most contributes "liberated people" like Rutilio Grande himself—Christian liberators who are inspired by the faith, motivated by love, and oriented "by a social doctrine that is the foundation of their wisdom and of their existence."[70] In trying to become the kind of Christian liberator *Evangelii Nuntiandi* calls for, the kind of liberator he thought Grande was, Romero did what the apostolic exhortation recommends: he tried to make Catholic social teaching the basis of his wisdom as he worked for land reform, translating this teaching into his own Salvadoran context.

Scholar and essayist Lewis Hyde has written, "How we imagine property is how we imagine ourselves." Discussions about property are never only about property, understood as objects to be possessed.[71] Such discussions also always implicate human agency, as well as the wider social world in which people live and move and make claims about what and how they possess.

The present work focuses on one particular conflict over property and

69. This study follows Romero in using the phrases "social doctrine" and "social teaching" in a specific sense: as shorthand for what Pius XI in *Quadragesimo Anno* calls the "doctrine on the social and economic question" that he receives from Leo XIII and defends and develops in *Quadragesimo Anno* (see no. 15); Pius XI, Encyclical Letter, *Quadragesimo Anno* (May 15, 1931).

70. Romero, *Homilías*, 1:32–33; Paul VI, Encyclical Letter *Evangelii Nuntiandi*, December 8, 1975.

71. Lewis Hyde, *Common as Air: Revolution, Art, and Ownership* (New York: Farrar, Strauss and Giroux, 2012), 26.

possession underlying a debate about land reform in El Salvador in the 1970s. But if Hyde is right about how property relates to our imagination of human existence and sociality, then we should expect the significance of this conflict to extend far beyond Romero's El Salvador or even the specific issue of land reform. As we will see, this struggle for a just distribution of land was not simply a struggle over the meaning of property in a small Central American country in the second half of the twentieth century. It was also a struggle over what it meant to be human, to live in society with others, and to be a member of Christ's ecclesial body.

At the heart of the conception of property shared by Catholic social teaching and Romero is a theological grammar of creation as common gift. Both assume and elaborate upon what *Gaudium et Spes*, the Second Vatican Council's Pastoral Constitution of the Church in the Modern World, calls the "common" or "universal" destination of created goods.[72] The phrase "theological grammar" signals how social teaching and Romero's own adherence to it hold together—in both explicit and implicit ways—in relationship to this axiomatic claim about creation. One of the main goals of this book is to render this grammar and its associated lexicon more perspicuous. Of particular importance is how this theological grammar of creation yields a politics of common use, which prioritizes the access of all people to the gift of creation. We will see how the call for land reform in social teaching emerges as one expression of this politics.

What follows also displays the fundamental consonance between this theological grammar of creation as common gift and how Romero's beliefs and actions in pursuit of land reform led to his martyrdom. In other words, consideration of the theological stakes of the debate about land reform helps us to approach the issue raised earlier about Romero's role in the drama of salvation, as well as to reflect theologically upon Romero as a witness—a martyr—who represents the Savior in Salvadoran form and who reveals God's ongoing work in the world to restore all things in Christ.[73] Consequently, in addition to examining how Romero reads Catholic social teaching, we will also be concerned with how social teach-

72. Vatican Council II, *Gaudium et Spes* (December 7, 1965), nos. 69, 71.
73. Todd Walatka, *Von Balthasar and the Option for the Poor: Theodramatics in the Light*

ing helps us to "read" Romero's witness and how Romero's witness, in turn, helps us to "read" social teaching. For if, as Romero believed, Catholic social teaching is an authentic expression of the gospel as it aims to guide Christian behavior, then it is also an important source for theological reflection upon Romero himself, who, as a martyr, exemplifies such behavior. And conversely, if a martyr like Romero is a true imitator of Christ, giving the gospel and the social teaching based upon it concrete form and application in the world, then lives like Romero's can also serve as important sources for reflection upon social teaching—perhaps even suggesting ways to extend and deepen the guidance it offers.[74]

That guidance for Christian behavior closely relates to the acknowledgment of creation as a common gift and how it gives rise to a politics of common use. Morozzo della Rocca suggests the contours and content of this politics as it pertains to Romero when he writes:

> As archbishop, Romero understands better than before that the poverty of his people is a product of social injustice. For this reason, he denounces social injustice strongly and publicly, as is well known. But he does not abandon the practice of charity, the aid of individuals. In his correspondence, he includes alms for those who write him. He happily signs letters of recommendation to help people find work, to introduce people to one another, to help needy families. He shelters the needy in a hospital for the sick and terminally ill, and he visits them each month. For Romero, petitioning for structural reforms was never an alternative to direct relief for those in need.[75]

In this passage, Morozzo della Rocca contends that Romero sought to address the injustice embedded in structures and institutions while also continuing to perform the work of mercy. Among my basic contentions is that structural reform and the work of mercy cannot be mutually exclusive alternatives because both manifest how creation is a gift that God gives to all human creatures for their common benefit. Both, in admit-

---

of Liberation Theology (Washington, D.C.: The Catholic University of America Press, 2017), 161–66.

74. Gutiérrez makes a related point in *Teología de la liberación*, 68–69.

75. Morozzo della Rocca, "La controvertida identidad de un obispo," in *Óscar Romero*, 41. See also Morozzo Della Rocca, *Primero Dios*, 285, 324–25.

tedly different ways, participate in a politics of common use. While this politics includes land reform, as well as the defense of workers' ability to organize for living wages and for the improvement of their working conditions, the privileged expression of the politics of common use under the conditions of sin and its damage to creation is the work of mercy—following Matthew 25:31–46, paradigmatically feeding the hungry, slaking the thirsty, clothing the naked, welcoming the stranger, tending to the sick, and visiting the imprisoned.

That the work of structural reform and the work of mercy are not mutually exclusive alternatives is important to underscore because one so often encounters the suggestion that charity is secondary to the pursuit of justice. Consider Martin Maier's comment that Romero underwent a conversion "from charity to structures,"[76] which seems to locate the significance of Romero's conversion in a movement away *from* the work of mercy and *toward* structural reform. Putting aside the controverted question of Romero's "conversion," the problem is not the suggestion that Romero increasingly recognizes the importance of structural critique and reform. We will see how Romero regards land reform as an urgent response to an injustice deeply embedded in the Salvadoran landscape. Rather, the problem is the idea that structural reform and the work of mercy are in tension and that charity does not presuppose and perfect justice. Such presumptions, however, make it difficult to perceive the politics of common use.

Romero's own life and pastoral ministry support the view that structural reform and the work of mercy both participate in a politics of common use. We will be looking at Romero's involvement in the debate about land reform at length. But to appreciate its shape entails seeing it in continuity with and growing out of mercy's work. From the beginning to the end of his life, Romero exhibits the twofold movement arising from the acknowledgment of creation as a gift of God's love for humankind in common: minimizing his own needs so as to have something to give

---

76. Martin Maier, *Monseñor Romero: Maestro de espiritualidad* (San Salvador: UCA Editores, 2005), 56–58, 39–41. Maier is rightly concerned with a false construal of charity, which assigns to charity alone the redress of injustice. On this point, see Pius XI's *Quadragesimo Anno*, no. 4.

others.[77] As a seminarian, he smuggled bread out of the dining hall at the Colegio Pío Latino Americano to feed the hungry.[78] As a priest in San Miguel, he welcomed the excluded at meals,[79] shared table and meals with beggars,[80] prioritized the most vulnerable in pastoral visits to villages and hamlets,[81] and attended to the sick and infirm in their homes.[82] He helped prostitutes leave the streets and alcoholics to overcome their addiction.[83] He criticized coffee growers who did not pay their workers just wages.[84] As bishop of Santiago de Maria, Romero traveled to the remotest parts of the diocese, often by horse or by foot,[85] where he visited the sick and the imprisoned,[86] helped the infirm find medical attention, and generally supported all those who approached him for help.[87] During the harvests, when migrant laborers in Santiago de Maria slept huddled up together in parks and by roadsides, Romero opened the cathedral rectory and diocesan offices and organized meals, sharing not only table with them but also the church's own buildings and property.[88] As archbishop, he refused the bishop's residence and opted instead to live on the grounds of a hospital founded to shelter and care for terminal cancer patients.[89] He received and intervened on behalf of families of the arrested, the tortured, and the disappeared.[90] Simply put, mercy helps make Romero's life and death intelligible. And as we will also see, Romero's call for structural changes like land reform, which he regarded as an invitation to use cre-

---

77. Delgado, *Óscar A. Romero*, 19–20; Morozzo della Rocca, *Primero Dios*, 302–3; Will, *Archbishop Óscar Romero*, 17.

78. Will, *Archbishop Óscar Romero*, 36; Delgado, "Romero, un joven aspirante a la santidad," *Orientación* 55, no. 5463 (March 25, 2007).

79. Delgado, *Óscar A. Romero*, 27.

80. Delgado, *Óscar A. Romero*, 32; Maier, *Monseñor Romero*, 39–41.

81. Delgado, *Óscar A. Romero*, 61, 105.

82. Delgado, *Óscar A. Romero*, 61.

83. Morozzo della Rocca, *Primero Dios*, 72.

84. Morozzo della Rocca, *Primero Dios*, 73.

85. Brockman, *Romero*, 58; Morozzo Della Rocca, *Primero Dios*, 140, 145.

86. Morozzo della Rocca, *Primero Dios*, 141.

87. Brockman, *Romero*, 59.

88. Brockman, *Romero*, 55–56; Maier, *Monseñor Romero*, 40; Morozzo Della Rocca, *Primero Dios*, 146; Wright, *Óscar Romero and the Communion of the Saints*, 18, 34.

89. Wright, *Óscar Romero and the Communion of the Saints*, 55.

90. Morozzo della Rocca, *Primero Dios*, 250.

ation in accordance with God's purpose for it, also grew from mercy's soil.

Romero had critics from across the Salvadoran political spectrum for his views on these matters, but none were more vocal or violent than those he refers to as *la oligarquía* (the oligarchy) or *los económicamente poderosos* (the economically powerful). By the mid-twentieth century, this group was often referred to as *las catorce familias* (the fourteen families), although there were more than fourteen.[91] Nevertheless, the phrase is helpful in capturing the extraordinary concentration of property and power in El Salvador.

The Salvadoran oligarchy has roots in nineteenth-century liberalism in Central America, which was associated with the rise of the commercial production of coffee and the social upheavals that accompanied its spread. The oligarchs characteristically saw themselves as civilizing modernizers bringing progress and enlightenment to their country. Agricultural production for export, they thought, was the path forward, and among the state's central tasks was to clear away any obstacles to it, including subsistence agriculture and communal land tenure, both of which kept El Salvador mired in backwardness.[92]

Here at the outset it is crucial to mention the views of property and possession associated with this group's espousal of economic liberalism or capitalism, ones that fueled its ferocious opposition to land reform of the kind Romero advocated. Political scientist Yvon Grenier comments on how oligarchs often saw themselves as "pioneers," "a truly national vanguard that developed the country single-handedly[,] ... creat[ing] whatever resources the poor country has to go around."[93] Consequently, they regarded their wealth as legitimately earned by the strength of their own hands, which led to the violent repudiation of all other claims upon their property, including those of the most destitute. This liberal view of property was therefore also fused with a form of nationalism—what we might

---

91. James Dunkerley, "El Salvador since 1930," in *The Cambridge History of Latin America* (New York: Cambridge University Press, 1990), 251–52.

92. Diario Oficial, "Ley de la extinción de ejidos," vol. 12, no. 62 (March 14, 1882).

93. Yvon Grenier, *The Emergence of Insurgency El Salvador: Ideology and Political Will* (Pittsburgh, Pa.: University of Pittsburgh Press, 1998), 39–40.

call "possessive nationalism." Because members of the oligarchy characteristically thought they had built El Salvador from scratch, they tended to regard the country as their property, which was their unique responsibility to manage.[94] "Their nationalism," Morozzo della Rocca writes, "was not based on the sense of belonging but on the sense of possession."[95]

At the same time, this view of property was also closely tied to the idea of the common good as the aggregate of the private holdings of those with secure property rights. The oligarchy's primary sense of the collective good was that the pursuit of its own material self-interest redounded to the benefit of all.

These are among the principal views that stoked opposition to Romero and resistance to land reform. Members of the Salvadoran oligarchy articulated them in public debate, as well as through the "language" of state repression and death-squad terror. Through consideration of the oligarchy, we will see how property relates to our imagination of ourselves and our societies, as well as how the views of those who opposed Romero have not been relegated to the mere past.[96] But what careful consideration of the oligarchy's opposition to Romero also makes abundantly clear is that not all of the church's members in Romero's day acknowledged creation as a common gift. Instead of understanding their land and property as given to humankind for common benefit, many members saw their land and property as given to themselves alone and for their own exclusive use, to be protected by law and defended from any encroachment by force. In other words, in Romero's El Salvador, like everywhere else, we see how property and the habits of possession are profoundly implicated in sin and the violence it does to God's creation.

---

94. Héctor Lindo-Fuentes and Erik Ching, *Modernizing Minds in El Salvador: Education Reform and the Cold War, 1960–1980* (Albuquerque: University of New Mexico Press, 2012), 37–38; Jeffery M. Paige, *Coffee and Power: Revolution and the Rise of Democracy in Central America* (Cambridge, Mass.: Harvard University Press, 1998), 44–46. On the liberals' relationship to the military, see Erik Ching, *Authoritarian El Salvador: Politics and the Origins of the Military Regimes, 1880–1940* (Notre Dame, Ind.: University of Notre Dame Press, 2014).

95. Morozzo della Rocca, *Primero Dios*, 16.

96. This phrase is from Artur Mrowczynski-Van Allen, *Between the Icon and the Idol: The Human Person and the Modern State in Russian Literature and Thought; Chaadayev, Soloviev, Grossman*, trans. Matthew Philipp Whelan, Theopolitical Visions (Eugene, Ore.: Cascade, 2013), xviii.

Facing the difficulty of this reality involves learning to see the church as, in Augustine of Hippo's words, a *corpus permixtum* (mixed body)—a society of wheat and weeds, saints and sinners, merciful and unmerciful alike.[97] In his 1993 encyclical *Veritatis Splendor*, John Paul II writes that the martyrs are an "eloquent and attractive example of a life completely transfigured by the splendor of moral truth," "light[ing] up every period of history by reawakening its moral sense."[98] If that is true, then Romero's case shows the light to be harsh and unflattering for the church itself. For one thing Romero's martyrdom lights up is the pervasive resistance to a politics of common use among its membership.

In Romero's El Salvador, those who spoke out against or otherwise opposed the ubiquity of the concentration of land and who advocated for the landless and land-poor to have access to land to cultivate suffered enormously as a consequence. This suffering points to how, under the conditions of sin and violence, the politics of common use can lead to the cross. In other words, those who hunger and thirst for others to have access to what is theirs in justice often risk laying down their lives in charity. As Romero himself said just months before he died, "The greatest sign of the faith in a God of life is the testimony of those who are willing to give their lives. 'No one has greater love than this, to lay down one's life for one's friends' (Jn 15:13). And this is what we see daily in our country."[99]

The way of charity conforms people to Christ, who restores what God has made not by withdrawing God's life but by giving it fully, even to the point of laying it down willingly for the good of what God has made. This is how Christ, the one through whom and for whom "all things were created" and in whom "all things hold together," brings peace to the violence sin unleashes in creation (Col 1:15–20). As we will see, it is also how Romero sought to bring peace to El Salvador. By walking the path of charity, he witnessed to the way God's merciful work to restore creation is cruciform. Therefore, while Romero's embrace of church teaching on

---

97. This phrase comes from Cora Diamond, "The Difficulty of Reality and the Difficulty of Philosophy," In *Philosophy and Animal Life* (New York: Columbia University Press, 2008).

98. John Paul II, Encyclical Letter *Veritatis Splendor* (August 6, 1993), no. 93.

99. Romero, "La dimensión política de la fe desde la opción por los pobres," in *La voz de los sin voz: La palabra viva de Monseñor Romero*, ed. Rodolfo Cardenal, Ignacio Martín-Baró, and Jon Sobrino (San Salvador: UCA Editores, 1980), 191.

property and possession begins with an emphasis upon creation as common gift and the claims of justice flowing from that belief, his testimony to this truth in word and in deed points beyond it, to the *telos* of the gift and the common life in the crucified and risen Lord in which it participates. What becomes perceptible in the process is how the entire economy of salvation, like God's work of creation, is ordered by and to gifts given in common.

This study consists of five chapters. Chapter 1 examines the notion of ordinary violence in the homiletical and literary corpus of Romero. Focusing especially on the reality of landlessness, this chapter attends to Romero's characterization of the inability of people to access land and livelihood as a form of violence, which he understands as an attack upon the dignity of those deprived of what they need to survive and to flourish. The chapter then turns to the assumptions that make the perception of ordinary violence possible, arguing that it is an elaboration upon the theological grammar of creation as common gift.

Chapters 2 and 3 turn explicitly to Catholic social teaching in order to explore this theological grammar further, along with its implications for property and possession. The purpose of these two chapters is to delineate the moral and theological landscape within which land reform emerges and to situate that emergence in relation to a wider politics of common use, because this is the landscape in which Romero walks. While both chapters discuss Romero, their primary concern is not Romero as an interpreter of social teaching, but rather how social teaching and the theological grammar of creation as common gift help us to interpret Romero.

Chapter 2 treats the line of reflection following Pope Leo XIII's 1891 encyclical *Rerum Novarum* and how its construal of property and possession derives from the claim that creation is a common gift. Chapter 3 tracks this same line of reflection, showing what kinds of laws, politics, and institutions support a politics of common use. Chapter 3 concludes by looking at the call for land reform, which Catholic social teaching first makes after the Second World War and which has continued ever since.

The purpose in addressing land reform in this manner is to convey that it is a new application of a much older and deeper set of concerns, and that it coheres with the wider moral and theological landscape of social teaching as a whole.

Chapter 4 returns to Romero's El Salvador in order to examine the debate about land reform and how the church's participation in the debate drew upon Catholic social teaching. The chapter considers Romero's homilies during the crucial period in Salvadoran history spanning the announcement of a major land reform initiative in December 1979 and its implementation in March the following year, during which time there was a massive escalation of state repression. These were also the final months of Romero's life. The chapter attends to Romero's interpretation both of the theological significance of land reform and of the repression accompanying the reform's implementation. An important theme of this chapter is therefore the cruciform character of a politics of common use.

Chapter 5 confronts this cruciformity directly by developing a theological interpretation of Romero's martyrdom, reflecting explicitly upon the question posed earlier: To what does Romero bear witness? The chapter offers an extended theological examination of Romero's martyrdom and its witness to Christ's abiding presence in the world. It argues that Romero's martyrdom lights up resistance to a politics of common use, revealing how such a politics follows the way of the cross and God's work to restore all things in Christ.

Part 1

GIFT OF
THE EARTH

–1–

"YOU POSSESS THE LAND THAT BELONGS TO ALL SALVADORANS"

The story of Naboth is an old one, but it is repeated every day.

—Ambrose of Milan, *On Naboth*

In February 1980, just two months before he was killed, Óscar Romero gave an address at the Université Catholique de Louvain in Belgium under the title "La dimensión política de la fe desde la opción por los pobres" ("The Political Dimension of Faith from the Perspective of the Option for the Poor"). The central argument of the address, as Romero memorably puts it, is that "the world of the poor … is the key to understanding the Christian faith, the activity of the Church, and the political dimension of this faith and ecclesial activity.… The poor are those who tell us what the *polis* is … and what it means for the Church to live truly in the world."[1]

Romero then goes on to make an important observation: by learning to orient its life in relationship to the world of the impoverished,

An earlier version of this chapter appeared in *Modern Theology* 35, no. 4 (2019): 638–62. Thanks to Wiley Blackwell for permission to publish it.

1. Romero, "La dimensión política de la fe desde la opción por los pobres," 185.

31

the church in El Salvador has come to discover another essential aspect of its vocation, which he calls the provision of *defensa* (defense). "The Church has not only incarnated itself in the world of the poor," he says, "but it has also firmly committed itself to their defense."[2] The violence the church defends the poor against, however, is not immediately clear in Romero's remarks. Although the world of the impoverished is replete with violence, he observes that this specific form of violence is difficult to perceive and therefore to defend against. It "has always been among us, but has often been hidden, even from the gaze of the Church."[3] Learning to see it, much less address it, entails first "turning toward the world of the poor—to their real, concrete world."[4]

Romero's words merit further reflection, because so much of the violence by the time of the Louvain address was not hidden but patently evident. Events in El Salvador were making international headlines as the country became synonymous with the violent assault on human dignity and state-sponsored repression. As Joan Didion reported two years later, with words that could just as easily describe El Salvador in 1980, "Terror is the given of the place.... The dead and pieces of the dead turn up everywhere, every day, as taken-for-granted as in a nightmare or in a horror movie."[5] The routine and public display of disfigured bodies—in vacant lots, roadsides, ditches, public restrooms, and beaches—was not simply about eliminating the opposition (or suspected opposition). It was also and especially about making a spectacle of violence by terrorizing and scattering the populace. Death squads linked to state security forces and landowners' associations announced their gruesome work by carving their initials into the corpses of victims.[6]

---

2. Romero, "La dimensión política de la fe desde la opción por los pobres," 187. Romero frequently employs similar language, speaking of the defense of the suffering, of the poor, and of human rights. For a sampling, see Romero, *Diario*, 114–15, 179–80; Romero, *La Iglesia, cuerpo de Cristo en la historia: Segunda carta pastoral*, in *La voz de los sin voz*, 88; Romero, *Iglesia y organizaciones políticas populares: Tercera carta pastoral*, in *La voz de los sin voz*, 94; Romero, *Homilías*, 5:193.

3. Romero, "La dimensión política de la fe desde la opción por los pobres," 185.

4. Romero, "La dimensión política de la fe desde la opción por los pobres," 185.

5. Joan Didion, *Salvador* (New York: Vintage, 1994), 14, 19.

6. Cynthia J. Arnson, "Window on the Past: A Declassified History of Death Squads in El Salvador," in *Death Squads in Global Perspective: Murder with Deniability* (New York: Palgrave

This violence was not only occurring in plain view, but much of it was focused on the church. During Romero's three-year tenure as archbishop, more than fifty priests had been attacked or threatened and six murdered. Many others were tortured or deported or both.[7] In 1977, a death squad known as the Unión Guerrera Blanca (White Warrior Union, UGB) claimed responsibility for the murder of one of the priests, Father Alfonso Navarro. Soon afterward, the UGB publicly called upon all Jesuits to leave the country within the month or become "military targets."[8] Along with the archdiocesan radio station YSAX, as well as numerous other educational and ecclesial institutions, the UCA was repeatedly bombed. Several parish communities had been raided, their altars desecrated.[9]

"If all this has happened to the Church's most visible representatives," Romero observes at Louvain, "imagine what has happened to ordinary Christians, to *campesinos*, catechists, lay ministers, and to the ecclesial base communities. There, the threats, arrests, tortures, and murders number in the hundreds and thousands. As always … it has been the poor among the Christians who have suffered the most."[10] Throughout the decade of the 1970s, public demonstrations and gatherings were repeatedly attacked by military and police forces.[11] By the late 1970s, these forces, especially the death squads, increasingly employed strategies of disappearance and torture, with the legal aid office of the archbishop monitoring hundreds of such cases.[12] By 1980, about one thousand civilians each

Macmillan, 2002), 86. See also Amnistía Internacional, *El espectro de los "escuadrones de la muerte"* (London, 1996).

7. Romero, "La dimensión política de la fe desde la opción por los pobres," 188.

8. Brockman, *Romero*, 65.

9. Romero, "La dimensión política de la fe desde la opción por los pobres," 188; Report of the Latin American Bureau, *Violence and Fraud in El Salvador* (London: Latin American Bureau, 1977), 1–2, 6–7, 65; *Persecución de la Iglesia en El Salvador* (San Salvador: Publicaciones del Secretariado Social Interdiocesano, 1977).

10. Romero, "La dimensión política de la fe desde la opción por los pobres," 177. José Luis Escobar Alas, the current archbishop of San Salvador, makes a similar point in Escobar Alas, *Ustedes también darán testimonio, porque han estado conmigo desde el principio* (San Salvador: Arzobispado de San Salvador, 2017), 93.

11. Paul Almeida, *Waves of Protest: Popular Struggle in El Salvador, 1925–2005* (Minneapolis: University of Minnesota Press, 2008), 103–73.

12. Almeida, *Waves of Protest*, 151–52, 158; Socorro Jurídico Cristiano, *El Salvador: La situación de los derechos humanos, octubre 1979–julio 1981* (Mexico City: Socorro Jurídico Cristiano,

month were being killed as a result of state-sponsored repression. Most of the victims were *campesinos*, members of grassroots organizations, leaders or members of trade unions, teachers, students, journalists, or anyone who spoke out against or challenged the existing order.[13]

In the Louvain address, Romero addresses the selectivity of the violence against the church, underscoring once again the church's role as defender. "Not any and every priest has been persecuted," he says, "not any and every institution has been attacked. That part of the Church has been attacked and persecuted that put itself on the side of the impoverished and went to their defense."[14] Once again, what Romero means by defense and even by violence is not immediately clear, for his words imply that persecution follows from the church's provision of defense against a prior form of violence being suffered.

What, then, is the violence in question? What is the best way to describe it and the kind of defense the church offers? And finally, why did this defense lead to further violence? At one point in the address, Romero offers the clue to an answer. Citing scripture and church teaching, Romero describes the violence in view this way:

> Just as elsewhere in Latin America, the words of Exodus have, after many years—perhaps even centuries—finally rung in our ears: *The cry of the sons of Israel has now come to me; I have also seen how the Egyptians oppress them* (Ex 3:9).... We have learned to see what is the first, basic fact about our world and, as pastors, we have made a judgment about it at Medellín and at Puebla: *that misery, as a collective fact, expresses itself as an injustice which cries to the heavens* [citing *Medellín*, "Justice," 1].... Experiencing these realities, and letting ourselves be affected by them, far from separating us from our faith, has returned us to the world of the poor as our true location.... It is [in the world of the poor] that we have encountered the real faces of the poor, about which

---

1981); Rafael Guidos Véjar, "La crisis política en El Salvador (1976-1979)," *Estudios Centroamericanos* 19 (July-August 1979): 519.

13. Aldo Lauria-Santiago, "The Culture and Politics of State Terror and Repression in El Salvador," in *When States Kill: Latin America, the U.S. and Technologies of Terror* (Austin: University of Texas Press, 2005); Almeida, *Waves of Protest*, 151.

14. Romero, "La dimensión política de la fe desde la opción por los pobres," 177.

Puebla speaks [see *Puebla*, 1.2.29–39]. There we have encountered *campesinos* without land and without steady work, without running water or electricity in their homes, without medical assistance when mothers give birth, and without schools when their children begin to grow. There we have met factory workers without labor rights, and who are fired if they demand them and then left at the mercy of cold economic calculations.[15]

In this passage, Romero suggests that impoverishment, along with its associated vulnerabilities and deprivations—the way lack of land and work, for instance, is tied to lack of water, housing, healthcare, and education—is itself a form of violence from which people need protection. In Romero's El Salvador, this violence was concentrated especially in the countryside, and its principal face was that of the landless.

Earlier, we saw Romero at several points speak to the hiddenness of this violence and the difficulties of perceiving it. One reason for this is simply the ordinariness of the violence. The landless and land-poor majority are oppressed and repressed *cotidianamente*, Romero observes.[16] The violence has become daily, routine, quasi-natural—part of what the French Catholic philosopher Emmanuel Mounier calls *le désordre établi* (the established disorder),[17] the silence of misery endured.[18] Romero draws upon the language of the prophets to describe it:

Among us the terrible words of the prophets of Israel remain true. Among us there are those who sell the just for money and the poor for a pair of sandals [Am 8:6]; those who hoard violence and spoil in their palaces [Am 3:10]; those who crush the poor [Am 2:7]; those who bring near the kingdom of violence, while they lie in beds of ivory [Am 6:3–4]; those who join house to house and annex field to field until they occupy everything and remain alone in the land [Is 5:8].[19]

15. Romero, "La dimensión política de la fe desde la opción por los pobres," 185–86.

16. Romero, "La dimensión política de la fe desde la opción por los pobres," 187.

17. Katherine Davies and Toby Garfitt, eds., *God's Mirror: Renewal and Engagement in French Catholic Intellectual Culture in the Mid-Twentieth Century* (New York: Fordham University Press, 2014), 7.

18. This phrase is from Leonel Gómez Vides, quoted in Carolyn Forché, *What You Have Heard Is True* (New York: Penguin Press, 2019), 52.

19. Romero, "La dimensión política de la fe desde la opción por los pobres," 187.

It is important to see that Romero's use of this prophetic language is not hyperbolic but points to quite literal features of the violence in question: it is enacted through institutions of exchange, stored up in buildings and structures, and embedded in landscapes.

This chapter focuses on Romero's depiction of landlessness as a form of violence from which the Salvadoran people need defense and on the reason Romero thinks a more just distribution of land is constitutive of that defense. Later chapters will return again to the topic of defense as it emerges in Catholic social teaching, paying particular attention to the role access to property—especially land—plays in it, as well as why the attempt to offer such defense in El Salvador led to persecution and martyrdom. We examine ordinary violence in this chapter because it is on this basis that Romero both resists the description that land reform disrupts a peaceful order with subversion and depicts the pursuit of a better distribution of land as the way toward peace in a context where there is no peace.

What *Gaudium et Spes* calls the "common" or "universal destination of earthly goods" (nos. 69, 71) is essential for understanding this account of ordinary violence. As we saw, the Pastoral Constitution of the Church in the Modern World uses these phrases to signal how creation is a common gift, which God gives for the use of humankind as a whole. Romero's understanding of ordinary violence assumes and develops this belief about creation; the axiom that creation is a gift given for common use is precisely what enables Romero's perception and description of such violence. Examining the theological grammar of creation as common gift and its relationship to ordinary violence therefore will help us clarify Romero's sense that true land reform contributes to the defense against ordinary violence as it simultaneously bears witness to the truth about creation and its implications for property. The purpose of this chapter is to begin to sketch the contours of the moral and theological landscape opened up by this conviction about creation and point to the possibilities it generates for moral description and agency, such as Romero's claim, from which the chapter's title is taken, that some oligarchs are like thieves because they possess land that belongs to all Salvadorans. To appreciate what Romero means, we must first attend more closely to the violence to which he thinks land reform is a defensive response.

ORDINARY VIOLENCE

One of the basic contentions emerging from Romero's homiletical and literary corpus is that it is impossible to understand El Salvador without attending to how injustice is—in its very ordinariness—a form of violence, which then crystalizes into structures, institutions, and even landscapes.[20] In this and in other ways, Romero sees ordinary violence as productive of and implicated in further violence. For this reason, Romero often makes statements in his homilies and his writings like the following: "As we analyze the real roots of violence in our society, we must remember that if we do not create social and political possibilities that enable the poorest members of our society and the *campesinos* to present their just demands and their urgent needs, then unfortunately violence will only increase."[21] Here Romero characterizes the exclusion of certain people from participation in social life—along with the chronic deprivation of what they need—as a violence they suffer, which, in turn, perpetuates additional violence.

In the same homily, Romero compares ordinary violence to an invasive weed that has infested a field—a weed like Bermuda grass, whose rhizomes branch downward from nodes beneath the field's surface. The image suggests that even when the top growth is removed or dies, the underground shoots survive, often for years, with a small piece sufficient for regeneration. The shoots can surface in the same space or move elsewhere to colonize, which leads to Romero's question: "When the roots are firmly in place, should we be surprised to find new weeds sprouting up everywhere?"[22] Violence continues to proliferate because its rhizomes are already lodged so deeply within the landscape.

The context for Romero's words is that in 1978, in the days before Holy Week in the town of San Pedro Perulapán, security forces attacked

---

20. See Romero, *Iglesia y organizaciones politicas populares*, 113–21.
21. Romero, *Homilías*, 2:383.
22. Romero, *Homilías*, 2:384–85.

a demonstration of *campesinos* who had arrived for an appointment at a bank to discuss the need for land to farm. Finding the bank closed, which they interpreted as a gesture of disdain, they took to the streets to protest, only to be met with repression. The violence continued throughout Holy Week with additional victims, including Tránsito Vásquez, who disappeared and was later found decapitated and hanging from a tree—a Salvadoran icon of the events of Good Friday.[23] "Because our people are hungry," Romero says in a homily reflecting upon what happened, "they need land to work; they need someone with whom they can dialogue to find a solution to their problems. Death and dismemberment is the response to those longings."[24]

This episode encapsulates the idea of ordinary violence as productive of and entangled with additional forms of violence: the ordinary violence of *campesinos* lacking land and livelihood—the violence of privation they suffer in the flesh, which is sustained by larger structural and institutional forms of violence—is systematically neglected. The protests that ensue as a response are interpreted by authorities as a form of violent disruption of a peaceful order—the agitation of subversives—and so repressed, which only stokes the flames of further violence.

In his homilies, Romero uses other images for ordinary violence as well, comparing it not only to weeds filling a field, but also to a thick smog filling "the air we breathe."[25] We inhale it, he says, in our "ordinary respiration."[26] And it enters us "through all the pores of our being."[27] The cumulative effect of these and other images is to unsettle a picture of violence as an interruption to the ordinary, peaceful course of events, as if it were a state of exception to the everyday rather than constitutive of it. Consider this description from the Truth Commission for El Salvador, *From Madness to Hope*, which describes the "fire [of civil war] that swept over the fields of El Salvador" as a *breach of the calm plenitude which accompanies the rule of law*," before going on to state that the "essential na-

---

23. Brockman, *Romero*, 107–8.
24. Romero, *Homilías*, 2:331.
25. Romero, *Homilías*, 5:60, 273.
26. Romero, *Homilías*, 4:435.
27. Romero, *Homilías*, 1:381.

ture" of this violence, like all violence, was *suddenly or gradually to alter the certainty which the law nurtures in human beings.*"[28] Romero's thought unsettles and recontextualizes this picture of violence as interruption or exception, and he pressures us, precisely on theological grounds, to attend to the blood-soaked character of what often passes as "order." In this way, he provides us with tools for understanding how what appear to be aberrant outbreaks of violence are anything but, because he reads the outbreaks that do occur in relation to these more mundane manifestations of violence.

By characterizing Salvadoran reality as saturated with violence, Romero's purpose is not to conflate distinct forms of violence, much less to exculpate the revolutionary violence of the regime's opponents. This is the concern of Mennonite theologian John Howard Yoder, who worries about "redefining the term 'violence'" from the "careful, traditional discussion" of it.[29] Yoder thinks that in the hands of "apologetes for violence in the interest of righteous revolution in the third world," this redefinition suggests a moral equivalence between structural/institutional violence and revolutionary violence and becomes a conceptual tool to legitimate the latter.[30] Perhaps this is true in some cases, but Romero appeals to ordinary violence in order to offer a clearer picture of the world, not to legitimize further violence. Moreover, his understanding of violence is not a *redefinition* of violence from its traditional uses but is better understood as an attempt to *recover* them. After all, he draws on the language of Amos and Isaiah to describe it.

Even the best readers and most ardent supporters of Romero tend to discount or overlook ordinary violence and its importance to the theological grammar of his thought, focusing instead upon forms of violence that, although more readily perceptible, Romero himself regarded as secondary. For instance, Morozzo della Rocca, arguably Romero's leading biographer, writes, "In the three years that Romero governed as archbishop,

---

28. Commission on the Truth for El Salvador, *From Madness to Hope: The 12-Year War in El Salvador: Report of the Commission on the Truth for El Salvador* (New York: UN Security Council, 1993), emphasis mine.

29. John Howard Yoder, "Fuller Definition of 'Violence'" (Goshen Biblical Seminary, March 28, 1973), 1.

30. Yoder, "Fuller Definition of 'Violence,'" 1–2.

there is a repressive violence [of the regime] and a subversive violence [of its revolutionary opponents]. The repressive is quantitatively greater and more brutal," which is why, Morozzo della Rocca explains, Romero more frequently condemns it.[31] Archbishop Vincenzo Paglia, the postulator for Romero's canonization cause, seems to second this view when he refers to these alone as the "two forms of violence in the country."[32]

As descriptions of Romero's social analysis of violence, these formulations are incomplete. In his third and fourth pastoral letters, for instance, Romero offers extended catecheses on violence that draw directly upon church teaching, including detailed typologies of violence.[33] All violence is the consequence of sin and the damage it does to what God has made, but in both letters, Romero emphasizes what Medellín calls "institutionalized violence,"[34] which he defines as the systematic and widespread deprivation of the basic necessities of life.[35] This is the primary form of violence the country faces, he argues, and it is closely related to the "idolatry of wealth and of property," which rejects the social function of property and lures people into the violent defense of their possessions.[36] But according to Romero—and this is crucial—institutionalized violence is not only the primary and "most acute" form of violence.[37] It is also "the source of innumerable other cruelties and violences."[38] Romero calls it *la raíz de la violencia* (the root of the violence).[39] It is like a taproot—the central tapering root from which other, lateral roots of violence ramify. Therefore, the priority Romero accords to ordinary violence is by no means a denial or minimization of other forms of violence. Rather, his point is simply that while there are indeed important and complex rela-

---

31. Morozzo della Rocca, "La controvertida identidad de un obispo," in *Óscar Romero: Un obispo entre guerra fría y revolución* (Madrid: Editorial San Pablo España, 2013), 19.

32. Vincenzo Paglia, "Sentir con la Iglesia," in *Un obispo entre guerra fría y revolución* (Madrid: Editorial San Pablo España, 2013), 126.

33. Romero, *Iglesia y organizaciones políticas populares*, 113–19; Romero, *Misión de la Iglesia en medio de la crisis del país: Cuarta carta pastoral*, in *La voz de los sin voz*, 156–59.

34. The phrase "institutionalized violence" is from *Medellín*, "Peace," 16.

35. Romero, *Iglesia y organizaciones políticas populares*, 114–15; Romero, *Misión de la Iglesia en medio de la crisis del país*, 156–57.

36. Romero, *Misión de la Iglesia en medio de la crisis del país*, 146.

37. Romero, *Iglesia y organizaciones políticas populares*, 114, 117.

38. Romero, *Misión de la Iglesia en medio de la crisis del país*, 157.

39. Romero, *Misión de la Iglesia en medio de la crisis del país*, 146.

tionships among various forms of violence, the primary one is ordinary, which often escapes notice.

The careful reader will have observed that there are terminological differences between Romero's words and my exposition of them. Although Romero does not use the phrase "ordinary violence," and he often associates, as we saw him do earlier, institutionalized/structural violence and ordinary violence, distinguishing among these forms of violence helps clarify Romero's reasoning and the grammar of the theological tradition he inherits and out of which he speaks.

In an unpublished paper entitled "Notes on the Violence in El Salvador," Ignacio Ellacuría, the Jesuit philosopher, contributor to the theologies of liberation and one of the Jesuits summarily executed in 1989 by the Salvadoran army, helps further conceptualize the notion of ordinary violence.[40] Ellacuría thinks the church in El Salvador has failed to distinguish adequately among different kinds of violence and to assimilate those differences into its moral imagination. While the church certainly condemns "structural violence and the violence against human dignity," these forms of ordinary violence, he writes, tend to "pass into the background."[41]

By violence against human dignity, Ellacuría means the deprivation of what is bodily necessary for life and flourishing, such as adequate food, water, clothing, shelter, and so on. Ellacuría's point is not that those who are deprived of what is necessary to live fully human lives are *particularly susceptible to violence* but that *this deprivation itself is a form of violence*. In the case of ordinary violence, what is being violated is the dignity of those who are deprived of what is necessary, which is distinct from, though closely related to, the structures and institutions that establish, preserve, and perpetuate this ordinary violence of deprivation.

Just as ordinary violence must be differentiated from structural/institutional violence, then, so too must it be differentiated from violence in the commonplace sense, as a physical force used to inflict injury or

---

40. See Ellacuría and Sobrino, eds., *Mysterium liberationis: Conceptos fundamentales de la Teología de la Liberación*, 2 vols. (San Salvador: UCA Editores, 1993).

41. Ellacuría, "Apuntes sobre la violencia en El Salvador," Ignacio Ellacuría Archives, Universidad Centroamericana, San Salvador, box 13, folder 30.4, n.d.

death. According to Ellacuría—and Romero would agree—when ordinary and structural/institutional violence recede to the background of the Christian moral imagination, what migrates to the foreground are other, more easily perceptible forms of violence. For instance, Ellacuría and Romero think that in El Salvador the interplay between repressive and revolutionary violence monopolizes analysis of the violence, becoming the primary and often exclusive lens through which to see and analyze the conflict. But this monopolization comes at a price, and the price is the profound distortion of the church's witness in a violent world.

In contrast, according to Ellacuría and to Romero, ordinary and structural/institutional violence must be the foreground, not the background, of the church's moral imagination. For this reason, Romero often and evocatively speaks of the church's work in the midst of the violence as "defending the image of God, which is each person."[42] Both Ellacuría and Romero want us to learn to perceive impoverishment as the primary form of violence with which Christians should be concerned, a violence that is a perpetual attack upon human dignity, which is generated and sustained by structures and institutions, and which is embedded in landscapes. In short, both Ellacuría and Romero are trying to offer the conceptual and linguistic tools to bring to the surface the violence woven into the ordinary. Something like this is what Romero means in his Louvain address when he says the impoverished are those who tell the church what the *polis* is and what the church's politics truly entails.

ENCLOSURE AND ITS LEGACIES

In the introduction, we considered Romero's return from Puebla and saw him suggest that the church's teaching about a social mortgage bearing upon all property is where the message of Puebla becomes the history of his people. What does he mean by this? What does property's social mortgage have to do with his people or its history?

In that same homily, Romero begins to offer some suggestive lines of thought. Through Christ, he tells his Salvadoran listeners, the history of the people of Israel has become their own history. They have been incor-

---

42. Romero, *Homilías*, 1:377, 299, 387; 2:147.

porated into it, and the site of incorporation is Christ's ecclesial body.[43] At another point, Romero reads a letter from his fellow Latin American bishops, which compares the people of El Salvador to Christ's ongoing suffering in the world, remarking, "This is history and the God of our history."[44] It is a history that includes the "terror" of the present—ongoing disappearances and assassinations of professors, hospital workers, and *campesinos*; their bodies appearing on the shores of lakes and beaches—and closely related to this terror, the struggle for a just distribution of land.[45]

In later chapters, we will continue to dwell on this history. But in order to understand the relationship between Puebla's message on property and the history of the Salvadoran people, we must continue our examination of ordinary violence by considering one of its paradigmatic expressions in Romero's El Salvador: landlessness. When Romero became archbishop in 1977, the country was, to the eyes of most observers, hurtling toward war, and conditions were desperate. The picture consistently emerging in the scholarship is extreme concentration of land and wealth in a country in which the livelihood of the vast majority depended upon agriculture.[46] Official data of the Ministry of Agriculture showed that less than 1 percent of the population owned about 40 percent of the land in 1979.[47] Closely associated with this concentration was landlessness. By 1975, about 40 percent of all rural households were classified as landless, and the percentage swelled to 65 percent by 1980.[48]

How did the distance between the many who have nothing and the few who have everything grow so vast? How did landlessness become so

43. Romero, *Homilías*, 4:205–10, 221.

44. Romero, *Homilías*, 4:211.

45. Romero, *Homilías*, 4:212–16.

46. According to the World Handbook of Political and Social Indicators, El Salvador was among the most unequal in the world at the time; *World Handbook of Political and Social Indicators, Cross-National Attributes and Rates of Change*, vol. 1 (New Haven, Conn.: Yale University Press, 1983). On the general conditions in El Salvador, see James Dunkerley, *Political Suicide in Latin America: And Other Essays* (London: Verso, 1992), 70–73; Roy Prosterman and Jeffery M. Riedinger, *Land Reform and Democratic Development* (Baltimore: Johns Hopkins University Press, 1987), 143; Elisabeth Jean Wood, *Insurgent Collective Action and Civil War in El Salvador* (New York: Cambridge University Press, 2003), 24.

47. "Presentación del Ministro de Agricultura y Ganadería, Enrique Álvarez Córdova, en la cadena de radio y televisión," *La Prensa Gráfica*, December 14, 1979.

48. Almeida, *Waves of Protest*, 90, 114.

pervasive, and why did the conflict over access to land intensify as the twentieth century progressed? An important part of the answer is the account given by most scholars of Salvadoran history about two expansions of export-agricultural production and the exclusion of the *campesinado* associated with them. The first expansion was the rise of coffee in the late nineteenth and early twentieth centuries. The second expansion—again in coffee, but also additionally in cotton, sugar cane, and cattle—occurred after the Second World War. This twofold expansion of export-agricultural production is indispensable for understanding not only Romero's account of ordinary violence, but also the agrarian conflicts he inherits upon becoming archbishop and the larger question about how the Puebla's message about property becomes the history of his people.

Of course, the roots of these problems sink into the history of conquest and colonialization. Bartolomé de las Casas offers a glimpse of that cataclysm in his depiction of the dispossession of peoples and the overturning of worlds, the blood and fire through which Christianity came to the Americas. This is his description of Pedro de Alvarado, the man who conquered Cuscatlán, which would later become El Salvador:

> If all these malicious and evil acts [of Alvarado]…[if] all the devastations, all the deaths, all the extirpations of peoples from their lands, [if] all such savage acts of injustice that inspire horror in the centuries present and to come were expressed and gathered together, they would make a great book indeed, for this captain exceeded all those of the past and present, both in quantity and number of abominations which he did, and in the peoples that he destroyed and lands that he laid waste and made a desert.[49]

Las Casas reports that, upon his arrival in Cuscatlán in 1524, Alvarez encountered people bearing gifts whom he burned alive, ran through with spears, cut into pieces, and fed to dogs.[50] Others he sold into slavery, or he put to work, loading them down with cargo or using them to wage

---

49. Bartolomé de las Casas, *An Account, Much Abbreviated, of the Destruction of the Indies with Related Texts*, trans. Andrew Hurley (Indianapolis: Hackett, 2003), 37.
50. Las Casas, *An Account*, 37.

war.[51] He razed whole villages as he made his way through much of what is today the isthmus of Central America.

At issue for Las Casas is not simply the cruelty of those like Alvarado, or the way that, as Las Casas claims in the last memorial he sent to the Council of the Indies, "every bit of gold and silver, pearls, and other wealth that has arrived in Spain is stolen property."[52] It is also the new world being built upon the violence and plunder, the structures and institutions arising as a result of them and serving to formalize and legitimize them.[53] Along these lines, Las Casas is especially critical of the *encomienda* system in which the conquered, as vassals of the Spanish crown, were entrusted to settlers (from the Spanish *encomendar*, "to entrust"), ostensibly for the purposes of catechesis in the faith. For Las Casas, this system was slavery by another name, functioning as an insurmountable obstacle to evangelization.[54]As Las Casas observes, the *encomienda* reveals the primary purpose of the Spanish presence in the Americas to be greed for gold and wealth rather than evangelization. The treatment of human beings as objects to be used up and then discarded, he thinks, follows from the covetousness of the *encomenderos*. For this reason, "the principal and most substantial remedy" to be sought, Las Casas insists, is the end of the *encomienda*. Violence and plunder not only established the *encomienda* system but are embedded in it. Without its abolition, "all other [remedies] will be worthless, as all are ordered to and arranged around this one."[55]

History took a different course from the one for which Las Casas advocated and hoped. In a 2016 pastoral letter, José Luis Escobar Alas, the sitting archbishop of San Salvador, argues that the colonial moment

51. Las Casas, *An Account*, 37–43.

52. Cited in Gutiérrez, *Las Casas: In Search of the Poor of Jesus Christ* (Maryknoll, N.Y.: Orbis, 1993), 314.

53. See Willie James Jennings, *The Christian Imagination: Theology and the Origins of Race* (New Haven, Conn.: Yale University Press, 2011).

54. Las Casas, "Octavo Remedio," in *Tratados de 1552: Impresos por Las Casas en Sevilla, Obras Completas*, vol. 10 (Madrid: Alianza, 1988).

55. Las Casas, "Octavo Remedio," 293. See also Antonio Montesinos, "Advent Sermon," in *A History of Christianity in Asia, Africa, and Latin America, 1450–1990: A Documentary Sourcebook*, ed. Klaus Koschorke, Frieder Ludwig, and Mariano Delgado (Grand Rapids, Mich.: William B. Eerdmans, 2007), 286–87.

indelibly shaped the current societies of Latin America, exposing the indigenous peoples and later generations to *una pedagogía de la muerte* (a pedagogy of death), by which he means a complex and still ongoing catechesis both in the perpetration of violence and its impunity. From colonialism onward, violence was used to solidify social exclusions and to establish legal and other institutions, authorizing an incalculable toll of death, which was left unpunished.[56] The archbishop's narrative is reminiscent of Walter Benjamin's angel of history, face turned toward the past, seeing "one single catastrophe which keeps piling wreckage upon wreckage." The angel would like to stay and repair the damage, but a storm keeps propelling him toward the future, with the wreckage continuing to rise skyward.[57]

Regarding the specific problems of this chapter—the concentration of land in vast holdings and the phenomenon of landlessness Romero confronted—it is especially necessary to survey strata of this wreckage related to the enclosure movement of the late nineteenth century.[58] "The existing literature," historian Adolfo Bonilla Bonilla writes, "is unanimous in its agreement that with coffee cultivation came the concentration of land in few hands, as well as the development of the agrarian oligarchy in El Salvador, which after the Second World War was well established as a coffee and agrarian oligarchy."[59]

Enclosure or what historians of El Salvador generally call "privatization" (*privatización*) refers to a series of laws passed between 1879 and 1882 abolishing what were known as *Tierras de Resguardo*—various forms of communal landholdings that had gradually developed after the conquest of the late fifteenth and early sixteenth centuries.[60] We will see in

56. Escobar Alas, *Veo en la ciudad violencia y discordia* (San Salvador: Arzobispado de San Salvador, 2016), 19–25.

57. Walter Benjamin, *Illuminations* (New York: Schocken, 1969), 257–58.

58. Pontifical Council for Justice and Peace, *Toward a Better Distribution of Land: The Challenge of Agrarian Reform* (Rome: Libreria Editrice Vaticana, 1997), no. 4.

59. Bonilla Bonilla, *Tenencia de la tierra y reforma agraria en El Salvador: Un análisis Histórico* (San Salvador: Centro Nacional de Investigaciones en Ciencias Sociales y humanidades, 2013), 8, 41–42.

60. David Browning, *El Salvador: Landscape and Society* (New York: Oxford University Press, 1971), 87–94; David Weeks, "European Antecedents of Land Tenure and Agrarian Organization of Hispanic America," *Journal of Land and Public Utility Economics* 23 (February 1947):

chapter 2 how similar processes transformed Europe centuries earlier before eventually spreading to Europe's colonial holdings. In the case of El Salvador, the *Tierras de Resguardo* were assigned to indigenous communities themselves.[61]

The idea of enclosure was not novel. There were precedents long before the late nineteenth century that can similarly be traced to colonialism. The *encomenderos* criticized by Las Casas were granted the labor of the subjects, not their land, which continued to remain in subjects' hands.[62] Rights to land came through separate grants, known as *Merced de Tierra*, which assigned private landholdings known as *estancias*. After a certain period of time, these lands could then be bought and sold.[63] The colonial *hacienda* or privately held landed estate, devoted principally to commercial agriculture, grew out of these forms of land tenure.[64] With the advance of economic liberalism in the nineteenth century, these holdings became individual private property in the modern sense of that phrase. In the twentieth century, they developed into the agrarian oligarchies for which El Salvador became known.[65]

However, until the enclosure legislation of the late nineteenth century, land tenure in El Salvador remained plural, consisting of a complex patchwork of formal and informal arrangements. What marked the new enclosure legislation in the late nineteenth century were its scope and ambition. In one fell swoop, it replaced this complex patchwork with a nationwide system based exclusively upon individual and exclusive private ownership.[66]

60–65; J. Friede, "Proceso de formación de la propiedad territorial en la América inter-tropical," *Jahrbuch für Geschichte von Staat, Wirtschaft und Gesellschaft Lateinamerikas* 2 (1965).

61. Browning, *El Salvador*, 77, 87–88, 196; Weeks, "European Antecedents of Land Tenure and Agrarian Organization of Hispanic America"; Friede, "Proceso de formacion de la propiedad territorial en la America inter-tropical."

62. James Lockhart and Stuart B. Schwartz, *Early Latin America: A History of Colonial Spanish America and Brazil* (New York: Cambridge University Press, 1983), 68.

63. Bonilla Bonilla, *Ideas económicas en la Centroamérica ilustrada, 1793–1838* (San Salvador: FLASCO Programa El Salvador, 1999), 41; Lockhart and Schwartz, *Early Latin America*, 68–69.

64. Lauria-Santiago, *An Agrarian Republic: Commercial Agriculture and the Politics of Peasant Communities in El Salvador, 1823–1914* (Pittsburgh: University of Pittsburgh Press, 1999), 230–32.

65. Bonilla Bonilla, *Tenencia de la tierra y reforma agraria en El Salvador*, 18.

66. Browning, *El Salvador*, 78–137.

Historian Aldo A. Lauria-Santiago has shown that by the end of the colonial period, the *hacienda* system was languishing, and indigenous and mestizo communities controlled extensive landholdings through legal title.[67] These lands consisted of *ejidos* or lands held by municipalities; *tierras communales* or lands held by communities, whether indigenous or mestizo; and finally *baldíos* or unclaimed, state-owned land.[68] The *ejidos* and *tierras communales* were based upon the recognition of the right of towns to have sufficient land for subsistence needs, as well as upon the idea, more pronounced in Hispanic-American than Anglo-American law, that continual occupancy and use of land are legitimate grounds for legal ownership.[69] These communally held lands preserved the notion that the use of land was part of communal organization itself, embedded in communal forms of life.

What is crucial to see is that while the land targeted for enclosure did not belong to households by legal title, the use of it did. As forms of land tenure, the *ejidos* and *tierras communales* were common lands in the sense of belonging to all members of the community. Land could not be subject to alienation by individuals claiming exclusive ownership over it.[70] However, families did have usufruct rights, which they depended upon to meet their own subsistence needs, focusing especially upon the cultivation of maize.[71] Additionally, households also had rights of access to common lands for grazing, hunting, fishing, timber, and so on.[72] For this reason, the historian David Browning writes of "a sense of possession"

67. Lauria-Santiago, *Agrarian Republic*, 17–33.

68. These different forms of land tenure experienced different processes of enclosure, but I treat them together for the purposes of the present chapter. For a more detailed portrait, see Lauria-Santiago, *Agrarian Republic*. The classic work on enclosure in El Salvador is Browning, *El Salvador*, to which Lauria-Santiago is responding.

69. Browning, *El Salvador*, 145–46, 150, 196.

70. However, communal leaders could petition for more land if the needs changed; Browning, *El Salvador*, 17, 150, 196; Lauria-Santiago, *Agrarian Republic*, 25.

71. Browning, *El Salvador*, 14–15, 18–19; Lauria-Santiago, *Agrarian Republic*, 17–33. The archbishop of Guatemala described such cultivation about a century earlier: "Everything they did and said so concerned maize that they almost regarded it as a god ... as though the *milpas* [the maize field] were their final purpose in life and source of their felicity"; Pedro Cortés y Larraz, *Descripción geográfico-moral de la diócesis de Goathemala*, A.G.I, Audiencia de Guatemala, leg. 940, fol. 35 (2001) [1770].

72. José M. Ots Capdequí, *El régimen de la tierra en la América Española durante el período colonial* (Ciudad Trujillo: Universidad de Santo Domingo-Editora Montalvo, 1946).

on the part of these households "as far as the use of land was concerned," as well as of the "ancient belief" in the "right of accessibility" to land.[73]

According to Browning, in the decades after independence the emerging Salvadoran state began to implement policies prioritizing commercial agriculture, removing any obstacles to its establishment and spread.[74] The state imagined progress primarily in terms of increased production of crops for export and justified its policies—agricultural and otherwise—through an appeal to *laissez-faire* economic theory.[75] At least at first, most newly independent republics, including El Salvador, did not challenge the legitimacy of the common lands.[76] The goal was reform rather than revolution.[77] But government officials increasingly regarded the complex patchwork of formal and informal land tenure arrangements to be a particularly problematic colonial legacy, so they set to work streamlining them to make agriculture more organized and efficient.[78] The principles undergirding common lands, such as sufficient land for subsistence needs and ongoing occupancy and use as grounds for possession, came under immense pressure.

The state's vision of progress is on clear display in the enclosure legislation itself. The 1881 decree declares that the existence of communal lands is "contrary to the economic, political, and social principles that the Republic has accepted," because these lands "impede the development of agriculture, obstruct the circulation of wealth, and weaken family bonds and the independence of the individual."[79] The abolition of the *ejidos* came the following year on the grounds that they were likewise an obstacle to the nation's development. The *ejidos*, according to the 1882 decree, "nullified the benefits of property (*anula los beneficios de la propriedad*) of the larger and most important lands in the Republic," which were dedi-

---

73. Browning, *El Salvador*, 16–17, 28–29. These rights were loosely defined, at least in part because the cultivation of maize and other subsistence crops, which was migratory. Households did not cultivate particular lands in perpetuity but were periodically assigned them by communal leaders.

74. Browning, *El Salvador*, 142–48.

75. Browning, *El Salvador*, 145–46.

76. Lauria-Santiago, *Agrarian Republic*, 14, 17–33.

77. Browning, *El Salvador*, 174–203.

78. Browning, *El Salvador*, 145–48; Lauria-Santiago, *Agrarian Republic*, 135.

79. Diario Oficial, "Ley de extinción de comunidades," vol. 10, no. 49, February 26, 1881.

cated to "crops of little value" or "abandoned altogether." The crux of the problem, in other words, was the very idea of communally held land and the perceived absence of property. As the decree states, the problem was the "precariousness of the right of [the possessors of communal land, which]…leads them to maintain land in isolation, apathy, and indifference to all improvement."[80]

As this language suggests, the architects of enclosure were members of the liberal revolution of nineteenth-century Latin America, who viewed themselves as the vanguard of modernity, leading those mired in backwardness into a new age of enlightenment.[81] The elevation of a characteristically modern understanding of property occupied a prominent place in this march of progress, and it functioned as a support column for a whole social vision. One of the defining features of this social vision was the power of owners to exclude others from the use of their property,[82] which is exactly what the enclosure legislation in El Salvador granted. This power to exclude, advocates of enclosure argued, guarantees private property.

In Latin America, like elsewhere, liberals closely associated—even conflated—liberty and private property, often arguing that a political economy based on private property and its protection both embodies liberty and enables it to flourish. As Arthur Lee writes about the U.S. Constitution, but with words that are likewise applicable to the Salvadoran context, "The right of property is the guardian of every other right, and to deprive a peo-

80. Diario Oficial, "Ley de la extinción de ejidos," vol. 12, no. 62, March 2, 1882.

81. Lindo-Fuentes and Ching, *Modernizing Minds in El Salvador*, 30–38; Paige, *Coffee and Power*, 44–45, 55–56. Liberalism interacted in novel and complex ways with its new environs. Latin American liberals tended to favor reliance upon a powerful, centralized state not only to enclose common lands so as to facilitate export agriculture, but also to embark on infrastructure projects, to intervene actively in labor markets (for instance, through vagrancy laws), and to maintain social order. Consequently, in addition to export agriculture and *laissez-faire* economics, Salvadoran liberalism was associated with authoritarianism and, later, with anticommunism.

82. Legal scholar Jedediah Purdy notes how many early-modern thinkers understood property in terms of an owner's exclusive control of access, use, and disposal over objects. This understanding of property became "the centerpiece" of a "new way of understanding society," "the keystone institution" of a whole "social vision"; Jedediah Purdy, *The Meaning of Property: Freedom, Community, and the Legal Imagination* (New Haven, Conn.: Yale University Press, 2011), 5, 16.

ple of this is in fact to deprive them of their liberty."[83] On this view, the relationship between private property and liberty is intimate, often indistinguishable. Private property guards freedom as it also expresses it.

Salvadoran liberalism fused *laissez-faire* economic theory and a vision of agricultural development centered upon diversification and agricultural export.[84] The common lands, liberals argued, hindered development principally because inalienability of land prevented the establishment of markets.[85] Common lands embedded cultivation within communities and municipalities, and this cultivation centered upon subsistence. Consequently, to the eyes of liberals, the whole system appeared inherently inefficient and wasteful.[86] Adán Mora, the minister of the interior at the time of the enclosure legislation, characterized the common lands as an "anti-economic institution, which kept large portions of land in the hands of a few people and which the system of administration regularly rendered unproductive, with negative consequences for public wealth."[87]

Liberals saw markets in land as the best way to ensure that equal citizens had equal access to it. Their vision was a nation of flourishing entrepreneurial farmers cultivating their own lands and pursuing their own private good, the accumulation of which would promote the good of the nation as a whole.[88] As Lauria-Santiago observes, theirs was a conception of the common good "defined clearly … in commercial terms," for which the protection of private property and the freedom to engage in commerce became the primary locus of collective purpose.[89] The idea was that markets for agricultural goods would automatically channel private self-interest toward socially desirable ends, as if by an invisible hand.[90]

This is why liberals often diagnosed the root of El Salvador's ills to be

83. Quoted in James W. Ely, *The Guardian of Every Other Right: A Constitutional History of Property Rights* (New York: Oxford University Press, 2007), 26. See also Lionel Robbins, *The Theory of Economic Policy in English Classical Political Economy* (London: Macmillan, 1961); Gerald F. Gaus, "Property, Rights, and Freedom," *Social Philosophy and Policy* 11 (1994): 209–40.

84. Browning, *El Salvador*, 145–48, 172; Lauria-Santiago, *Agrarian Republic*, 6–7, 207, 230–31.

85. Browning, *El Salvador*, 196.

86. Lauria-Santiago, *Agrarian Republic*, 164–69.

87. Quoted in Lauria-Santiago, *Agrarian Republic*, 168.

88. Lauria-Santiago, *Agrarian Republic*, 231.

89. Lauria-Santiago, *Agrarian Republic*, 231.

90. Adam Smith, *The Wealth of Nations* (New York, N.Y: Bantam Classics, 2003), book IV, chap. II.

the very idea of common property itself. To them, the paucity of private landowners was the primary source of El Salvador's backwardness. This diagnosis frequently appears in the pages of the government-sponsored publication *Boletín de Agricultura*. In the lead article of an early issue, an anonymous author states that common lands have "no particular owners, since their possessors cannot consider them as their own."[91] Despite the frequency of this claim, it is in fact untrue. Common lands are a particular form of property, not its absence. Community members had usufruct rights over land to cultivate, to graze cattle, and so on—rights that were regulated communally. Nevertheless, the perceived absence of property leads the same author to assert that the very existence of common lands "deprives farmers of the benefits of cultivating their own property, defrauding (*defraudando*) both the state and the individual."[92] With the establishment of a system of individual property, however, "a rich and extensive source of prosperity will be opened to the Nation," because individual cultivation makes land more "productive."[93] Notice the moral outrage in the article's criticism of the inefficiency and wastefulness of common lands. By this logic, common lands are not only obsolete, but their mere existence is a kind of thievery—taking from the state and citizens what is rightfully theirs.

In this way, liberals tended to draw moral lessons from communal tenure. The inefficiency and wastefulness of common property, they thought, bred inefficiency and wastefulness in the habits of those who participated in it. *Campesinos* content with cultivating maize for subsistence on existing landholdings were often viewed as mired in their traditions or simply lacking in the industriousness indispensable to the nation's flourishing.[94] Versions of this view were frequently articulated, such as in this editorial of a leading Salvadoran daily, for which communal land "prejudices and diminishes [the value of land] through encouraging vagrancy, providing excuses for disputes, and thereby daily eroding

91. Lauria-Santiago, *Agrarian Republic*, 165.
92. Lauria-Santiago, *Agrarian Republic*, 165–66.
93. Lauria-Santiago, *Agrarian Republic*, 165–66.
94. Browning, *El Salvador*, 180; Lauria-Santiago, *Agrarian Republic*, 136.

man's progressive spirit."[95] Communal and *ejidal* lands, then, not only prevented progress; they also generated moral decay.

We have already noted that an emphasis on productivism characterized the liberal vision of agricultural development in El Salvador—the notion that production was the exclusive lens through which to evaluate agriculture. By production, however, liberals did not mean the increased production of what most Salvadorans relied upon for their subsistence— namely, maize, beans, sorghum, rice, manioc, and so on. These crops, like the people who cultivated them, were implicated in backwardness and traditionalism. What liberals meant by production was production of crops for export, especially coffee.

This liberal agricultural vision of progress and productivism was also tied to a pervasive racialized discourse inherited from the colonial past, which erected a racial scale collapsing all darker-skinned rural inhabitants into the category *indio*.[96] On this view, indigenous and rural mestizo communities were practically indistinguishable. Together, they formed "the lower class," as one *cafetalero* put it, whose existence was "a drag on and a denial of progress." This "primitive mass" would have to be led— even compelled by force, if necessary—into modernity.[97] This attitude impacted rural life, among other ways, in the passage of labor laws whose purpose was to control and to recruit those dispossessed from lands they formerly farmed and keep them bound to privately owned estates by means of local agricultural judges backed by the military.[98]

Gould and Lauria-Santiago argue that as households lost land in the wake of enclosure and increasingly depended upon wage labor in coffee plantations, such racialized discourse shaped arguments in defense of an order characterized by low wages, deteriorating living and working conditions, and an unjust distribution of land. The belief that all so-called *indios* would waste higher wages or revert to idolatry if given access to land was

<hr>

95. Quoted in Browning, *El Salvador*, 185.

96. Gould and Lauria-Santiago, *To Rise in Darkness*, 12–13, 14, 20, 47–49, 100–101, 116–18, 191, 209, 227, 257, 283. On this point, see Jennings, *Christian Imagination*.

97. Gould and Lauria-Santiago, *To Rise in Darkness*, 12.

98. Browning, *El Salvador*, 217.

"the commonsense of the Central American planter class."[99] As the U.S. military attaché reported in 1931, the arguments of the wealthiest landowners can be distilled to this: "If we sell our land to these *mozos* [workers] we will have nobody to pick our coffee for us. The best thing for everybody is to keep things as they are. As a matter of fact, we paid our *mozos* very high wages three years ago ... [and] they simply stayed drunk two days a week longer than they do now. These *mozos* are not unhappy and as long as they do not know any better, why go out of our way to change matters?"[100]

Enclosure has often been understood by historians of El Salvador in terms of a land grab by the elite—a process of legalized theft that dispossessed the *campesinado* and forced them into wage labor. Social unrest following the legislation attests to the truth of this depiction. Abelardo Torres reports *campesino* uprisings throughout the 1870s and 1880s due to "the abolition of communal and *ejidal* lands, the dispossession of its cultivators, and the conversion of common land into coffee plantations."[101] The widespread disregard for the new legislation led to the establishment of a rural police force in western El Salvador, which later expanded to the rest of the country, whose purpose was to enforce the legislation.[102] However, the recent work of Lauria-Santiago has helpfully pointed to how the process of enclosure was more complex and open-ended than has been previously understood.[103]

According to Lauria-Santiago, among the most significant consequences of enclosure was the generation of new forms of vulnerability on the part of the *campesinado*—particularly in terms of the risk of land loss. Under the new property regime, private property was the only legal form of land tenure, and possessors of land (*poseedores actuales*) became the sole owners of it (*proprietarios*). Not only did they have the power to

---

99. Gould and Lauria-Santiago, *To Rise in Darkness*, 12, 49; Paige, *Coffee and Power*, 46.

100. Quoted in Gould and Lauria-Santiago, "'They Call Us Thieves and Steal Our Wage': Toward a Reinterpretation of the Salvadoran Rural Mobilization, 1929–1931," *Hispanic American Historical Review* 84, no. 2 (May 2004): 205.

101. Abelardo Torres, *Tierras y colonización* (San Salvador: Instituto de Estudios Económicos, 1961), 25.

102. Browning, *El Salvador*, 218.

103. Lauria-Santiago, *Agrarian Republic*, 9–10, 17–33, 132–221, 230–34.

exclude others from their land, but they also had the power to alienate it.[104] Moreover, because land was alienable, it could also serve as collateral, and so commercial agriculture in the wake of enclosure involved potential forfeiture of land to creditors.[105] Another consequence, closely associated with the establishment of a market in land, was land scarcity. In late nineteenth-century El Salvador, the implementation of a land market led to a rush to stake and title claims, with vast tracts of land being sold at low prices to claimants, many of whom were not farmers but speculators or investors. Because of this and a growing population, the agricultural frontier was shrinking rapidly and would close by the early twentieth century.[106] All the available land was being claimed and titled. And in the new property regime, the basic currency to acquire more was no longer the subsistence needs of households but capital.[107]

Especially during the first decades of the twentieth century, mid-level producers of coffee consolidated smaller farms and increased productivity, which led to a conspicuous concentration of land ownership.[108] A coffee elite began to emerge that controlled credit, along with the processing, marketing, and exporting of coffee. As coffee boomed, land values rose and profits soared. El Salvador became a leader in the application of new technologies to coffee. Due to these developments, Salvadoran coffee *fincas* became among the most productive in the world, and El Salvador's coffee elite grew fabulously wealthy. The wealth generated led not only to reinvestments in coffee, but also in crops such as cotton and sugar cane, as well as in finance, real estate, commerce, tourism, and manufacturing.

Consequently, the property regime resulting from enclosure, combined with coffee's expansion, presented an unprecedented opportunity to turn land into capital, which could then be used not only to build more wealth, but also—and especially pertinent to our present consider-

104. Browning, *El Salvador*, 207–8, 212.
105. Lauria-Santiago, *Agrarian Republic*, 157, 193, 233–34.
106. Lauria-Santiago, *Agrarian Republic*, 159, 191, 233–34.
107. Lauria-Santiago, *Agrarian Republic*, 193; Browning, *El Salvador*, 213.
108. This paragraph draws upon Browning, *El Salvador*, 138–221; Lauria-Santiago, *Agrarian Republic*, 132–33, 153–57, 228–29, 233–34; Hector Lindo-Fuentes, *Weak Foundations: The Economy of El Salvador in the Nineteenth Century, 1821–1898* (Berkeley: University of California Press, 1991), 152–86; Paige, *Coffee and Power*, 1–95.

ations—to expand landholdings. The concentration of credit, processing, marketing, and export of crops like coffee was therefore closely related to the concentration of land. As one newspaper described coffee's expansion, "The conquest of territory by the coffee industry is alarming. It has already occupied all the high ground and is now descending to the valleys, displacing maize, rice, and beans. It moves in the manner of the *conquistador*, spreading hunger and misery, reducing the former proprietors to the worst conditions."[109]

Indebted smallholders steadily lost their mortgaged farms to many of these same elite coffee families.[110] "About forty-five years ago," the Salvadoran scholar Alberto Masferrer wrote in 1928, "the land in the country was distributed among the majority of Salvadorians, but now it is falling into the hands of a few owners.... El Salvador is moving toward *latifundia* [from the Latin for "large estates"] at a time when most countries are attempting to move away from it."[111] Miguel Mármol, a prominent communist, concurred, observing that by the 1920s *latifundism* was widespread. The land hunger of the elite was so intense that he referred to it as *geophagia*—literally, the eating of the earth.[112]

By the 1920s, the *campesinado* was clearly in the midst of what Gould and Lauria-Santiago describe as an "agonizing decomposition."[113] The dispossessed increasingly turned to wage labor to survive. Many became *colonos* or permanent resident laborers on coffee *fincas*—an arrangement in which landlords typically provided land in exchange for work and a portion of the harvest of the *colono*.[114] By 1938, nearly 20 percent of the entire rural population in the west lived on coffee *fincas* as *colonos* or administrators.[115] Others migrated to the hot and humid coastal plains, to the cities, or to the banana and sugar plantations of Honduras.[116]

109. Quoted in Everett Alan Wilson, "The Crisis of National Integration in El Salvador, 1919–1935" (Ph.D. diss., Stanford University, 1970), 122.

110. Gould and Lauria-Santiago, "'They Call Us Thieves and Steal Our Wage,'" 200.

111. Quoted in Wilson, "Crisis of National Integration in El Salvador," 121.

112. Roque Dalton, *Miguel Mármol* (New York: Curbstone, 1995), 99.

113. Gould and Lauria-Santiago, *To Rise in Darkness*, 3.

114. Segundo Montes, *El agro salvadoreño: 1973–1980* (San Salvador: UCA Editores, 1986), 265, 318.

115. Gould and Lauria-Santiago, "'They Call Us Thieves and Steal Our Wage,'" 200.

116. Molly Todd, *Beyond Displacement: Campesinos, Refugees, and Collective Action in the Salvadoran Civil War* (Madison: University of Wisconsin Press, 2010), 27–29.

In summary, while the advocates of enclosure sought to facilitate a better distribution of land, they in fact facilitated concentration and established the conditions whereby access became more difficult. Enclosure effectively locked *campesinos* into landholding patterns that permitted little flexibility or possibility for expansion as needs changed. In Lauria-Santiago's words, enclosure "institutionalized and rigidified a decidedly flawed system," perpetuating "many of the limitations, contradictions and inequalities of the community land system and creat[ing] new problems as well."[117] Among the new problems was widespread dispossession. In 1882, Teodoro Moreno, the author of the enclosure legislation, stated on the floor of the National Assembly that the common lands were established to defend Salvadoran sons and daughters "from the ambitions of the conquerors."[118] Because "there are now no longer any conquerors," he continued, it has become necessary to enclose the commons and establish a market in land.[119] Apparently, he did not envision the new kind of conqueror that would emerge as a consequence of enclosure.

Historians continue to discuss and debate the intricacies of this process. But the result is uncontroversial: an elite that controlled not only coffee, but much of the rest of the country as well—including its arable land—with the vast majority of Salvadorans working for these families or finding a way to survive on land marginal to coffee cultivation. The benefits brought by enclosure therefore came with a heavy price as *campesinos* lost their lands and the subsistence guarantees of the old order. Widespread land concentration and chronic landlessness prevailed as the twentieth century progressed.

We have been examining the first expansion of export-agricultural production. The second expansion is also important to consider, because the rise of sugar cane, cattle, and cotton production after World War II ushered in another intensive period of land concentration and further contributed to the trends we have been examining.[120] The coastal plain,

117. Lauria-Santiago, *Agrarian Republic*, 191, 193; Lindo-Fuentes and Ching, *Modernizing Minds in El Salvador*, 32, 233.

118. Quoted in Lauria-Santiago, *Agrarian Republic*, 167.

119. Quoted in Lauria-Santiago, *Agrarian Republic*, 167.

120. For more on this second expansion, see Browning, *El Salvador*, 224–69; Charles D.

to which many of those dispossessed by the first wave migrated, was the principal site for the cultivation of these new crops. According to Browning, this second expansion of export-oriented agriculture therefore largely completed not just the dispossession of the Salvadoran *campesinado*, but the process initiated by conquest and colonization: the domination of the landscape by privately owned agricultural land dedicated principally to export crops.[121] During the first expansion of coffee cultivation in the late nineteenth and early twentieth centuries, the large plantations could absorb those dispossessed because of the high demand for labor. In contrast, the widespread use of agrochemicals and higher-yielding crop varieties in the second expansion meant landholders were considerably less reliant on labor. Therefore, instead of absorbing people, this second expansion tended to expel them, further contributing to the swelling numbers in search of land and work.

Another significant contributor to landlessness was the disintegration of the *colonato* system, in which permanent resident laborers typically exchanged work and a portion of their harvest for usufruct. By the 1950s, many throughout El Salvador were heavily dependent upon this institution for their livelihood. But, according to Marcelo Germán Posada and Mario López, in response to governmental reform measures—especially the establishment of a minimum wage law—large landowners began to evict *colonos* and rely instead exclusively on wage workers. Consequently, between the 1950s and 1970s, the *colonato* system went into rapid decline and had virtually disappeared by 1971.[122] With the disintegration

---

Brockett, *Land, Power, and Poverty: Agrarian Transformation and Political Conflict in Central America* (Boulder, Colo.: Westview, 1998), 41–65; Robert G. Williams, *Export Agriculture and the Crisis in Central America* (Chapel Hill: University of North Carolina Press, 1986); William Durham, *Scarcity and Survival in Central America: Ecological Origins of the Soccer War* (Stanford, Calif.: Stanford University Press, 1979), 21–62; Paige, *Coffee and Power*, 29, 92–93; Ridgeway Satterthwaite, "*Campesino* Agriculture and *Hacienda* Modernization in Coastal El Salvador, 1949–1969" (Ph.D. diss., University of Wisconsin, 1971); Santiago Ruíz Granadino, "Modernización agrícola en El Salvador," *Estudios Sociales Centroamericanos* 22 (1979): 71–95; Walter LaFeber, *Inevitable Revolutions: The United States in Central America* (New York: W. W. Norton, 1984), 176–77.

121. Browning, *El Salvador*, 225, 248.

122. Marcelo Germán Posada and Mario López, "El Salvador 1950–1970: Latifundios, integración y crisis," *Revista de Historia de América* 115 (1993): 37–62.

of the *colonato* system, thousands of families were forced to leave the lands they had previously farmed.[123]

What did the landless do to survive? Some remained in rural areas, but had weak ties to land or steady employment. When they found land to farm, they did so typically as renters or squatters. Moreover, the land itself was usually marginal, like hillsides, with thin, rocky soils and steep inclines—especially susceptible to degradation and erosion—and almost always insufficient for households' subsistence needs.[124] Others among the landless found migratory and seasonal wage work in the booming agro-export economy. Still others left rural areas altogether, joining the exodus of migrants to the cities, typically squatting in settlements and finding work in a growing urban informal sector of merchants, artisans, day laborers, and so on.[125]

Attending to enclosure and its legacies helps us to appreciate why scholars consistently characterize the Salvadoran political-economic system as exclusionary.[126] The sociologist Segundo Montes, another of the Jesuits killed in 1989, summarized the developments we have just been surveying: "The entire economic and financial system, as well as the state apparatus, functions to reproduce this capitalist mode of agricultural production."[127] What is especially important to see for our purposes is that this particular mode of export-agricultural production did not just produce coffee, cotton, sugar, and beef; it also produced people without

123. Browning, *El Salvador*, 248–53; Durham, *Scarcity and Survival in Central America*, 50–78; Brockett, *Land, Power, And Poverty*, 68–76; Dunkerley, *Power in the Isthmus* (New York: Verso, 1989), 179–201; Victor Bulmer-Thomas, *The Political Economy of Central America since 1920* (New York: Cambridge University Press, 1987), 201–7; Williams, *Export Agriculture and the Crisis in Central America*.

124. Durham, *Scarcity and Survival in Central America*; Jenny Pearce, *Promised Land: Peasant Rebellion in Chalatenango, El Salvador* (London: Latin America Bureau, 1986); Carlos Rafael Cabarrús, *Genesis de una revolución: Análisis del surgimiento y desarrollo de la organización campesina en El Salvador* (México, D.F.: Centro de Investigaciones y Estudios Superiores en Antropologia Social, 1983); Williams, *Export Agriculture and the Crisis in Central America*; Posada and López, "El Salvador 1950–1970," 45, 54–57; Paige, *Coffee and Power*, 90–94.

125. Durham, *Scarcity and Survival in Central America*, 56–62; Paige, *Coffee and Power*, 29–30, 94; Posada and López, "El Salvador 1950–1970," 42–43.

126. Posada and López, "El Salvador 1950–1970," 46; Durham, *Scarcity and Survival in Central America*, 50; Lauria-Santiago, *Agrarian Republic*, 238.

127. Montes, *El agro salvadoreño*, 104.

land—and it produced them in abundance. For this reason, descriptions of these developments as exploitative or oppressive are, strictly speaking, inaccurate. People were not simply being abused or treated unfairly by their societies; they were being excluded and discarded altogether by them. The production of landlessness is similar to what Pope Francis has described as a "throw away culture," in which those like the landless "are no longer society's underside or its fringes or its disenfranchised ... [but its] 'leftovers.'"[128] The basic institutions the exploited and the oppressed count upon were being devastated, the very idea of society in the minimal sense of shared social membership attacked.[129]

Writing in the early 1970s, Browning notes that in order to survive, the landless increasingly turned to squatting, settling upon and even cultivating land for which they had no legal title. Everywhere the landscape evidenced this phenomenon: the eroded hillsides, the deforestation, the makeshift huts of sticks and straw by the sides of the roads, maize and beans planted in every available patch of land, and the settlements at the outskirts of cities and towns. Large landowners lived with the constant threat of spontaneous occupation of land left untended. To keep land free of *paracaidístas* (parachutists), landowners patrolled boundaries or relied upon police or private security. In the cotton-growing lowlands, crop dusters reportedly bathed squatters with agrochemicals as if they were weeds or pests to be eradicated.[130]

By definition, squatters have no legal title to the lands they occupy, so their position is always insecure before the law. Salvadoran civil code did recognize the law of *usucapio* or adverse possession, whereby a person possessing land owned by others can legally acquire it after a period of time.[131] However, under the new property regime and in the context of

---

128. Francis I, Apostolic Exhortation *Evangelii Gaudium* (Washington, D.C.: United States Conference of Catholic Bishops, November 24, 2013), no. 53.

129. For this reason, Karl Polanyi points to parallels between the devastation of enclosure and the devastation of colonialism, in Polanyi, *The Great Transformation: The Political and Economic Origins of Our Time* (Boston: Beacon, 2001), 158–60. See also Jennings, *Christian Imagination*, 72–73.

130. Browning, *El Salvador*, 256. For a similar account, see Michael Samers, *Migration* (New York: Routledge, 2010), 176. For a fictional one, see Leslie Marmon Silko, *Almanac of the Dead* (New York: Simon and Schuster, 1991), 459.

131. Adverse possession attests both to the utility and the normative weight of de facto

land scarcity, access to land was increasingly fraught, and the squatter came to prominence as a new kind of problem plaguing the nation.[132] Acquiring land in this manner therefore became both difficult and dangerous. With the onset of the Cold War, at a time when questioning the justice of existing property arrangements involved risks, the bodily transgression of them was especially perilous. But a growing group of people had little choice. Survival involved breaking the law of property and the consequent criminalization of their need.

Browning makes an important observation when he writes that the landless often behaved as though any unused land was theirs—as if access to it belonged to them. When evicted from one place, they would simply move to the margins of another to establish themselves.[133] Of course, they were fully aware of the precarity of their position, knowing they lacked legal title to these lands. The kinds of dwellings they built and crops they planted evinced the sense that they could be evicted and forced to move at a moment's notice. Nevertheless, as Browning writes, "They continued to act in accordance with the belief in their ancient right of access to land."[134] Their need was its own law. To disobey it would have been like trying to disobey the preservation of themselves in existence.

On this basis, the landless behaved as though any unoccupied land was theirs—and in an important sense, it was.[135] Their need had effectively made it so de facto, even if not de jure. "The squatter family," Browning continues, "regard[s] the entire countryside as its 'common land': it will settle where it may, it will resist eviction, it will use every means possible to assert its belief that it has as much right to land as

---

possession, recognizing that in circumstances it should lead to de jure possession; Nomi Stolzenberg, "Facts on the Ground," in *Property and Community* (New York: Oxford University Press, 2010), 120.

132. Browning, *El Salvador*, 260–64.

133. Browning, *El Salvador*, 220.

134. Browning, *El Salvador*, 256, 145–46, 150.

135. For similar reasons, *campesinos* in neighboring Honduras spoke not of *occupying* land belonging to others but of *recovering* land belonging to them; Philip McManus and Gerald Schlabach, eds., *Relentless Persistence: Nonviolent Action in Latin America* (Philadelphia: New Society, 1991), 64–77; Anders Corr, *No Trespassing: Squatting, Rent Strikes, and Land Struggles Worldwide* (Cambridge, Mass.: South End, 1999), 39–50. On a recent trip to Chiapas, Mexico, I heard people speak in similar terms.

have all other members of the community."[136] Therefore, although the *ejidos* and the *tierras communales* had long since been enclosed and their legal basis dismantled by the Salvadoran state, the imperatives that led to their establishment continued and found new forms of expression outside the protection of positive law. The production of an excluded people, whose way of life was marked by landlessness, migration, and squatting, served as an ongoing reminder of this reality.

In this way, the phenomenon of squatting underscores what is at stake in a politics of common use—a politics based on the belief that creation is a common gift that seeks to ensure all have access to the material support they need to survive and to flourish. Squatting also points to the complex relationship of this politics to positive law. The squatter's intention, after all, is not to flout property law, but to secure material support in circumstances where there is no other means of doing so. Legal scholars Eduardo Peñalver and Sonia Katyal refer to this as the "redistributive value" property lawbreaking can have.[137] In the case of squatters, the lawbreaking is acquisitive; squatters take from others' excess and so redistribute goods from where they are less to more needed. Squatters tend to settle where property is abandoned or otherwise neglected, which suggests the owner's need of the land is not as immediately pressing as that of squatters themselves.

On this basis, Peñalver and Katyal argue that situations where property lawbreaking is persistent and widespread can communicate important lessons—for instance, about the failure or the injustice of a given property regime. In response to those lessons, a polity might pursue land reform or some other measure to ameliorate the problem. Among the possible courses of action for affected owners is to ask themselves whether squatters' claims upon their surfeit is just and to act accordingly. In these ways, property lawbreaking can have persuasive power and can even lead to greater justice. For property lawbreaking can help people reimagine their relationships to what they possess, to the needs of oth-

---

136. Browning, *El Salvador*, 221.

137. Eduardo M. Peñalver and Sonia Katyal, *Property Outlaws: How Squatters, Pirates, and Protesters Improve the Law of Ownership* (New Haven, Conn.: Yale University Press, 2010), 18, 127, 143, 183.

ers, and to the sources of sustenance upon which all people depend. Of course, property lawbreaking can lead to other responses as well, such as the use of coercion as deterrence. However, this response not only eliminates the redistributive value such lawbreaking can have, but also mutes its communicative power, thwarting its potential for societal and personal transformation.

These are admittedly complex matters, but the production of landlessness is important for understanding Romero's characterization of ordinary violence, especially as it affects the "difficult and desperate situation of the *campesinado*," whose members have no land upon which to subsist and who must therefore sell their labor for "miserable wages, insufficient to meet the most minimal necessities of subsistence."[138] Socorro Jurídico, the legal aid office of the archdiocese, frequently dealt with situations of *campesinos* looking for land to farm and standoffs between squatters and landowners.[139] These considerations also help us to appreciate the seriousness with which Romero took the struggle of his people to secure the land and tools needed to farm and to organize around the "vital problems of subsistence, of land, of wages"[140] in resistance to a throwaway culture producing people without land or livelihood. As Romero puts it in his third pastoral letter on the church and what at that time were referred to as "popular organizations" (*organizaciones populares*)—a topic to which we will turn in later chapters—"what forced [these organizations] to unite in the first place was not just their civil right to participate in the political and economic development of their country, but simply the vital necessity of subsistence, exercising the right to make their conditions of life at least tolerable. Here in this vital necessity is where the necessity for legislation and the necessity for organization coincide."[141] "The people are organizing themselves," Romero memorably puts it elsewhere, "not for subversion but for survival."[142]

We have been attending so closely to landlessness because for Romero

138. Romero, *Homilías*, 5:178.
139. Romero, *Homilías*, 2:291. Personal communication with Roberto Cuéllar, who worked closely with Romero as the director of Socorro Jurídico.
140. Romero, *Homilías*, 3:153, 346; 2:384; 4:103.
141. Romero, *Iglesia y organizaciones políticas populares*, 99.
142. Romero, *Homilías*, 5:168.

it is among the clearest signs of ordinary violence—a violence perpetrated against the dignity of those deprived of what they need to survive and to flourish, one that is sustained by structural and institutional forces. Once again, as forms of violence, these are distinct from the repressive violence of the state and the revolutionary violence of its opponents, both of which Romero interprets as violent responses to a violence already lodged in the landscape. Precisely because of their ubiquity, ordinary and structural-institutional forms violence tend to be normalized, associated with the orderly functioning of social and economic life, such as, in this case, export-agricultural production. This at least partially accounts for the hiddenness of such violence, the way it tends to recede into the background of moral consideration.

The problem of the ordinary violence of landlessness is also indispensable for understanding Romero's understanding of land reform. Much in the way Peñalver and Katyal suggest, Romero thinks phenomena like landlessness and squatting have a kind of communicative power that conveys important lessons about injustices that need redress. Perhaps the most important of these lessons concerns what property is and what it means to possess it. As Romero says in one homily regarding a standoff between squatters and landowners in Azacualpa, Chalatenango, "I know that those who are occupying lands … are respecting private property. They only want an agreement that enables them to have a place to plant and give food to their families."[143] In interpreting this reality, Romero quotes Paul VI's 1967 encyclical *Populorum Progressio* about how "the right to private property is not absolute and unconditional," such that "no one may appropriate surplus goods solely for his own private use when others lack the bare necessities of life."[144] As we will see, Romero thinks that those who possess the world's goods must constantly evaluate what they have in relationship to those who lack them, because God gives the gift of creation in common.

In addition to the justice of the claims being made upon people's surfeit by those in need, Romero thinks landlessness and squatting com-

143. Romero, *Homilías*, 1:408.
144. Romero, *Homilías*, 2:291, quoting Paul VI, Encyclical Letter *Populorum Progressio* (March, 26, 1967), no. 23.

municate other lessons regarding the imperative to enact land reform or some other legal measure to ameliorate the problem. The reason Romero advocates land reform from "above," through the action of the Salvadoran governmental and entities like ISTA, is that he is responding to an informal and widespread land reform already welling up from "below," through the actions of ordinary people to make ends meet, for instance, by farming on land for which they have no legal title out of necessity. Earlier we saw Romero say that it is in the vital necessity of subsistence where the need for legislation and organization coincide. As Romero sees it, such legislation is necessary not only for ensuring his people can organize, but also for attaining access to the land they need.

The pursuit of a better distribution of land through law and policy is therefore not, as Romero's critics repeatedly charge, the blatant thievery of what hard-working people have legitimately earned by the strength of their own hands, or an alliance forged with the forces of revolutionary violence and subversion. Rather, at least for Romero, the purpose of land reform is to address a violence already rooted in the landscape, to work for peace where there is presently no peace. Commenting upon what happened in San Pedro Perulapán, Romero states unequivocally that in defending the access of *campesinos* to land to work and their ability to organize to secure it, "the Church is not sowing violence; unjust situations are sowing violence."[145] The church is simply indicating how deep the roots of violence go, a process that is indispensable for the attainment of true peace, because peace is the fruit of justice, and justice entails sharing what God has given to all.[146]

THE GRAMMAR OF CREATION

The remainder of this chapter explores the theological grammar informing the notion of ordinary violence we have been exploring. Romero's purpose in characterizing reality in these terms is not to suggest a moral equivalence between distinct forms of violence, nor is it to wield the language of ordinary violence as a weapon to make the case for liberating

145. Romero, *Homilías*, 2:384.
146. Romero, *Homilías*, 2:385, 387.

violence. Rather, his purpose is to convey a clearer picture of the way the world truly is: how through goodness the God who makes all things gives the earth and its harvests to humankind as a whole, for all to be nourished from them; how God gives human creatures not only their land and its fruits, but also their lives and their agency in order to participate in the diffusion of God's goodness; and finally, how sin and the violence it unleashes hinder God's purpose for creation. Romero's analysis of ordinary violence derives from this theological grammar, specifically the conviction that creation is a common gift. Ordinary violence becomes perceptible precisely as a breach of the original goodness of God's gift of the earth and its harvests for common use.

In terms of the church's social teaching, perhaps the most authoritative articulation of the common character of creation is this passage from *Gaudium et Spes*:

> God intended the earth with everything contained in it for the use of all human beings and peoples. Thus, under the leadership of justice and in the company of charity, created goods should be in abundance for all in like manner. Whatever the forms of property may be, as adapted to the legitimate institutions of peoples, according to diverse and changeable circumstances, attention must always be paid to this universal destination of earthly goods. In using them, therefore, man should regard the external things that he legitimately possesses not only as his own but also as common in the sense that they should be able to benefit not only him but also others. On the other hand, the right of having a share of earthly goods sufficient for oneself and one's family belongs to everyone. The Fathers and Doctors of the Church held this opinion, teaching that men are obliged to come to the relief of the poor and to do so not merely out of their superfluous goods. If one is in extreme necessity, he has the right to procure for himself what he needs out of the riches of others. Since there are so many people prostrate with hunger in the world, this sacred council urges all, both individuals and governments, to remember the aphorism of the Fathers, "Feed the man dying of hunger, because if you have not fed him, you have killed him," and really to share and employ their earthly goods, according to the ability of each, especially

by supporting individuals or peoples with the aid by which they may be able to help and develop themselves.[147]

The foregoing describes creation in terms of the *telos,* or end, of created goods, the idea that they have a common or universal purpose. As Romero explains, "There are not two categories of people: those who have been born to have everything and leave the rest with nothing, while those with nothing are unable to share what God has created for all."[148]

The construal of property and possession flows directly from this conviction about creation. On the terms of *Gaudium et Spes,* people should learn to see their possessions not exclusively as their own, but as common, which means they must learn to see and to use them both for their own good and for the good of others. Following Catholic social teaching, Romero refers to this variously as the social "sense" or "function" of property, or its "social mortgage."[149] He often criticizes what he calls the "abuse," "aberration," or "absolutizing" of property, which he associates with the idea that possessions belong exclusively to their owners, for owners to use in whatever way they determine.[150] On *Gaudium et Spes*'s view, people can legitimately possess what they need for the survival and flourishing of themselves and their dependents—for they too are members of the commons to which God gives the gift of creation. But the acknowledgment of membership in the commons means possessors must learn to hold possessions lightly, always being open to the claims of others upon what they have. At its heart is the conviction that God creates heaven and earth as a gift given to humankind in common and that the commonality of the gift must be realized to every extent possible. All created goods—including land and the work of human hands—must be held up to this measure.

For the purposes of this chapter, I am isolating this conviction about the commonality of creation as it relates to land and its fruits. But when

---

147. Vatican Council II, *Gaudium et Spes,* nos. 69, 71.
148. Romero, *Homilías,* 5:61.
149. Romero, *Homilías,* 4:216; 5:178, 191, 209, 260, 381–82; 6:357–58.
150. Romero, *Homilías,* 1:341–45; 5:382–83, 386.

Romero speaks of creation, it often opens into new creation—that is, into the theological landscape of God's work of salvation in Israel and in Christ and of humankind's calling to share God's life in Christ and through the Spirit—the common life that creates and sustains creation and that loves it toward consummation. To take a single example from a homily in which Romero is reflecting upon God's triune life of eternal donation and re-donation: "To Christ we owe the great revelation that God is love … — love because God gives and hands over Godself. Without losing it, the Father gives all the divine nature to the Son and to the Holy Spirit. Without losing it, the Son gives it to the Father and to the Holy Spirit. And without losing it, the Spirit gives it to the Son and to the Father."[151] God, without ceasing to be God, creates the world in love to offer creatures a share in God's own life. Despite humankind's refusal of God's gifts, and despite the death and violence that ensues, God's response is not to withdraw but to give the fullness of God's own life by giving Christ.[152] God's purpose in doing so, Romero continues, is to create a "family communion" with human creatures.[153] It is in relation to the common destination of humankind to communion with the triune God that Romero remarks upon the common destination of created goods and "how the earth groans under the weight of sin because people have not understood that creation is for the flourishing of all and not for a few to set themselves up (*instalarse*) in comfort."[154]

In this homily, as elsewhere, Romero locates the gift of creation within the wider divine economy of salvation, which is ordered by and to common gifts, and whose *telos* is eternally sharing in God's life. Sin is the refusal of this reality. Among its paradigmatic expressions for Romero is the appetite of mastery or ownership in which people cling to their possessions, like their lives, as if they were exclusive property. This posture profoundly wounds creatures' capacity for the common life into which God calls them. To use Romero's language, instead of opening their property and their lives to the needs of others, acknowledging the gift-character

---

151. Romero, *Homilías*, 2:515.
152. Romero, *Homilías*, 2:515–16.
153. Romero, *Homilías*, 2:516.
154. Romero, *Homilías*, 2:516.

of both, *se instalan*—they set themselves up apart from others, they settle into their comforts as if the earth were their true home rather than a place of pilgrimage.[155] But in doing so, they operate with a false picture of themselves and the world they inhabit. According to Romero, this is the deepest source of the violence affecting his country.

The idea that creation is a common gift indelibly shapes Romero's social analysis. To take one representative instance: in 1975, Romero started publishing a weekly periodical for the archdiocese of San Salvador called *La Voz del Pastor* (The Pastor's Voice). In the midst of the coffee harvest in 1976, he describes the situation of the Salvadoran coffee harvesters or *cortadores* (cutters):

> The coffee harvest is in full swing … and what is certain is that God, whose works are always full of splendor, is giving us this year a splendid rain of rubies that attracts thousands of workers from all parts to gather the rich gift of our mountains.
>
> Here we see how sin makes God's beautiful creation groan—God's creation which is destined for the freedom of the glory of God's children [Rom 8:19–23]. For this reason, the Church cries out that God's command be heeded: "God intended the earth with everything contained in it for the use of all human beings and peoples. Thus, under the leadership of justice and in the company of charity, created goods should be in abundance for all in like manner. Whatever the forms of property may be … attention must always be paid to this universal destination of earthly goods" (*Gaudium et Spes*, no. 69).
>
> For this reason, the happiness the harvest brings makes us happy. It is not only the happiness of the large landowners but the height of the happiness of so many "cutters" among us, who with this harvest attain their only hope of income for the year. For this same reason, therefore, we are saddened and preoccupied by the selfishness with which methods are devised to deprive workers of their just wages.…
>
> How we would like that the happiness of this rain of rubies and of all the harvests of the earth not to be darkened by the tragic words from Scripture: "Listen! The wages of the laborers who mowed your fields,

---

155. Romero, *Homilías*, 1:272, 483; 2:39, 164; 3:268; 5:264.

which you kept back by fraud, cry out, and the cries of the harvesters
have reached the ears of the Lord of hosts" (Jas 5:4).[156]

As the economic center of gravity, coffee gathers workers from all over El
Salvador to its fields. These workers must move from harvest to harvest,
and what moves them is bodily need. Wherever they reside, their own
lands and opportunities for livelihood are insufficient, so they follow the
harvest, migrating to make ends meet.

In one sense, the coffee harvest is a sign of the goodness of God's
creation, and of God's gift of the land of El Salvador and its harvests for
the happiness of all who dwell in it. Romero shares in the happiness of
the workers for whom the harvest is the only source of income for the
year.[157] But this passage also recalls the problems associated with coffee's
conquest of the Salvadoran landscape. For in the migrants' movement to
make ends meet, in the need that compels it, and especially in the lack
of adequate remuneration for their work, Romero perceives creation's
groaning under the weight of sin.

What is crucial to see is that the very perception of the groaning
derives from the belief that creation is a common gift, which Romero
discusses in relation to the already-cited passage from *Gaudium et Spes*.
That the basic needs of whole groups of people are systematically ignored
means that God's purpose for creation is being blocked. Notice also that
the verses from James about unpaid wages crying out—as if to protest
the thievery being perpetrated in the fields—are not mere ornament or
hyperbole. The belief that creation is a common gift generates this language, alerting us to a violence that, although right before our eyes, might
nevertheless escape notice. Such descriptions serve to unsettle everyday
perceptions of the world, which are habituated to violence by offering a
clearer picture of how the world really is, conforming human perception,
we might say, to God's. Although landowners do not log stolen wages in
their ledgers, God does. God sees the misery and hears the cries of the
workers, just as God observes the misery of the children of Israel under
bondage in Egypt, knows their oppression, and does not turn away from

156. Romero, *La Voz del Pastor*, no. 62, November 28, 1976.
157. Romero, *Homilías*, 6:63.

them in their time of need (Ex 3:7–10). God does not let the wreckage of history pile up without attending to the anguish buried in it. Careful attention to the words Romero uses is important theological work, among other reasons, because the words open a landscape and expand possibilities for agency that would otherwise be imperceptible.

In this article, Romero enacts the kind of social analysis of violence we see throughout his homiletical and literary corpus, which he explicitly describes in a December 1979 homily as the agrarian crisis intensified. Commenting on the gospel passage from Luke 3:10–18—especially John the Baptist's injunction to share ("Whoever has two coats must share with anyone who has none; and whoever has food must do likewise"; 3:11) in preparation for the advent of the Lord—Romero speaks about a "society of solidarity" that is based upon "sharing what God has given to all." The formation of such a society, Romero continues, not only requires sharing, but also fostering a *sentido crítico* (critical sense), which is guided by *criterios cristianos* (Christian criteria) that can help "expose the social mechanisms that marginalize workers and *campesinos*." "Why are *campesinos* only able to earn wages during the harvests of coffee, sugarcane, and cotton?" Romero asks. "Why does our society need *campesinos* without work, poorly paid workers, and people without just wages? These mechanisms must be discovered … in a Christian way, in order to avoid being accomplices in this machinery."[158]

One of Romero's principal criteria in this regard is the common destination of created goods. Although he does not always explicitly cite *Gaudium et Spes*, its theological grammar of creation shapes Romero's social analysis of ordinary violence and the structures and institutions that sustain it. Romero's language often echoes that of the passage about the migrant harvesters. El Salvador's land, like its harvests, he continually says, is for the flourishing of all Salvadorans, not just for the enrichment of the few, which is a purpose they at best only partially fulfill.[159] Throughout his homilies and writings, we therefore frequently find Romero making statements that assume this theological grammar, such as: "God has

158. Romero, *Homilías*, 6:60–63.
159. Romero, *Homilías*, 1:217, 243; 2:191, 197; 3:351, 357, 408; 5:103, 428; 6:393.

made the earth for all peoples."[160] Or: "The products this land produces are for the well-being of the whole community, with justice."[161] Moreover, Romero's conviction that creation is a common gift applies to all land, not just to the land of El Salvador, which relativizes national boundaries. In one homily, he observes that if God gives the earth for all, and if in El Salvador land is scarce while in other countries it is not, then it follows that those who need land should be able to access it elsewhere.[162] On this view, people's ability to access what God gives in common takes precedence over the borders of nations.

This conviction about creation is why Romero's homilies repeatedly return to the vital problems of subsistence, land, and wages, and it is also what animates his concern about the conditions of *campesinos*. Scattered throughout his homilies, for instance, we find comments about migrant workers lacking shelter as they travel in the cold season from farm to farm looking for work and being forced to sleep on tarps or on improvised hammocks.[163] We find comments upon inadequate protections for those whose bodies are routinely exposed to agrochemicals.[164] "I have seen it up close," Romero says, "on the farms."[165]

In the background of these and similar comments is the whole question of why migrant workers must move in the first place, why the land and the wages where they live are insufficient, and why their vulnerability and need have become a site of further violence. As Romero sees it, land concentration is at the heart of the matter. The "enormous injustice of the distribution of land" and the stark polarizations it produces, he thinks, are a reality that "dominates" El Salvador.[166] In discussing official government statistics about the dire state of the *campesinado*—the absence of prenatal and postpartum care for women, the high rates of infant and childhood mortality and malnutrition, the lack of access to water and adequate shelter, and so on—Romero contends that this ordi-

160. Romero, *Homilías*, 3:78.
161. Romero, *Homilías*, 1:423.
162. Romero, *Homilías*, 3:78; 1:217, 423; 2:19.
163. Romero, *Homilías*, 4:103.
164. Romero, *Homilías*, 5:178.
165. Romero, *Homilías*, 5:178.
166. Romero, *Homilías*, 4:280.

nary violence must be understood in relation to "the unjust and dispro-portionate distribution of the land of this country."[167] Inequality in the distribution of land is not only an injustice coterminous with the status quo; it is an injustice that is productive of further injustice, like a taproot.

In this regard, Romero characteristically understands the struggles both of rural and urban workers in relation to what has happened in the Salvadoran countryside. In one homily, he draws upon the 1980 document of the Brazilian Bishops Conference, *Igreja e problemas da terra* (Church and Land Problems) to speak of the plight of urban workers as the "fruit of the injustice in the rural areas," a consequence of the way "people have had to abandon their land and now seek to earn a living in the city."[168] According to Romero, the inhabitants of the countryside have collective-ly shared the fate of the man going down from Jerusalem to Jericho in Luke's Gospel, who was stripped, beaten, and left half-dead by a gang of thieves (10:30). "We, too, find ourselves today," Romero observes in anoth-er homily, "with a whole people lying wounded by the roadsides of this country."[169]

As Romero sees it, land concentration and landlessness, as well as workers' struggles for living wages and dignified working conditions, are all manifestations of a deep-seated refusal to acknowledge the com-monality of God's gift of creation. In El Salvador, a country in which the vast majority of people depend upon agriculture for survival, the fact that land is so concentrated stands as a stark countersign to God's purpose for creation. Such concentration obscures the whole reason God gives land, which is to meet the needs of all who live on it and from it. This is why, as Romero puts it in his penultimate dominical homily, the land "groans": some have "hoarded it (*la acaparan*), leaving nothing for others."[170] Once again, belief in the God who gives creation in common is what makes the groaning audible, removes the blockage from the ears so the sound

---

167. Romero, *Homilías*, 6:70.

168. Romero, *Homilías*, 6:396–97; Conferência Nacional dos Bispos do Brasil, *Igreja e problemas da terra* (Itaici: Conferência Nacional dos Bispos do Brasil, February 14, 1980).

169. Romero, *Homilías*, 2:381. Adolfo Bonilla Bonilla describes the Salvadoran *campesina-do* as "crushed without misery" and "on the brink of extinction"; Bonilla Bonilla, *Tenencia de la tierra y reforma agraria en El Salvador*, 22.

170. Romero, *Homilías*, 6:393.

of it can be heard. In the homily, Romero goes on to speak of land re-form as a "theological necessity" for the same reason: the goal of reform is likewise to manifest the commonality of the gift, in however limited a fashion, by pursuing a more just distribution of land.[171] It is to testify to how, in *Gaudium et Spes*'s words, God intended the earth and everything contained in it for the use of all peoples.

Of course, the refusal to acknowledge the commonality of the gift is not a recent development, nor is it restricted to El Salvador. It long predates the agrarian crisis Romero inherits as archbishop, just as it predates enclosure and even colonization. Romero's view can be helpful-ly summarized by the words with which Ambrose of Milan begins *On Naboth*: "The story of Naboth is an old one, but it is repeated every day."[172] The story is an old one because it is the story of covetousness, the story of having enough and yet wanting more. Ahab sees a tract of land, the in-heritance of Naboth's ancestors, and desires it for his own. When Naboth refuses to relinquish it, Ahab and Jezebel concoct a scheme to seize it from him by violence (1 Kg 21). The roots of covetousness sink deep into human history.

The story is not only an old one; it is still ongoing. In the Louvain address, in reference to Amos's rebuke of those who devour the poor (2:6, 3:10, 8:6) and Isaiah's of those who amass land at the expense of others (5:8), Romero comments on the contemporaneousness of the prophets' words. "Passages like these … are not distant voices from many centuries ago," he writes. "They are ordinary realities, whose cruelty and intensity we live daily."[173] According to Romero, then, the story of covetousness continues, and it merges with the message of Puebla to speak to the his-tory of the Salvadoran people. One of the major plotlines of this story is the abuse of property, the cumulative effects of which are written indel-ibly into the landscape. Land concentration and landlessness are among its unmistakable signs.

171. Romero, *Homilías*, 6:393.

172. Ambrose of Milan, *On Naboth*, in *Ambrose* 7.37, ed. Boniface Ramsey (New York: Routledge, 1997).

173. Romero, "La dimensión política de la fe desde la opción por los pobres" 187. See also Romero, *Homilías*, 1:340–42.

"YOU POSSESS THE LAND THAT BELONGS
TO ALL SALVADORANS"

The careful reader will have already noticed that the inner logic of Romero's belief that God gives creation as a common gift leads to statements like the following: a sufficient share of created goods *belongs* to those in need; it is *theirs*; when it is lacking, it is what is *due* them; and so on. In other words, the theological grammar of creation we have been considering implies an account of justice.

Thus, a sufficient share of created goods belongs to those who need it, not because of what they have done or failed to do or because of the kind of people they are. Nor does it belong to them on account of the laws or institutions of the polities in which they live, though these laws and institutions can facilitate—and hinder—people's access to what is theirs. Rather, a sufficient share of created goods belongs to them because they are members of the community of humankind to which God gives the gift of creation for common use. The basis of this belonging is bodily need. Human creatures need food, drink, clothing, and shelter to survive, and the privation of these goods impairs human flourishing.[174]

For this line of thought, one of the principal works of justice is to open others' access to the goods they need—to what is theirs in justice—but that they lack for whatever reason. For if God intends the earth and its fruits for the benefit of humankind in common, it directly follows that created goods have an intrinsic and inescapable orientation to the alleviation of bodily need, and it further follows that those who are chronically hungry, thirsty, naked, shelterless, and so on, have a unique claim upon those goods. This claim—the claim of bodily need—is the most basic and fundamental claim human creatures can have upon the created order. Among all other possible claims, this one takes precedence.

The foregoing account of justice intimately relates to a prominent strand of thinking about almsgiving or the work of mercy in the Christian tradition, which is patterned on Matthew 25:31-46: feeding the

---

174. For a helpful discussion, see Brian Tierney, *The Idea of Natural Rights: Studies on Natural Rights, Natural Law, and Church Law* (Atlanta: Scholars Press, 1997), 69-76, 84-85.

hungry, slaking the thirsty, clothing the naked, welcoming the stranger, tending to the sick, and visiting the imprisoned. According to this strand, to give alms is not to give what belongs to the almsgiver, but to give to others what is theirs. It is to return to them that from which they have been excluded because of the injustice of the world, presupposing and responding to a previous injustice as it aims to recover an equality between people that has been lost, denied, or otherwise obscured. To ignore or to dismiss the justice that is presupposed and perfected by mercy undermines charity itself, for charity alone cannot veil the violation of justice. In this way, then, mercy is a work of justice transfigured by love for those deprived of basic needs. At the same time, as Maria Clara Bingemer explains, such feeding, slaking, clothing, welcoming, tending, and visiting "entails nothing less than restoring a piece of the cosmos to those who have been deprived."[175] This is because the merciful reveal God's original purpose for the created order, which is to meet the needs of all.

We have been considering this account of justice from the perspective of those with the world's goods. But what about from the perspective of those without such goods? Are they to wait patiently to receive what is theirs in justice? What happens when what is theirs does not arrive? Might they justifiably take what belongs to them? And if so, in the name and under the protection of what law? Along these lines, another implication of this account of justice—which relates to the problematic of landlessness, squatting, and the criminalization of need—can be found in *Gaudium et Spes*'s allusion to the law of necessity (*ius necesitatis*). According to this law, when such aid is lacking, the destitute need not wait for what belongs to them but can legitimately take what they need from the excess of others. Taking simply facilitates their access to what they need when such access is otherwise lacking—when human laws, property regimes, or the goodness of others fail them.

The foregoing briefly sketches the theological grammar that informs a politics of common use. My contention has been that this grammar shapes Romero's thought, leading to descriptions of land reform as a theological necessity, of landlessness as relativizing the borders of na-

---

175. Bingemer, *Latin American Theology*, 99.

tions and requiring a reconsideration of property law, and of the denial of sufficient land and just wages as a violence that has become ordinary.

Romero's reflections on justice often begin with the reality of its absence, with the fact that so many people have been denied their rightful share of the created goods given to them by God. He thinks the ordinary refusal to acknowledge creation as a common gift, which is especially evident in the vice of covetousness, is among the main forms of violence that saturate El Salvador's fields with blood.[176] The covetous take more than what they need and continue to want more. In so doing, they take what belongs to others in justice.[177] At the same time, as Romero says, "they subvert the sense of property," substituting a pagan conception of property as *ius utendi et abutendi* (the right to use and abuse) for a Christian one. The Christian sense of property begins and ends not with the self, but with God as creator, and conforms itself to God's purpose in creating, which is for common benefit.[178]

Habitual taking and wanting more also cultivate what Romero calls *insensibilidad*—"insensitivity," "indifference," "callousness," or to use the scriptural idiom, "hard-heartedness." "Besides this false concept of property," Romero therefore says, "the most terrible thing [about covetousness] is this: it hardens, it makes us insensitive (*insensibles*) to the needs of others."[179] He thinks *insensibilidad* affects anyone, irrespective of wealth. To guard against it, Romero therefore counsels cultivating the habits of justice infused by mercy: "Here I am not only speaking to those with great wealth, but to all of us, so when we have something to eat— even an ice cream, a piece of bread, or a tortilla—we, too, can become insensitive (*insensibles*) to those who do not have even this. Why not share … even our poverty?"[180] Or to return once more to what happened in San Pedro Perulapán, Romero exhorts his hearers to respond to the violence by following the example of the people of the community of Illopango,

<hr>

176. Romero, *Homilías*, 1:450.

177. Friedrich Nietzsche translated covetousness as "having and wanting to have more (*haben und mehrwollhaben*)"; quoted in Alasdair MacIntyre, *After Virtue: A Study in Moral Theory* (Notre Dame, Ind.: University of Notre Dame Press, 2007), 137.

178. Romero, *Homilías*, 1:342.

179. Romero, *Homilías*, 1:342.

180. Romero, *Homilías*, 1:343.

who fasted in order to have something to offer the families of the victims, fulfilling the words of the prophet Isaiah: "Is not this the fast I choose: ... to share your bread with the hungry?" [Isa 58:6–7].[181]

Earlier we saw Romero compare ordinary violence to weeds colonizing a field, with new shoots continually springing up because the rhizomes are lodged beneath the field's surface. We are now in a better position to see why: Romero thinks the deepest, most intractable roots of violence reside in the enclosure of the self and its possessions, as well as the process of privatization and exclusion underlying it, all of which wounds the human creature's capacity for communion.[182] Because of the kind of creatures humans are, whose bodies embed them in a natural order and whose lives make them members of manifold societies, the damage done by such enclosure extends beyond the self, crystallizing in structures, institutions, and landscapes. What is more, because sin is an old story that continues to be repeated daily, the constancy of the repetition means that the damage also accumulates across time, piling wreckage upon wreckage.

According to Romero, this is why we must attend not only to the role of structures and institutions in the violence, but to the role of people in it as well—to violence's personal, as well as its impersonal, sources. As important as the transformation of structures, institutions, and landscapes is, Romero's primary focus is uprooting the sin that enslaves the human heart and leads to the enclosure of the self and its possessions. As he puts the point in one of his final homilies, "As bold as an agrarian transformation may seem ... beyond this God is giving us ... freedom from sin."[183]

It is on this basis that Romero, precisely as a proponent of liberation, criticizes other construals of liberation, which he thinks insufficiently grasp the damage sin does and the merciful shape of God's intervention in Christ to heal it.[184] Romero consistently argues, against what he char-

---

181. Romero, *Homilías*, 2:385–87.

182. Romero, *Homilías*, 1:164.

183. Romero, *Homilías*, 6:256.

184. As Michael Lee writes, "If liberation theology is understood broadly as a theology committed to understanding faith as exercised in the pursuit of justice, with principles pro-

acterizes as earthbound visions of liberation, that true liberation centers upon God's graceful work in Christ and in the Spirit to uproot sin and to liberate people from death's hold upon human life. The problem for Romero is not that these terrestrial visions of liberation are completely false, but rather that they only partially grasp the fullness of the liberation Christ brings. To paraphrase Herbert McCabe, the disagreement regards the nature of liberation and what Romero thinks is an overly superficial understanding of it. In Romero's view, these earthbound visions have yet to reckon with the liberation inaugurated by the advent of Christ, which breaks the bonds of death and makes all things new.[185]

"The liberation for which the Church hopes and proclaims," Romero therefore says, "begins in the true freedom of the human heart, which is liberation from sin. For this reason, the Church's hope is in a God who forgives sin."[186] The merciful intervention of God in Christ, which forgives sin and gracefully endows humans with the capacity to imitate this mercy, "is true liberation."[187] It forms a liberated people, whose lives take a merciful—and therefore cruciform—shape in a sinful and violent world. As Romero argues in his funeral homily for Rutilio Grande, this is what the church most contributes to the struggle for liberation: a liberated people, who live by the faith that bears fruit in works of love, and who find guidance in Catholic social teaching.[188] According to Romero,

---

claimed in magisterial teaching of bishops' conferences, and even echoes in papal teaching, then Romero can be seen as an exemplar of liberation theology"; Lee, *Revolutionary Saint*, 190.

185. Herbert McCabe, *Love, Law, and Language* (New York: Continuum, 2003), 133–35. For an early articulation of this view, see Óscar Romero, "La más profunda revolución social," *Diario del Oriente*, no. 30867, August 28, 1973.

186. Romero, *Homilías*, 2:93. Or as he puts it in another homily, "True liberation begins … in the heart of those whose faith has made them the possessor of the heavenly life"; Romero, *Homilías*, 3:85. See also Romero, *Homilías*, 1:164; 2:118, 297, 356, 408–10, 414.

187. Romero, *Homilías*, 3:38–39.

188. Romero, *Homilías*, 1:32–33. The funeral homily for Grande is not an aberration in Romero's thought. Until his own death, Romero continues to speak similarly about liberation. He emphasizes transcendence as a distinguishing mark of true liberation (Romero, *Homilías*, 6:26, 56, 282, 286, 434–36); he draws on *Evangelii Nuntiandi* and other church documents to articulate it (Romero, *Homilías*, 6:26, 256); and he critically engages what he characterizes as earthbound forms of liberation, which rely exclusively on Marxist analytical tools (Romero, *Homilías*, 6:153), refuse to be opened to liberation's heavenly horizon (Romero, *Homilías*, 6:83), and reject Christ as the way and the goal of liberation (Romero, *Homilías*, 6:85, 233, 435). Additionally, Romero frequently turns to Cardinal Pironio's *Escritos Pastorales* in explicating the form of liberation theology he espouses, referring to Pironio as "the great

Grande is himself such a liberator. He witnesses to how "only from the forgiveness of the cross is it possible to hope for the liberation of Latin America and its peoples."[189] For this forgiveness produces people like Grande who collaborate in the great liberation of Christ by their willingness to bear crosses for love of God and neighbor. Christian liberators like Grande do not mete out violence; they absorb it.

Other liberation theologians might very well regard Romero's understanding of how Christ uproots sin and defeats death as distractions from the real demands of history, as symptomatic of a lack of seriousness about structures and institutions. But for Romero, this criticism betrays an incomplete understanding of liberation, because it fails to see how God's grace dislodges the deepest roots of sin and violence. Moreover, according to Romero, the liberation Christ brings does address structures, institutions, and landscapes—first and foremost by cultivating people who follow Christ in the way of love and willingly share what God has given to all.[190] A letter Romero received from an ecclesial base community puts the point well, commending Romero's message of "build[ing] a more just order, beginning with ourselves."[191] "Economic liberation, political liberation, social liberation—all this is good," Romero insists, "but it comes in addition (*por añadidura*)," as a kind of cascade effect of the gospel's proclamation.[192] Once again, Grande exemplifies this understanding of liberation. For what must come first, according to Romero, is the formation of people like him, who live on the basis of the belief that death has been swallowed up in victory. Because of the kind of creatures humans are, such lives can, in turn, effect changes in structures, institutions, and even landscapes, as Grande's did in Aguilares.[193] For this reason, the pas-

---

promoter of authentic liberation theology in Latin America" (Romero, *Homilías*, 1:298, 215–17; 3:80, 317). On Romero's understanding of liberation, see also Óscar Romero, "Liberación es salvación," *Diario de Oriente*, no. 30896, April 14, 1974. See also "Education Liberadora," *Diario de Oriente*, May 30, 1973; and "De acuerdo con una teología de la liberación," *Diario del Oriente*, no. 30905, June 18, 1974.

189. Romero, *Homilías*, 1:304; 2:426.

190. Romero, *Homilías*, 1:93; 3:107.

191. Quoted in José Inocencio Alas, *Iglesia, tierra, y lucha campesina: Suchitoto, El Salvador, 1968–1977* (San Salvador: Asoc de Frailes Franciscanos OFM de C.A., 2003), 269.

192. Romero, *Homilías*, 3:38.

193. See Thomas M. Kelly, *When the Gospel Grows Feet: Rutilio Grande, SJ, and the Church*

sage from Medellín Romero frequently cites is, "We will not have a new continent without new and renewed structures. But above all, there will be no new continent without new people."[194] What Romero most appreciates about this passage is that, while keeping in full view the violence of structures and institutions and the need for their transformation, it underscores God's merciful response in Christ to sin and the violence it unleashes, a response that recreates human life by water and the Spirit.[195]

More remains to be said about how sin encloses the self and its possessions from the claims of others. We have been examining how Romero thinks the new people for which Medellín calls will be just and that among the most characteristic features of justice's work is to open access of the landless to what is theirs but has been denied them because of sin. Conversely, the covetous who, as Romero puts it, "take for their own (*acaparan*) what God has given for the flourishing of all"[196]—and especially those who use violence to defend the taking—epitomize the problem he faces. In this regard, it is important to see how Romero's belief that creation is a common gift implies a conception of thievery that is importantly distinct from the unlawful taking of another's personal property criminalized by positive law. Not only is this particular conception of thievery distinct, but—and this is crucial—it can exist in tension with or even in outright contradiction to ordinary assumptions about what thievery is. For instance, in the same homily in which Romero speaks of the theological necessity of a just distribution of land, Romero addresses the oligarchy's refusal to permit land reform to proceed without bloodshed. The members of the oligarchy, he says, must realize "that they possess the land that belongs to all Salvadorans" (*están poseyendo la tierra que es de todos los salvadoreños*).[197]

---

of El Salvador (Collegeville, Minn.: Michael Glazier, 2013); Rodolfo Cardenal, *Rutilio Grande: Mártir de la evangelización rural en El Salvador* (San Salvador: UCA Editores, 2015).

194. *Medellín*, "Justicia," 1.3. See Romero, *Homilías*, 1:177, 315, 416; 2:58, 102, 201; 3:72, 187, 277; 4:35; 5:31, 182; 6:63, 275, 349.

195. *Medellín*, "Justicia," 1.4. See Romero, *Homilías*, 1:141; 6:281.

196. Romero, *Homilías*, 1:217. Here Romero is drawing on the Argentine cardinal Eduardo Pironio's *Escritos Pastorales* (Madrid: BAC, 1973), 92.

197. Romero, *Homilías*, 6:420. In Oaxaca, John Paul speaks of "powerful classes" who possess lands that "hide the bread that so many families lack" (*que esconden el pan que a tantas familias falta*); John Paul II, *Address in Cuilapan, Mexico*, January 29, 1979.

In what sense do they do this? Romero's words raise issues that are more complex than they might first appear. Like the language of creation groaning and unpaid wages crying out for redress, the accusation of thievery similarly conveys important, interpersonal features of the moral and theological landscape we are considering. Of course, Romero does not think members of the oligarchy lack legal title to their lands or that they could not easily defend their possessions in a court of law. Romero well knows that, by law, they are the rightful owners. Rather, Romero is trying to catechize his people about a law concerning property and possession more primordial than that enshrined in Salvadoran law—a law to which all positive law is ultimately accountable. It is in relation to this more primordial law that the oligarchs are like thieves, unjustly possessing the land that belongs to all Salvadorans, excessively taking for their own exclusive use what God has given for the survival and flourishing of all. The point can be put as a question: If God gives the earth in common, is not the first and most fundamental form of thievery holding goods in ways that habitually fail to acknowledge their intrinsic and inescapable orientation to those deprived of material support?

This question haunts the tradition of reflection about property and possession upon which Romero draws. According to this tradition, the failure of those with the world's goods to acknowledge the claims of the needy upon their possessions is a grave violation of justice. It amounts to a form of thievery, a violent taking of what belongs to others. Additionally, we can also say that such thieves are complicit in a kind of murder. As the passage from *Gaudium et Spes* above states, "Since there are so many people prostrate with hunger in the world, this sacred council urges all … to remember the aphorism of the Fathers, 'Feed the man dying of hunger, because if you have not fed him, you have killed him'" (no. 69). In the moral and theological landscape disclosed by the belief that creation is a common gift, God holds people accountable, not only for what they have done, such as taking too much of what belongs to all. God also holds them accountable for what they have failed to do, such as neglecting the needs of others by means of what they have.

As we have seen, one important implication of the belief that creation is a common gift is therefore a manner of using created goods that is guided by justice and accompanied by mercy, which is characterized by a simultaneous twofold movement—both "downward," as people learn the habits of taking only what they need, and "outward," as they work to ensure all people, especially those without the world's goods, have access to what is theirs. However, in the account of thievery and murder we have just been considering, it is possible to discern the inversion of this manner of use. Instead of taking only what is sufficient for their needs, these thieves take in vast excess of them. And instead of working to ensure that the needs of others, especially those without the world's goods, are met, these murderers take for their own use exclusively, ignoring or spurning others' claims. Such thievery and murder are particularly insidious, not only because they can coexist with positive law, but also because positive law often protects such ordinary violence with additional violence.

In the meantime, what emerges in the forms of thievery and murder we have been examining is admittedly a rather strange conception of property and possession. Consider again Romero's statement that the oligarchy possesses the land that belongs to all Salvadorans. In what sense does land *belong* to some people while others presently *possess* it? What is the relationship between this belonging and possessing and the gap that opens up between them—a gap that can even remain permanently in place? What does the work of suturing the gap look like? What risks does it run? These are just some of the questions raised by the theological grammar of creation we have been examining. What must be emphasized for our purposes is that, at least on these terms, the work of suturing the gap between belonging and possessing by working for a more just distribution of land is an attempt to manifest the commonality of the gift of creation even in the face of its ongoing refusal. Because of the sheer magnitude of the refusal, such work, it would seem, will always be provisional, incomplete, unending.

Once again, the language of thievery and murder, like the language of creation's groaning, might be tempting to ignore or dismiss. But doing so neglects the work the words are doing in disclosing a landscape that would otherwise remain hidden. It would leave us beholden to some other grammar, ensnared in structures, institutions, and landscapes that make it difficult for us to see the world for what it really is: a gift God gives in common.

The landscape into which Romero wants to invite us is one in which deprivation of what is bodily necessary for life, along with the institutions and structures that preserve and perpetuate that deprivation, is the heart of our concern. Orienting ourselves within this landscape requires new modes of perception. As Romero evocatively puts it at the funeral mass for one of his priests, Father Rafael Palacios, it involves seeing that "the voice of blood is the most eloquent of words" and that this voice is an "ordinary" one. In this same homily, Romero even represents his whole ministry along these same lines: "From this cathedral we have simply tried to interpret the language of so much blood being poured out in our country in the mountains, the streets of our cities and our roadways, on our beaches."[198] For Romero, this bloodshed certainly includes the repressive violence of the state and the terror of its associated death squads, as well as the subversive violence welling up like a wave to topple it. But true interpretation of this language, he thinks, must attend to violence's or-dinary utterances, the bloodletting enacted by those who possess and refuse to relinquish what belongs to all.

As I have tried to show in this chapter, the theological grammar of creation as common gift generates these descriptions, just as it points to a politics of common use, which responds to sin's damage to what God gives for the benefit of all. Romero's preaching and ministry attempt to disclose this moral and theological landscape and to help his people walk within it. But Romero is no innovator. He is laboring to recover a neglected Christian grammar, which he finds in the church's social teaching. It is to a closer examination of this teaching that we now turn.

198. Romero, *Homilías*, 5:25.

-2-

THE GRAMMAR OF CREATION

This mercy, therefore, is called justice because the giver knows that
God has given all things to all in common.

—Ambrose of Milan, *Commentary on Second Corinthians*

In its consideration of ordinary violence, chapter 1 began to locate Romero's sense of the theological necessity of a more just distribution of land within the wider framework of Catholic social teaching. It examined how the theological grammar of creation as a common gift shapes Romero's social analysis of violence, as well as his approach to property and possession. Romero's description of landlessness as a form of violence derives from this theological grammar and provides an important rationale for the church's support of land reform under his leadership. For this reason, Romero insists that the promotion of access to land, as well as the defense of rural workers and their ability to organize, is not communism but the message of Puebla and the popes. "Romero was coming aboard in the midst of a storm," writes James Brockman about Romero's installation as archbishop,[1] and in charting a course through it, Romero clung to Catholic social teaching.

1. Brockman, *Romero*, 2.

Romero's continual insistence upon his fidelity to this teaching is it-self noteworthy. It reflects the fierce resistance he faced from a power-ful group of Catholics who were convinced that Romero and his sympa-thizers were communists posing a grave threat to property, nation, and church. But it raises a host of other questions as well. Why did Romero's adherence to social teaching on these matters generate such controver-sy and provoke such resistance in this predominantly Catholic country in the first place? Why was this teaching not better known, understood, and disseminated? And at an even more basic level, what is the place of land reform within social teaching? How and why did the call for it even emerge? Is this call a peripheral feature of the teaching's moral and theo-logical landscape, which can be easily ignored or even removed without altering the landscape's fundamental features?

To address these questions, this chapter and the following one fo-cus upon, in Romero's words, those "Church documents beginning with Leo XIII's [1891] encyclical *Rerum Novarum* ... which attempt to orient us regarding ... the crucial problems facing our societies."[2] From *Rerum No-varum* onward, as Romero says in a 1979 homily, social teaching has shone its "light upon the injustice of Latin America and the world"[3]—a light to which we must attend. Of course, Romero thinks that there were many profound changes in the church's life as a consequence of the Second Vatican Council and its application to Latin America at CELAM's 1968 gathering in Medellín.[4] But he understands these changes as a renewal in the church's life, which is why he describes them as helping the church "recover its most profound Christian essence,"[5] and which is also why he characterizes the Council and Medellín as contributing to the *conci-entización* (conscientization) about social teaching and its implications.[6] Understanding Romero's advocacy of land reform therefore involves see-

---

2. Romero, *La Iglesia, cuerpo de Cristo en la historia*, 80; Romero, *Homilías*, 1:453.

3. Romero, *Homilías*, 5:67.

4. Romero, *La Iglesia, cuerpo de Cristo en la historia*, 71–75.

5. Romero, *La Iglesia, cuerpo de Cristo en la historia*, 71.

6. Quoted in Morozzo Della Rocca, *Primero Dios*, 103. The Brazilian educator, philoso-pher, and activist Paulo Freire uses and popularizes the term *conscientização* in his 1970 book *Pedagogia do Oprimido* (*Pedagogy of the Oppressed*, trans. Myra Bergman Ramos [New York: Bloomsbury, 2000]). See also Romero, *Iglesia y organizaciones políticas populares*, 94.

ing it *both* in relation to the Second Vatican Council and its application to Latin America *and* in relation to an older line of thinking about property and possession resourced by Leo XIII in *Rerum Novarum*. As we will see, this older line of thinking was itself carried through by the Second Vatican Council and then again at Medellín and Puebla. Indeed, Romero's support for land reform cannot be understood apart from it.[7]

While turning to social teaching might seem to take us far afield from Romero, it is in fact crucial for understanding him.[8] And this is not sim-

7. Just as Catholic social teaching precedes the Second Vatican Council and Medellín, it also extends beyond them. On the topic of land reform, it includes statements of episcopal conferences in Latin America and throughout the world. In addition to the documents of the General Conferences of Latin American Bishops held in Santo Domingo (October 12–28, 1992) and the Basilica of Aparecida in São Paulo, Brazil (May 13–31, 2007), see also Conferencia Episcopal de Paraguay, *La tierra, don de Dios para todos* (Asunción, June 12, 1983); South Andean Bishops, *La tierra, don de Dios* (March 30, 1986); Conferencia Episcopal de Guatemala, *El clamor por la tierra* (Guatemala de la Asunción, February 29, 1988); Apostolic Vicariate of Darien, Panama, *Tierra de todos, tierra de paz* (Darien, December 8, 1988); Conferencia Episcopal de Costa Rica, *Madre tierra: Carta pastoral sobre la situación de los campesinos y indígenas* (San José, August 2, 1994); Conferencia Episcopal de Honduras, *Mensaje sobre algunos temas de interés nacional* (Tegucigalpa, August 28, 1995). The Conferência Nacional dos Bispos do Brasil (National Episcopal Conference of Brazil), and particularly the Comissão Pastoral da Terra (Pastoral Land Commission), have spoken out several times on the subject of land reform: *Manifesto pela terra e pela vita a CPT e a reforma agrária hoje* (Goiânia, August 1, 1995); *Pro-memória da Presidência e Comissão Episcopal de Pastoral da CNBB sobre as consequências do Decreto n. 1775 de 8 de Janeiro de 1996* (Brasília, February 29, 1996); *Exigências Cristãs para a paz social* (Itaici, April 24, 1996). See also the Pontifical Council of Justice and Peace, *Toward a Better Distribution of Land: The Challenge of Agrarian Reform* (1997), Benedict XVI, Encyclical Letter *Caritas in Veritate* (June 29, 2009), and most recently, Francis I, Encyclical Letter *Laudato Si'* (May 24, 2015), as well as Francis's addresses at the world meetings of popular movements, among other documents.

8. A growing number of scholars have appreciated Romero's dependence upon Catholic social teaching and its sources. Given the minimal attention devoted to Romero's support for land reform or its sources, the failure to perceive his reliance on social teaching in arguing for a better distribution of land is unsurprising. Additionally, that this teaching even addresses land reform remains relatively unknown in English-language scholarship. The situation is different in Spanish- and Portuguese-language scholarship, where the topic has received much more extensive engagement. For Romero's reliance on Catholic social teaching in general, see Kevin F. Burke, "Archbishop Óscar Romero: Peacemaker in the Tradition of Catholic Social Thought," *Journal for Peace and Justice Studies* 13, no. 2 (2003): 105–24; Armando Márquez Ochoa, *No basta la justicia, es necesario el amor: Compendio de la catequesis social de Mons. Romero* (San Salvador: Comunidades eclesiales de base de El Salvador, 2007); Carlos F. Mejía, *La doctrina social en la Iglesia universal y en la Iglesia particular de San Salvador* (San Salvador: Imprenta Criterio, 2006), 220–31. On Romero's use of and relation to early church sources, see Thomas Greenan, "La opción por los pobres en las homilías de Monseñor Romero y de San Juan Crisóstomo: Análisis de la convergencias y de las peculiaridades en los presupuestos teológicos y en las orientaciones morales" (Ph.D. diss., Universidad

ply because of how he clings to social teaching as he navigates the agrarian crisis of his day, making that teaching, as Paul VI writes in *Evangelii Nuntiandi*, the foundation of his wisdom and experience, and translating it into forms of action, participation, and commitment. It is also because one of my primary purposes in this work is to show how social teaching and its politics of common use illumine Romero's role in the drama of salvation. He is, after all, a martyr of the church, a witness to what the church holds to be true, and so considering what the church holds to be true with respect to its social teaching is helpful for understanding that witness. However, in order to appreciate the light social teaching offers in this regard, it is first necessary to familiarize ourselves with the teaching itself. My purpose in chapters 2 and 3 is therefore to do exactly that: to show how the theological grammar of creation as common gift structures social teaching in its deepest pattern and to examine land reform's relationship to it, with an eye toward our examination in chapter 5 of Romero himself as an icon of God's creating and saving work.

Chapters 2 and 3 narrate the emergence of social teaching's call for land reform in relationship to a distinctive approach to property and possession articulated by Leo XIII in *Rerum Novarum*. Whereas previously we saw Romero say Puebla's message about property is the history of his people, in this chapter we step back to consider the story of church teaching on property, placing Puebla's message in relationship to it. Over the course of the twentieth century, a subsequent line of commentary preserves, clarifies, and applies Leo's approach—a line that helps constitute Catholic social teaching. The reason these chapters dwell at such length

---

Pontificia Comillas, 2003); Claudia Marlene Rivera Navarrete, "La denuncia profética de la riqueza: Resonancia de la patrística en la teología Latinoamericana de la liberación" (Master's thesis, Universidad Centroamericano, 2015). For brief examinations of Catholic social teaching's understanding of land reform that focus mainly on the United States, see John Hart, *The Spirit of the Earth: A Theology of the Land* (Mahwah, N.J.: Paulist Press, 1984); Mark E. Graham, *Sustainable Agriculture: A Christian Ethic of Gratitude* (Eugene, Ore.: Wipf and Stock, 2009), 142–47. For a brief examination that focuses on Brazil, see Roy H. May, *The Poor of the Land: A Christian Case for Land Reform* (Maryknoll, N.Y.: Orbis, 1991), 75–105. Much more comprehensive treatments can be found in Marcelo de Barros Souza and José Luis Caravias, *Teología de la tierra* (Madrid: Ediciones Paulinas, 1988), 336–84; F. Bastos de Ávila, "Igreja e propriedade: Fundamentação doutrinal," in *A Igreja e a propriedade da terra no Brasil* (São Paulo: Edições Loyola, 1980).

upon *Rerum Novarum*, then, is because Leo's great encyclical establishes the theological grammar and lexicon that subsequent teaching assumes and develops.[9] Leo's successors—and Romero himself—repeatedly refer to it as that teaching's Magna Carta.[10]

Tracing the development of this line of commentary on *Rerum Novarum* also has the additional benefit of locating land reform within a wider moral and doctrinal context, as well as conveying how it participates in a more comprehensive politics of common use. The claim that *Rerum Novarum*'s account of property and possession exhibits the theological grammar of creation as common gift might appear counterintuitive, because it is often suggested that this belief about creation had long been abandoned by the church. For instance, Brian Matz traces its introduction into social teaching to the pontificate of Pius XI (1922–39),[11] Donal Dorr to that of Pope Pius XII (1939–58),[12] and René Laurentin to the promulgation of *Gaudium et Spes* in 1965.[13] While this chapter offers no similar genealogical account of this belief's disappearance and (re)emergence, it does demonstrate that this theological grammar structures Leo's ap-

9. There have been and continue to be debates about continuity and discontinuity within Catholic social teaching before and after Leo's pontificate, which this chapter does not adjudicate. Instead, it takes up the more modest task of following the line Leo's successors explicitly trace to *Rerum Novarum*. One way to appreciate *Rerum Novarum*'s significance is by attending to the line of thinking it occasions within the broader ambit of the church's social doctrine. The line includes, but is not limited to, Pius XI's Encyclical Letter *Quadragesimo Anno* (May 15, 1931), Pius XII's *Discourse of His Holiness Pius XII to Commemorate the 50th Anniversary of the Encyclical "Rerum Novarum" of Pope Leo XIII on the Social Question*, in *Acta Apostolicae Sedis* 33 (June 1, 1941); John XXIII's Encyclical Letter *Mater et Magistra* (May 15, 1961), Paul VI's Encyclical Letter *Octogesima Adveniens* (May 14, 1971), and John Paul II's Encyclical Letter *Laborem Exercens* (September 14, 1981) and Encyclical Letter *Centesimus Annus* (May 1, 1991).

10. Óscar Romero, "La *Rerum Novarum* perene y urgente," *El Chaparrastique*, May 26, 1961. See also Pius XI, *Quadragesimo Anno*, no. 39; Pius XII, *Discourse to Commemorate the 50th Anniversary of the Encyclical "Rerum Novarum" of Pope Leo XIII on the Social Question*, June 1, 1941, 220–21; Pius XII, *Radiomensaje del Santo Padre Pío XII a los trabajadores de España*, in *Acta Apostolicae Sedis* 43 (March 11, 1951), 1–3.

11. Brian Matz, "The Principle of Detachment from Private Property in Basil of Caesarea's Homily 6 and Its Context," in *Reading Patristic Texts on Social Ethics: Issues and Challenges for the Twenty-First Century* (Washington, D.C.: The Catholic University of America Press, 2011), 180–83.

12. Donal Dorr, *Option for the Poor: A Hundred Hears of Vatican Social Teaching* (Maryknoll, N.Y.: Orbis, 1983), 83.

13. René Laurentin, *Liberation, Development, and Salvation* (Maryknoll, N.Y.: Orbis, 1972), 94–101.

proach to property and possession in *Rerum Novarum* at the most fundamental level, along with the line of reflection following it.

Another reason such a reading of *Rerum Novarum* might appear counterintuitive is because it is commonplace to characterize Leo's criticisms of socialism and his arguments for private property in terms of the church's defense of "itself and the status quo against unwelcome forces of change."[14] But my argument is that this interpretation basically gets it backward by presuming that the meaning of property is univocal. As we will see, what Leo means by property differs significantly from how that term is ordinarily used, and he challenges this ordinary usage by resourcing a much older and neglected approach to property found in the writings of Thomas Aquinas and elsewhere, which assumes the compatibility between a qualified version of personal property and God's gift of creation for common use. For this approach, property is what enables creaturely participation in and mediation of God's giving of the gift to humankind for its common benefit. As Leo writes in *Rerum Novarum*, "the blessings of nature and the gifts of grace belong to the whole human race in common."[15] And, as we will see, for Leo these blessings include the access of as many as possible to productive property like land. The commentarial tradition upon *Rerum Novarum* takes up this approach, preserving, clarifying, and applying it anew in light of changing circumstances. The teaching on land reform that Romero inherits and for which he advocates is one such application.

Leo's understanding of property and his argument for increasing access to it underlie his response to developments associated with the spread of capitalism in Europe and beyond, which is yet another reason it is a mistake to regard him as a defender of the status quo and of propertied interests. For in the face of the massive dispossession of the peasantry and the increasing concentration of productive property like land—developments closely related to our consideration of enclosure in chapter 1—Leo argues for the diffusion of property, not its abolition. He

---

14. Thomas A. Shannon, "Commentary on *Rerum Novarum*," in *Modern Catholic Social Teaching: Commentaries and Interpretations* (Washington, D.C.: Georgetown University Press, 2005), 135.

15. Leo XIII, Encyclical Letter *Rerum Novarum* (May 15, 1891), no. 25.

wants those dispossessed of property to be repossessed, to have a share in the land they work. In so arguing, Leo is effectively restating for his own day, and for subsequent social teaching, the vision of Isaiah and the prophets of Israel: "They shall build houses and inhabit them; they shall plant vineyards and eat their fruit. They shall not build and another inhabit; they shall not plant and another eat" (Is 65:21; see also 32:18, 37:30; Jer 12:15, 31:5; Am 9:14).

ENCLOSURE

Rerum Novarum directs itself to what at the time was called "the social question," which was the subject of much debate.[16] We immediately get a sense of the phrases's meaning in the opening sections of the encyclical, where Leo famously states that "some opportune remedy must be found quickly for the misery and wretchedness pressing so unjustly on the majority of the working class: for the ancient workingmen's guilds were abolished in the last century, and no other protective organization took their place."[17] As a consequence of these and other developments, he continues, "it has come to pass that working men have been surrendered,

16. For Leo on the social question, see Matthew Habiger, *Papal Teaching on Private Property (1891–1981)* (Lanham, Md.: University Press of America, 1990), 4–8; Shannon, "Commentary on *Rerum Novarum*," 128–29, 134. On the social question more generally, see John Augustine Ryan and Raymond Augustine McGowan, *A Catechism of the Social Question* (Mahwah, N.J.: Paulist Press, 1921); Douglas Moggach and Paul Leduc Browne, *The Social Question and the Democratic Revolution: Marx and the Legacy of 1848* (Ottawa: University of Ottawa Press, 2000); Warren Breckman, *Marx, the Young Hegelians, and the Origins of Radical Social Theory: Dethroning the Self* (New York: Cambridge University Press, 2001), 149–50.

17. Notice how Leo mentions the abolition of the guilds, not because he is pining for their reestablishment, but out of concern that "no other protective organization took their place." In other words, the problem for him is that many see no need for the protection of workers and even oppose the idea that a society, as Leo puts it later in the encyclical, should "shield from misery those on whom it so largely depends for the things that it needs." On Leo's terms, there is an absence of societies where societies should exist. This is one important reason that, he thinks, employers are able to exploit the vulnerability of the migrants flooding into the cities; Leo, *Rerum Novarum*, nos. 3, 34, 48–57. The term "society" as Leo uses it embraces social memberships within polities, as well as diverse kinds of human community: families (nos. 12–14), organizations and associations of employers and workers (nos. 48–57), and even the church (nos. 16, 19, 29, 38, 53). As William Cavanaugh explains, "Society, for Leo, is not an aggregate of individuals but a society of societies"; Cavanaugh, "Dispersed Political Authority: Subsidiarity and Globalization in *Caritas in Veritate*," in *Jesus Christ: The New Face of Social Progress* (Grand Rapids, Mich.: Wm. B. Eerdmans, 2015), 101–2.

isolated and helpless, to the hardheartedness of employers and the greed of unchecked competition" and "a small number of very rich men have been able to lay upon the teeming masses of the laboring poor a yoke little better than that of slavery itself."[18]

How did this happen? What has generated this misery and wretchedness, in which people have been uprooted from societies that previously offered them at least some measure of protection? What brought "the teeming masses of laboring poor" to the cities? It is instructive to begin our consideration of *Rerum Novarum* by reading it against the backdrop of what had been happening in Europe over the previous several centuries—what Karl Polanyi refers to as "the great transformation."[19] An important part of this transformation concerns the enclosure of common fields and pastures upon which commoners throughout Europe and elsewhere had previously relied for sustenance, which was enacted in the name of progress, agricultural and otherwise.[20] Enclosure, we will recall from chapter 1, refers to the privatization of land—surrounding, bounding, and containing it—usually with fences or hedges. The enclosed land is then deeded to owners, and the claims of others upon it are curtailed or eliminated altogether.

Enclosure movements began in England around the fifteenth century before expanding to continental Europe and the rest of the world.[21] In Europe, enclosure typically replaced "open field" agriculture, the specific characteristics of which varied considerably across place and time.[22] The

18. Leo, *Rerum Novarum*, no. 3.

19. Polanyi, *Great Transformation*.

20. Of course, this understanding of progress is hotly contested; see E. P. Thompson, *The Making of the English Working Class* (New York: Vintage, 1963), 217; J. M. Neeson, *Commoners: Common Right, Enclosure and Social Change in England, 1700–1820* (New York: Cambridge University Press, 1996), 41, 157.

21. Helpful treatments of enclosure include Karl Marx, *Capital*, vol. 1 (New York: Penguin, 1976); Polanyi, *Great Transformation*; Thompson, *Making of the English Working Class*; J. L. Hammond and Barbara Hammond, *The Village Labourer, 1760–1832: A Study of the Government of England before the Reform Bill* (London: Longman Green, 1911); Neeson, *Commoners*; Mark Overton, *Agricultural Revolution in England: The Transformation of the Agrarian Economy, 1500–1850* (New York: Cambridge University Press, 1996); E. C. K. Gonner, *Common Land and Inclosure* (Abingdon on Thames: Taylor and Francis, 1912).

22. Carl J. Dahlman, *The Open Field System and Beyond: A Property Rights Analysis of an Economic Institution* (New York: Cambridge University Press, 2008); Warren Ortman Ault, *Open-Field Farming in Medieval England* (London: Allen and Unwin, 1972); Grenville Astill,

lands on which people practiced this agriculture were common; although the lands were either owned collectively or by a particular person, others known as commoners had rights to access and use them. While it is often thought that common land belongs to no one in particular or that it belongs in some diffuse way to the community, which results in excessive use and degradation, this is a misconception.[23] Common land is owned as other land is owned. What distinguishes it is that people besides the owner(s) have rights in it. Common land is a form of property in which more than one person has rights of use, not the absence of property. What this means for our purposes is that while the land targeted for enclosure did not belong to commoners in the sense that they had a legal title to it, the right to access it and use it *did* very much belong to them—a use referred to as common right. This was a *profit à prendre*, or a right of taking, which amounted to a nonpossessory interest in land.[24] Over the centuries and across Europe, common law and custom came to protect these and numerous additional rights in the commons, which is why J. L. Hammond and Barbara Hammond refer to the commons as "the patrimony of the poor."[25]

With enclosure came the loss of these rights to access and use common land, as well as the ascendancy of a conception of ownership that prioritized the exclusivity of possession and the power to exclude others from what was possessed. Enclosure therefore not only fundamentally transformed the European landscape, delimiting fields with fences,

---

The Countryside of Medieval England (Cambridge, Mass.: Blackwell, 1992); Rosemary Lynn Hopcroft, *Regions, Institutions, and Agrarian Change in European History* (Ann Arbor: University of Michigan Press, 1999); Tom Kemp, *Industrialization in Nineteenth Century Europe* (New York: Routledge, 1997), 32–78; Trevor Rowley, *The Origins of Open-Field Agriculture* (London: Croom Helm, 1981); Tom Scott, *The Peasantries of Europe: From the Fourteenth to the Eighteenth Centuries* (London: Longman, 1998).

23. As Hyde puts it, "Use rights in the common were typically stinted, rarely absolute. No common was 'open to all' and no 'rational herdsman' was ever free to increase his herd at will. A true commons is a stinted thing; what [Garrett] Hardin [in "The Tragedy of the Commons"] described is not a commons at all but what is nowadays called an unmanaged common-pool resource"; Hyde, *Common as Air*, 35, 32–35. For more on these matters, see Elinor Ostrom, *Governing the Commons: The Evolution of Institutions for Collective Action* (New York: Cambridge University Press, 1990).

24. Neeson, *Commoners*, 1.

25. Hammond and Hammond, *Village Labourer, 1760–1832*, 103–4.

hedges, or other markers, but it also brought important changes in how ownership was understood, as the use of land was increasingly restricted to the owner alone and centered upon profit-making rather than subsistence.[26] Moreover, because enclosure led to the disappearance of common lands upon which people had previously relied for their livelihoods, enclosure was closely tied to dispossession and migration to urban centers, along with the increasing and often exclusive reliance of people upon wages to make ends meet.[27] The increased labor supply stemming from the production of landlessness was an important factor fueling the Industrial Revolution,[28] and it is also behind Leo's depiction of the misery and wretchedness pressing down unjustly upon the majority of the working class in *Rerum Novarum*.

In Germany and elsewhere in Europe, problems surrounding the new agricultural production system and its underlying property regime became particularly acute in the decades just before Leo wrote his encyclical. Unlike in Britain and France, where enclosure began earlier and extended over a longer period, industrialism in Germany, according to Ralf Dahrendorf, "occurred late, quickly, and thoroughly."[29] Various factors, including enclosure and the abolishment of guilds, contributed to the rise of a new class of landless workers.[30] People spoke of *landflucht* or land flight to describe the rural exodus.[31] These were major topics discussed by the Fribourg Union—a circle of scholars that met in Fribourg, Switzerland, beginning in 1884, which had an important influence upon *Rerum Novarum*.[32]

Enclosure is extraordinarily complex, and doing justice to it is well

---

26. See Overton, *Agricultural Revolution in England*, 165.

27. Neeson, *Commoners*, 22–23, 34.

28. Douglas Fisher, *The Industrial Revolution: A Macroeconomic Interpretation* (New York: Springer, 2016), 45–46.

29. Ralf Dahrendorf, *Society and Democracy in Germany* (Garden City, N.Y.: Anchor, 1992), 33.

30. Breckman, *Marx, the Young Hegelians, and the Origins of Radical Social Theory*, 149–50.

31. Ludwig von Mises, *Economic Policy: Thoughts for Today and Tomorrow* (Auburn, Ala.: Ludwig von Mises Institute, 2006), 8; George F. McLean and John Kromkowski, *Cultural Heritage and Contemporary Change*, vol. 5, *Urbanization and Values* (Washington, D.C.: Council for Research in Values and Philosophy, 1991), 56.

32. Normand J. Paulhus, "Social Catholicism and the Fribourg Union," Selected Papers from the Annual Meeting of the Society of Christian Ethics, 1980; Paulhus, *The Theological and Political Ideals of the Fribourg Union* (University Microfilms, 1986).

beyond the scope of this chapter. But even our brief consideration of enclosure helps to highlight the background conditions of *Rerum Novarum* and connect them to Romero's context. John Paul II makes a similar move in his 1991 encyclical *Centesimus Annus* when he compares the "inhuman exploitation" described in *Rerum Novarum* to parts of the contemporary world where "the rules of the earliest period of capitalism still flourish in conditions of 'ruthlessness' in no way inferior to the darkest moments of the first phase of industrialization." In such places, he continues, "land is still the central element in the economic process, but those who cultivate it are excluded from ownership and reduced to a state of quasi-servitude."[33] Romero's El Salvador fits this description quite aptly.

Enclosure is also important for our consideration because of the conception of property it advances and inscribes into the landscape, which the jurist William Blackstone describes as "that sole and despotic dominion which one man claims and exercises over the external things of the world, in total exclusion of the right of any other individual in the universe."[34] Blackstone's is the quintessential picture of classical liberal property.[35] Although by no means limited to modernity, this picture acquires a new kind of power and pervasiveness during that period, occupying a prominent place in a new vision of social and economic life centered upon markets. Among the main characteristics of this vision are that property involves private ownership and that an owner's control over its access, use, and disposal is absolute—or as Blackstone would have it, "despotic." This understanding of property is marked by the dyad of "owner" and "owned," from which the picture emerges of the owner standing at the center, over and against a world of passively arrayed objects. The owner's absolute control can be seen especially in the power to exclude others—"any other individual in the universe." On this view, ownership of land becomes synonymous with the exclusive right to its use.

One reason enclosure continues to be a locus of such controversy is

33. John Paul II, *Centesimus Annus*, no. 33.

34. William Blackstone, *Commentaries on the Laws of England* [1765] (Chicago: University of Chicago Press, 1979), 2:3.

35. Of course, in actual practice, Blackstone's sole and despotic dominion is hedged with restrictions: easements, covenants, nuisance laws, zoning laws, regulatory statutes, and so on.

that it so conspicuously enacts the power to exclude people who were once included in the use of property by common right. The bishop of Mainz, Wilhelm Emmanuel von Ketteler, an important influence both on the Fribourg Union and on *Rerum Novarum*, called Blackstone's understanding of property a "crude doctrine" because it "sanctions the right to steal, since … stealing means not only to take what belongs to others, but also to hold back what rightfully ought to belong to them."[36] It is therefore noteworthy that opponents of enclosure frequently resorted to the language of thievery to describe it. Enclosure, after all, took what they once had a right to access and use, what they understood to be theirs.[37]

READING RERUM NOVARUM

Our consideration of enclosure helps to clarify what is at stake in Leo's defense of property in *Rerum Novarum*. What is crucial to underscore in this regard is that developments associated with enclosure and the advance of capitalism threaten property as Leo understands it. In the *Communist Manifesto*, Karl Marx and Friedrich Engels respond to those who are "horrified" at their proposal to abolish private property with the following riposte: "But in your existing society private property is already done away with for nine-tenths of the population."[38] At least on this point, Leo agrees with their assessment. *Rerum Novarum* and social-

---

36. Wilhelm Emmanuel von Ketteler, "The Six Sermons," in *The Social Teachings of Wilhelm Emmanuel von Ketteler* (Washington, D.C.: University Press of America, 1981), 16. As Ketteler observes, the person who fails to give alms "is likened in Christian teaching to a thief"; von Ketteler, "The Labor Problem and Christianity," in *The Social Teachings of Wilhelm Emmanuel von Ketteler*, 367.

37. In a 1796 letter entitled, "Reflections on the Cruelty of Inclosing," an anonymous author wrote to the bishop of Lincoln in Lincolnshire evoking a range of scripture—especially the episode of Ahab's robbery of Naboth's vineyard in 1 Kings 21—to describe the "unchristian practice" of enclosure: "It is not doing as we would be done unto: it is not loving our neighbor as ourselves; but is removing his landmark, contrary to his inclination; and therefore joining field to field by iniquity. The history of Ahab and Naboth is not altogether inapplicable here. It does not appear from the sacred pages, that the wicked prince intended to rob his subject of his vineyard; but to make him, as he supposed, a proper recompense. Under an act of parliament, the poor man's land is frequently taken from him; and what is allotted to him is by no means a compensation for his loss"; quoted in Neeson, *Commoners*, 221. See also MacIntyre, *After Virtue*, 251; Polanyi, *The Great Transformation*, 35; Thompson, *The Making of the English Working Class*, 218.

38. Marx and Engels, *Communist Manifesto*, 98.

ism both oppose the forces of dispossession and dislocation, which have atomized societies and scattered people and which have generated the conditions within which people have nothing to sell but their labor to strangers who exploit them. According to Leo, these forces represent a greater threat to property than does socialism.[39]

As Leo puts the point, "To exercise pressure upon the indigent and the destitute for the sake of gain, and to gather one's profit out of the need of another, is condemned by all laws, human and divine. To defraud any one of wages that are his due is a great crime which cries to the avenging anger of Heaven."[40] Yet this is what is happening in the emerging industrial order on a massive scale: workers are being systematically exposed to those who would exploit their vulnerability, as we saw Leo say at the outset of the encyclical.[41] In characterizing this order, he even cites James 5:4 about the unpaid wages of laborers crying out to God[42]—the same verse we saw Romero use in the previous chapter to describe the situation of Salvadoran coffee harvesters. For his part, Leo is suggesting that this order, which denies workers living wages and exploits their needs, is criminal, haunted by the cries of those who have been robbed of what is theirs. Although Leo does not use the language of ordinary violence, this language is apposite, for as Gustavo Gutiérrez argues, *Rerum Novarum* centers upon violence suffered by the poor, which continues to characterize the present.[43]

Yet Leo does not harbor any illusions about socialism, and he frames the encyclical by calling it a false remedy to an injustice of which it is not itself the source.[44] According to Leo and his successors, socialism has a parasitic character, feeding upon the injustices associated with the advance of capitalism. Socialism is therefore not so much an evil threatening civilization, as Romero's opponents often suggest, as an indicator that

39. On this point see also Pius XI, *Quadragesimo Anno*, nos. 3–4.

40. Leo, *Rerum Novarum*, no. 20.

41. Leo, *Rerum Novarum*, no. 3.

42. Leo, *Rerum Novarum*, no. 44.

43. Gustavo Gutiérrez, "New Things Today: A Rereading of *Rerum Novarum*," in *The Density of the Present: Selected Writings* (Maryknoll, N.Y.: Orbis, 1999), 44.

44. Leo, *Rerum Novarum*, no. 4; Habiger, *Papal Teaching on Private Property*, 15, 19; Dorr, *Option for the Poor*, 14.

things are already rotten. Pius XI later writes in *Divini Redemptoris* (1937) that if we want to understand socialism's appeal, "we must remember that the way had been already prepared for it by the religious and moral destitution in which wage-earners had been left by liberal economics."[45] According to him, the best way to overcome socialism is therefore to address the injustices of capitalism.[46]

It is for this reason that one of Leo's central arguments in *Rerum Novarum* is for the proliferation of property rather than its elimination. "The law," he writes, "should favor ownership, and its policy should be to induce as many as possible of the people to become owners."[47] While certainly recognizing property rights as natural rights,[48] Leo insists upon the rights of *all* people to property. In other words, an enduring distributive concern underlies his articulation of the fundamental right to property. Moreover, in arguing for the proliferation of property, Leo is speaking not only of movables such as food and clothing, but also, and especially, of immovables such as land and houses.[49]

The imaginative reach of *Rerum Novarum* is therefore as striking as it is ambitious. Leo is effectively trying to renew the reality of common right in a world being built upon its repudiation. He is trying to imagine how a new society might emerge within the shell of the industrial one. Consequently, as Leo states repeatedly throughout *Rerum Novarum*, the solution to the social question is the "protection" of property.[50] But pro-

---

45. Pius XI, Encyclical Letter *Divini Redemptoris* (March 19, 1937), no. 16. See Romero, "La *Rerum Novarum* perenne y urgente."

46. See Pius XI, *Quadragesimo Anno*, nos. 62, 122; Pius XII, *Discourse to Commemorate the 50th Anniversary of the Encyclical "Rerum Novarum" of Pope Leo XIII on the Social Question*, 219; John XXIII, *Mater et Magistra*, no. 14.

47. Leo XIII, *Rerum Novarum*, no. 46.

48. Leo, *Rerum Novarum*, no. 6.

49. Leo, *Rerum Novarum*, nos. 5, 10, 47. On the centrality of land to Leo's social vision, see Pius XII, *Discourse to Commemorate the 50th Anniversary of the Encyclical "Rerum Novarum" of Pope Leo XIII on the Social Question*, 224. This emphasis is one of the reasons *Rerum Novarum* had such influence upon Catholic agrarian movements; see *Flee to the Fields: The Faith and Works of the Catholic Land Movement; A Symposium* (London: Heath Cranton, 1934). An important figure associated with such movements was the Dominican priest Vincent McNabb. For a general overview of his Catholic agrarianism, see Matthew Philipp Whelan, "Land, Economy, and the Measure of Christ: The Catholic Agrarianism of Vincent McNabb, O.P.," *Nova et Vetera* 10, no. 1 (2012): 253–77.

50. Leo XIII, *Rerum Novarum*, nos. 8, 13, 15, 38, 46–47.

tection for him does not mean defense of the status quo, but a radical expansion of ownership and the goods flowing from it—the facilitation of property's ongoing circulation and distribution to meet the needs of all. Property's protection is synonymous with laws, institutions, and policies that promote a better distribution of property and that counter dispossession.[51] In short, it is because industrial capitalism threatens property that Leo thinks property must be protected.

To appreciate this, consider the benefits Leo thinks will follow from a better distribution of land. "If working people can be encouraged to look forward to obtaining a share in the land," he writes, "the consequence will be that the gulf between vast wealth and sheer poverty will be bridged over, and the respective classes will be brought nearer to one another."[52] Notice the echoes of this passage in Romero's homily upon his return from Puebla. Although Leo does not specify how obtaining a share in the land might be accomplished—and he certainly makes no mention of land reform—he clearly thinks that increasing access of workers to productive property like land will begin to bridge the distance between classes and ameliorate the conflict between them. Additionally, Leo observes that people not only tend to work harder on what is theirs, but they also know and care for it better as well. Having a share in the land, he thinks, leads people to "love the very soil" that brings forth the "abundance of good things" upon which their lives depend. In this way, widespread distribution of land facilitates practical wisdom in its care and use.[53] Finally, and

51. This point is especially important for the movement known as Distributism, for which the defense of property became synonymous with its diffusion. Classic Distributist texts include G. K. Chesterton's *What's Wrong with the World* (New York: Dodd, Mead, 1912) and his *The Outline of Sanity* (New York: Dodd Mead, 1927); see also Hilaire Belloc, *The Servile State* (Boston: Le Roy Phillips, 1913), and his *An Essay on the Restoration of Property* (Norfolk, Va.: IHS, 2012).

52. Leo XIII, *Rerum Novarum*, no. 47.

53. There are important affinities here with agrarians like Wendell Berry. Berry explains his position in an essay in terms similar to Leo's: "I believe that land that is to be used should be divided into small parcels among a lot of small owners; I believe therefore in the right of private property. I believe that, given our history and tradition, a large population of small property holders offers the best available chance for local cultural adaptation and good stewardship of the land—provided that the property holders are secure, legally and economically, in their properties"; Berry, "Private Property and the Common Wealth," in *Another Turn of the Crank: Essays* (Berkeley, Calif.: Counterpoint, 2011), 49. Central to Berry's work is the sense that people care for that which belongs to them and that property rightly understood

closely related to the previous benefits, Leo is convinced that if people have enough land to live well, they will set down roots and "cling to the country in which they were born" instead of being forced to move to survive,[54] like the migrant workers we saw Romero discuss. In other words, having land binds people to places, which not only promotes good use of land, but also helps establish a mutuality of belonging between people and the places from which they draw the gift of their lives.

We are examining *Rerum Novarum* because it sets the terms that are preserved, clarified, and applied by subsequent Catholic social teaching. So far, we have seen that the dispossession associated with enclosure is a threat to property as Leo understands it and that his response is to call for a more just distribution of property—paradigmatically property in land. A distributive concern animates his arguments for the right to property. Although Leo himself does not advocate land reform, this distributive concern is what enables later social teaching to do so, which we will examine in the following chapter. However, the deeper issue we must first address is what property is and what possession of it entails, because Blackstone and Leo do not mean the same thing by these terms. We must therefore look more closely at Leo's understanding of property and possession and how the theological grammar of creation as common gift informs it.

Near the beginning of *Rerum Novarum*, Leo makes an important statement about this theological grammar and its relationship to property, an axiomatic claim that church teaching will continue to reiterate. God has given the earth for the use and enjoyment of the whole human race, Leo writes, but this "can in no way be a bar to the owning of private property."[55] At first glance, this statement seems paradoxical, even oxymoronic. How can the earth be given to all and yet this not ipso facto bar the possession of private property? Does not the adjective "private" suggest a use that is

---

can therefore safeguard, as he puts it, the "mutual belonging of people and places without which there can be no lasting and caring human communities"; Berry, *Sex, Economy, Freedom and Community: Eight Essays* (New York: Pantheon, 1993), 96.

54. Leo XIII, *Rerum Novarum*, no. 47.

55. Leo XIII, *Rerum Novarum*, no. 8.

restricted to a particular person or persons and so opposed to "common"? In short, how does Leo understand the commonality of the gift of creation, and what does that commonality have to do with property?

Because Leo assumes the theological grammar of creation as common gift and its implications for property and possession, he sees no need for further elaboration, simply observing that God, in giving the earth to all, does not assign specific parts of it to particular peoples but leaves the precise arrangements up to them.[56] What increasingly becomes evident as the discussion proceeds is that Leo thinks the institutions and structures devised by distinct societies regarding the use of the earth internally relate to God's giving of the earth for common use, and that these institutions and structures play an indispensable role in mediating access to the gift. For this reason, Leo writes that even as different peoples use the earth in different ways, the earth "ceases not thereby to minister to the needs of all, inasmuch as there is not one who does not sustain life from what the land produces." "All human subsistence," he continues, "is derived either from labor on one's own land, or from some toil, some calling, which is paid for either in the produce of the land itself, or in what is exchanged for what the land brings forth."[57] Notice how these statements convey the elemental sharing of all creaturely life in land that precedes and conditions particular property arrangements—the way land is *sui generis* in its contribution to the giving of life. At the same time, these statements also convey how Leo thinks particular property-holding arrangements are indispensable in order to facilitate this elemental creaturely sharing and the life it makes possible. Property's whole point and purpose are to advance this sharing.

What therefore begins to emerge from close attention to these initial sections of *Rerum Novarum* is that Leo thinks all property derives from and must be ordered to God's gift of the earth for common use.[58] The underlying assumption is that God enables human participation in the giv-

56. Leo XIII, *Rerum Novarum*, no. 8.
57. Leo XIII, *Rerum Novarum*, no. 8.
58. Habiger thinks that Leo is not as clear as he could be on this point: "Leo does not closely differentiate between the principle of private property and the more fundamental principle of the common use of all material goods. The source he draws upon for *Rerum Novarum* [*ST* II-II, q. 66, aa. 1, 2] is clear about this distinction, but that is not reflected as clearly

ing of the gift of creation to humankind in common. Consequently, even as Leo and his successors affirm private property, they also insist that God gives the earth for common use, that human agency participates in God's giving of the gift, and that the purpose of property and its associated institutions is to facilitate the access of all people to what God gives to them. The influence of the theological grammar of creation as common gift upon this pattern of thinking is unmistakable. But if all this is true, it raises questions, not just about what property most fundamentally is, but also about what duties possession of it entails. Among the central questions for this whole line of thought is, how can people use what God gives in a manner that acknowledges the gift as a common one?

Later in the encyclical, Leo addresses precisely this question, and in doing so, his larger theological vision of human flourishing and property's derived status becomes especially apparent. In this part of *Rerum Novarum*, Leo turns to what he takes to be the solution to the social question: the common life of the church itself, a society founded upon and sustained by a communion more determinative than class conflict.[59] Although the church's task in the world certainly involves reminding people of their obligations to one another in justice, the church, Leo argues, "aims higher" than the mere cessation of conflict. For it aims to incarnate—in an admittedly limited and imperfect way—the communion at the center of all reality, and to remind all people that their destiny is to share in it.[60] It is through the cultivation of charity among people, which is the love most characteristic of that communion, that the church works to overcome the "separation" between people, establishing "friendly concord" and promoting unity in "bonds of friendship."[61] As the Jesuit philosopher and economist Heinrich Pesch observes in his *Lehrbuch der Nationalökonomie*, the solidarity that results is established on the basis of the common origin and destiny of humankind and of a common Redeemer and a common church.[62]

---

in *Rerum Novarum*"; Habiger, *Papal Teaching on Private Property*, 32–33. Note that both here and elsewhere I've put "aa" when there are multiple articles from the *Summa*.

59. Leo XIII, *Rerum Novarum*, nos. 15–19.

60. Leo XIII, *Rerum Novarum*, nos. 19–21.

61. Leo XIII, *Rerum Novarum*, nos. 24–25.

62. Quoted in Heinrich Pesch, *Heinrich Pesch on Solidarist Economics: Excerpts from the*

Informing Leo's discussion is Thomas Aquinas's account in the *Summa Theologiae* of God's love that in Christ "communicates" across the infinite distance between Creator and creation, establishing the possibility of a mysterious form of friendship between God and human beings (Jn 15:15).[63] Any friendship is based upon some kind of sharing (*aliqua communicatio*), Thomas observes, and what is being shared in this case is God's own common life. According to Aristotle, Thomas's interlocutor here, friendship exists both when someone wills the good of another and when that willing is mutual and ordered to a good shared in common.[64] However, in arguing for the possibility of friendship between God and humans, Thomas departs radically from Aristotle, citing 1 Corinthians 1:9 ("God is faithful; by him you were called into the fellowship of his Son, Jesus Christ our Lord") to emphasize the uniqueness of this friendship, whose conditions of possibility have been wholly established by God's work in Christ.[65]

Although this friendship begins on earth, Thomas believes it will be perfected in the land of heaven.[66] In making this point, Thomas appeals to Paul's discussion in Philippians 3:20 of a common life in heaven (in Latin, *conversatio*; in Greek, *politeuma*). This is yet another departure from Aristotle, for whom friendship is political in the sense that the common life of most concern is that of the earthly *polis* or city-state. Indeed, friendship for Aristotle is impossible between citizens of different *poli*, just as it impossible between those who are citizens of a given *polis* and those who are not, whether they are women, slaves, children, or strangers. Thomas's understanding of the friendship between God and humankind is not political in Aristotle's sense, but it does have important political ramifications. Sharing in God's common life means that friendship on earth becomes possible across distances that might previously have seemed insurmountable, such as between people of different polities or

---

Lehrbuch der Nationalökonomie, trans. Rupert J. Ederer (New York: University Press of America, 1998), 43.

63. *ST* II-II, q. 23, a. 1, resp.

64. Aristotle, *Nicomachean Ethics*, trans. Martin Ostwald (Upper Saddle River, N.J.: Prentice Hall, 1962), VIII.2.

65. *ST* II-II, q. 23, a. 1, resp., ad. 1.

66. *ST* II-II, q. 23, a. 1, resp., ad. 1.

different statuses within them, because it is possible across the infinite distance between God and humankind. The politics of this friendship, although not of the world, can nevertheless unsettle and transfigure it, which is why Leo believes that the church embodies the solution to the social question and that its life shows how the distances separating people can be surmounted. Above all, this politics is exemplified in the love most characteristic of God's common life as it works within a world groaning from sin: a love that extends as far as the enemy and even forgives those who crucify it, because even enemies belong, or potentially belong, to Christ.[67]

Thomas's understanding of friendship in Christ is at the heart of Leo's concerns in *Rerum Novarum*, and as the encyclical develops, it becomes the horizon under which Leo locates his discussion of the proper use of property. For Leo identifies the solution to the social question in the acknowledgment of the higher goods people hold or might one day hold in common with one another in Christ. In Christ, Leo thinks, people have more in common than a Creator who brings them into existence, sustains them in it, and gives the earth for the use and enjoyment of all. They also have in common a Redeemer. Sharing in Christ's life is not only their ultimate destiny and final flourishing, but it is the ground of Leo's hope that those whose lives are separated by property can learn to acknowledge that "the blessings of nature and the gifts of grace belong to the whole human race in common."[68]

According to Leo, humankind's destiny to share more fully in God's common life in Christ transfigures commonplace conceptions of earthly treasure. "The things of earth," Leo writes, "cannot be understood or valued aright without taking into consideration the life to come, the life that will know no death.... God has not created us for the perishable and transitory things of earth, but for things heavenly and everlasting."[69] Even for those still on pilgrimage, the life for which they are destined should shape how they understand and use their property. "So far as eternal happiness is concerned," Leo writes, "the only important thing [regarding posses-

---

67. *ST* II-II, q. 23, a. 1, ad. 1.
68. Leo XIII, *Rerum Novarum*, no. 25.
69. Leo XIII, *Rerum Novarum*, no. 21.

sions] is to use them aright."[70] In this regard, he extols Christians who have "despoiled themselves of their possessions in order to relieve their brethren."[71] Citing the explicit teaching of Jesus (Mt 19:23–24; Lk 6:24–25), Leo even argues that riches can become an obstacle to participation in God's life.[72] As far as Leo is concerned, then, the crucial issue is not how people think about their possessions or whether they are attached to them in some abstract sense, but how they use them.

Underlying Leo's understanding of property is a fundamental distinction between possession and use. As Leo explains, "It is one thing to have a right to the possession of money and another to have a right to use money as one wills."[73] Leo takes this distinction from a passage in the *Summa Theologiae*, in which Thomas discusses what he calls a "twofold competence (*duo competunt*) in relation to material things." "The first [competence]," as Thomas writes, "is the power to procure and dispense (*procurandi et dispensandi*) them. Understood in this way, it is not merely legitimate for a man to possess things as his own (*propria possideat*), it is even necessary for human life."[74] This tracks with what Leo has said earlier in *Rerum Novarum* in defense of possession of property and the way property is meant to facilitate access to the natural gifts God gives to humankind in common. However, Leo's concern here is the second competence, which Thomas calls the use (*usus ipsarum*) of material things and describes this way: "No man is entitled to manage things merely for himself, but as common (*ut proprias, sed ut communes*), so that he is ready to share them easily (*facili*) with others in the case of necessity. This is why Paul writes to Timothy, 'As for the rich of this world, charge them to give easily [*facile*], to communicate to others, etc.' [1 Tm 6:17–18]."[75]

Consider the claim Thomas is making with regard to the second competence. It is one thing *that* people possess material goods, along with the capacity to manage them. However, Thomas is now raising a different,

---

70. Leo XIII, *Rerum Novarum*, no. 21.

71. Leo XIII, *Rerum Novarum*, no. 29.

72. Leo XIII, *Rerum Novarum*, no. 22.

73. Leo XIII, *Rerum Novarum*, no. 22.

74. *ST* II-II, q. 66, a. 2, resp. The reasons Thomas gives are from Aristotle, *Politics*, trans. T. A. Sinclair (New York: Penguin, 1981), 1262b37–64b25.

75. *ST* II-II, q. 62, a. 1, resp.

though related issue, which concerns *how* people possess material goods. In other words, he is addressing the habits governing use. Regarding these habits, Thomas contends that people should manage what they have as if it were common, as if their possessions belonged not exclusively to themselves but to others as well. In making decisions about the use of what they have, people must draw others into the orbit of concern, taking them into account in the very use of what they have.

This is a very different picture of property and possession than Blackstone's, and the influence of the theological grammar of creation as common gift upon it is clear. In contrast to Blackstone's prioritization of the power to exclude, Leo/Thomas prioritize the power to include others in the use and enjoyment of property. Although Leo/Thomas endorse a certain conception of private property, in which particular persons possess and use things, they do not believe owners have absolute and exclusive control over it. Among other reasons, this is because the God who gives the earth for the benefit of all people is at the center of the picture, and Leo/Thomas enfold property and possession—like human life and agency more generally—into the way God gives the gift. People must manage things as common because they hold what they have not as isolated individuals, but as members of a wider constellation of societies to which the gift has likewise been given, whose horizon is humankind. Consequently, for people to learn to hold what they have as common means using it to support the life of these societies, beginning, but not ending, with their households and those nearest to them.[76] In this picture, the primary rationale for property is God's exclusion of no one from the blessings of nature.

As members of the community of humankind, particular people have claims upon the earth, just as others do, which is why Leo observes that even as they manage material things as common, people are not bound

---

76. That humankind is a unity is not self-evident. But as Henri de Lubac observes, "The supernatural dignity of one who has been baptized rests, we know, on the natural dignity of man, though it surpasses it in an infinite manner: *Recognize, O Christian, your dignity—God, who in a wonderful manner created and ennobled human nature.* Thus, the unity of the Mystical Body of Christ, a supernatural unity, supposes a previous natural unity, the unity of the human race"; de Lubac, *Catholicism: Christ and the Common Destiny of Man* (San Francisco: Ignatius Press, 1988), 25.

to distribute what they need for themselves or their dependents.[77] This is because they are likewise recipients of God's gift of creation. However, while people are not bound to distribute what they need, they are bound to distribute what they do not, which requires the ability to distinguish between the two—a complex cultural accomplishment. As Jean-Yves Calvez and Jacques Perrin remind us, needs have a "discipline," which means that "the order of needs can be debased and true needs exploited."[78] An additional complication is that the very criteria people use to distinguish between need and excess can shift over time. The tradition under consideration here is no exception. In the determination of what is superfluous, Leo counsels taking into account social station and what it means to live well within it.[79] In contrast, as Catholic social teaching develops into the twentieth century, the maintenance of social station drops out of view as a legitimate criterion, and as Pope John XXIII puts it, the "measure of the needs of others" becomes paramount.[80]

The crucial point at this juncture is that the formation of people who are able to distinguish between what they need and what they do not is indispensable to this theological grammar. Owners are also members of a community of common use, along with others who have legitimate claims upon the goods of creation. Ensuring fellow recipients of the gift have access to what is theirs is constitutive to what it means to regard material goods as common. But such a manner of use is not possible without the existence of a people who can discriminate between true and false needs and who can acknowledge that what they possess in excess of their needs belongs to others. As Leo explains, "When what necessity demands has

77. Leo XIII, *Rerum Novarum*, 22.

78. Jean-Yves Calvez and Jacques Perrin, *The Church and Social Justice: The Social Teaching of the Popes from Leo XIII to Pius XII (1878–1958)* (Chicago: Henry Regnery, 1961), 190. For a beautiful meditation on what humans need in order to flourish, see Michael Ignatieff, *The Needs of Strangers* (New York: Penguin, 1986). See also Pius XII, *Adscriptis Sodalitati Catholicae ex Operariis Italicis: Ob Commendationem Litterarum Encyclicarum "Rerum Novarum" Coadunatis*, in *Acta Apostolicae Sedis* 45 (1953), 406–8.

79. Leo XIII, *Rerum Novarum*, no. 22.

80. The full quotation reads, "The urgent obligation of the Christian man is to reckon what is superfluous by the measure of the needs of others, and to see to it that the administration and the distribution of created goods serve the common good"; John XXIII, "Radio-Television Message," in *Acta Apostolicae Sedis* 54 (1962), 682; Vatican Council II, *Gaudium et Spes*, no. 69.

been supplied … it becomes a duty to give to the indigent out of what remains over. 'Of that which remaineth, give alms.'"[81] This pattern of reasoning is the basis of the simultaneous twofold movement characteristic of the politics of common use: "downward" as people discern their true needs, and "outward" as they return the surplus to those to whom it belongs. Following Thomas, Leo therefore suggests that the best evidence of the management of material things as common is people's willingness to open their hands and release what they have when faced with the need of others. In Thomas's words, in such situations, people must learn not to cling to their possessions but rather to part with them *facili*—readily, without difficulty.

THOMAS AQUINAS

We have been surveying *Rerum Novarum*'s articulation of the wider moral and theological landscape within which God gives the blessings of nature for the common use of humankind. In this landscape, property essentially derives from the grammar of creation as common gift, with commonality inhering in what property essentially is and what proper use of it entails. However, before considering how subsequent social teaching takes up this approach, we must briefly examine Thomas's treatment of this topic in the *Summa Theologiae* (*Summa*), because it also sheds considerable light upon some of the features of the landscape we are surveying. Once again, my interest in this chapter is not only Leo's reliance upon Thomas or Thomas's influence upon Catholic social teaching—as important as these are—but also how the theological grammar of creation as common gift gives rise to a politics of common use and how that politics illuminates the struggle for a better distribution of land in El Salvador and Romero's role in it. That theological grammar is on full display in the *Summa*.

The passages from the *Summa* upon which *Rerum Novarum* draws are from the question on theft and robbery in the treatise on justice. There is an important shift between the first and the second articles of the ques-

---

81. This verse is Lk 11:41 from the Douay-Rheims edition, a translation from the Vulgate; Leo XIII, *Rerum Novarum*, no. 22.

tion. While the first article concerns whether the possession (*possessio*) of created goods is natural for humankind, the second concerns whether it is natural for particular persons to possess things as their own. What is significant about this shift is how Thomas begins the question by framing his whole discussion of *possessio* in relation to God's provision of sustenance for humankind in common. Only then—and always in relation to God's *possessio*—does he consider *possessio* as it pertains to particular persons.

The distinction between God's possession and humankind's governs the entirety of what follows. Regarding whether possession is natural for humankind, Thomas contrasts dominion (*dominium*) over the nature of a thing, which pertains to God alone, with *dominium* in the use of a thing (*usum ipsius rei*), which pertains to humankind.[82] We are once again encountering the notion of use, which Thomas relates to how possessions are a means to an end. "All possessions," as Thomas notes elsewhere, "come under the heading of the useful."[83] In this case, their usefulness is for the support of human life. As embodied creatures, humans need food, drink, shelter, clothing, and similar goods for survival and for the practice of virtue.[84] However, Thomas thinks the use of possessions must

82. Marcus Lefébure notes that while the terms *dominium* and *possessio* are largely interchangeable for Thomas, *proprietas* is a species of *possessio*, and it is typically contrasted with terms like *communitas rerum*, *possidere communiter*, and so on; Thomas Aquinas, *Summa Theologiae*, ed. Marcus Lefébure, vol. 38 (New York: Cambridge University Press, 1975), 63, note a. On this point, Thomas's understanding of *possessio* and *dominium* must be distinguished from that of his Franciscan contemporaries, who tended to associate these terms with possessive lordship, absolute control, exclusive use, and so on. In contrast to the Franciscans, Thomas understands *dominium*, as Christopher A. Franks puts it, "in a more minimal sense as any power—however limited and subordinate—to use goods." *Dominium* is characteristically "limited, social, and defined by the power of use that is necessary to human beings in order to accomplish the purpose of sustenance established for them by the divine order. It is a *dominium* whose contours are defined by a yielding to the prior fabric of natural and social membership that encompasses human beings. In short, this *dominium* is nonproprietary"; Franks, *He Became Poor: The Poverty of Christ and Aquinas's Economic Teachings* (Grand Rapids, Mich.: William B. Eerdmans, 2009), 58–59. For an exposition of Franciscan thought on this point, see Giorgio Agamben, *The Highest Poverty: Monastic Rules and Form-of-Life*, trans. Adam Kotsko (Stanford, Calif.: Stanford University Press, 2013).

83. *ST* II-II, q. 62, a. 5, ad. 1; q. 117, a. 3, resp.

84. Because human creatures are embodied, sufficient sustenance is indispensable to human flourishing. As Thomas sees it, the virtues do not float free of the body. Their operation is bodily and depends upon bodily needs being met (*ST* I-II, q. 4, a. 7, resp.). Thomas distinguishes himself from the Stoics on this point. While the Stoics hold that the only

ultimately be understood in light of the true end of human creatures, which is not the preservation of the body but union with God in beatitude.[85] The important point is that, according to Thomas, God's *possessio* over the nature of things relates to God's creation of heaven and earth and how God holds all things in existence. In contrast, humankind's *possessio* is not power over the nature of things, but rather the power to make use of things for humankind's benefit, by which Thomas principally means for bodily sustenance.[86]

Thomas therefore ties humankind's *possessio* to its creaturely status, to its ontological dependency upon God for being and agency. In other words, human *possessio*, like human existence more generally, is itself an expression of God's *possessio* over creation.[87] What is also crucial to see is that Thomas relates humankind's *possessio* to its embodiment and particularly to how human beings are embedded within and reliant upon the wider created order to meet needs. For Thomas, *possessio* begins with the relationships that sustain life, with humans in need of basic "material support," such as food, drink, shelter, clothing, and so on.[88] God in God's goodness gives this support, and God calls upon human creatures to imitate this goodness that makes provision for all. It is no exaggeration to say that human *possessio* on Thomas's terms simply is participation in and conformity to God's provisioning for creation in common, from which human *possessio* derives its essential rationale and takes it shape.[89]

---

human good is virtue, such that bodily goods are not really goods at all, Thomas contends that because humans are creatures in which soul and body are united, whatever preserves the life of the body, though not a final good, is still a good. Humans should therefore feel sorrow whenever those goods are lacking (*ST* I-II, q. 59, a. 3, resp.).

85. *ST* I-II, q. 3, a. 8.

86. *ST* II-II, q. 66, a. 1, resp., ad. 1.

87. As the Fourth Lateran Council states, "For between creator and creature there can be noted no similarity so great that a greater dissimilarity cannot be seen between them"; Norman P. Tanner, ed., *Decrees of the Ecumenical Councils: Nicaea I to Lateran V* (Washington, D.C.: Sheed and Ward, 1990), 1:2.

88. *ST* II-II, q. 66, a. 1, ad. 1. Thomas bases his comments here on the initial chapters of Genesis: "Behold, I have given you every plant yielding seed that is on the surface of all the earth, and every tree which has fruit yielding seed; it shall be food for you; and to every beast of the earth and to every bird of the sky and to everything that moves on the earth which has life, I have given every green plant for food"; Gen 1:29–30, 2:9, 16–17.

89. *ST* II-II, q. 66, a. 1, ad. 1.

Thomas is not alone in this understanding but inherits a much older and deeper line of reflection. Drawing not only on scripture but also on Greek and Latin sources, many early Christian theologians regarded it as axiomatic that God created the sun, moon, sky, water, wind, and even land as common—*koina, communia*—making them accessible to all, and that humankind's vocation was to imitate God's manner of giving. Cyprian of Carthage's words from *Works and Almsgiving* are representative:

> For whatever belongs to God, belongs to all by our appropriation of it, nor is anyone kept from God's benefits and gifts, nor does anything prevent the whole human race from equally enjoying God's goodness and generosity. Thus, the day illuminates equally; the sun radiates, the rain moistens; the wind blows, and for those who sleep there is one sleep; and the splendor of the stars and the moon is common. With this example of equality the possessor on the earth who shares his returns and fruits, while he is fair and just with his gratuitous bounties, is an imitator of God the Father.[90]

In clarifying the difference between God's *possessio* and humankind's, Thomas repeatedly turns to one of these early Christian theologians for help: Basil the Great, especially his homily *Destruam horrea mea* ("I Will Tear Down My Barns"). The title refers to the rich fool's words as recounted in Luke's Gospel—a parable that became a *locus classicus* for later discussions of covetousness:

> Then Jesus told them a parable: "The land of a rich man produced abundantly. And he thought to himself, 'What should I do, for I have no place to store my crops?' Then he said, 'I will do this: I will pull down my barns and build larger ones, and there I will store all my grain and my goods. And I will say to my soul, *Soul, you have ample goods laid up for many years; relax, eat, drink, be merry.*' But God said to him, 'You fool!

90. Cyprian of Carthage, *Works and Almsgiving*, in *Treatises*, trans. Roy J. Deferrari, Fathers of the Church 36 (New York: Fathers of the Church, 1958), 25. See also Clement of Alexandria, *Paedagogus* 2:12 (Boston: Brill, 2002); Ambrose, *On Naboth* 1:2, 3:11, 12:53. Charles Avila compiles and comments on much of this material in Avila, *Ownership: Early Christian Teaching* (Maryknoll, N.Y.: Orbis, 1983).

This very night your life is being demanded of you. And the things you have prepared, whose will they be?' So, it is with those who store up treasures for themselves but are not rich toward God" (12:16–21).

For both Basil and Thomas, the problem with the rich fool is not merely his practical atheism but that his *possessio* is a parody of God's.[91] To use Thomas's language, he aspires to have power over the nature of things, rather than over the use of them for the support of human life. Or to use Blackstone's, he wants sole and despotic dominion over his grain and goods, in total exclusion of the right of any other individual in the universe. According to Luke, God asks the fool a single question: "And the things you have prepared, whose will they be?" (Lk 12:20). This question, like the entire parable, suggests the fool is engaged in an impossible task, striving for a control that in principle he cannot attain. As Thomas puts it, he behaves as though what he has is his "absolutely" rather than "received from another, namely God."[92] He is about to die, and God seems to be telling him that if his grip over the grain and goods in his possession does not loosen in life, then it will loosen in death, when his possessions will inevitably end up in the hands of others.

Significantly, Thomas cites Basil as asking two additional but closely related questions: "Tell me, what is your own? What did you bring into this life?"[93] These questions highlight how the fool is trying to establish himself as the organizing center of the world, treating possessions as if they were exclusively his own, as if he brought them into existence and sustained them in it. According to Basil, sin has so darkened the fool's intellect and warped his will that he is blind to the gifts God shares with him to benefit others besides himself, such as "fertile soil, temperate weather, plenty of seeds, cooperation of the animals, and whatever else is required for successful cultivation."[94] Yet God continues to share with such fools,

91. Avila, *Ownership*, 52. Basil puts the problem this way: "You deny God, since you neither recognize your Creator, nor are grateful to the One who gives these things to you"; Basil the Great, "I Will Tear Down My Barns," in *On Social Justice*, trans. C. Paul Schroeder (Crestwood, N.Y.: St. Vladimir's Seminary Press, 2009), 7.

92. *ST* II-II, q. 66, a. 1, ad. 2.

93. *ST* II-II, q. 66, a. 1, obj. 2; Basil the Great, "I Will Tear Down My Barns," 7. Informing these questions is surely Paul's: "What do you have that you did not receive?" (1 Cor 4:7).

94. Basil the Great, "I Will Tear Down My Barns," 1.

manifesting a patient and forgiving love, which makes the sun rise on both good and evil, and sends rain on the just and unjust (Mt 5:43–48).[95]

The indication that the fool's *possessio* is a parody of God's is not only the absoluteness of the control he seeks but also his futile attempt to wall off his possessions from the needs of others. As Basil writes, instead of saying, "I will satisfy the souls of the hungry, I will throw open the gates of my barns and summon all those in need,"[96] the fool regards his land and crops as his alone and tries to exclude others from benefiting from them. He wants nothing to "slip through his fingers" or "trickle down" to others,[97] and his actions ramify outward, implicating fields and barns, shaping landscapes and structures. The picture is of a person being showered by gifts well in excess of his needs. Although he frenetically gathers everything for his own exclusive benefit, his efforts ultimately will be futile. He misconstrues himself and his possessions because he misconstrues the world God has made.

Having established that human *possessio* participates in and is meant to conform to God's provisioning for all, the next article of the question turns to *possessio* as practiced by particular persons. This is the same article that Leo discusses in *Rerum Novarum* concerning the twofold competence regarding material goods: the power to procure and dispense and the power to use. While the former renders it necessary and legitimate for people to possess goods, the latter relates to the habits that govern people's use of their possessions. As Leo presents these habits, people must learn to see and to hold what they have not for themselves alone but as common, for commonality inheres in what property is and what proper use of it entails. To possess anything at all is to do so as the recipient of a common gift—as the member of a wider commons—which is why the hallmark of good use is inclusion rather than exclusion.

While the horizon of this wider commons is humankind, sin separates humankind from God, breaking and scattering this unity. Thomas's discussion of *possessio* presupposes these damaging and disintegrating

95. Basil the Great, "I Will Tear Down My Barns," 1.
96. Basil the Great, "I Will Tear Down My Barns," 2.
97. Basil the Great, "I Will Tear Down My Barns," 1.

effects of sin. A state of affairs in which some have goods in vast excess of their needs while others die from lack of them is inexplicable for him apart from sin. Humankind's long and ongoing refusal to conform its *possessio* to God's is the only "reason" for these disparities and the distances between people they generate. Given these conditions, Thomas finds a providential purpose for *possessio* by particular persons: "Those who suffer want are so numerous and they cannot all be supplied out of one stock, and this is why it is left to each individual to decide how to manage his own things [*dispensatio propriarum rerum*] in such a way as to supply the wants of the suffering."[98] The damage that sin has done to human life is deep and pervasive, and those who lack what they need are many and everywhere. In light of this, it is crucial for people in all places to address this lack by learning to conform their *possessio* to God's. For Thomas, God wants to involve as many people as possible in God's giving of the gift of creation in common.

On Thomas's picture, then, *possessio* assumes the conditions of sin, while also addressing some of its deleterious effects through the leaven of mercy. Once again, we see mercy's intimacy to the work of justice understood in the sense of opening others' access to the material goods they lack because of sin. Ambrose expresses this intimacy in the epigraph to the chapter when he writes of a mercy that is also called justice, because "the giver knows that God has given all things to all in common—that his sun rises for all, his rain falls on all, and he has given the earth to all."[99] The merciful uniquely acknowledge God's gift of the earth to feed, slake, clothe, shelter, and comfort humankind in common. For this reason Cyprian of Carthage calls mercy "the eye-salve of Christ" because its healing effects help people see the world as it truly is.[100]

All this becomes particularly clear in almsgiving. According to Thomas, almsgiving embraces all work that brings about the good of those in need, involving both bodily and other forms of relief.[101] As a work of

---

98. *ST* II-II, q. 66, a. 7, resp.

99. Quoted Avila, *Ownership*, 77.

100. Cyprian of Carthage, *Works and Almsgiving*, 14. Cyprian is drawing on Rv 3:17–18.

101. *ST* II-II, q. 32, a. 2.

mercy, almsgiving is obligatory for all Christians, a matter of precept.[102] The traditional corporal works of mercy—feeding the hungry, slaking the thirsty, clothing the naked, welcoming the stranger, visiting the sick and imprisoned, and burying the dead—are not exhaustive of mercy's work, but Thomas does think the particular sufferings addressed by these works to be representative of the lack of basic material support afflicting humankind because of sin.[103] In his treatment of almsgiving, Thomas observes that the merciful reflect as they become like God, imitating God's work on behalf of the wounded in Christ.[104] Mercy unites people to Christ by helping to heal the damage sin has done—in this case, the deprivation of material support—and therefore collaborates with Christ in the restoration of creation. In the work of mercy, we simultaneously glimpse the world in its created form, sin's damage to it, and the contours of God's ongoing work of restoration and renewal.

Another question emerging out of Thomas's discussion is whether *possessio* is compatible with the work of mercy, because such work seems to entail giving property away rather than possessing it.[105] In his response, Thomas reiterates the distinction between the power to procure and dispense and the power to use. People can and do possess material goods, he observes, and with regard to the fact of possession, the goods are theirs. But with regard to how people are to use the goods they hold, what people possess is not exclusively theirs. The rule governing use is that possessions "belong not to us alone but also to such others as we are able to succor out of what we have over and above our needs."[106] This is the claim of Romero and Leo: although people may possess these goods, the surfeit belongs to others—especially those whom sin has deprived of what they need. Thomas cites Basil's famous formulation: "The bread you are holding back is for the hungry, the clothes you keep put away are for the naked, the shoes that are rotting away with disuse are for those

---

102. *ST* II-II, q. 32, a. 5.

103. *ST* II-II, q. 32, a. 2, ad. 2. He also includes leading the blind, supporting the lame, and coming to the aid of those who are oppressed.

104. *ST* II-II, q. 30, a. 4, ad. 3.

105. *ST* II-II, q. 32, a. 5, ad. 2.

106. *ST* II-II, q. 32, a. 5, ad. 2.

who have none, the silver you keep buried in the earth is for the needy. You are thus guilty of injustice toward as many as you might have aided, and did not."[107] The theological grammar of creation as common gift generates this arresting language, casting in stark and personal terms the imperatives of the politics of common use. Although people need not give everything away, depriving themselves and their dependents of necessary material support, they must learn to distinguish between what they need and what they do not, because the latter belongs to others. Taking seriously the common character of the gift of creation clearly places demands upon those with the world's goods, who must be engaged constantly in the difficult and complex work of assessing their own needs and returning what they have in surfeit to those to whom it belongs. This work of returning necessarily draws those with the world's goods out of themselves into greater intimacy with those who lack what they need and, consequently, with God.[108]

As a final objection to the legitimacy of *possessio* by particular persons, Thomas cites the axiom that by natural law "everything is common to all" (*omnia sunt communia*).[109] In his response, Thomas does not oppose

---

107. *ST* II-II, q. 66, a. 7, resp. See Basil the Great, "I Will Tear Down My Barns," 7. Here, as elsewhere in his discussion, Thomas erroneously attributes passages to Ambrose that are actually from Basil.

108. Although the language of the preferential option for the poor comes much later in Catholic thought, the grammar of creation as a common gift implies something very much like it. As Maria Clara Bingemer observes, the concept has "remote roots," and it was among "the basic principles of Catholic social teaching" long before it was resourced by Leo XIII in *Rerum Novarum* in his engagement with industrialism. What Leo and subsequent social teaching did "was to call the faithful back to the origins of their faith, to the sources of their salvation"; Bingemer, *Latin American Theology*, 48–49. See also Peter Hebblethwaite, "Liberation Theology and the Roman Catholic Church," in *The Cambridge Companion to Liberation Theology* (New York: Cambridge University Press, 2007), 179.

109. *ST* II-II, q. 66, a. 2, obj. 1. The relevant texts from Gratian's *Decretum* read, "The Law of Nature stands apart from Custom and Ordinance. *For by the Law of Nature everything is shared by everyone.* This is believed to have been observed not only by those of whom it is written: 'Among the multitude of believers there was one heart and soul,' etc., but it is also found in an earlier tradition handed down by philosophers. In Plato that polity is said to be most justly ordered in which each person does not know his own attachments. By contrast, by the Law of Custom and Ordinance, this is mine, while that is another's"; Gratian's *Decretum*, Dist. 8, col. 12. And: "Many authorities pronounce that clergy should possess nothing.... *All men ought to have the use in common of all that is in this world.* It is through iniquity that one thing came to be called one man's and another thing another's"; Gratian's

this axiom, only the notion that it necessarily entails common ownership, such as that found in monastic communities.[110] Particular property arrangements, he thinks, are not a matter of natural law but of convention and, as such, contingent and diverse. Thomas calls them "additions" to the natural law.[111] But additions do not subtract from natural law or contradict it; their purpose is still to mediate God's giving of creation in common. Thomas agrees that monastics and all those who model their life together upon the first Christians in Jerusalem who shared "all things in common" and who distributed the proceeds "as any had need" (Acts 2:44–45, 4:31–35) most perfectly incarnate the axiom that everything is common to all. However, while such communities are the best examples of this axiom, they are not the only ones. As we have seen, the work of mercy that is incumbent upon all Christians is likewise compatible with a certain construal of *possessio* and based upon the conviction that creation is a common gift. Through mercy, even those with the world's goods can participate in and conform their *possessio* to God's. For their destiny, like that of all people, is to share in God's common life.[112]

Before leaving the *Summa*, one final feature of Thomas's treatment of property and possession deserves comment. This is his explicit account of thievery, which can help develop the implicit one we encountered in Romero's homilies in chapter 1 and guide us in navigating the terrain we will be traversing in subsequent chapters.

Toward the end of his treatment of *possessio*, Thomas returns to Ba-

---

Decretum, Causa 12, qu. 1, col. 676–77; quoted in Peter Garnsey, *Thinking about Property: From Antiquity to the Age of Revolution* (New York: Cambridge University Press, 2007), 81.

110. *ST* II-II, q. 66, a. 2, resp.

111. *ST* II-II, q. 66, a. 2, ad. 1.

112. This sense is bolstered by the *sed contra* of the article, in which Thomas cites Augustine's critique of those he calls the "apostolic." As the name suggests, the apostolic model themselves upon the Christian community Acts describes; Acts 2:37–47, 4:32–37. What troubles Thomas about this group is not their embrace of common ownership or celibacy, but that they exclude others from their fellowship. They "cut themselves off from the Church," Thomas writes, because they allege that those who possess property "have no hope of salvation"; *ST* II-II, q. 66, a. 2, s.c. In other words, Thomas defends the hope that those who possess property (and get married) might likewise be saved. What therefore becomes especially clear in this article is that Thomas's overarching aim in his discussion is to envision how *possessio* by particular persons can be compatible with following Christ.

sil's homily on Luke 12, citing Basil's observation that those like the rich fool who keep for themselves alone what God gives for the benefit of all in common "seize common goods before others have the opportunity, then claim them as their own by right of preemption."[113] Basil compares them to those who take a seat in a theater and then prevent others from attending and watching the performance.[114] Thomas agrees with Basil and attempts to clarify the conception of *possessio* implicit in it.

According to Thomas, the crucial issue is use—not taking as such but the character of the taking. To continue with Basil's theater image: A person might go to the play, take a seat, and allow others to do the same, realizing that the performance is a good best enjoyed not alone in an empty theater but together with others. Thomas observes that people might arrive first "to get things ready," busying themselves with making preparations so that the performance might be enjoyed by all.[115] In doing so, such people acknowledge the performance as a common good, which in turn shapes the manner of taking.

We can elaborate the image still further in light of Romero's martyrdom. Given a reality in which some clamor for entry into the theater while others hoard seats and block entry, it is possible to imagine people who decide to forgo their seats out of love, making room for others. For the same reason, these same people might also defend the ability of those barred entry to access their seats. In the process, these defenders might be threatened and even attacked, but refuse to defend themselves, patiently bearing persecution and violence rather than responding in kind. They might even forgive their attackers for what they have done, thereby demonstrating a love that extends to enemies.

What is especially significant about this elaboration of the theatre image is that it conveys how the work of mercy presupposes and even perfects justice, as well as how the work of justice can be deepened Chris-

---

113. *ST* II-II, q. 66, a. 2, obj. 2. See Basil the Great, "I Will Tear Down My Barns," 7.

114. This metaphor appears in Cicero, Seneca, and Epictetus, among others, and Basil's use of it is grafted onto these older narratives about humankind's original state. On the image's Stoic background, see A. A. Long, "Stoic Philosophers on Persons, Property-Ownership, and Community," in *Aristotle and After* (London: Institute of Classical Studies, 1997). On the use of the image more generally, see Garnsey, *Thinking about Property*, 113–17, 132, 137, 216.

115. *ST* II-II, q. 66, a. 2, ad. 2.

tologically.[116] The important point for this chapter is that while Thomas defends a certain conception of *possessio*—understood in terms of taking a seat in the theater—the characteristic mark of such taking is sufficiency and inclusion, in other words, taking only what is necessary and ensuring there are enough seats for others as well.[117] This is why, on Thomas's terms, hoarding seats and excluding others from entering the theater is not *possessio* at all but what he calls "violent expropriation."[118]

This violent expropriation comes more clearly into view in the question's article on theft. Following Aristotle and Isidore, Thomas defines theft as the surreptitious taking of another's property, in contrast to robbery, in which the taking is done in the open.[119] Thomas cites Basil's claim that "it is just as wrong to take something from somebody else as it is to refuse to give to the needy when you are in plenty and could do so."[120] An adequate understanding of thievery must include the category of refusal. Once again, Thomas is in fundamental agreement with Basil. "Retaining what one owes another," Thomas observes, "does the same sort of harm as taking something from another, and this is why unjustifiable taking must be held to include unjustifiable retention."[121] In other words, keeping for one's own exclusive use what belongs to others in justice is a form of thievery.

On Thomas's account of *possessio*, then, there are two distinct but related forms of thievery involved, just as we saw with Romero. The first is the more commonplace view of the thief who takes in secret what is possessed by another. Basil's theatergoer, who occupies the seats and re-

116. For an insightful development of this point in the context of Christian rights talk of the sixteenth-century School of Salamanca, see David Lantigua, "The Image of God, Christian Rights Talk, and the School of Salamanca," *Journal of Law and Religion* 31, no. 1 (2016): 39–40.

117. *ST* II-II, q. 66, a. 2, ad. 2; Basil the Great, "I Will Tear Down My Barns," 7.

118. *ST* II-II, q. 66, a. 2, ad. 3. Here Thomas is quoting a passage from Gratian's *Decretum*, which he attributes to Ambrose but is in fact from Basil the Great. In it, Basil condemns those who "charge more than the expenses warrant." The context of the articles on theft and robbery in the *Summa* concern vices opposed to commutative justice (*ST* II-II, q. 64, pr.)—that is, to the mutual dealings between people (*ST* II-II, q. 61, a. 1). In this article, Thomas, like Basil, regards buying cheap and selling dear to be a violation of it.

119. *ST* II-II, q. 66, aa. 3–4.

120. *ST* II-II, q. 66, a. 3, obj. 2.

121. *ST* II-II, q. 66, a. 3, ad. 2.

fuses entry to others, epitomizes the second.[122] Basil articulates the latter in the following passage from "I Will Tear Down My Barns," in which he addresses the rich fool and the covetous more generally:

> Who are the greedy? Those who are not satisfied with what suffices for their own needs. Who are the thieves? Those who take for themselves what rightfully belongs to everyone. And you, are you not greedy? Are you not a thief? The things you received in trust as a stewardship, have you not appropriated for yourself? Is not the person who strips another of clothing called a thief? And those who do not clothe the naked when they have the power to do so, should they not be called the same?[123]

The lines immediately following are those already cited about the bread held back being for the hungry, the clothes stored away for the naked, the unused shoes for the discalced, and so on. Clearly, the belief that creation is a common gift shapes Basil's articulation of a form of thievery that often escapes notice. Among other things, Basil is addressing the extent to which sin distorts human *possessio* as it is commonly practiced. Those who take in excess of what they need, who take in ways that refuse to hold open what they have to the needs of others, also engage in a kind of thievery.

Notice also how Basil closely associates covetousness (*pleonexia*) with thievery. This might seem a strange association, but it also reveals the influence of the theological grammar of creation as common gift. The object of Basil's critique is not just taking too much in the abstract but taking too much of what God has given for all—from what belongs to others in justice. Under the conditions of sin and violence, this means taking too much from what belongs to those who lack basic material support. In *On Naboth*, a treatise that itself draws heavily on Basil's homilies, Ambrose identifies the problem this way: "You [the rich fool, the covetous] keep for yourself what God wished to grow for the many through you."[124] Such

---

122. Such a view casts in a different light the issue of first acquisition in property law. See von Ketteler, "The Six Sermons," 16.

123. *ST* II-II, q. 66, a. 7, resp. I slightly alter the passage as it appears in Basil the Great, "I Will Tear Down My Barns," 7. The word Basil uses here to designate the thief are derivations of the Greek *apostereó*, which means to defraud or deprive.

124. Ambrose, *On Naboth* 7:37.

taking rejects the common life that it is property's purpose to enable and support.

Thomas approaches this matter from a different angle in discussing whether theft is legitimate in cases of necessity. Earlier we saw that, according to natural law, everything is common, and that Thomas regards particular property arrangements as a matter of convention, diverse attempts to facilitate common access to the earth. That these arrangements are what he calls "additions to the natural law" does not abrogate this overriding purpose, in relationship to which they must be evaluated and judged. Regarding the issue of whether theft is legitimate in cases of necessity, Thomas cites a variant of the axiom we have seen: "In the case of necessity everything is common" (*in necessitate sunt omnia communia*). This is the so-called law of necessity we discussed in chapter 1 in relation to landlessness and squatting, according to which those in need can take from what others have in excess of their needs.[125] In elaborating upon the implications of this law, Thomas argues that humans depend on the created order to meet their needs, a purpose that property arrangements exist to facilitate. But the claim of need is so paramount that it can even relativize these arrangements. It follows for Thomas that those who are in extreme need and who have no other recourse can justifiably take what they need from another's property, either openly or furtively.[126]

Thomas's position is not that *people can justifiably steal in cases of necessity* but rather that in taking what they need from another's property *they are neither thieves nor robbers*. The descriptions "thief" and "robber" are inaccurate because in such cases there is "strictly speaking no theft or robbery."[127] While those involved take what others possess, the goods actually belong to them; they take what "necessity has made common" (*necessitatem sibi factam commune*).[128] Taking facilitates their access to what they need when human laws, property regimes, or the mercy of par-

---

125. *ST* II-II, q. 66, a. 7. For medieval debates about the *ius necessitatis*, see Tierney, *Idea of Natural Rights*, 69–77; Virpi Mäkinen, "Rights and Duties in Late Scholastic Discussion on Extreme Necessity," in *Transformations in Medieval and Early-Modern Rights Discourse*, New Synthese Historical Library 56 (Dordrecht: Springer, 2006).

126. *ST* II-II, q. 66, q. 7.

127. *ST* II-II, q. 66, q. 7, resp.

128. *ST* II-II, q. 66, a. 7, s.c.

ticular property holders fail them. What Thomas is suggesting, in Marcus Lefébure's words, is that "a particular human system of distribution of [the world's goods] may be … resolved back into the primitive state of undifferentiated community in the case of blatant and extreme necessity."[129] Property arrangements are meant to mediate God's gift of creation to everyone. For this reason, those who take out of necessity are not thieves, even if they do so in violation of property law, because they are acting in accordance with a higher law, the law of necessity. What is more—and perhaps paradoxically to some—this violation even witnesses to God's overriding purpose for creation.

Thomas seems to envision such taking as a last resort, which should only occur in extreme cases. But if this is true, then the contexts of Catholic social teaching and Romero's El Salvador press important questions. What happens when the extreme cases are not occasional but commonplace—and the situation is deteriorating? When property arrangements structurally and institutionally prevent people from accessing what is theirs? When the advance of capitalism does away with property for the many? These and other questions raised by *Rerum Novarum* and its sources are taken up by the tradition of Catholic social teaching, and as we have already begun to see, by Romero himself. It is to a closer consideration of this tradition that we now turn.

BEYOND *RERUM NOVARUM*

Forty years after *Rerum Novarum*, Pope Pius XI writes in *Quadragesimo Anno* of a "doctrine on the social and economic question" he inherits from Leo. The reasons for returning to this doctrine now, Pius states, are numerous. Among other things, he wants to remember the encyclical's benefits; to defend it against doubts that have subsequently emerged about its teaching; to develop certain points at greater length; to clarify its critique of the "idols" of capitalism and socialism while pointing the way to "sound restoration"; and above all, to give thanks for it.[130] Pius not only *receives* this doctrine; the ongoing process of returning to this

---

129. *ST* II-II, q. 66, a. 7, note a.
130. Pius XI, *Quadragesimo Anno*, nos. 14–16.

doctrine by Pius and his successors also helps *constitute* it as a tradition that develops by way of clarification and application. We must therefore examine how the tradition of commentary on *Rerum Novarum* preserves and develops Leo's account of property and possession. Along the way, we will continue to see the governing influence of the theological grammar of creation as common gift upon social teaching as a whole.

When Pius XI in *Quadragesimo Anno* turns to *Rerum Novarum*'s treatment of property and possession, the first misreading he attempts to clarify relates to the accusation that, in their defense of the right of property, "the Supreme Pontiff [Leo], and the Church … had taken and were still taking the part of the rich against the non-owning workers," effectively endorsing "a pagan concept of ownership."[131] This is the view mentioned at the outset of this chapter, which depicts *Rerum Novarum* as the church's defense of itself, property, and the status quo against the threat of socialism.

One way social teaching develops is by way of clarification, which is exactly Pius's purpose in *Quadragesimo Anno* when he takes up the topic of property and possession. According to Pius, Leo neither denies nor questions "the twofold character of ownership (*duplicem dominii rationem*) called usually individual or social according as it regards either separate persons or the common good."[132] This is an alternative description of the distinction Leo draws from Thomas Aquinas between possession and use, which underlies his argument in *Rerum Novarum*.[133] What is especially crucial to see is that the twofold character of ownership is for Pius a distinction *within* ownership. In other words, the individual character (as ownership pertains to particular persons) and the social character (as it pertains to the common good) are not two separate characteristics or rights extrinsically related to one another. We can consider ownership either from the perspective of a person's support for herself and her de-

---

131. Pius XI, *Quadragesimo Anno*, nos. 44, 46.

132. Pius XI, *Quadragesimo Anno*, no. 45.

133. The distinction between possession and use is one Pius endorses. Pius associates possession with commutative justice, which entails respect for the "division of possessions," and he associates use with virtues like social justice (*Quadragesimo Anno*, nos. 57, 58, 71, 74, 88, 101, 110, 126). In this way, possession and use, he thinks, have distinct "boundaries" (no. 47).

pendents—a support that never disembeds them from membership in a community of common use—or from the perspective of God's overriding purpose for creation, which is to provide support for humankind as a whole.[134] These distinct vantages, however, are not mutually exclusive. God's gift of creation for common use and the duties associated with it always shape the individual character of ownership and how people use what they have.

The language Pius uses to integrate the twofold character of ownership should be familiar by now: in their possession and use of things, people must consider both their "own advantage" and the "common good."[135] They must do so because the goods they possess and use are not exclusively theirs but given to humankind in common. The common destination of these goods is prior to any appropriation of them by particular people, which should shape the character of the appropriation. True ownership therefore necessarily entails taking others into account, especially those who are deprived of what they need. Here Pius is simply assuming and clarifying Leo's view that ownership entails "inherent duties" because "the earth, even though apportioned among private owners, ceases not thereby to minister to the needs of all."[136]

That the twofold character is a distinction within ownership is important to stress given the tendency among interpreters to formulate it as a division, according to which the individual character of ownership is essentially private and subsequently limited and circumscribed by property's social character. From this perspective, the social character appears as if it is an extrinsic feature of ownership, exerting influence upon it from the outside. Among the problems with this picture is that it imagines the individual character of ownership in Blackstonian terms. Sole and despotic dominion remains the default position, even if it is combined with an ethical break—the general right of all people to the goods of the earth—to curb its excesses.

When commentators construe the twofold character in these terms,

---

134. Pius XI, *Quadragesimo Anno*, no. 45.
135. Pius XI, *Quadragesimo Anno*, no. 49.
136. Pius XI, *Quadragesimo Anno*, nos. 47, 56, quoting *Rerum Novarum*, no. 8.

a conundrum immediately arises regarding the proper relationship between the individual and social characters of ownership. Manfred Spieker articulates this conundrum when he asks how the natural right to private property relates to the universal destination of goods, to which he responds, "It is not easy to determine their proper relationship."[137] On this problematic construal, discrete rights—some individual and others social—seem to be in inherent tension with one another, such that compromises between them must be sought. Along these same lines, Albino Barrera writes that *Quadragesimo Anno* follows *Rerum Novarum*'s defense of the right to private property, "counterbalancing" it with the conviction that God gives the earth to meet the needs of all.[138] The word "counterbalance" mistakenly suggests separate weights, forces, or influences that offset, check, or balance each other. But what Leo writes about ownership does not need to be counterbalanced with the conviction that creation is a common gift because these are not separate principles to be offset, checked, or balanced. Leo's whole understanding of ownership rests upon the belief that creation is a common gift and that private property is the personal use of these gifts. Similarly, Pius XI emphasizes throughout *Quadragesimo Anno* that the personal and social characters are different facets of a unified understanding of ownership, which is why they cannot be pried apart in the ways capitalism and socialism attempt to do.[139]

Spieker and Barrera are representative of the way some scholars of Catholic social teaching still imagine property as essentially private, with the social character impinging upon property extrinsically. According to

137. Manfred Spieker, "The Universal Destination of Goods: The Ethics of Property in the Theory of a Christian Society," *Journal of Markets and Morality* 8, no. 2 (2005): 334.

138. Albino Barrera, *Modern Catholic Social Documents and Political Economy* (Washington, D.C: Georgetown University Press, 2001), 197.

139. In *Quadragesimo Anno*, Pius treats both liberalism and socialism as products of a modernism that separates the twofold character of ownership, with liberals emphasizing the individual and socialists the social. The former Pius calls "Manchesterian Liberals," who hold that the law of capital is to appropriate everything to itself and leave workers with only enough to sustain their ability to work—a way of thinking, Pius notes, that has in the modern world increasingly taken institutional form (no. 54). In contrast, socialists seek to remedy this state of affairs by flipping the liberal position on its head and claiming that all products and profits belong to workers (no. 55). According to Pius, the denial of property's social character results in "individualism," while the denial of property's personal character results in "collectivism" (no. 46).

this construal, the decisive debates revolve around whether there should be limitations upon private ownership and how to determine what they should be. What unites all sides is how they imagine limitations as an extrinsic feature of ownership, curbing it—or not—from the outside.[140] Consequently, they unwittingly assume the Blackstonian picture of ownership and fail to appreciate how, on social teaching's terms, what Blackstone is describing is thievery, not ownership. Expositing the tradition under consideration therefore requires considerable care, because the commonality in question inheres in what property is and shapes what possessing it entails at the most fundamental level. The failure to discern this commonality obscures the moral and theological landscape this approach to property opens to perception and the politics of common use it seeks to enact.

Beginning with Pius XI's *Quadragesimo Anno*, a tradition of commentary upon *Rerum Novarum* therefore begins to clarify and apply Leo's approach to property and possession—a process that contributes to the making of social teaching. In this way, the conviction that God gives the earth for common use becomes part of that teaching's very substance and structure. Reflecting back upon the development of social teaching, John Paul II refers to the common destination of created goods as "the first principle of the whole ethical and social order,"[141] "the characteristic principle of Christian social doctrine."[142] As we will see in chapter 3, the impact of this conviction about creation decisively shapes this tradition's treatment of work; justice in wages, partnership contracts and other efforts to facilitate co-ownership; workers' associations and organizations like unions; and even land reform. But for the moment, we must continue to attend to property and possession, briefly surveying how Leo's successors clarify the influence of the theological grammar of creation as common gift upon it.

---

140. Matthew Philipp Whelan, "Jesus Is the Jubilee: A Theological Reflection on the Pontifical Council for Justice and Peace's *Toward a Better Distribution of Land*," *Journal of Moral Theology* 6, no. 2 (2017): 218–19.

141. John Paul II, *Laborem Exercens*, no. 19.

142. John Paul II, Encyclical Letter *Sollicitudo Rei Socialis* (December 30, 1987), no. 42.

Pius XII, Pius XI's successor, articulates this theological grammar's implications for property and possession in new ways, which we see, for instance, in his call for land reform in order to favor ownership and to help as many as possible become owners—a call we will examine at greater length in chapter 3. During and after Pius XII's pontificate (1939–58), we encounter a new insistence in Catholic social teaching upon private property's derived status.[143] Earlier we saw Pius XI speak of the twofold character of ownership in order to clarify Leo's approach to property and possession, as well as to refute the accusation that Leo's understanding of ownership was pagan and amounted to a preferential option for the rich and the status quo. For his part, Pius XII joins in this effort, further clarifying Leo's distinctive approach.

Perhaps the most important formulation in this regard can be found in Pius XII's 1939 encyclical *Sertum Laetitiae*. In addressing the social question and the prevalence of class conflict, Pius follows his predecessors in highlighting the contributing role of the maldistribution of land and its fruits. In addressing the roots of the conflict, he states that "the fundamental point of the social question" is that "the goods created by God for all peoples should in the same way reach all, justice guiding and charity helping."[144] In this passage, which figures prominently in the text from *Gaudium et Spes* that we have already considered, Pius writes of God's purpose for creation in terms of the relationship between justice and charity. Pius also implies that this purpose has yet to be accomplished and that doing so requires creaturely involvement through the exercise of these virtues, which together enable creaturely *possessio* to image God's.

What does Pius mean by justice guiding? In the previous chapter, we examined how Romero's belief that creation is a common gift implies an account of justice according to which the material goods people need belong to them simply because they are members of the community of hu-

---

143. Though Pius XII issued no major social encyclical, he delivered many addresses to farmers and workers over the course of his pontificate. Detailed treatment of them can be found in Habiger, *Papal Teaching on Private Property*, 146–96; Rupert J. Ederer, *Pope Pius XII on the Economic Order* (Lanham, Md.: Scarecrow, 2011).

144. Pius XII, Encyclical Letter *Sertum Laetitiae* (November 1, 1939), no. 34.

mankind to which God gives the gift of the earth for common use. Therefore, such goods are due to those in need; when people give alms, they are returning what belongs to others; and finally, when people accumulate possessions in excess of their needs, they are practicing a kind of thievery. Pius means something similar when he refers to justice as offering a kind of guidance. Without these sorts of claims and the guidance they offer, people would stray from accomplishing God's purpose for creation. Discerning the grammar of creation would be difficult, and understanding God's work in creation and in salvation would be impoverished.

However, the need for justice's guidance is not the whole story. According to Pius, charity, especially as it bears fruit in mercy, is an additional gift from God that helps fulfill God's purpose for creation. God is charity, and in Christ's coming to the aid of those in need, we see its merciful face. Creaturely mercy is the love that follows the way of Christ, the sorrow that moves someone's heart to enter into and willingly bear the misery of others as if it were their own.[145] Like God's merciful work in Christ, creaturely mercy presupposes sin and its effects, including humankind's refusal to conform its *possessio* to God's. Mercy does not negate justice's guidance, but affirms and deepens it as it works to repair sin's damage and restore creation. Mercy's corporal works—feeding the hungry, slaking the thirsty, clothing the naked, welcoming the stranger, visiting the sick and imprisoned, and burying the dead—point toward this restoration as they also manifest it, which is why they are such a privileged site of encounter with Christ (Mt 25:40), the one who makes all things new (Rv 21:5).

The basic insight behind the pairing of justice and charity is that in a world in which the story of Naboth is ongoing, in which actions like those of the rich fool in the Lucan parable are considered to be prudent, justice offers important guidance in finding the right path forward. But in a world so damaged by sin, justice alone is insufficient to accomplish God's purpose for creation, and walking the path of justice requires additional help. What is required in the context of a creation groaning with

---

145. See Augustine, *The City of God against the Pagans*, IX.5, ed. R. W. Dyson (New York: Cambridge University Press, 1998). See also Aquinas, *ST* II-II, q. 30.

sin is above all the love that goes out toward the groaning, the formation of a people who have been liberated by God's merciful work in Christ to share their possessions and their lives with one another. In this way, the pairing of justice and mercy coheres with the axiom that grace does not destroy nature but presupposes and perfects it.[146] For in addition to preparing people to share more fully in God's common life in Christ, mercy also restores and transforms their natural capabilities, which have been wounded by sin—in this case, their ability to use what God gives in common in a way that acknowledges and preserves it as common.[147]

This formulation from *Sertum Laetitiae* about justice guiding and charity helping structures Pius XII's remarks on "the use of material goods" in his 1941 Pentecost message, which commemorates the fiftieth anniversary of *Rerum Novarum*.[148] Pius regards the encyclical's teaching on property and possession to be among its most important legacies. And the heart of that teaching, according to Pius, is that "the goods created by God for all peoples should in the same way reach all, justice guiding and charity helping."[149] Throughout the message, Pius retains *Rerum Novarum*'s emphasis upon people's access to and possession of productive property like land—"the holding in which the family lives, and from the products of which it draws all or part of its subsistence"—and the numerous benefits that follow from it.[150]

Tied to Pius's prioritization of the axiom that creation is common gift, there are other notable shifts in his language regarding the fundamental right to property. Like his predecessors, Pius speaks of the natural right to property and the individual character of that right,[151] but he prefers language like "the fundamental right to make use of the material goods of the

---

146. *ST* I, q. 1, a. 8, ad. 2; q. 2, a. 2, ad. 1.

147. *ST* I-II, q. 109, a. 7 ad 3.

148. *Discourse to Commemorate the 50th Anniversary of the Encyclical "Rerum Novarum" of Pope Leo XIII on the Social Question*, 221.

149. *Discourse to Commemorate the 50th Anniversary of the Encyclical "Rerum Novarum" of Pope Leo XIII on the Social Question*, 220–21.

150. *Discourse to Commemorate the 50th Anniversary of the Encyclical "Rerum Novarum" of Pope Leo XIII on the Social Question*, 224.

151. Pius XII, *Radiomessaggio di Sua Santità Pio XII nel V anniversario dall'inizio della guerra mondiale*, September 1, 1944, 20; Pius XII, *Radiomensaje del Santo Padre Pío XII a los trabajadores de España*, 2.

earth" and "the native right to the use of material goods."[152] As Calvez and Perrin persuasively argue, Pius is simply restating the position of his predecessors, but stressing the category of use rather than that of property or ownership.[153] At the same time, these discernable shifts in language are also an attempt to distinguish social teaching's understanding of property and possession from the Blackstonian one that undergirds capitalism. In his 1944 address, for instance, Pius calls capitalism's conception of property "totally false" (*tutto falso*) because it arrogates to itself an "unlimited right," refusing "any subordination to the common good."[154]

These various, novel formulations that Pius uses to convey the theological grammar of creation as common gift and its significance for property and possession exemplify one way Catholic social teaching develops: by clarification. In this case, what Pius is clarifying is how social teaching's account of property and possession derives from this theological grammar, as well as how ensuring the common use of creation is the fundamental imperative from which all other considerations regarding property and possession flow. According to Pius, the right of common use is prior to and more elemental than the institutions of private property, commercial exchange, and state regulation. All these institutions are "subordinate to the natural purpose of material goods" and should never "supersede" it. They exist to "serve" and "secure" common use and must always be evaluated in light of it.[155] Only by serving and securing common use, Pius contends, can there be "peace" where presently there is not.[156]

The subsequent tradition continues to clarify and emphasize how social teaching's understanding of property and possession derives from the theological grammar of creation as common gift and how that under-

---

152. *Discourse to Commemorate the 50th Anniversary of the Encyclical "Rerum Novarum" of Pope Leo XIII on the Social Question*, 221–22.

153. Calvez and Perrin, *The Church and Social Justice*, 194–200.

154. Pius XII, *Radiomessaggio di Sua Santità Pio XII nel V anniversario dall'inizio della guerra mondiale*, 22.

155. Pius XII, *Discourse to Commemorate the 50th Anniversary of the Encyclical "Rerum Novarum" of Pope Leo XIII on the Social Question*, 221–22. Barrera regards Pius XII's subordination of these institutions to common gift as a "step further" than his predecessors; Barrera, *Modern Catholic Social Documents and Political Economy*, 198.

156. Pius XII, *Discourse to Commemorate the 50th Anniversary of the Encyclical "Rerum Novarum" of Pope Leo XIII on the Social Question*, 221.

standing differs from Blackstone's sole and despotic dominion. In *Mater et Magistra* (1961), for instance, John XXIII writes that the right of private ownership "naturally entails a social obligation (*munus*)," which means "it is a right which must be exercised not only for one's own personal benefit but also for the benefit of others."[157] John is particularly concerned with the "social function inherent in the right of private ownership," and he repeatedly draws on the language of *munus*, which implies both rights and duties, to underscore it.[158] This is no abstract, free-floating entitlement to ownership, but a conception of ownership that is embedded in a larger vision of natural and supernatural sociality.[159] Citing both *Gaudium et Spes* and *Sertum Laetitiae* on the common destination of created goods, Pope Paul VI in *Populorum Progressio* (1967) similarly underscores how property and free trade are "subordinated to" and must "actively facilitate" common use. All people, he declares, must have the right to "glean" what they need from the earth, which is, after all, the "original purpose" (*primigenium finem*) of property and its associated institutions. As a consequence, redirecting these institutions back to their original purpose is "an important and urgent social duty."[160] Additionally, there are brief but fundamentally comparable discussions of property—particularly property in land—in the final documents of Medellín.[161]

Regarding Puebla, we have already seen how Pope John Paul II uses a striking phrase in his 1979 Puebla address to describe the derivative status of ownership: that all private property bears a "social mortgage"—a teaching he associates with Ambrose's *On Naboth* and Thomas Aquinas's *Summa Theologiae*, as well as with "the social encyclicals of the recent popes."[162] After Puebla, Romero adopts this phrase and repeatedly in-

157. John XXIII, *Mater et Magistra*, no. 19.

158. John XXIII, *Mater et Magistra*, nos. 119–20. For more on the language of *munus* and *munera*, see Russell Hittinger, "Social Roles and Ruling Virtues in Catholic Social Doctrine," *Annales Theologici* 16 (2002): 385–408.

159. Pius XII, *Discourse to Commemorate the 50th Anniversary of the Encyclical "Rerum Novarum" of Pope Leo XIII on the Social Question*, 221–22.

160. Paul VI, *Populorum Progressio*, no. 22.

161. *Medellín*, "Justicia," 1.3; 3.14.

162. John Paul II, *Address at the Opening of the Third General Conference of the Latin American Bishops*, Puebla, Mexico, January 28, 1979, 3.4. On John Paul's use of this phrase, see Edward J. O'Boyle, "Blessed John Paul II on Social Mortgage: Origins, Questions, and Norms," *Logos: A Journal of Catholic Thought and Culture* 17, no. 2 (2014): 118–35.

vokes it until his death.[163] The word "mortgage" is of French provenance and means "dead pledge" (*mort gaige*). It is established when a person (the mortgagor) borrows from another (the mortgagee) a specific sum and grants the mortgagee land in pledge. In the case of nonpayment, the land is "dead" to the mortgagor, while in the case of payment, it is "dead" to the mortgagee. What is interesting about John Paul's use of this phrase is the suggestion that the social mortgage on property—the pledge to fulfill the debt owed to others—never dies in the ordinary sense. The pledge on property endures even after all debts upon it are paid or foreclosed upon because the pledge inheres in property *in se*—in what it means for property to be property. It is a pledge that binds property and its use to others' flourishing. As Romero explains, "Everything we have is not for ourselves alone. What we have is a gift God has given us to manage in service to the common good."[164] "The common good is *la pauta* (the standard, pattern, guideline, rule) for the use of private property."[165]

This same understanding of property figures prominently in Puebla's final documents, which discuss the social mortgage on property in relation to how "the goods and the wealth of the world" are given by God for the "use and the advantage of all."[166] Such use and advantage are the most "fundamental" claim creatures have on created goods—a claim that is "absolutely inviolable," the "first purpose" of property. Consequently, Puebla characterizes the pervasive and growing tendency in Latin America to construe property in "absolute or unlimited"[167] terms as nothing but an "idol."[168] After Puebla, Romero similarly adopts this language as well. Until his death, he continues to speak of the idolatry of property—or what he also calls the "abuse," "aberration," or "absolutizing" of property—which he associates with the idea that possessions belong exclusively to their owners, for owners to use in any way they determine.[169]

---

163. Romero, *Homilías*, 4:216; 5:166–67, 178, 192, 209, 260, 381–382; 6:73, 213; Romero, "Misión de la Iglesia en medio de la crisis del país," 44.

164. Romero, *Homilías*, 5:209.

165. Romero, *Homilías*, 5:303.

166. *Puebla*, 4.4.492; see also 3.4.1224, 3.4.1271, 3.4.1281.

167. *Puebla*, 4.4.492.

168. *Puebla*, 4.4.494–97, 5.5.542–57.

169. Romero, *Homilías*, 1:38, 98–99, 141, 164, 430, 434; 2:239, 255, 449, 508–9; 3:44–45, 77, 87, 130–33, 336; 4:48–49, 149, 207, 230–33, 293–94, 463–64; 5:91, 107, 191–92, 246, 254–56, 418,

We have been assessing how Catholic social teaching assumes, clarifies, and underscores *Rerum Novarum*'s distinctive approach to property and possession, and how the theological grammar of creation as a common gift consistently influences the whole process. As social teaching develops over the twentieth century, we encounter an increasingly explicit critique of capitalism and how its Blackstonian conception of property obstructs the common destination of created goods. The basis of this critique is, as Calvez and Perrin put it, that if "the institution [of property] does not allow of the exercise of this right [to property] by *all*, it is in some disorder. There would then be an obligation to reform social life."[170]

The imperative for social renewal is clearly present in *Rerum Novarum*, which is what leads Leo to decry the violence of capitalism and argue for the proliferation of property in contrast to socialism's call for its abolition. But what subsequent commentators make even clearer than Leo did is how deeply established the disorder is. As we will see in the following chapter, this is the essential context for understanding land reform's emergence in social teaching as one way law and policy can favor ownership so as to enable as many people as possible to become owners.

The theological grammar of creation as common gift as we have been examining it in these pages implies a vision of the common good, which is important to specify. Of course, in one sense, the common good of all creation is simply God, the one in whom all created things live, move, and have their being (Acts 17:28). We have already encountered the language of creation's common destiny in God at various points—for instance, in Leo's hope that the church itself offers the solution to the social question. But we have also encountered the language of the common good employed in a much more mundane sense—for instance, in Thomas's discussion of Basil's theater image. In contrast to those who seize seats and block others from entry, Thomas and Basil counsel taking a seat and allowing others to do the same, enabling appreciation of the performance

---

494–99, 509–11; 6:156, 176, 254, 281, 309, 398; Romero, *Misión de la Iglesia en medio de la crisis del país*, 43–45.

170. Calvez and Perrin, *Church and Social Justice*, 200. On this point, see John XXIII, *Mater et Magistra*, no. 113.

as a good that is best enjoyed in common. Additionally, in explaining John Paul II's phrase "social mortgage," we saw Romero say that the common good is the guide for the use of property. In the case of the theatre and the social mortgage on property, the common good implicates ordinary social existence. Therefore, by way of conclusion to this chapter—and with an eye toward what is to come—it is necessary to say more about the common good implied by the theological grammar of creation as common gift and its vision of sociality.

To this end, it is helpful to return to Pius XI's *Quadragesimo Anno* and the reasons he gives for why "not every distribution ... of property and wealth is of a character to attain either completely or to a satisfactory degree of perfection the end which God intends."[171] Because creation is a common gift, which implies a community that shares in it, Pius argues that "the riches that economic-social developments constantly increase ought to be so distributed among individual persons and classes that the common advantage of all ... will be safeguarded." Such distributions, which enable all those to whom the gift is given to share in it, is the basis—the minimum requirement—for the care of what he calls the "common good" (*bonum commune*).[172]

What Pius means by this phrase is an indivisible and undistributable good that can be held only in common with others. This means it is a good that cannot be held exclusively; to try to possess for oneself alone is to fail to possess it at all. As William J. Ferree explains, "It is something which each of us possesses in its entirety, like light, or life itself."[173] People can only participate in it by engaging with others in a common activity for a common purpose. Consequently, the common good is neither a good that comes after some other purpose is achieved nor the sum total of the particular goods of each person gathered together with others. Rather, it is the good that is being aimed at and sought by their gathering together. On this basis, the common good (*bonum commune*) can be distinguished from common goods (*bona communia*). The lands and harvests

---

171. Pius XI, *Quadragesimo Anno*, no. 57.

172. Pius XI, *Quadragesimo Anno*, no. 57.

173. William J. Ferree, *Introduction to Social Justice* (Arlington, Va.: Center for Economic and Social Justice, 1997), 30.

of El Salvador are instances of the latter. They are common goods, given by God for the benefit of the Salvadoran people, and they are capable of being divided and distributed, unlike the common good, which is not. But how these lands and harvests are divided and distributed, and whether it promotes a good that the people of El Salvador can possess only together, implicates the common good in Pius's sense.

According to Pius, the virtue that cares for the common good is social justice. "By this law of social justice," Pius writes in *Quadragesimo Anno*, "one class is forbidden to exclude the other from sharing in the benefits [of the circulation of property and wealth]."[174] The problem Pius is identifying is quite specific and very easily missed. It certainly relates to the widespread and systematic deprivation of basic material support, as we saw with the production of landlessness in the previous chapter. However, such deprivation, as we also saw there, is often symptomatic of a more fundamental problem, which is the attack upon societies as shared social memberships and upon the goods that can only be sought and enjoyed together by them. This is the basis of Leo's plea in *Rerum Novarum* that "it cannot but be good for the commonwealth to shield from misery those on whom it so largely depends for the things that it needs."[175] Along these same lines, Pius and Catholic social teaching more generally devote particular attention to the exclusions affecting rural areas throughout the world, frequently singling out those Pius in *Quadragesimo Anno* calls "the huge army of rural wage workers, pushed to the lowest level of existence and deprived of all hope of ever acquiring 'a share in the land.'"[176] Social teaching reads this exclusion from land as emblematic of other forms of social exclusion.[177]

Formulated negatively, the virtue of social justice therefore entails resisting the exclusion of those like the landless from what must be enjoyed in common or not at all. For the production of landlessness not only deprives people of the land that belongs to them and exacerbates the distance between the many with nothing and the few with everything, but

---

174. Pius XI, *Quadragesimo Anno*, no. 57.
175. Leo XIII, *Rerum Novarum*, no. 34.
176. Pius XI, *Quadragesimo Anno*, 59, quoting *Rerum Novarum*, no. 47.
177. A similar analysis can be found in Romero, *Homilías*, 1:217.

it also excludes the many from social life in the process. It imperils the possibility that people can share a common good at all. This is precisely Romero's point in a 1962 article entitled, "Which Homeland?," in which he decries the "brutal social inequality" that makes the wealthy and powerful "strangers to the immense majority of those born in their own soil."[178] Like Pius, Romero thinks that the failure of societies to share the benefits of common goods like land and wealth, which are divisible and distributable, intimately relates to the failure to share a higher, common good, which is not. The underlying assumption is that the greater the distance between people—a distance epitomized by disparities in the distribution of created goods like land—the more difficult it will be to share the highest goods of all with one another.

Formulated positively, the "very essence" of social justice, Pius XI writes in *Divini Redemptoris*, is therefore "to demand for each individual all that is necessary for the common good"—to demand what is necessary for full participation in social life. Although closely related to distributive justice, social justice most fundamentally concerns not the distribution of goods but rather the end sought by the distribution: the pursuit and love of a good that can only be held in common with others.[179] It is for this reason, Romero says, the church in El Salvador works with the landless and land-poor, even if it is seen as subversive. "All people have received from God a capacity to contribute to the common good," and preventing anyone from realizing this capacity and so contributing is "an abuse of power," a "hoarding of goods that God has given for all." Each Salvadoran must therefore learn to say, "I too am a child of God, … I too have to be a participant in the politics of the common good of my country (*la política del bien común de mi patria*), and I too have a right to the goods God has created for all." According to Romero, "This is a matter of life or death for the kingdom of God on this earth."[180] It strikes at the heart of the question with which Gutiérrez says liberation theology

178. Romero, "¿Cuál patria?," *El Chaparrastique*, September 8, 1962.
179. Pius XI, *Divini Redemptoris*, no. 51. See also Hittinger, "The Coherence of the Four Basic Principles of Catholic Social Doctrine: An Interpretation," in *Pursuing the Common Good: How Solidarity and Subsidiarity Can Work Together* (Vatican City: Pontifical Academy of Social Sciences, 2008), 14:112.
180. Romero, *Homilías*, 1:216–18. Ferree comments that one of the "great laws" of social

begins: "How to say to the poor, the oppressed, the insignificant person, 'God loves you'?"[181]

A vision of sociality centered upon the pursuit and love of the common good helps clarify Romero's concern about the distances between people in El Salvador; or Leo's in *Rerum Novarum* about the "immense chasm," "the gulf between vast wealth and sheer poverty"; or Pius XI's in *Quadragesimo Anno* about "the huge disparity between the few exceedingly rich and the unnumbered propertyless."[182] Over the course of the twentieth century, voices from this tradition repeatedly inveigh against mounting inequalities in the distribution of land and wealth, along with the exclusion of so many from sharing in their benefits. While such dichotomous language clearly fails as a detailed sociological investigation of class, it does offer, as Calvez and Perrin observe, "an outline of a pathology."[183] The pathology is that the growing inequalities and exclusions threaten not only the common destination of created goods, but also forms of life that share goods in common, as well as the justice and charity that enable and constitute those forms of life. Expanding distances, widening chasms, and deepening gulfs make it increasingly unlikely for people to have anything in common at all as their lives and concerns drift apart. This is why the failure of a society to distribute goods like land among its members and to shield its most vulnerable from misery is symptomatic of its failure to be a society at all, to share life together in any meaningful sense, to establish spaces for nearness and intimacy.

In *Populorum Progressio*, Paul VI helps concretize what is at stake in this account of social justice and the common life it is property's purpose to foster. The aim of social justice, he writes, is the establishment of forms of life "where the needy Lazarus can sit down with the rich man at the same banquet table."[184] The reference is to the parable in Luke's Gospel, in which Lazarus the beggar lies at the gate of a rich man—tradi-

---

justice is that "every individual, regardless of his age or occupation or state in life, is directly responsible for the Common Good"; Ferree, *Introduction to Social Justice*, 38.

181. Mev Puleo, "An Interview with Gustavo Gutiérrez," *St. Anthony Messenger*, February 1989, 10.

182. Leo XIII, *Rerum Novarum*, no. 47; Pius XI, *Quadragesimo Anno*, no. 58.

183. Calvez and Perrin, *The Church and Social Justice*, 345.

184. Paul VI, *Populorum Progressio*, no. 47.

tionally known as Dives (Latin for "rich man")—who fails to offer Lazarus even the scraps from his luxurious banquet table (Lk 16:19–31). When both Lazarus and Dives die, the great though bridgeable distance between them in life becomes unbridgeable in death, with Lazarus at Abraham's side and Dives separated from them in agony. In drawing upon Luke's parable in this way, Paul suggests that the pursuit of social justice is inseparable from Lazarus's need for basic material support, as well as from the indifference of Dives and the wider society. But more fundamentally still, social justice ultimately concerns what the distribution of wealth and property aims at, which in this case is for Lazarus to be able to contribute to the common good, for Lazarus and Dives to overcome the distances that divide them, and for both to share a form of life in which they can hold goods beyond simply food and drink in common.[185]

On the terms of this tradition, the cultivation of such forms of life is made possible by the discovery of the highest good of all: what Augustine refers to as the "really great and profitable common estate," which is God.[186] As Pius XII puts it in a speech commemorating the sixtieth anniversary of *Rerum Novarum*, Leo teaches that the church wants justice. But even more, the church wants what exceeds justice and what must be built upon it: a "bringing together" (*ravvicinare*) in charity that "derives entirely" (*deriva interamente*) from a destiny that is "common to all" (*a tutti comune*). The crucial imperative is for people to discover that they are fellow pilgrims journeying toward a "common homeland" (*comune patria*), which can only be shared.[187] This common heavenly homeland transcends and relativizes the claims of the lands where people presently live. But it can be entered into wherever the gospel is proclaimed and baptism begins to break down the barriers between people, whether those barriers are between Jew and Greek, slave and free, male and female (Gal 3:28)—or between poor and rich, worker and owner, landless and landed.

As we have seen in this chapter, Leo argues in *Rerum Novarum* that

185. See John Paul II's treatment of this parable in Encyclical Letter *Redemptor Hominis* (March 4, 1979), nos. 51–52, as well as Benedict XVI's in *Caritas in Veritate*, no. 31.

186. Augustine, *Sermons 341–400 on Various Themes* vol. III, part 10, in *The Works of Saint Augustine* (New York: New City Press: 1995), 355.2

187. Pius XII, *Adscriptis Sodalitati Catholicae Ex Operariis Italicis: Ob Commendationem Litterarum Encyclicarum "Rerum Novarum" Coadunatis*, 405.

the diffusion of property contributes to the cessation of social conflict, which he bases on the belief that God gives the blessings of nature to humankind in common. But more than simply the cessation of conflict, the church aims at establishing friendship among people, which Leo bases upon the belief that the gifts of God's graceful work in Christ are likewise common. God's mercy in Christ not only gathers the church as a body, but it is also the very communion of love that creates and sustains heaven and earth, along with all things visible and invisible. While sharing in this common good begins on earth, taking imperfect shape in the lands through which people pilgrim, it will be perfected in the heavenly land received in Christ. According to social teaching, the church's mission in the world is to announce this land and to prepare people for sharing in it. Property's most fundamental purpose is to build up bodies that bear witness to it.

Part 2

WORK OF HUMAN HANDS

–3–

LAND REFORM AND THE POLITICS OF COMMON USE

Without taking into account what work is . . . it is impossible to approach adequately the problem of land reform.

—Ignacio Ellacuría, *Veinte años de historia en El Salvador*

The present chapter continues our examination of the call for land reform in Catholic social teaching as part of a more comprehensive politics
of common use. Chapter 2 argued that the theological grammar of creation as common gift informs Leo and his successors' approach to property and possession. In *Rerum Novarum*, Leo contends that all property
derives from this gift and is internally ordered to God's giving of it to
meet the needs of all. This leads him to formulate a distinctive response
to the dispossession associated with capitalism's spread and to the new
forms of exploitation associated with these developments: to call for a
just distribution of property, especially land. The tradition of commentary upon *Rerum Novarum*, like Catholic social teaching more generally,
follows Leo on these points.

Chapter 2 therefore also began to display the governing influence of
this theological grammar of creation upon the very shape of social teach-

143

ing. The purpose of this chapter is to trace how the governing influence of this grammar extends even further, ordering social teaching's account of a host of related matters, such as work as a path to ownership of property, justice in wages, partnership contracts and other efforts to facilitate co-administration and co-ownership of businesses, workers' associations, organizations like unions, and finally, even land reform—always with an eye to their pertinence for Romero and El Salvador. What follows is by no means an exhaustive treatment of these matters but an attempt to display the influence of theological grammar of creation as common gift upon social teaching as a whole.

Along the way, we will see that we have not left the concerns of chapter 2 but find ourselves within the same moral and theological landscape. We will continue to see how God makes provision for the material support of all people, both through the gifts of the earth and the work of human hands. Indeed, not only does human action presuppose and make use of God's gifts, but human creatures are themselves gifts, whose lives and work are called to play a role in how God gives the gift of creation in common. In this way, God's graceful work in Christ and in the Spirit incorporates people into God's life, preparing them to share in it more fully by collaborating in God's work of making provision for all.

One reason we are continuing to familiarize ourselves with the landscape within which land reform emerges, then, is to continue to display how this theological grammar of creation shapes Catholic social teaching in its deepest pattern. Another is that doing so clarifies how the call for land reform is no isolated topic but participates in a more expansive politics of common use. While in chapter 2 we saw how social teaching proceeds by clarification, in this chapter we see how it also precedes by application. During the pontificate of Pius XII in the mid-twentieth century, land reform emerges as a new expression of the politics of common use in light of the increasing concentration of land throughout the world and the resulting widespread and chronic problems for many who lack access to land. In this context, social teaching considers land reform a tool for law and policy to facilitate ownership—but by no means the only tool.

Finally, continued familiarization with this landscape helps us appreciate why land and work were so central to Romero's ministry as arch-bishop, as well as the nature of the conflicts that occasioned his martyr-dom. For Romero insists that the church teaches that *campesinos* should have access to land and workers should be able to organize and receive sufficient remuneration for their labor. But this very same teaching became a source of acute conflict and division within the church, with Romero's detractors characterizing it as evidence of a communist infil-tration. That social teaching's message about land and work became the locus of such controversy is yet another reason to provide an account of it here. Once again, while my ultimate interest in these pages is to show how the politics of common use and Romero's witness mutually illumi-nate one another, doing so necessitates that we continue to attend to the emergence of the call for land reform in social teaching and the politics in which it participates.

WORK AND THE POLITICS OF COMMON USE

One of the central contentions of chapter 2 is that Catholic social teach-ing's response to the forces of dispossession and dislocation—which have disrupted social bonds, dispersed people, and generated conditions in which the propertyless work for wages—is to advocate for the diffusion of property. Leo and his successors want the dispossessed to be repos-sessed through laws and policies that expand access to land and other forms of productive property. They do not see propertylessness as a static social condition to which an entire class of people is permanently rele-gated. Rather, they share a vision of restoration in which societies facil-itate ownership, helping as many as possible become owners, especially the landless.

The notion of restoration implies the repair of something damaged or disordered by way of return to a prior or original condition. What is prior or original in this case is God's purpose for the created order and a use of created goods that conforms to this purpose. Restoration therefore presumes an understanding of property and possession that derives from the theological grammar of creation as common gift, in which property's hallmark is the inclusion and gathering of others in its very use, because property is meant to facilitate creaturely participation in and mediation of God's giving of the gift in common. As Barrera eloquently puts the point, "God not only supplies our needs but also uses our mutual responsibility for each other as a channel for bestowing such provisions upon us.... God provides for us through each other; God elicits human participation in effecting divine providence."[1] This entails that those who already have a share in land must work to enable others to obtain one as well—a logic exemplified by the Movimento dos Trabalhadores Rurais Sem Terra (Landless Worker's Movement, or MST), in which those who have gained access to land work to extend that access to others.[2] The important point is that the vocation of all people is to participate in the politics of common use, which begins with their management of what they possess not merely for themselves, but for the common benefit of all, especially those who lack what they need.

Articulated in these terms, we see how this theological grammar governs not just social teaching's account of property and possession but of human work as well. The management of material things as common is an important instance of how all work is meant to pursue and love the common good. For work is not simply for the exclusive benefit of the worker's household but for others as well, classically articulated in Paul's exhortation in Ephesians that the reformed thief no longer steal but perform "honest work with his hands, so that he may be able to give to those in need" (Eph 4:28). Similarly, in words attributed to him in Acts, Paul says that in working with his hands to minister to his and others' needs, he shows how "one must help the weak, remembering the words of the Lord Jesus, how he said, 'It is more blessed to give than to receive'" (Acts 20:34–35).

The resonance between these Pauline passages and Leo/Thomas's treatment of proper use is apparent. Social teaching follows Paul and Leo/Thomas in understanding work as an extension and elaboration of such management of what is common. Calvez and Perrin's observation

---

1. Barrera, *Economic Compulsion and Christian Ethics* (New York: Cambridge University Press, 2007), 77.

2. Peter Rosset, Raj Patel, and Michael Courville, eds., *Promised Land: Competing Visions of Agrarian Reform* (Oakland, Calif.: Food First, 2006), 271.

that "the work relationship is … internal to the property relationship" highlights how the relationship to the material world that this tradition calls "work" presupposes and builds upon the relationship that it calls "property."[3] Therefore, as Paul suggests, having something to give others is not simply the product of work or something to think about after work is over but is work's source and wellspring, ordering it from the inside. Work is how people provide for themselves and for others—a conception of work patterned upon the inclusion of others in its provisioning.[4] The work of human hands participates in the politics of common use.

This section examines how the vision of restoration that Leo and his successors share hinges upon a renewed understanding of work and its role in the politics of common use. Indeed, in order to understand the emergence of the call for land reform in social teaching, we must attend to the intimate and complex relationship between property and work, along with the way work should promote the diffusion of property. Ellacuría means something similar in the epigraph beginning this chapter when he states that without accounting for work and what it represents in human life, we cannot understand how the church's call for land reform is meant to facilitate work. Once again, *Rerum Novarum* sets the terms for subsequent social teaching, so we must begin with it, focusing upon how and why Leo thinks that people should be able to acquire productive property like land through work and that property's purpose is to serve work.[5]

Leo's treatment of the relationship between property and work in *Rerum Novarum* begins with a careful, almost phenomenological examination of work itself. Why do the dispossessed who are streaming into the cit-

3. Calvez and Perrin, *Church and Social Justice*, 193.

4. For additional examples, see Athanasius, *The Life of Antony*, trans. Robert C. Gregg, Classics of Western Spirituality (Mahwah, N.J.: Paulist Press, 1980), 3; Basil the Great, *The Rule of St. Basil* (Collegeville, Minn.: Liturgical Press, 2013), 243–44, 253–54, 386–87, 410, 422–23. For more on Basil's understanding of work as a source for social teaching, see Andrew Dinan, "Manual Labor in the Life and Thought of St. Basil the Great," *Logos: A Journal of Catholic Thought and Culture* 12, no. 4 (2009): 133–57.

5. On work as a route to property, see Calvez and Perrin, *Church and Social Justice*, 242; Michael Naughton, *The Good Stewards: Practical Applications of the Papal Social Vision of Work* (Lanham, Md.: University Press of America, 1992), 12.

ies want to work in the first place? What does a close consideration of their work reveal? They work for wages, Leo observes, in order to receive what is necessary for their basic material support, "for the purpose of receiving in return what is necessary for the satisfaction of [their] needs."[6] Since these workers do not own productive property, wages become essential, because the only way for them to satisfy the needs of themselves and their dependents is through wages paid for work done.

Leo examines the intentionality implicit in these ordinary exchanges of work for wages. In return for work, people receive remuneration, which they use to satisfy their needs. But even more fundamentally, this process presupposes people's ability to use the remuneration received in determining how their needs are to be best met—what Leo calls the power "over the disposal of such remuneration."[7] Implicit in the very institution of wage work is the stable and secure hold upon wages, as well as the ability to manage them, which is synonymous with the wages belonging to *this worker* rather than *that one.* Of course, Leo does not endorse the typical wage contracts of his day, which he regards as criminal. But Leo begins with these ordinary exchanges in order to suggest that wages earned are the property of the worker and that workers therefore possess (along with their wages) the power to manage them and so participate in the process of making provision for themselves and others. This power to manage is the essential precondition for using wages—or anything at all—not just for individual benefit but also for the common good.

This analysis serves as an argument for personal property, which Leo compares to the power to manage that is implied in wage contracts. Leo posits a scenario in which workers, both through their wage work and the virtue of temperance, save and invest in a small landholding—a "little estate"—for the purpose of achieving "greater security" than could be achieved through reliance upon wages alone.[8] Leo argues that just as the power to manage applies to wages, so too should it apply to land. In this scenario, Leo is not eliding the significant differences between wages and

---

6. Leo XIII, *Rerum Novarum*, nos. 5, 12–13.
7. Leo XIII, *Rerum Novarum*, no. 5.
8. Leo XIII, *Rerum Novarum*, no. 5.

land but drawing an analogy regarding a person's relationship to them. At issue is the relationship people have to the goods upon which they depend and whether their possession of such goods is stable and secure enough to be able to rely upon them in the process of making provision. Leo thinks that people should be able to have stable and secure power to manage land just as they have in managing their wages. However, this management is not Blackstone's sole and despotic dominion but something much more modest and centered upon sustenance. If people cultivate land, they should be able to enjoy its harvests, and if they build houses, they should be able to inhabit them. As Leo sees it, ideally, such stability and security in cultivating and inhabiting should unfold across generations, passing down to others as an inheritance.[9]

There are several important features of this scenario that underlie the discussion of work in *Rerum Novarum* and beyond. First, the scenario suggests that, when rightly ordered, wage work can and should lead to possession of land. The workers in question are paid a wage sufficient to live well and eventually to afford land themselves. In other words, Leo assumes there should be a path from wage work to possession of land. Second, the scenario suggests that reliance upon land offers workers more stability and security in meeting needs than does reliance upon wages alone. The heart of the matter is the satisfaction of needs, the sources that best facilitate it, and enabling stable and secure access to these sources—in this case, land. Last, the scenario suggests that the work of agriculture presupposes property in the sense described previously of a stable and secure hold upon the land being worked. People who work land and dwell upon it should not live in fear of dispossession. All the features just noted exhibit the influence of the theological grammar of creation as common gift.

Let us look more closely at the first—the path from wage work to possession of land—because it is crucial to see how Leo and his successors encourage both broadening that path and clearing any obstacles that block movement along it. In the initial sections of *Rerum Novarum*, Leo argues for personal property through an analysis of human work, sug-

---

9. Leo XIII, *Rerum Novarum*, no. 13.

gesting that property and work are closely related to one another and characterize human forms of life. Humans use created goods, he writes, "not merely for temporary and momentary use, as other living things do, but to have and to hold them in stable and permanent possession; … not only things that perish in the use, but those also which, though they have been reduced into use, continue for further use."[10] In this passage, Leo is working with two sets of distinctions. The first concerns the kinds of relationships creatures have with the created order that sustain them. One relationship is temporary and momentary, in which goods are consumed in the act of use. Leo contrasts this consumption relationship with a more stable and permanent one, in which goods are had, held, or possessed across time. He calls this property. While the distinction between consumption and property concerns the relationships people have to the world that sustains them, the second set of distinctions concerns the kinds of goods upon which they depend for sustenance. Regarding the latter, some goods are consumed in the act of using them, such as food when it is eaten or water when it is drunk. However, other goods bear repeated use, such as land that is cultivated with care, aquifers that are not over-drafted, or fisheries that are not depleted of their stocks. Leo takes it as axiomatic that both kinds of relationships—consumption and property—and dependence upon both kinds of goods—those consumed in the act of use and those that are not—characterize human forms of life.

All this becomes clearer, Leo thinks, when we consider how human beings make provision, understood in the sense of providing before-hand, arranging in advance. Human life, he observes, depends upon de-cision-making not only regarding present needs but anticipated future needs. Such decision-making is imperative given the constitutive need-iness of human creatures and their bodily dependence upon the wider world. Bodily needs "do not die out, but forever recur; although satisfied today, they demand fresh supplies for tomorrow." Because of the tem-poral unfolding of these needs, humans must rely upon "a source that is stable and remaining" and that can provide "continual supplies" to meet them, which is found "solely in the earth and its fruits." This line of

10. Leo XIII, *Rerum Novarum*, no. 6.

thought becomes yet another argument for personal property, showing why it is fitting for people to possess not just "the fruits of the earth," but also "the very soil" upon which they rely to meet their needs—once again, possession not in the sense of sole and despotic dominion but stable and secure hold over land in order to manage it for present and future sustenance.[11] We also continue to see how land uniquely contributes to the bodily support of human life, serving as a trope for the wider created order within which all human life is embedded and upon which it depends. Human creatures both depend upon land and are also bodily constituted by it, living from land as they live in flesh.

Attending to the constitutive neediness of human life, along with the importance of stability and security in the possession of land, leads Leo from the topic of property to the topic of work, the analysis of which provides additional justification for possession of land. In articulating what work has to do with possession, Leo reiterates land's vital role in the material support of human life before further specifying the material conditions necessary for land to fulfill this role. One of these conditions is that people must engage in an even more complex relationship with the created order than either consumption or property: work. In Leo's words, they must bring land into "cultivation" through "solicitude and skill."[12] For the material support of human life, people must have a stable and secure hold over the land upon which they depend, and they must also work it, modifying and adapting land in order to supply their needs. Moreover, human work must also always defer to the land's own "work"—the way "the earth produces of itself, first the blade, then the ear, then the full grain in the ear" (Mk 4:28). Nevertheless, the work of human hands is necessary in order for land to produce. People must prepare it for cultivation, plant seed, and perform the innumerable other necessary tasks to encourage and collaborate with the land's own work.

According to Leo, it is therefore not just *land* but *agriculture* that sustains human life by supplying the bodily needs of humankind, which is why he argues that "all human subsistence is derived either from labor

11. Leo XIII, *Rerum Novarum*, no. 7.
12. Leo XIII, *Rerum Novarum*, no. 9.

on one's own land, or from some toil, some calling, which is paid for either in the produce of the land itself, or in that which is exchanged for what the land brings forth."[13] Throughout these initial sections of the encyclical, which attend with such care to human dependence upon and bodily embeddedness within the creation, most of Leo's examples are agricultural. His analysis points to how all human life and work trace their debt to agriculture and how it uniquely conjoins the work of land and human hands, epitomizing God's provision for humankind by means of this twofold work.

Because of the intimacy and complexity of agricultural work, Leo proceeds to argue that it is a matter of justice for the possession of land to follow directly from work upon it, and he opposes those who contend that "it is unjust for anyone to possess outright either the land on which he has built or the estate which he has brought under cultivation." Those who deny this are "defrauding" workers of what their own "labor has produced," because it is unjust whenever others permanently possess the fruit of a person's "own sweat and labor." "As effects follow their cause," Leo concludes, "so it is just and right that the results of labor should belong to those who have bestowed their labor."[14]

Though he offers little detail, Leo's position is that houses should belong to those who build them and fields to those who cultivate them. We have seen that his understanding of work presupposes the use of created goods as common gifts and that he envisions work as participating in the diffusion of property. But here we also see how Leo crucially assumes there should be some kind of path from wage work to the possession of land. In other words, a distributive concern, which is informed by the theological grammar of creation as common gift, underlies both his articulation of the right to property and how work should lead to property. At least on the surface, there are suggestive affinities between Leo's position and Ellacuría's description of a Salvadoran land reform proposal in the mid-1970s: "The aim is that those who work the land become owners and active agents in the agrarian transformation. It is only a step from this to

13. Leo XIII, *Rerum Novarum*, no. 8.
14. Leo XIII, *Rerum Novarum*, nos. 9–11.

the adage, 'the land belongs to those who work it.'"[15] An additional implication of Leo's view would seem to be that if the institution of wage work systematically obstructs access to property, it is in need of fundamental reform.

JUSTICE IN WAGES

If one of the assumptions undergirding Leo's discussion of property and work in *Rerum Novarum* is that work should lead to the possession of property, then this vision of restoration depends in large measure upon a renewed understanding of work and its contribution to the politics of common use, specifically in relation to work's facilitation of ownership for as many people as possible. This becomes especially evident in the topic of justice in wages.

Leo thinks the remuneration of workers as it exists in his time suffers from a profoundly malformed conception of justice. As Leo characterizes this position, the parties arrive at a wage contract, and the demands of justice are met by mere consent to the contract. Injustice occurs when the employer holds the agreed-upon wages back or when the agreed-upon work is left incomplete or performed inadequately. Only in such circumstances should public authority intervene to ensure compliance with justice.[16] Michael Naughton observes that this understanding "presupposes the infallibility of the market, that is, whatever the labor market determines as the wage is the just wage."[17] In contrast to this problematic view of justice, Leo argues that the consent of the parties involved, while necessary, is ultimately insufficient for the wage to be just. In other words, the problem for Leo is with the reduction of justice to consent alone, which neglects crucial considerations such as the dignity of workers and what they need for material support. For wages are not simply payment

---

15. Quoted in John J. Hassett and Hugh Lacey, *Towards a Society that Serves Its People: The Intellectual Contribution of El Salvador's Murdered Jesuits* (Washington, D.C.: Georgetown University Press, 1991), 122. The phrase "land belongs to those who work it" is often associated with the Mexican revolutionary leader Emiliano Zapata, but its provenance is likely much older; see Samuel Brunk, *The Posthumous Career of Emiliano Zapata: Myth, Memory, and Mexico's Twentieth Century* (Austin: University of Texas Press, 2008), 71, 76, 122, 164, 167, 183.

16. Leo XIII, *Rerum Novarum*, no. 43.

17. Naughton, *Good Stewards*, 19.

for work but the income workers require for satisfying the needs of their families.

In elaborating upon this more comprehensive view of justice, Leo returns to the situation of the propertyless, whose only access to what they and their dependents need to survive is through wages: "The preservation of life is the bounden duty of one and all, and to be wanting therein is a crime," he writes. "It necessarily follows that each one has a natural right to procure what is required in order to live, and the poor can procure that in no other way than by what they can earn through their work."[18] What Leo is suggesting is that material support that is sufficient to meet needs is a demand of commutative justice. Such support is due, irrespective of any other consideration.[19] On his terms, wage theft is not simply the failure to pay the wages that are contractually owed but the failure to pay the wages that are sufficient for the support of the worker and the worker's dependents. As Romero explains this rationale for justice in wages in a 1971 article, "Human Solutions," "The worker is not a commodity, who is subject to the vagaries of the economy, but a human person, who by the mere fact of being human is entitled to a just wage, which is sufficient to cover material and cultural needs."[20]

This understanding of the just wage is therefore yet another entailment of the theological grammar of creation as common gift in the context of the emerging industrial order. The most fundamental consideration is neither the demands of the contract nor what market forces dictate but what is due workers as God's creatures, to whom the gift of creation is likewise given and for whom access to the gift is primarily through wages. Leo begins with the belief that the blessings of nature belong to humankind in common and on this basis formulates an account of justice in wages. That Leo is drawing out the implications of the grammar of creation can additionally be seen in how he thinks wages should be sufficient to support workers' families as well.[21]

18. Leo XIII, *Rerum Novarum*, no. 44.

19. For a helpful discussion of the problems with a conception of commutative justice reduced to contractual obligations alone, see Calvez and Perrin, *Church and Social Justice*, 154–55.

20. Romero, "Soluciónes humanas," *Orientación*, October 24, 1971.

21. Leo XIII, *Rerum Novarum*, no. 46; see also Calvez and Perrin, *Church and Social Justice*, 242–44.

On the question of justice in wages, once again we see *Rerum Novarum*'s imaginative reach as Leo tries to envision what justice demands in the midst of the new situation the church faces. Leo is disputing the thesis, often associated with Marxism, that class conflict necessarily follows from the wage system, such that wherever there is wage work, there is exploitation of surplus value and the relegation of workers to misery.[22] To be clear, Leo certainly thinks this describes the wage system of his day, which is criminal. But Leo's response to this situation is not to reject the wage system and replace it with another system but to imagine the conditions that would make it just—conditions wholly derived from the belief that creation is a common gift. Hence Leo's concern that the wage system he faces fails to consider a "more imperious and ancient" justice. Regarding this deeper justice, wages must be sufficient for the material support of workers and their dependents, and if they are not, or "if through necessity or fear of a worse evil" workers must accept degrading conditions, they are the victims of "force and injustice."[23] The language of ordinary violence is apposite. Because of this deeper justice, Leo categorically rejects as violence all "pressure upon the indigent and the destitute for the sake of gain," all gathering of profit "out of the need of another."[24]

Of course, another way a wage system might accord with this deeper justice is by facilitating access to property like land, because as we have seen, Leo thinks land affords greater stability and security for workers than reliance upon wages alone. It is therefore no coincidence that in the midst of a discussion of wages, Leo returns to the subject of work's role in facilitating access to land, arguing that wages must also be sufficient for the landless "to look forward to obtaining a share in the land."[25] Indeed, this discussion of justice in wages precedes and directly leads to

22. Calvez and Perrin, *Church and Social Justice*, 244.

23. Leo XIII, *Rerum Novarum*, no. 45.

24. Leo XIII, *Rerum Novarum*, no. 20. For an examination of ordinary violence or coercion in exchange, see Odd Langholm, *Economics in the Medieval Schools: Wealth, Exchange, Value, Money and Usury According to the Paris Theological Tradition 1200–1350* (New York: Brill Academic, 1992), 578–79; Langholm, *The Legacy of Scholasticism in Economic Thought: Antecedents of Choice and Power* (New York: Cambridge University Press, 2006), 52–132. For a contemporary articulation of "economic compulsion," see Barrera, *Economic Compulsion and Christian Ethics*.

25. Leo XIII, *Rerum Novarum*, no. 47.

Leo's programmatic conclusion that law and policy should favor ownership.[26] Even in *Rerum Novarum*'s treatment of justice in wages, then, we find a defense of property. However, the rationale for such defense is to signal the path whereby those without property might one day share more stably and securely in it. Work is meant to promote the proliferation of property and to play a decisive role in the politics of common use. But for work to play this role and facilitate access to what God gives in common, justice in wages is paramount.

Catholic social teaching will continue to reiterate the basic shape of this understanding of justice in wages and its underlying theological rationale. For instance, when Pius XI addresses in *Quadragesimo Anno* how the propertyless might acquire property and defend themselves from ordinary violence, he turns immediately to the topic of wages.[27] The shift from property to wages and salaries is both subtle and important. Until this point, Pius treats property,[28] how the disparity between the propertied and the propertyless imperils the common good,[29] and how this problem cannot be addressed unless the propertyless might "advance to the state of possessing some little property."[30] The topical shift at this juncture conveys that wage justice is so central to the politics of common use in an industrial order because apart from wages and salaries, workers have no other way to "obtain food and the necessaries of life," much less property.[31] Underlying the whole discussion is a vision of restoration, in which justice in wages also helps to establish and maintain the path from propertylessness to property. Accordingly, Pius interprets the fact that rural wageworkers are being "pushed to the lowest level of existence" as symptomatic of how workers are being "deprived of all hope of ever acquiring 'a share in the land.'"[32] The wages are insufficient to obtain the material support workers need in the present, but they are also insufficient for workers to walk the path from propertylessness to property.

26. Leo XIII, *Rerum Novarum*, no. 46.
27. Pius XI, *Quadragesimo Anno*, no. 63.
28. Pius XI, *Quadragesimo Anno*, nos. 44–53.
29. Pius XI, *Quadragesimo Anno*, nos. 58, 59–63.
30. Pius XI, *Quadragesimo Anno*, no. 63.
31. Pius XI, *Quadragesimo Anno*, no. 63.
32. Pius XI, *Quadragesimo Anno*, no. 59.

Injustice in wages is therefore an attack upon the politics of common use, obstructing workers' access to what is theirs as fellow recipients of the gift of creation.

Pius XII follows his predecessors in stressing these same points. One of the "practical conclusions" he draws in his 1942 Christmas message is the need to establish "a social order that will make possible an assured, even if modest, private property for all classes of society"[33] in which property is "a natural fruit of work."[34] When it is rightly ordered, wage work can and should lead to the possession of property. In his March 11, 1951, Radio Message to Spanish workers, he states, "There are many factors which should contribute to a wider diffusion of property. However, the principal one will always be the just wage." Together, the just wage and a better distribution of created goods are "two of the most urgent requirements in the social program of the Church."[35] Pius likewise continues to emphasize access to land—"the holding in which the family lives, and from the products of which it draws all or part of its subsistence."[36]

In accordance with the vision of restoration we have been examining, which involves as many people as possible becoming owners, Catholic social teaching continues to emphasize how justice demands wages sufficient to support workers and their dependents, as well as to establish a path to property for all people.[37] This understanding of justice in wages, like the vision of restoration more generally, bears the clear imprint of the theological grammar of creation as common gift. In *Rerum Novarum*

33. Pius XII, *Radiomessaggio di Sua Santità Pio XII alla vigilia del Santo Natale*, December 24, 1942. Here and elsewhere, Pius indexes "social order" to God's purposes for creation. Social order is therefore fundamentally threatened by dispossession and dislocation because such order, as Pius understands it, presupposes sufficient access for all to the earth's land and harvests.

34. Pius XII, *Radiomensaje en el V aniversario del comienzo de la guerra*, September 1, 1944. See also Pius XII, "The Problem of Fair Distribution," *A Letter Addressed to Semaine Sociale of Dijon, France*, July 7, 1952, in *Pope Pius XII on the Economic Order*, ed. Rupert J. Ederer (Lanham, Md.: Scarecrow, 2011).

35. Pius XII, *Radiomensaje del Santo Padre Pío XII a los trabajadores de España*, 2.

36. Pius XII, *Discourse to Commemorate the 50th Anniversary of the Encyclical "Rerum Novarum" of Pope Leo XIII on the Social Question*, 224–25.

37. Pius XII, *Discourse to Commemorate the 50th Anniversary of the Encyclical "Rerum Novarum" of Pope Leo XIII on the Social Question*; Pius XII, "The Church and Labor," *Address to Workers in Rome*, June 13, 1943, in Ederer, *Pope Pius XII on the Economic Order*; John XXIII, *Mater et Magistra*, nos. 71, 112; John Paul II, *Laborem Exercens*, no. 19.

and beyond, ensuring justice in wages becomes one decisive way for law and policy to favor ownership—an understanding Romero inherits. We have seen its influence upon him in the homily upon his return from Puebla when he says that workers must be able to organize and to be paid just salaries. But even when he was a priest in San Miguel in the 1950s and 1960s, Romero criticized large landowners of the diocese for their treatment of workers and for their refusal to pay just wages.[38] And as the agrarian crisis in El Salvador worsened in the late 1960s and early 1970s, Romero continued to voice this understanding of justice in wages, criticizing those who opposed the ability of *campesinos* to organize to improve their wages and working conditions, and insisting upon the need to address the "hunger wages" (*salarios de hambre*) they receive.[39]

PARTNERSHIP CONTRACTS

We have been examining how social teaching sees work and justice in wages as central to the politics of common use in an industrial order because wages are workers' primary means of access to the created goods that are their due as God's creatures. At the same time, we have also seen how this tradition tends to regard reliance upon wage work alone as a precarious means of access to such goods and, relatedly, how wage workers are more susceptible to ordinary violence than those who possess property. Landlessness therefore represents not only a failure of adequate access to material support, but also insecurity and instability in the limited access that does exist. The landless face a more acute form of defenselessness before a social world that refuses to shield them from misery and that exploits their vulnerability, using them, in Leo's words, "as though they were things."[40] This is why social teaching articulates its

38. Morozzo della Rocca, *Primero Dios*, 73, 84–85. On this point, see Óscar Romero, "La Iglesia va al campesino," *Chaparrastique*, December 12, 1952; Romero, "La *Rerum Novarum* perenne y urgente."

39. This phrase is from Romero, "Los campesinos no son parias," *Orientación*, July 4, 1971; but see also Romero, "La *Populorum Progressio*," *Chaparrastique*, April 21, 1967; Óscar Romero, "Hacia una mejor política agraria," *Diario de Oriente*, October 11, 1974; Romero, *Homilías*, 3:356–57; 6:396–97.

40. Leo XIII, *Rerum Novarum*, no. 20.

underlying vision of restoration in terms of a movement from property-lessness to property, from landlessness to obtaining a share in it.

My treatment of social teaching has attended closely to land and landlessness—themes that emerge straightforwardly from the documents under consideration and that bear obvious relation to social teaching's later call for land reform and to Romero's application of it in El Salvador. But land is only one form of property that provides the requisite stability and security in the support of material needs through time, and so it is important to consider how social teaching's vision of restoration is not limited to increasing access to land alone.

This becomes clearer in relation to developments following upon Leo's critique of wage contracts in *Rerum Novarum*. Some interpreted Leo as suggesting that wage contracts and the wage system were unjust *in se*, and that they should be replaced by what Pius XI in *Quadragesimo Anno* refers to as a "partnership contract" (*societatis contractum*)—or similar approaches involving the co-ownership or co-management of property and the co-sharing in the profits therefrom.[41] For his part, Pius XI thinks that this characterization misconstrues what Leo actually argues in *Rerum Novarum*. According to Pius, while commutative justice demands that workers receive wages sufficient both to support themselves and to walk the path from wage work to property, it does not require partnership contracts or related approaches such as worker participation in ownership, management, and profits of the enterprise for which they work. Nevertheless, Pius does think that partnership contracts should be promoted "so far as is possible" in order that "workers and other employees ... become sharers in ownership or management or participate in some fashion in the profits received."[42]

This stress upon increased worker participation in ownership, management, and profit-sharing in all aspects of economic life continues after *Quadragesimo Anno*, and social teaching consistently looks to foster forms of organization and association that embody alternatives to what

41. Pius XI, *Quadragesimo Anno*, no. 65.
42. Pius XI, *Quadragesimo Anno*, no. 65.

it sees as the widespread antagonism between work and capital. Along these lines, in his 1951 address to Spanish workers, Pius XII states that "the Church encourages all that which, as far as circumstances allow, tries to introduce elements of partnership contracts into work-contracts and improves the general condition of workers."[43] In *Mater et Magistra*, John XXIII similarly advocates that workers share in the ownership of the firms for which they work in order to ensure that they not be excluded from what God gives for common use.[44] The trajectory of social teaching is always toward greater sharing on the part of workers in ownership, management, and profit-sharing in all aspects of economic life, agricultural and otherwise.[45]

All of these proposals envision genuine sharing on the part of workers in the ownership and management of productive property, as well as in the profits deriving from it. And we continue to see the vision of restoration informed by the theological grammar of creation as common gift in the discernable movement from propertylessness to property. What these proposals also display is how social teaching develops by way of application. For these proposals seek to implement Leo's call in *Rerum Novarum* for the diffusion of property and to imagine new ways for law and policy to favor ownership.

This emphasis upon partnership contracts and increased worker participation in economic life also underscores social teaching's understanding of what property is and the common life the use of it is meant to foster. This is well articulated by the anonymous author of an article that appeared in *Orientación*, a weekly publication of the Archdiocese of San Salvador, about the cooperative movement—cooperatives being one example of what sharing on the part of workers in ownership, management, and profit-sharing looks like. In the article, the author points out that

43. Pius XII, *Radiomensaje del Santo Padre Pío XII a los trabajadores de España*, 2.

44. John XXIII, *Mater et Magistra*, no. 75–77.

45. On this point, see John XXIII, *Mater et Magistra*, no. 31–33; Vatican Council II, *Gaudium et Spes*, no. 68; John Paul II, *Laborem Exercens*, no. 14; *Centesimus Annus*, no. 41.

cooperatives do not destroy private property but rather generalize it; they realize property's social function. Members of cooperatives are not at any moment divested of what belongs to them. Rather, they come to understand that it belongs to all of them in common, and so they practically discover that the common good is above the personal good because the common good includes the personal good and fulfills it.[46]

As this description suggests, cooperatives promote the diffusion of property in a way that prioritizes mutual responsibility such that personal possession of property neither comes at the expense of others nor denies duties toward them. This approach resonates with the understanding of property and possession that Leo conveys in *Rerum Novarum* and that subsequent social teaching preserves, which holds that creation is a common gift and that the hallmark of possessing property is including and gathering others in its use.

Social teaching's general emphasis on expanding worker participation in all aspects of economic life even inflects Romero's advocacy of a particular approach to land reform centered upon producers' cooperatives. As we will see in chapter 4, Romero tends not to intervene in the debate about land reform with particular policy details, which he thinks is not his competence as a pastor. An exception to this tendency, however, is an article he wrote in 1974 in anticipation of President Molina's agrarian transformation project, the fallout over which plunged El Salvador into violence for the rest of the decade and beyond. In the article "Rural Parcelization, the Great Enemy of Land Reform," Romero critiques an approach he calls "parcelization"—a process of partitioning land into small parcels—for failing to achieve what land reform aims at, which is for landless workers to have a share in the land of their country and to contribute to the common good. Romero's concern with parcelization is that his people will leave "*latifundia* only to enter into *minifundia* [small farms]." In other words, if how we imagine property is how we imagine ourselves, then the problem with parcelization is how it encourages *campesinos* to imagine themselves as isolated indi-

46. "El cooperativismo: Una realización obrera," *Orientación*, San Salvador, December 29, 1969.

viduals with sole and despotic dominion over their little parcels of land.

Instead of parcelization, Romero favors an approach to land reform centered upon the formation of producers' cooperatives—an approach he takes from Medellín[47]—which he thinks would enable workers truly to share in the land of El Salvador and support the common good. For land reform, Romero argues, "is not a matter of dividing the land but dividing ownership of it," a process meant to enable as many as possible to share together in this land and its harvests.[48] As Romero will put the point years later in one of his homilies, the goal is not the distribution of the land into equal allotments for every Salvadoran but "the transformation of private property," which "knows how to give property a true social sense (*un verdadero sentido social*)."[49]

AGRICULTURE AND SOCIAL JUSTICE

My main goal in this chapter is to show how the church's social teaching begins to support land reform as one expression of a politics of common use. Up to this point, we have been tracing the influence of the theological grammar of creation as common gift and its governing influence upon social teaching's treatment of work as a path to property ownership, justice in wages, partnership contracts, and related efforts to facilitate co-administration and co-ownership of property. This provisional survey of the theological and moral landscape within which land reform emerges has continually underscored how God provides for the material support of all people, both through the fruits of the earth and the work of human hands.

Over the course of the twentieth century, the problems to which Leo was responding in *Rerum Novarum* did not go away but grew increasingly worse. The path from wage work to property ownership was narrowing and becoming more obstructed. In rural areas throughout the world, the path ceased to exist altogether, as the problem of insufficient access to

---

47. *Medellín*, "Justicia," 3.14.

48. Romero, "Parcelaciones rurales, un gran enemigo de reforma agraria," *Orientación*, March 31, 1974. See also Romero, "Reformas estructurales y salvación," *Orientación*, October 28, 1973.

49. Romero, *Homilías*, 1:217.

land became more widespread and acute. Even by the time Pius XI wrote *Quadragesimo Anno* in 1931, this disorder was well established. Pius mentions the complex and manifold modern forces of dispossession that have "rapidly pervaded and occupied" other parts of the world, as a consequence of which numbers of "non-owning working poor" have "increased enormously," "their groans cry[ing] to God from the earth."[50] Pius singles out the effects of these developments in the countryside, writing about a rising number of rural wageworkers permanently bound to landlessness and about those who derive their livelihood from agriculture "crushed with hardships and with difficulties."[51] These words certainly apply to El Salvador, where, as noted earlier, conditions were deteriorating rapidly around this time following enclosure and coffee's conquest of the landscape. In 1932, one of the largest *campesino* insurrections in Latin American history occurred in western El Salvador. It ended with the Salvadoran army marching through the countryside, systematically killing suspected participants, sympathizers, and many others.

During the twentieth century, new questions therefore arise and clamor for a response. These questions lie behind Pius XI's general assessment of the state of the world in 1931: "The immense multitude of the non-owning workers on the one hand and the enormous riches of certain very wealthy men on the other establish an unanswerable argument that the riches which are so abundantly produced in our age of 'industrialism' … are not rightly distributed and equitably made available to the various classes of the people."[52] We saw that in cases of extreme necessity, Thomas Aquinas thinks it is appropriate for people to take the excess property of others, because need has made the goods common. As the maldistribution of created goods worsens as the twentieth century progresses, social teaching effectively starts to ask whether, in certain extreme cases, states might take the excess property of others in order to help facilitate common use. While Leo argues in *Rerum Novarum* that law and policy should favor ownership, he does not address the possibility that states might expropriate and redistribute land. However, by mid-century,

---

50. Pius XI, *Quadragesimo Anno*, no. 59.
51. Pius XI, *Quadragesimo Anno*, nos. 59, 102.
52. Pius XI, *Quadragesimo Anno*, no. 60.

the situation has grown so dire that social teaching does address this possibility. And for the first time law reform enters social teaching as yet another way law and policy might enable as many people as possible to become owners.

These are crucial considerations for understanding why social teaching begins to call for land reform as a new application of the politics of common use. It is also helpful to situate this call within the context of Pius XII's numerous addresses to farmers and farmworkers. These addresses gather many of the themes we have been examining and focus them on the problems facing the rural world. In one of these addresses, Pius articulates what is arguably his central purpose when he references a passage from Pius X's encyclical *Il Fermo Proposito* (1905) about how "the work of restoring all things in Christ"—a reference to Paul's statement in the Letter to the Ephesians about God's plan "to unite all things in Christ" (Eph 1:10)—must especially consider "the working and agricultural classes" and endeavor "to dry their tears, to alleviate their sufferings, and to improve their economic condition."[53] Their particular form of affliction merits special attention. During Pius XII's pontificate, social teaching reflects in a more focused and sustained manner upon the problems facing rural communities throughout the world, and for the first time, the call for land reform emerges.

As we have already seen, agriculture is of profound importance for the tradition of social teaching, especially since the land's capacity to support human life hinges on the work of human hands. What especially comes to the fore in these addresses is the communal shape of this work and how the loss of communities living upon the land imperils both the preservation of land and its capacity to support others.[54] Pius continually reminds his listeners of the centrality of agriculture to human life, as well as of the importance of farmers and farming communities—a

---

53. Pius XII, "'Economic and Cultural Self-Help on the Part of the Rural Community,' A Letter to the Organization of Irish Agricultural People," July 14, 1954, in Ederer, *Pope Pius XII on the Economic Order*. See Pius X, Encyclical Letter *Il Fermo Proposito* (June 11, 1905), no. 7.

54. For more on the significance of agriculture beyond Pius XII, see Matthew Philip Whelan, "The Grammar of Creation: Agriculture in the Thought of Pope Benedict XVI," in *Environmental Justice and Climate Change* (New York: Lexington, 2013), 103–23.

centrality he sees as a direct entailment of the grammar of creation as common gift.[55] The crucial issue for him is how these communities might continue their work of supporting themselves and others, which is impossible without supporting the ongoing existence of the communities themselves.[56] What also begins to emerge in these addresses is a thematization of how communities deriving their living from agriculture are being decimated.[57] Pius frequently discusses topics like the appropriation and concentration of land by capital, the rural exodus, and the vast expansion of modern cities.[58]

The general decline in farming populations throughout the world was accelerating rapidly during the second half of the twentieth century, a phenomenon the historian Eric Hobsbawm refers to as "the death of the peasantry."[59] In chapter 1, we considered this phenomenon in El Salvador in relation to the postwar period of land concentration in coffee, as well as in sugar cane, cattle, and cotton. Agricultural modernization through higher-yielding varieties and heavy reliance on agrochemicals and machinery expelled rather than absorbed labor, contributing to the exodus of people in search of land and work. Between the 1950s and the 1970s, the *colonato* system, an arrangement in which resident laborers would exchange work or part of the harvest for the use of another's land, was

55. Pius XII, "The Basis and Importance of a Healthy Agricultural Class," *Speech Delivered by His Holiness to the Delegates at the Convention of the Address to the National Farmers' League of Italy in Rome*, November 15, 1946; Pius XII, "The Farmer's Status as a Pressing Problem of Social Order," *Letter to the Leaders of the Social Week of Canada*, August 31, 1947; Pius XII, "Problems in the World of Agriculture," *Address before the First International Congress for the Problems of Agriculture*, July 2, 1951; Pius XII, "Farming: Model of Human Effort," *Discourse to the Italian Catholic Federation of Farmers*, May 18, 1955; and Pius XII, "The Problems of Rural Life," *An Address to the Social Week of Italy*, September 18, 1957. All of these documents can be found in Ederer, *Pope Pius XII on the Economic Order*.

56. Pius XII, "Problems in the World of Agriculture."

57. Pius XII, "The Basis and Importance of a Healthy Agricultural Class"; Pius XII, "Problems in the World of Agriculture."

58. Pius XII, "The Basis and Importance of a Healthy Agricultural Class"; Pius XII, "Problems in the World of Agriculture."

59. Eric Hobsbawm, *The Age of Extremes: A History of the World, 1914–1991* (New York: Vintage, 1994), 289–95. For a more detailed look at developments of what the authors call "the pillage of agriculture in the developing nations," see Marcel Mazoyer and Laurence Roudart, *A History of World Agriculture: From the Neolithic Age to the Current Crisis* (New York: Monthly Review, 2006), 441–97.

disintegrating. Its demise meant that many whose livelihood depended upon this arrangement lost employment. Subsequently, those affected joined the labor force of landless workers who had to migrate to make ends meet, relying upon whatever temporary employment they could find. Similar developments occurred throughout Latin America. In analyzing these trends in land and labor between the 1950s and the 1980s, the eminent agricultural economist Alain de Janvry and his colleagues describe this period as one in which the Latin American *campesinado* became a massive "refugee sector."[60]

According to Pius XII, one practical ramification of these developments is that the loss of land by those who had once lived stably and securely upon it necessarily entails the additional loss of practical wisdom in the use and care of land, with deleterious effects for agricultural practice. "After the land has been so abandoned," he says, "capital hastens to make it its own; the land then becomes no longer the object of love but of cold exploitation." Land increasingly produces for the purpose of "speculation," and profit becomes the sole standard for its use, which Pius calls a "perversion of private rural property."[61] Notice the distinction between two rival conceptions of property: one that enables the use and care of land by communities across time and another that has "no love or concern for the plot that so many generations had lovingly tilled, and is heartless towards the families who till it and dwell upon it now."[62] Pius is also attentive to the ecological consequences of the latter form of land use and how it has occasioned "too much experimentation with mass production, with the exploitation, to the point of exhaustion, of every resource of the soil and subsoil."[63]

The deleterious effect of transformations in agricultural practice—especially regarding agriculture's *telos*—is a frequent theme of these addresses. In this regard, Pius especially critiques the idea of productivism,

---

60. De Janvry, Sadoulet, and Young, "Land and Labour in Latin American Agriculture from the 1950s to the 1980s," 423.

61. Pius XII, "The Basis and Importance of a Healthy Agricultural Class." On this point, see also Pius XII, "Problems in the World of Agriculture."

62. Pius XII, "The Basis and Importance of a Healthy Agricultural Class."

63. Pius XII, "Production for Human Needs," *Address for the Catholic International Congress of Social Study*, Rome, June 3, 1950, in Ederer, *Pope Pius XII on the Economic Order.*

which is the privileging of constant increases in agricultural productivity above all other ends for agriculture.[64] Productionism has roots in the enclosure movements in Europe, and it is deeply implicated in an account of property that prioritizes the owner's exclusive control of access, use, and disposal.[65] According to Pius, the problem with productionism is not production per se, which is indispensable to the practice of agriculture, but rather the failure to perceive any other end for agriculture besides production. "Productivity is not an end in itself, nor does it regulate itself," he says. Exclusive emphasis upon production therefore obscures the true end of agriculture, which is the material support of human life, in relation to which production must constantly be evaluated.[66] The fact that workers do not necessarily share in gains from rising production is a very important reason Pius thinks production alone is an inadequate criterion upon which to base agricultural practice.[67] Indeed, the exclusive prioritization of production tends to increase the concentration of productive property, which in turn results in the exclusion of the many from access to it.[68]

Romero shares a similar view, contending that the social sense of property "does not consist only in producing more, but in producing more for the common good."[69] With this distinction between producing more and producing more for the common good, Romero is contrasting the liberal vision of the common good, according to which maximizing production of privately held agricultural estates redounds to the benefit of all Salvadorans—the common good understood as the aggregate of the private good—with a different vision, according to which production serves the common good understood as a good that can only be held in common.

<hr>

64. Pius XII, "Farming: Model of Human Effort"; Pius XII, "The Basis and Importance of a Healthy Agricultural Class"; Pius XII, "Problems in the World of Agriculture."

65. Paul B. Thompson, *The Spirit of Soil: Agriculture and Environmental Ethics* (New York: Routledge, 1994), 47–71.

66. Pius XII, "The Problem of Fair Distribution." On this point, see also Pius XI, *Quadragesimo Anno*, nos. 88, 132; John XXIII *Mater et Magistra*, nos. 10–14, 71; *Gaudium et Spes*, no. 64.

67. Pius XII, "Human Claims on Economic Expansion," *Letter to the President of French Social Week*, July 10, 1956, in Ederer, *Pope Pius XII on the Economic Order.*

68. Pius XII, "The Vocational Tasks and the Cultural Mission of the Farmer," *Address to the Italian Farmers' Association*, April 16, 1958, in Ederer, *Pope Pius XII on the Economic Order.*

69. Romero, *Homilías*, 1:217.

This latter vision has dramatically different implications for sharing in the land and harvests of El Salvador than the former. For according to this latter vision, human creatures and what they need to share in the common good are the primary measures for agricultural production. And in an agriculturally-based society characterized by pervasive landlessness such as El Salvador, sharing in the common good would involve ensuring that people have access to land to farm.

Pius's understanding of the common good therefore leads him to support ends for agriculture besides production, including a more just distribution of land. Production in agriculture, he thinks, must always defer to goods apart from production itself, such as facilitating people's access to land.[70] Furthermore, Pius assumes that increases in production and more just distributions of property are not mutually exclusive alternatives; giving ownership of land to those who work it can both decrease poverty and at the same time potentially increase production.[71] As Ellacuría explains this position in response to its Salvadoran opponents, "The argument [that a better distribution of land necessarily leads to productivity declines] ignores the fact that people who live and die cultivating the soil know how to make it produce."[72] However, according to Pius, it is above all because of agriculture's centrality to the politics of common use and to God's provisioning for all people that justice in the distribution of land is of paramount importance.

For Pius, the disintegration of agricultural communities throughout the world is symptomatic of a pathology that he repeatedly refers to as "social injustice."[73] Recall that social teaching's use of this phrase has a specific meaning that points to the exclusion of whole groups of people from social life as well as to how this exclusion imperils the pursuit and care of goods that can only be held in common. Therefore, while certainly including a society's failure to protect those in need, social injustice relates principally to a society's failure to regard those in need as wor-

---

70. See also Pius XI's comments in *Quadragesimo Anno*, nos. 57, 61.

71. Pius XII, "The Vocational Tasks and the Cultural Mission of the Farmer."

72. Ignacio Ellacuría, *Veinte años de historia en El Salvador (1969–1989): Escritos políticos* (San Salvador: UCA Editores, 1992), 1:574.

73. Pius XII, "The Basis and Importance of a Healthy Agricultural Class."

thy of protection, as sharers in a common life. Pius thinks this especially applies to rural communities throughout the world whose members have been systematically excluded from sharing in the benefits of what they produce. The vulnerabilities and dependencies particular to these communities have been exploited rather than protected, undermining the very notion of society as a shared membership. Consequently, such communities have been decimated and their inhabitants dispossessed.[74] Social injustice refers to this ubiquitous structural and institutional exclusion and the upheavals in rural life with which it is associated.

The charge of social injustice implies that those communities involved in the provision of sustenance have legitimate demands upon the societies in which they live. These demands include the assurance of sufficient material support as well as the ability to gather in associations and organizations of various kinds without fear of reprisal. This is of a piece with Leo's belief in a kind of moral economy governing social life, in which it is good and right for a society to support those upon whom it depends for what it needs—an understanding that hinges upon the recognition of a shared social membership. But that rural communities have such demands presupposes that the communities exist in the first place, and that there is a sociality proper to them that must be acknowledged by their societies. A related problem, we will recall, is part of what prompts Leo to write *Rerum Novarum*: developments associated with enclosure and industrialism have not only undone property for the many but have also dissolved their societies and scattered their members, generating the conditions in which people have nothing to sell but their labor to strangers. It is both because people have been dispossessed of their land and disembedded from their societies that Leo thinks they are without protection—surrendered, isolated, and helpless before those who would prey upon their vulnerability.

One way to understand what Pius XII is doing in these addresses to farmers and farmworkers is that he is effectively trying to prevent further dispossession and dissolution by arguing, first, that these farming

74. Pius XII, "The Basis and Importance of a Healthy Agricultural Class"; Pius XII, "The Farmer's Status as a Pressing Problem of Social Order"; Pius XII, "The Problems of Rural Life."

communities exist and their existence should be acknowledged; second, that their existence brings with it demands upon the societies to which they belong; and finally, that the ongoing existence of such communities depends upon their demands being met. Among the needed reforms Pius repeatedly cites in support of such farming communities are a wider diffusion of agricultural land through land reform, stable work contracts, and remuneration for wageworkers and tenants that is sufficient for them to become landowners themselves eventually.[75] John XXIII's *Mater et Magistra*[76] and Paul VI's *Octogesima Adveniens*[77] follow and expand upon Pius XII's analysis of social injustice as it affects the rural world.

In addition to the just demands rural communities have upon their societies, Pius also emphasizes their duties.[78] "Your principal help must come from yourselves," he says, "from your cooperative unions, especially from your credit unions."[79] The survival of rural communities requires new forms of "solidarity."[80] Viewed from this vantage, the work of preserving and proliferating rural organizations and associations

75. Pius XII also mentions a host of other reforms, such as access to forms of insurance and assistance common to other laborers; technical training; and other measures to address the disparities between agricultural and industrial income; Pius XII, "A Farmer's Three Duties," *Address to the Confederations of Italian Tenant Farmers*, April 11, 1956, in Ederer, *Pope Pius XII on the Economic Order*.

76. In *Mater et Magistra*, John XXIII observes that the question of justice pertains not simply to relationships between workers and their employers, but also to relationships among various kinds of productive activities within the same political community, and even to the relationships among political communities themselves (no. 122). These relationships in their current form, he thinks, are characterized by injustice. It is within this context that he begins to address what he calls "the depressed state of agriculture" (nos. 123–24).

77. Near the beginning of *Octogesima Adveniens*, Paul VI asks, "Is sufficient attention being devoted to the arrangement and improvement of the life of the country people, whose inferior and at times miserable economic situation provokes the flight to the unhappy crowded conditions of the city outskirts, where neither employment nor housing awaits them?" (no. 8). The answer is clearly "no." Paul devotes particular attention to the problems being generated by the "inordinate" and "disordered" growth of cities, including the production of what he calls "new proletariats" (nos. 9–10).

78. Pius XII, "The Basis and Importance of a Healthy Agricultural Class." See also Pius XII, "The Value of Agricultural Science for the World Economy," *Address to the Ninth International Congress of Agricultural Industries*, May 29, 1952, in Ederer, *Pope Pius XII on the Economic Order*; Pius XII, "Farming: Model of Human Effort."

79. Pius XII, "The Basis and Importance of a Healthy Agricultural Class"; Pius XII, "Economic and Cultural Self-Help on the Part of the Rural Community"; Pius XII, "The Problems of Rural Life." See also John XXIII, *Mater et Magistra*, nos. 145–47.

80. Pius XII, "The Problems of Rural Life."

contributes to the amelioration of social injustice by the simple fact of gathering together those who are presently being scattered and by protecting isolated individuals through their incorporation into social bodies. Such preservation and proliferation resist the reduction of civil society to, in Leo XIII's words, "one dead level," and stems the tide of what Pius XI describes as "the overthrow and near extinction of that rich social life which was once highly developed through associations of various kinds."[81]

But the preservation and proliferation of such organizations and associations afford aid in other ways, too—including, but not limited to, increasing workers' access to property and basic material support. In gathering together, members of such groups can more effectively clear the path between work and property of obstacles and so participate in the movement of restoration themselves. In this regard, Pius thinks landowners in particular must "make every effort to improve the living standard of those who devote themselves to agriculture" and support much-needed land reforms on behalf of the landless and day-laborers. Therefore, in addition to farming, the work of landowners must also include advocating for justice in the distribution of property and promoting independent farm ownership.[82] For the politics of common use, those who already have land play an indispensable role in extending that access to others.

We have already begun to see how Pius XII explicitly and repeatedly calls for land reform, which represents for him one measure among others to address the social injustice affecting rural communities.[83] In his 1944 radio message, Pius narrates *Rerum Novarum*'s demand for laws and policies that favor ownership specifically in terms of land reform, which Pius articulates as a prominent example of state participation in the politics of common use. The goal of such reform is to protect, preserve, and promote "small- and medium-sized properties" in agriculture, as well as in social life more generally. The aid land reform offers is therefore of a

81. Leo XIII, *Rerum Novarum*, no. 17; Pius XI, *Quadragesimo Anno*, no. 78.

82. Pius XII, "The Vocational Tasks and the Cultural Mission of the Farmer."

83. See Pius XII, "The Question of Agricultural Reform," *Papal Letter Transmitted by J. B. Montini to the 22nd Social Week at Naples*, September 15, 1947, in Ederer, *Pope Pius XII on the Economic Order*; Pius XII, "Problems in the World of Agriculture"; Pius XII, "The Vocational Tasks and the Cultural Mission of the Farmer."

very specific kind: it seeks to support the rural communities that receive it and so to help build up societies where societies should exist. Because inequality detracts from property's "vital function" in personal and social life, Pius explains, "the state may, in the common interest, intervene to regulate [the use of property], or even, if it is impossible to arrive at another solution, decree expropriation, giving a fair and equitable indemnity."[84] States certainly do not have carte blanche to expropriate land. In the 1944 radio message, Pius presents land reform's place in a politics of common use as a last resort that should be employed only when stakeholders have arrived at an impasse, such that there is no other clear way forward. It is a final expedient when other attempts to attain a more just distribution of property have failed.

What is also important to note about Pius's support for land reform is that he sees it as arising directly and straightforwardly from the concerns of his predecessors, an entailment of the theological grammar of creation as common gift.[85] It is a response to the growing distances between the many who have little or no land and the few who have excessive amounts of it, the closure of the path between wage work and ownership of productive property like land, and the ongoing decline and disintegration of rural communities throughout the world. Land reform represents a new and now necessary application of social teaching's understanding of property and possession. Land reform is admittedly a last resort, to be employed only in extreme cases. But one reason the call for it enters social teaching is precisely because extreme cases have become so ordinary and social injustice has become so pervasive.

Not everyone, however, shared this assessment. In commenting upon Pius XII's suggestion in the 1944 radio message that there are times when land reform might be pursued, the economist Rupert J. Ederer writes that Pius "injected the Church's social teaching into what has always represented a controversial position for some."[86] Ederer's comment raises many questions. In what way was land reform *injected* into the teaching? Clearly, it is a new application, but the language of injection makes it

---

84. Pius XII, *Radiomensaje en el V aniversario del comienzo de la guerra.*
85. See especially Pius XII, "The Question of Agricultural Reform."
86. Ederer, *Pope Pius XII on the Economic Order*, 59, 190.

sound as though land reform is an alien substance, potentially contaminating or compromising the integrity of social teaching. Moreover, who are the people to whom Ederer refers, and why is land reform so controversial to them? What reasons do they give for their concerns? What understanding of property and possession do these reasons imply? Unfortunately, Ederer does not say.

These unanswered questions are important to bear in mind because they are relevant to the debate about land reform in El Salvador and the conflicting visions of property and possession underlying it. Romero faced wealthy and powerful members of his own church who found the idea of advocating for or organizing on behalf of a better distribution of land not just controversial, but subversive. These members represented those who questioned the justice of existing property arrangements or of the wages and conditions of agricultural workers as threats to the faith, the nation, and Western civilization. As Morozzo della Rocca observes, the ruling classes of El Salvador did not bother to distinguish between the various social movements of the time. "Each and every one of the *campesino* meetings were, at a minimum, suspect of subversion, each demand for justice was an outstretched hand toward communism."[87]

For his part, Romero thought many of these critics of land reform subscribed to the "economic dictatorship" Pius XI discusses in *Quadragesimo Anno*, according to which "the right ordering of economic life" must be left "to a free competition of forces"—a view that, in Romero's estimation, neglected the social mortgage on all property and the embeddedness of markets in social life.[88] But this was not simply a conflict over different visions of property and possession. Romero thought it was a conflict over different visions of Christianity itself. For this reason, he refers to supporters of this economic dictatorship as "baptized pagans" who make an idol of their property and bow down before it.[89] Gutiérrez describes situations like those Romero faced as the radical challenge of

---

87. Morozzo della Rocca, *Primero Dios*, 32.

88. Letter of Óscar Romero to Cardinal Baggio, May 21, 1978. The Romero-Baggio correspondence can be found in Series 5, Boxes 25 and 27, Brockman-Romero Papers, Special Collections and Archives, DePaul University, Chicago, Illinois. See also Romero, *Homilías*, 3:77.

89. Romero, *Homilías*, 6:176.

proclaiming the gospel in the face of "the poverty, misery, and exploitation in which the immense majority of Latin Americans live," but doing so within "a society that claims to be Christian" and resists the proclamation.[90]

We have been examining the emergence of land reform not only to draw attention to a neglected topic of social teaching, but above all to show land reform's theological stakes, the problems to which the call for it is a response, and its place within a wider politics of common use. When viewed in this way, land reform is a fitting feature of the moral and theological landscape we have been surveying, and its emergence only underscores one of social teaching's fundamental claims: that particular property arrangements and systems of distribution are meant to facilitate common use. As we have seen, the theological grammar of creation as common gift governs the tradition's teaching on property and possession, the path between work and property in land, partnership contracts, justice in wages, and the social injustice affecting rural communities. Our purpose in considering these matters has been to familiarize ourselves with the underlying belief about creation and its implications for property and possession, which is continuing to be clarified and applied when taken up in support of land reform.

LAND REFORM AND THE STATE

In attending to the emergence of the call for land reform in Catholic social teaching, we have seen how the problems to which Leo sought to respond in *Rerum Novarum* had grown so acute by the mid-twentieth century that Pius XII began to include land reform among the laws and policies states might pursue in order to favor ownership. We have also seen that although social teaching integrates land reform into its politics of common use, land reform is not the central expression of this politics. It is a response to extreme cases when other measures have failed. Relatedly, just as land reform is not the central expression of this politics, neither is it an ideal one. A deep ambivalence about the modern state pervades social teaching, which is important for us to consider. Among other rea-

---

90. Gutíerrez, *Los pobres y la liberación en Puebla* (Bogotá: Indo-American Press, 1979), 8.

sons, this is because of the state's complicity in the very problems Leo is addressing in *Rerum Novarum*. That laws and policies of states clearly have not favored ownership helps explain why Leo even issues the encyclical.

Regarding the problem of the modern state in social teaching, the work of Russell Hittinger is especially helpful. In a series of essays and book chapters, he maintains that social teaching developed largely in response to the French Revolution's creed of "liberty, equality, and fraternity." Catholic thinkers were especially alarmed by the creed's notion of fraternity and its equation with citizenship at a time when other social memberships were being suppressed by the state. In nineteenth-century France, workers' corporations were widely regarded as a threat to public order, and the attack on the privileges of the old regime morphed into an attack on corporations themselves. In the words of historian William H. Sewell, this implied "the annihilation of any sense of common interest intermediate between the individual and the nation. Loyalties to provinces, estates, orders, communities, corporations, all were to vanish before the interests of individual citizens and the supreme loyalty of every citizen to the nation."[91] In this context, workers' corporations were seen as counterrevolutionary, and workers' freedom to assemble in pursuit of common interests was opposed. In a nation of free individual citizens, wages and working conditions had to be contracted with employers on an individual basis. Hittinger explains the crux of the problem with this understanding of fraternity: "Insofar as the state permitted the existence of other social entities only by the concession and in the pattern of state sovereignty, the state was implicitly claiming to be the exemplary cause of the good." For this reason, Catholic thinkers tended to depict the modern nation-state as "a neo-pagan expression of state sovereignty," "a demonic rival to the divinity."[92]

Leo XIII undertakes a distinctive response to this problem—what Hit-

91. William H. Sewell Jr., *Work and Revolution in France: The Language of Labor from the Old Regime to 1848* (New York: Cambridge University Press, 1980), 88–89.

92. Hittinger, "Toward an Adequate Anthropology: Social Aspects of *Imago Dei* in Catholic Theology," in *Imago Dei: Human Dignity in Ecumenical Perspective* (Washington, D.C.: The Catholic University of America Press, 2013), 60.

tinger characterizes as "a scissors-like approach" to the state and its ambition to exercise monopoly over fraternity—whereby the church sought to limit and to contextualize the claims of citizenship by defending societies other than the state, such as marriage and family, workers' associations and organizations such as unions, and the church.[93] "Regarding these social spheres," Hittinger writes, "the church could say to the state, *noli me tangere*, 'don't touch me.'"[94] Both during and after Leo's pontificate, concerns about the state and its ambition to exercise monopoly over fraternity continue to shape social teaching in profound ways.

In light of Hittinger's attention to the overreach of the modern state, it is important to point out that social teaching's misgivings about the state do not result in the rejection of its role in social life. The church certainly chastises the state for its overreach, but it also appeals to it regarding its moral vocation.[95] As we have seen, Leo thinks the laws and policies of states have a role to play in promoting a politics of common use. Moreover, social teaching's defense of societies other than the state is not reducible to the state's lack of interference with them. In *Rerum Novarum*, Leo even goes so far as to argue that the state is required to provide assistance where it is needed but not forthcoming:

> When there is question of defending the rights of individuals, the poor and badly off have a claim to especial consideration. The richer class have many ways of shielding themselves, and stand less in need of help from the State; whereas the mass of the poor have no resources of their own to fall back upon, and must chiefly depend upon the assistance of the State. And it is for this reason that wage-earners, since they mostly belong in the mass of the needy, should be specially cared for and protected by the government.[96]

93. Hittinger, "Toward an Adequate Anthropology," 41, 60; Hittinger, "Leo XIII (1810–1903)," in *The Teachings of Modern Roman Catholicism on Law, Politics, and Human Nature* (New York: Columbia University Press, 2007).

94. Hittinger, "Toward an Adequate Anthropology," 41.

95. I am indebted to Jason Heron for this formulation.

96. Leo XIII, *Rerum Novarum*, no. 37.

In this passage, Leo offers, in Gutiérrez's words, a "witness to … a preferential option for the poor" and most vulnerable by the state.[97] In the emerging capitalist order, widespread dispossession and dissolution of social bonds have left many without property and protective organizations, and what Leo calls the human creature's "weakness" has become the site of systematic exploitation. Under these conditions, Leo's reason for calling upon the state for help is not that the state is particularly adept at helping, but that nothing else is doing so on the scale necessary to address the disaster.[98]

The key point for our purposes is that misgivings about the state coexist with the belief that there are important tasks to be done and goods to be promoted by it. According to social teaching, the purpose of all social authority, including the state, is to promote the common good.[99] But this does not imply that the modern state is particularly amenable to this purpose or that it must not be constantly and insistently goaded regarding it—often at great personal cost. In this connection, the Argentinian priest Carlos Olivero speaks of "the evangelization of the state," by which he means "help[ing] the state to occupy the place it should have, and to do its job."[100] This is similar to Romero's posture. By no means naïve to its pathologies, Romero never ceases to remind the Salvadoran state of its moral vocation or to engage it as if it were capable of pursuing the common good. After Grande's death, Romero refused to appear aligned with or supportive of the state in public in any way. However, as Morozzo della Rocca observes, "Romero did not want to, in any way, break the lines of commu-

---

97. Gutiérrez, "New Things Today: A Rereading of *Rerum Novarum*," 43.

98. Leo XIII, *Rerum Novarum*, no. 50. On this point, see also *Quadragesimo Anno*, no. 25; Pius XII, "The Problem of Fair Distribution."

99. While the form of polity is not fixed—there are various forms of legitimate government—the end of polity is, which is to promote the common good; see Leo XIII, Encyclical Letter *Sapientiae Christianae* (January 10, 1890), 28; Leo XIII, Encyclical Letter *Au Milieu* (February 16, 1892), 14, 28–29; John XXIII, *Pacem in Terris*, no. 54. A different, more instrumental understanding of the state begins to appear in social teaching during and after World War II. See Pius XII, Encyclical Letter *Summi Pontificatus* (October 20, 1939), no. 59; John XXIII, *Pacem in Terris*, no. 68; Jacques Maritain, *Man and the State* (Chicago: University of Chicago Press, 1951); William T. Cavanaugh, "Killing for the Telephone Company: Why the Nation-State Is Not the Keeper of the Common Good," *Modern Theology* 20, no. 2 (2004): 243–74.

100. Quoted in Andrea Tornielli and Giacomo Galeazzi, *This Economy Kills: Pope Francis on Capitalism and Social Justice* (Collegeville, Minn.: Liturgical Press, 2015), 143.

nication with the authorities.... In private he received everyone—ministers, soldiers, oligarchs, all those who called upon him ... —and explained, asked, mediated, directed, and pleaded. Indeed, one must recognize in him a great patience with the authorities."[101] We see this especially with regard to the land reform we will examine in chapter 4. Romero worked extensively behind the scenes with the minister of agriculture and other government officials who were involved in its planning.[102]

All this amounts to social teaching's profound ambivalence about the modern state, which is well beyond the scope of this chapter to examine in detail.[103] At the moment, our concern is a related but more precise issue: the place of land reform in the politics of common use as a tool that states can use to facilitate ownership. As previously noted, Leo does not envision the involvement of states in taking the excess property of others and giving it to those who need it for the sake of the common good, because he thinks that distinguishing between what is sufficient and superfluous to a person's needs is a task best left to property owners themselves. However, Leo's successors do envision the involvement of states in this matter, and it is important to understand why.[104]

In *Quadragesimo Anno*, Pius XI engages this question in a way that is not altogether clear. At times, he seems to oppose state expropriation and redistribution of property, such as when he distinguishes between ownership of property and its use to argue that ownership cannot be "destroyed or lost by reason of abuse or non-use."[105] It would seem to follow

---

101. Morozzo della Rocca also adds that "with regard to [President] Molina, even in the moments of maximum indignation and disappointment, Romero continued speaking to him, writing him, sending him documentation, and proposing to him common work. He behaved in the same way with Molina's successor [General Carlos Humberto Romero]"; Morozzo della Rocca, *Primero Dios*, 179–80, 185–95.

102. Romero, *Diario*, 391–92, 409–10, 413–14, 417–18.

103. Among Catholic thinkers, William Cavanaugh has offered perhaps the most eloquent and sustained criticisms of the modern state, though there are points in his corpus where he articulates an ambivalence similar to that of social teaching; see, for instance, Cavanaugh, "Killing for the Telephone Company," 266. For a critical response to Cavanaugh's work for its failure to articulate this ambivalence about the state in a sustained manner, see Matthew A. Shadle, "Cavanaugh on the Church and the Modern State: An Appraisal," *Horizons* 37, no. 2 (2010).

104. For an overview, see Calvez and Perrin, *Church and Social Justice*, 214–17.

105. Pius XI, *Quadragesimo Anno*, no. 47.

that states must tolerate those who abuse or even destroy their property. Such misuse, while clearly morally problematic, is unenforceable by the state. As far as positive law goes, ownership of property does not depend upon the use that is made of it.[106]

By way of example, consider a group of landowners in El Salvador who, in the midst of rampant landlessness and pervasive hunger, possess estates so extensive that they decide to leave some land idle or to cultivate crops for export with such intensity that the practice of doing so degrades and exhausts the soil. It would seem that Pius's response would be that they clearly misuse their land and neglect property's social function. But they do not forfeit their right to property, and the state should not compel them to relinquish their lands on behalf of those who need them. Although a scandalous situation clearly exists, the state has no direct role in redressing the situation. Human law, he might respond, cannot uproot all evil.[107]

Instead of state action, Pius seems to favor responding to the scandal by way of the catechetical power and moral suasion of the church itself. He praises those who, while preserving "the integrity of the traditional teaching of the Church," take it upon themselves to live in "the inner nature of these duties and their limits whereby either the right of property itself or its use, that is, the exercise of ownership, is circumscribed by the necessities of social living."[108] In other words, while the state and its laws should not compel landowners to relinquish their lands, the church might convince its landowning members to do so of their own volition. Presumably, someone like Enrique Álvarez Córdova fits the description. Álvarez, a wealthy Salvadoran landowner from a prominent family, who served as vice minister and minister of agriculture under three different administrations, enacted a land reform on his family's farm, El Jobo. After training the farm's workers, Álvarez handed over management and ownership of the farm to them through a cooperative structure. His ef-

---

106. According to Habiger, this is the position of both Leo and Pius XI; Habiger, *Papal Teaching on Private Property*, 79. However, the position of Pius XII and his successors differ, all of whom share a sense that non-use and even misuse can negate the right and that property can be lawfully taken away from its possessors in certain circumstances.

107. See Thomas Aquinas, *ST* I-II, q. 96, a. 2.

108. Pius XI, *Quadragesimo Anno*, no. 48.

forts to realize a just polity involved his own family and the way it held its lands, apart from any compulsion by the state.[109] The Salvadoran bishops responded in a similar fashion to the 1969 war between El Salvador and Honduras that sent thousands of undocumented Salvadoran immigrants in Honduras streaming back into El Salvador. The bishops did not propose that the state expropriate and redistribute land but that church members voluntarily hand over land, capital, and equipment and that they lay these at the church's feet to be distributed to *campesino* families as they had need.[110]

However, later in *Quadragesimo Anno*, Pius XI's position seems to shift subtly. When he turns to the role of the state in the determination of the common good, Pius's language suggests a much more involved role in the realization of property's social function. For instance, after commenting upon the injustice of burdensome taxation schemes, Pius goes on to write:

> Yet when the State brings private ownership into harmony with the needs of the common good, it does not commit a hostile act against private owners but rather does them a friendly service; for it thereby effectively prevents the private possession of goods … from causing intolerable evils and thus rushing to its own destruction; it does not destroy private possessions, but safeguards them; and it does not weaken private property rights, but strengthens them.[111]

The immediate context for this passage is a discussion of taxation, but Pius's words suggest a much broader application.[112] Given the freedom Pius grants to the state in the determination of the common good, potential applications extend beyond taxation to include (possibly) expropriating and redistributing land. Although Pius does not explicitly advocate land

---

109. John W. Lamperti, *Enrique Alvarez Córdova* (Jefferson, N.C: McFarland, 2006), 121–45.

110. Conferencia Episcopal de El Salvador, "Llamamiento del Episcopado Salvadoreño en nombre del país," *Estudios Centroamericanos* 254–55 (1969). The allusion being drawn to Acts 4:33–35 is mine, though it is consistent with the document's message. Instead of Acts, the bishops frame their appeal in terms of the Beatitudes and peacemaking (Mt 5:9).

111. Pius XI, *Quadragesimo Anno*, no. 49.

112. Habiger, for instance, thinks it includes placing limits upon the amount of property people own; see Habiger, *Papal Teaching on Private Property*, 83.

reform, the language of harmonizing private property with the common good and helping property fulfill its purpose in support of life certainly suggests this possibility.

According to Pius, states clearly have a role to play in the politics of common use, but that role as it relates to land reform is unclear. What is clear is that Pius's language undermines any construal of property as essentially private, whose social character is an extrinsic feature of it. On Pius's terms, in taxing or otherwise seeking to harmonize ownership with the common good, the state safeguards and strengthens ownership. The state is not a threatening, alien presence, stealing what others have rightfully earned. Rather, the state helps property to be what it is, which is given by God for common use. We can even say that private property in the Blackstonian sense of sole and despotic dominion—not state action—is the real hostile act in response to God's gift of creation, the gravest threat to common use. For Pius, capitalism's practice of private property causes "intolerable evils" and tends toward its own "destruction." As a result, state involvement in pursuing the common good is necessary.

Regarding *Quadragesimo Anno*, questions certainly remain about the state's role in facilitating property's social function, which the encyclical does not fully resolve. Less than ten years later, however, Pius XII assumes the papacy, and we have seen how he endorses land reform as one tool among others to favor ownership. Subsequent social teaching follows him, and in the remainder of this chapter, we examine the two most important passages in it on land reform at the time Romero was archbishop. The first is from *Gaudium et Spes* (1965), and the second is from Paul VI's encyclical *Populorum Progressio* (1967). Of course, social teaching contains many other important discussions of this topic—in Medellín and Puebla, as well as in numerous statements by episcopal conferences. But for the most part, these other discussions simply reiterate the key passages from *Gaudium et Spes* and *Populorum Progressio*.[113]

We have repeatedly returned to *Gaudium et Spes*, no. 69, which foregrounds the axiom that creation is common gift, described in terms of

---

113. For the relevant passages in *Medellín*, see "Justicia" 1.3, 3.14; "Paz" 2.16. For the relevant passages in *Puebla*, see John Paul II, *Address at the Opening of the Third General Conference of the Latin American Bishops*; *Puebla*, 2.2.35, 2.4.68, 4.2.1263.

the universal or common destination of created goods. In its articulation of the politics of common use, the Pastoral Constitution begins with the participation of particular persons in this politics, especially through the work of mercy. Under the guidance of justice and with the help of charity, people must learn to regard what they possess as common, given for their good and for the good of others. Moreover, in terms of articulation of the politics of common use, *Gaudium et Spes*, no. 69, not only focuses on the obligations of those with the world's goods, but also on the prerogatives of those without them in its invocation of the law of necessity.

After this passage, *Gaudium et Spes* goes on to discuss land reform. The prime example of the failure to heed property's common destination is found in situations where there are

> large or even extensive rural estates which are only slightly cultivated or lie completely idle for the sake of profit, while the majority of the people either are without land or have only very small fields, and, on the other hand, it is evidently urgent to increase the productivity of the fields. Not infrequently those who are hired to work for the landowners or who till a portion of the land as tenants receive a wage or income unworthy of a human being, lack decent housing, and are exploited by middlemen. Deprived of all security, they live under such personal servitude that almost every opportunity of acting on their own initiative and responsibility is denied to them and all advancement in human culture and all sharing in social and political life is forbidden to them. According to the different cases, therefore, reforms are necessary: that income may grow, working conditions should be improved, security in employment increased, and an incentive to working on one's own initiative given. Indeed, insufficiently cultivated estates should be distributed to those who can make these lands fruitful; in this case, the necessary things and means, especially educational aids and the right facilities for co-operative organization, must be supplied. Whenever, nevertheless, the common good requires expropriation, compensation must be reckoned in equity after all the circumstances have been weighed.[114]

---

114. Vatican Council II, *Gaudium et Spes*, no. 71.

The passage indicates that the main problems with these landholdings are their size and lack of cultivation. Those who hold them possess land in vast excess of their needs, which they use for the sake of private profit or fail to use at all. At the same time, others lack access to land to farm altogether or they possess insufficient land to meet their needs. Moreover, wage work, with its meager remuneration and degrading conditions, does not offer them hope of obtaining land or, for that matter, any possible path out of their predicament. Like *Rerum Novarum*, *Gaudium et Spes* associates this lack of access to property in land and injustice in wages and working conditions with lack of protection and agency—a situation that renders workers particularly vulnerable to exploitation. This passage was written over seven decades after *Rerum Novarum* and addresses rural rather than urban conditions, but the workers under consideration are in the same position as those described by Leo. They are surrendered, isolated, and helpless; with little in the way of protection; and with little hope of ever acquiring a share in the land they work. Once again, landlessness is intimate with other, more insidious forms of social exclusion, for according to the Pastoral Constitution, landlessness produces a people for whom "all sharing in social and political life is forbidden."

One conclusion of *Gaudium et Spes* is that the productivity of idle or insufficiently used lands should be increased. But observe carefully how the path to the increased productivity it proposes is not the application of the latest agricultural technology, nor is it planting fields from fencerow to fencerow. Rather, the path to increased productivity is primarily through the distribution of land to those who presently lack access to it but who are willing to work it. "Indeed, insufficiently cultivated estates should be distributed to those who can make these lands fruitful." Implicit here is Pius XII's critique of productivism, which we discussed earlier. Because of agriculture's centrality to the politics of common use, the common good involves not only producing more, but producing more for the common good by increasing people's access to land.

What is especially important to see is that *Gaudium et Spes*'s call for the diffusion of property takes as its point of departure the participation of particular persons in the politics of common use through the work of mercy, which is the lifeblood of this politics. But the specific tasks enumerated in no. 71—income growth, improvements in working conditions, increased security in employment, better incentives, educational aids, the facilitation of cooperative organization, and the distribution of idle or insufficiently cultivated landholdings—also involve the state in the politics of common use, enacting laws and policies that favor ownership and securing the path from work to possession of productive property. Ultimately, however, the success of land reform and these other measures depends upon much more than the state. And their aim is not simply to enable the landless or land-poor to access land, but also to access other goods from which they are excluded, to foster fuller sharing in social and political life.

The second important passage about land reform in Catholic social teaching is from *Populorum Progressio*, which explicitly patterns itself upon *Gaudium et Spes*, nos. 69–71, in locating its discussion within a larger account of the common destination of created goods. The passage begins by stating that "all other rights, whatever they may be, including the rights of property and free trade, are to be subordinated to [the common destination of created goods]. They should in no way hinder it; in fact, they should actively facilitate its implementation," for common use is their "original purpose."[115]

In concretizing the implications of this understanding of property and possession, Paul VI, like the Pastoral Constitution, begins with the work of mercy:

> "He who has the goods of this world and sees his brother in need and closes his heart to him, how does the love of God abide in him?" [1 John 3:17] Everyone knows that the Fathers of the Church laid down the duty of the rich toward the poor in no uncertain terms. As St. Ambrose put it: "You are not making a gift of what is yours to the poor man, but you are giving him back what is his. You have been appropriating things that are meant to be for the common use of everyone. The earth belongs to everyone, not to the rich." [*On Naboth*, 12.53] These words indicate that the right to private property is not absolute and unconditional. No one may

---

115. Paul VI, *Populorum Progressio*, no. 22.

appropriate surplus goods solely for his own private use when others lack the bare necessities of life.[116]

The verse from 1 John states that when those with the world's goods distance themselves from those without them, they distance themselves from God's love. Among other reasons, this is because in distancing themselves from those in need, they withdraw from God's purpose for creation, which is the nourishment of all people. As Ambrose puts it here, they appropriate for themselves alone what God gives for common use. The problem Paul VI identifies in this passage therefore has to do both with the excess of the goods and the exclusivity with which they are held, an understanding of private property he calls "absolute and unconditional," with clear Blackstonian overtones. People who have the world's goods and yet close their hearts to those in need possess what belongs to others. They keep for themselves what God wishes to grow for the many through them. In this way, they withdraw not only from God's purpose for creation, but also from God's work in gathering what has been scattered by sin, especially those who have been made strangers to one another because of disparities in the possession of property.

According to *Populorum Progressio*, there will be situations in which conflicts arise between the property rights secured by positive law and the needs of communities themselves. In such situations, the encyclical envisions states playing an indispensable role in adjudicating the conflicts, the success of which will depend upon "the active involvement of citizens and social groups."[117] Just as in *Gaudium et Spes*, the single example given of such a conflict is the following: "If certain landed estates impede the general prosperity because they are extensive, unused or poorly used, or because they bring hardship to peoples or are detrimental to the interests of the country, the common good sometimes demands their expropriation."[118] Once again, these landed estates or *latifundia* exemplify how private property can go awry, claiming for itself absolute and un-

116. Paul VI, *Populorum Progressio*, no. 23.
117. Paul VI, *Populorum Progressio*, no. 24.
118. Paul VI, *Populorum Progressio*, no. 25.

conditional rights and refusing to subordinate itself to God's purposes for creation. Especially important in the passage from *Populorum Progressio* is the expansion of the criteria according to which expropriation is deemed a legitimate action on the part of states. While *Gaudium et Spes* poses the problem principally in terms of size and insufficient cultivation, *Populorum Progressio* cites yet additional grounds for appropriation: the poor use of the land, the impoverishment of the inhabitants, and even the harm *latifundia* cause to the country—all of which suppress property's social function.[119]

Gaudium et Spes and *Populorum Progressio*'s contention that there are times when state action is necessary in order to address property conflicts and to facilitate property's social function is an outworking of subsidiarity, a principle in social teaching that coordinates a plurality of societies in relation to one another.[120] Positively formulated, subsidiarity means that there are times when some societies must give assistance (*subsidium*) to others.[121] In the case of land reform, assistance is from the state in the form of an expropriation and redistribution of land on behalf of landless or land-poor families. Negatively formulated, subsidiarity requires that the assistance provided should seek to preserve and build up the recipient societies, never doing for them what they can do for themselves.[122] Regarding land reform, the purpose of the assistance is not to supplant the work of these societies but to help them make provision

---

119. In *Populorum Progressio*, Paul VI writes that *Gaudium et Spes* "affirms [these criteria] emphatically" (no. 24). Perhaps this is the spirit of the text, but it is certainly not its letter. The difference between *Gaudium et Spes* and *Populorum Progressio* was not lost on the church's representatives in the National Land Reform Congress in El Salvador in 1970; see Asamblea Legislativa, *Memoria del primer congreso nacional de reforma agraria*, 178–79.

120. Commentators often articulate subsidiarity in terms of devolution—namely, that judgments, actions, and decisions should be performed at the lowest possible level—and usually privilege the private initiative of individuals. But this is a misunderstanding. Subsidiarity concerns not the *lowest* level but the *proper* level, and it applies not so much to *individuals* as to *societies* and how they stand in relation to one another and to the state.

121. The *Compendium of the Social Doctrine of the Church* puts the matter this way: "Various circumstances may make it advisable that the State step in to supply certain functions.... One may [for instance]... envision the reality of serious imbalance or injustice where only the intervention of the public authority can create conditions of greater equality, justice and peace" (no. 188).

122. Pius XII, *Discourse to Commemorate the 50th Anniversary of the Encyclical "Rerum Novarum" of Pope Leo XIII on the Social Question*, 223.

for themselves and others. The purpose is to reestablish the conditions under which property can fulfill its social function within the life of the societies involved—conditions that benefit both the recipient societies and those whose lands have been expropriated. The common good, after all, can only be held in common, and the expropriation of part of their land might be the only way for some owners to discover what sharing in such a good involves.

Subsidiarity also implies a recognition that some forms of assistance do more harm than good.[123] In terms of land reform, state involvement in the expropriation and redistribution of land on a large scale not only might leave the problem prompting the involvement unresolved, but even exacerbate it.[124] As we will see in chapter 4, in the months prior to his murder, one of Romero's main concerns was how factions in the military and their government allies were harnessing the land reform order to militarize the countryside and to surveil and repress opponents.[125] It became increasingly clear to Romero that the land reform was deepening the injustice rather than helping to uproot it. The case of Romero's El Salvador therefore raises important questions and concerns about land reform as an outworking of subsidiarity and how such assistance can harm the societies it is supposed to benefit.

With respect to church teaching on land reform, there is a final implication of subsidiarity that deserves comment. Critics of land reform like those Ederer mentions frequently articulate their opposition on the basis of a defense of absolute property in the Blackstonian sense. Relatedly, they tend to see the state as a hostile actor, unjustly depriving private owners of what is rightfully theirs. However, at least in terms of social teaching, this understanding is misguided. For the crucial issue according to social teaching is not that the state infringes upon private property but that so many people have. Too many have failed to regard

---

123. Barrera makes this point regarding agricultural policy and the effects of the "anti-rural bias of the import-substitution strategy" in his insightful analysis of *Mater et Magistra*; see Barrera, *Modern Catholic Social Documents and Political Economy*, 15–33.

124. For extensive discussion of this issue, see James C. Scott, *Seeing Like a State: Why Certain Schemes to Improve the Human Condition Have Failed* (New Haven, Conn.: Yale University Press, 1988).

125. See Romero, *Homilías*, 6:383–85.

their possessions as given for common use and have kept what God wants to grow for the many through them. The ongoing accumulation of these ordinary infringements—the daily dispossessions of the Naboths of the world from their lands, the great piling up of wreckage upon wreckage—has generated the pressure for which land reform functions like a release valve. In its call for land reform, social teaching appeals to the state to play this particular role in the politics of common use because so many people and societies have failed to play theirs.

Many unanswered questions remain regarding the state's role in the reform of agriculture. But this discussion makes plain that the implementation of the politics of common use is not exclusively or primarily the task of the state but is the common work of all people. From this vantage, the state's involvement in expropriating and redistributing land is perhaps best understood by Christians as a limited and insufficient response to a widespread and collective societal failure, to a reality that church members must face and even embrace with weeping and mourning, sackcloth and ashes.

In this chapter and in chapter 2, we have explored the moral and theological landscape within which the call for land reform emerges in Catholic social teaching in order to show that it is not an incongruous feature of this landscape. Along the way, we have seen how the theological grammar of creation as common gift shapes social teaching's approach to property and possession, which has implications for a host of other issues.

The end of this chapter examined land reform itself, attending closely to the role of states in the expropriation and redistribution of land. There we saw that while the politics of common use implicates states, it is not state-centered. Rather, such a politics centers upon how persons, households, and societies acknowledge and pursue the common good by managing possessions as common and facilitating the access of others to them. Consequently, to fixate exclusively upon the state and its action of expropriating and redistributing land misconstrues social teaching's articulation of the politics of common use by giving the mistaken impression that such a politics is state-centered when it is not. There is no politics of common use without commoners.[126] All this is especially evident in *Gaudium et Spes* and *Populorum Progressio*, which place land reform within this wider framework. Both documents underscore the imperative that persons and households regard what they have as common. They also convey the fact that the support of the common good at times requires land reform. Neither document envisions common use either exclusively or even primarily through state action. My own presentation of land reform in these pages has followed suit.

Understood in these terms, social teaching's call for land reform represents far more than an exercise in the expropriation and redistribution of land through the agency of the state. Rather, land reform has most fundamentally to do with the way the church catechizes—or fails to catechize—the faithful to acknowledge that God's gift of creation is a common one, which should lead them to use what they have been given—including their very selves—to build up the life of the societies of which they are members. Land reform opens out into this more expansive politics of common use, in which the call for the reform of agriculture is inseparable from the reform of persons and societies more generally. As we will see, for Romero the society of central concern is the church, a body in need of continual reformation to be what it is.[127]

---

126. Along these lines, the Jesuit economist Bernard W. Dempsey critiques the notion that "common use is attained only through state action"; Dempsey, *The Functional Economy: The Bases of Economic Organization* (Englewood Cliffs, N.J.: Prentice-Hall, 1958), 183.

127. The phrase "continual reformation" (*perennem reformationem*) comes from the Second Vatican Council's decree on ecumenism, *Unitatis Redintegratio*, nos. 6, 4; see also *Lumen Gentium*, no. 7, and *Gaudium et Spes*, no. 21. Romero discusses this matter, among other places, in Romero, *Homilías*, 2:227; 5:360; Romero, *La Iglesia, cuerpo de Cristo en la historia*, 74–75; Romero, *Misión de la Iglesia en medio de la crisis del país*, 22.

–4–

THE LAND OF THE SAVIOR

Like Moses, the ministry that has been entrusted to me is that of
leading the people to the promised land.

—Óscar Romero, *Letter to Ernestina R.*

This chapter returns to Romero's El Salvador to continue the task initiated in chapter 1. There we looked at the production of landlessness in the wake of the enclosure legislation and Romero's depiction of lack of land to farm as a form of violence from which the Salvadoran people need defense. The chapter offered a brief historical narrative of the concentration of land and wealth in El Salvador, and it suggested, without examining in detail, how land reform became one particularly salient response on the part of the church to this concentration and the associated ordinary violence. The intervening chapters have prepared us to appreciate this response further, its grounding in Catholic social teaching, and its theological import. The purpose of the present chapter is to continue to examine the societal and ecclesial conflict about land reform in El Salvador and especially how social teaching was Romero's primary point of reference in advocating for justice in the distribution of land.

An important lesson to be drawn from chapters 2 and 3 is that the call for land reform arises out of a much wider set of concerns regarding the common destination of created goods. It is one part of a politics of common use, which implicates states but centers upon how all peoples learn to acknowledge creation as a common gift and use what they possess to build up the societies of which they are members. As we will see in this chapter, for Romero, the society with which he is most preoccupied is the church, Christ's ecclesial body. The process whereby its earthly members learn to acknowledge and use creation in this way speaks to the church's pilgrim character and how it is still undergoing continual reformation on earth as its members learn to anticipate life in the land of their destiny: the common life of God in Christ. Ultimately, Romero reads the struggle for land reform in El Salvador in relation to the heavenly life that Christians hold in hope, the life for which Christ liberates them.

Our examination of social teaching has also enabled us to understand why land reform as well as the defense of workers' associations and organizations were so important for Romero as archbishop. For the itinerary Romero sets for the pilgrim church in El Salvador traverses the same moral and theological landscape we have been exploring in chapters 2 and 3. But what will additionally become apparent is the cost of practicing the politics of common use—a topic that has received considerably less attention by social teaching itself. In El Salvador, the church's support for land reform and its role in rural organizing were among the main sources of the repression that led to Romero's death and plunged El Salvador into civil war. Romero himself is witness to how, in his words, "by defending this line of the archdiocese [in support of land reform], which is the line of the Church, those who have identified themselves with it have suffered and will continue to suffer."[1] The issue Romero identifies here is certainly implied by the language of justice guiding and of charity helping the goods

---

1. Romero, *Homilías*, 6:72. The link between land reform and repression can be seen in many high-profile assassinations during this period besides Romero's. For instance, Enrique Álvarez Córdova (examined briefly in chapter 3) was killed in November 1980. Michael Hammer and Mark Pearlman, two land reform experts from the United States, were also killed, along with José Rodolfo Viera, the president of El Salvador's Institute for Agrarian Transformation (ISTA), in January 1981; Lamperti, *Enrique Álvarez Córdova*; "The Sheraton Murder Case," *New York Times*, September 6, 1981.

created by God to reach all people, for charity, especially its work of mercy, presupposes sin and violence. But the fact that this violence so often targets practitioners of the politics of common use—particularly advocates of land reform like Romero—is seldom reflected upon by social teaching.[2] However, as Gutiérrez observes in reference to Romero and countless others like him, "In contemporary Latin America, supporting the defense of the right of the poor to life easily leads to suffering and even death."[3] At the heart of our consideration in chapters 4 and 5 is therefore the persecution of practitioners of the politics of common use and its theological significance.

Close readings of two of Romero's homilies—from December 16, 1979, and March 16, 1980—frame the present chapter. Romero was killed on March 24, 1980, so these homilies also frame Romero's final months. These months also mark a crucial period in Salvadoran history for other reasons. In December 1979, the government announced and began to implement in March 1980 a massive, nationwide land reform. Rafael Menjívar Ochoa refers to the fifteen months from October 1979 to the onset of civil war in January 1981 as *los tiempos de locura* (the times of madness), "the most convulsive period in the history of El Salvador."[4] Romero discusses the land reform at length in these two homilies, which together constitute his most sustained treatments of the topic in his homiletical and literary corpus. Consideration of these homilies therefore helps bring into focus the relationship between the reform, the escalation of violence, and the reasons for Romero's death.

Another important feature of these two homilies is that they are delivered during the Advent and Lenten seasons, respectively. These are times when the church prepares to celebrate the central mysteries of the Christian faith: the nativity of God in Christ and his crucifixion, death,

2. The *Compendium of the Social Doctrine of the Church* alludes to situations in which human authority makes itself a "deity" and demands "absolute submission," and how the peaceful resistance of the martyrs witnesses to the victory of Christ (nos. 515, 570). But the frequency of the abuse, the multitude of the martyrs, and its implications for social teaching are underexamined. This topic is explored at greater length in Whelan, "Jesus Is the Jubilee."

3. Gutiérrez, *Beber en su propio pozo: En el itinerario espiritual de un pueblo* (Salamanca: Ediciones Sigueme, 2007), 154.

4. Rafael Menjívar Ochoa, *Tiempos de locura, El Salvador 1979–1981* (San Salvador: FLASCO-Programa, 2006), 13.

and resurrection on the third day. My treatment of these homilies attends to how Romero reads the land reform liturgically, especially regarding the moral implications of sharing in Christ's life and the disciplines required for his people to be Christ's witnesses in the world. As we will see, the heart of Romero's concerns in these homilies is how church members should welcome the reform with lament and repentance; how their embrace of it can prepare them to participate more fully in the celebration of Christmas and Easter; and finally, what it can reveal to them about the land they share in Christ, toward which they are on pilgrimage.

"GOD BRINGS THE JOY OF SALVATION TO ALL PEOPLE, LET US BE CONVERTED"

In his December 16, 1979, homily, "God Brings the Joy of Salvation to All People, Let Us Be Converted," Romero comments, "Without a doubt, the central event this week … has been the announcement of the land reform. This promise has awoken great hope among the majority of the population: those who work the land; but it has also generated fear and even aggression among the powerful but small minority: the great *latifundistas*."[5]

On October 15, 1979, a coup d'état organized by junior army officers toppled the government of General Carlos Humberto Romero and brought reformist civilians into the government for the first time in almost five decades. The young military officers behind the coup warned the archbishop in advance. With the coup's success, and with civilians like Román Mayorga—president of the UCA and advisor to Romero—integrated into the new government, Romero was cautiously optimistic.[6]

Combining military and civilian leadership, the Junta Revolucionaria de Gobierno (Revolutionary Government Junta, JRG) promised reform and an end to the repression.[7] The group's *Proclama* (Proclamation) begins with these words: "The social political situation in El Salvador is ex-

5. Romero, *Homilías*, 6:69. See "Presentación del Ministro de Agricultura y Ganadería, Enrique Álvarez Córdova, en la cadena de radio y televisión," *La Prensa Gráfica*, December 14, 1979.

6. See Romero, *Diario*, 273–74; Brockman, *Romero*, 200–202.

7. The JRG's initial members were colonels Adolfo Arnaldo Majano Ramos and Jaime Abdul Gutiérrez Avendaño, along with three civilians, Guillermo Ungo, Mario Antonio Andino, and Román Mayorga Quirós.

tremely critical because of the inadequate structures of national income and land tenancy. These grave circumstances are the true origin of the dissatisfaction of the multitude." Of the numerous reform measures proposed by the JRG, land reform is the most important: "There will be initiated a program of land reform, whose purpose is to give the multitude of *campesinos* access to land." The reform will target idle and unproductive land, as well as the *latifundia*, and it will facilitate access to land, credit, and technical assistance, and establish cooperative associations. The purpose of the reform, the *Proclama* declares, is for the land of El Salvador to fulfill "a social function."[8]

In the months both preceding and following the coup, Romero met on numerous occasions with those involved in planning the land reform and with other stakeholders: *campesino* groups,[9] the minister of agriculture and other government officials,[10] the members of the JRG,[11] and technical specialists in land reform from the United States.[12] All of them called upon Romero to mediate and offer leadership and especially to evaluate the reform in light of "Christian social doctrine," as Romero puts it in his diary.[13] In this regard, he sought the counsel of Ignacio Ellacuría and Ricardo Urioste, among many others.[14]

On December 7, 1979, the JRG passed Decree 43, which froze large land transactions, the preliminary step in the implementation of the reform. The purpose was to prevent what had happened repeatedly in the past: landowners titling their holdings to family and friends to avoid relinquishing them. Enrique Álvarez Córdova, whom we briefly encountered in chapter 3, was the minister of agriculture at the time, and he

---

8. Primera Junta Revolucionaria del Gobierno, *Proclama del 15 de octubre 1979*; typed copy in possession of author. See also Rodrigo Guerra y Guerra, *Un golpe al amanecer: La verdadera historia de la Proclama del 15 de octubre 1979* (San Salvador: Índole Editores, 2009), 58–59. On the influence of the UCA on the reform movement, see William Stanley, *The Protection Racket State: Elite Politics, Military Extortion, and Civil War in El Salvador* (Philadelphia: Temple University Press, 1996), 4–5.

9. Romero, *Diario*, 198–99.

10. Romero, *Diario*, 392, 409–10, 413–17.

11. Romero, *Diario*, 413–14, 426–29.

12. Romero, *Diario*, 409–10, 412–13.

13. Romero, *Diario*, 391–94.

14. Romero, *Diario*, 402, 413–14.

went on television to sketch the plan. A week later the JRG nationalized control of coffee and sugar exports.[15]

In his homily on December 16, the third Sunday of Advent, Romero reflects at length on the theological significance of the land reform. Advent is a time in which Christians prepare for the coming of God's kingdom in Christ, to receive him anew liturgically in the Feast of the Nativity. Although God reveals Godself in the "eloquence" of the created order, Romero says, God's revelation of Godself in Christ is infinitely more "intimate." For in Christ is the fullness of God. And God sends Christ to free creation from sin and to liberate humankind to share more fully in God's life.[16] In this way, the incarnation implicates the end for which humankind was created. It is part of what Romero calls "God's project of salvation for all people," in which God calls humankind to collaborate.[17] This discussion of creation and its restoration in Christ becomes the theological framework within which Romero situates his commentary upon the JRG's announcement of land reform.

Throughout the homily, Romero uses the language of liberation to describe the advent of Christ, and among Romero's questions in this homily, like in his funeral homily for Rutilio Grande, is how "to incorporate the struggle of our people" into "the great liberation of Christ."[18] In the funeral homily, Romero's response is to affirm the church's solidarity with the struggle for liberation, while also arguing that the church is distinct from the struggle, because the church aims to elevate and transfigure it in the light of Christ. The basis of the church's solidarity is the promotion of human dignity, while the basis of its distinction is the gospel's transcendent end of eternal sharing in God's life. What the church most offers the struggle, Romero therefore contends, are liberators like Grande, who have been made new by the liberation of Christ and who can help

---

15. Enrique A. Baloyra, *El Salvador in Transition* (Chapel Hill: University of North Carolina Press, 1982), 91.

16. Romero, *Homilías*, 6:53. Romero quotes *Dei Verbum*, the Dogmatic Constitution on Divine Revelation, to describe such liberation: "God is with us to free us from the darkness of sin and death, and to raise us up to life eternal" (no. 4).

17. Romero, *Homilías*, 6:51–52.

18. Romero, *Homilías*, 6:56.

locate the struggle for liberation in the lands of Latin America in relationship to the heavenly land humankind receives in Christ.

As Romero puts the point in one of his final homilies, the path of Christ's liberation "passes through the cross and through Calvary," but ends "beyond history." This does not mean, however, that Christians are "alienated" from history or its struggles for liberation. Rather, in faith, they perceive their "definitive meaning." "From the day Christ rose," Romero says, "a light of eternity began to shine within history," such that people can engage these struggles with the hope that "Christ lives and that those who work with him will live eternally."[19] It is "through their faith in the resurrection of Jesus Christ" that Christian liberators like Grande "do not fear suffering" and "embrace the cross … like Mary did, who, in her poverty and suffering, knew how to say: 'He has sent the rich away empty and filled the lowly with good things. He has removed the powerful from their thrones whenever they become idolaters of their own power' [see Lk 1:52–53]."[20] In these claims, Romero is articulating what Margaret Pfeil refers to as his "theology of transfiguration."[21]

Romero speaks of liberation in similar terms in the December 16 homily, calling on those who have been made new in Christ to transfigure the popular organizations that are clamoring for liberation from within, like "yeast" leavens bread, "giving faith to the liberating forces of the world." This, Romero thinks, is how the struggle for liberation in El Salvador will be incorporated into the great liberation of Christ, suggesting a changed struggle as a result of the incorporation.[22] Romero's point is that those involved in this struggle must carefully discern the kind of

19. Romero, *Homilías*, 6:348.

20. Romero, *Homilías*, 6:349.

21. According to Pfeil, this theology of transfiguration stems from three interlocking theological commitments: first, an eschatological understanding of Salvadoran history and its integration into salvation history; second, an ecclesiology of the people of God on pilgrimage in El Salvador as Christ's ecclesial body; and third, an acknowledgment of the moral implications of Jesus' invitation to his disciples to follow him on the road to Jerusalem and to Calvary. Pfeil argues that these commitments inform Romero's whole homiletical and pastoral practice; Margaret R. Pfeil, "Óscar Romero's Theology of Transfiguration," *Theological Studies* 72 (2011): 89. See also Colón-Emeric, *Óscar Romero's Theological Vision*.

22. Romero, *Homilías*, 6:56.

justice for which they hunger and thirst and that the Christian pursuit of justice is above all for the justice of the kingdom of God.[23]

Romero therefore warns that Christian liberation cannot be conflated with "revolutionary attitudes that do not believe in God." What distinguishes these visions of liberation is neither the identification of injustice nor the struggle against it but the differences in their respective hopes and how those differences shapes their struggles—among other ways, in terms of whether they embrace violence or the cross. For the revolutionary, Romero says, has abandoned Mary's hope. Mary, too, belonged to an oppressed people, but she hopes in the God who brings down the powerful and lifts up the lowly, who satisfies the hungry and sends away the wealthy—a hope made flesh in Christ. In contrast, Romero thinks some liberators in El Salvador have located their hope exclusively in "concrete projects of the earth," forfeiting hope's heavenly "horizons."[24] However, while Romero is critical of earthbound visions of liberation, he does not dismiss them, and he takes the justice of their demands with absolute seriousness. Such liberators might have a limited and imperfect grasp of the liberation Christ brings, but it is a sign of the fullness of Christ's liberation that even what is limited and imperfect can be incorporated into it and transfigured by it.

All of this is important for understanding how Romero approaches the JRG's land reform, which is a concrete project of the earth. The first thing to notice is that Romero claims no competence with respect to the specifics of the project, nor does he discuss its details. "That is not up to me; I'm not a technician," he says. "But it is my duty to speak as a pastor regarding God's plan for the goods of the earth."[25] In light of God's plan, Romero thinks the vast disparities in land and wealth that characterize

23. Romero, *Homilías*, 3:150.

24. Romero, *Homilías*, 6:55–56.

25. Romero, *Homilías*, 6:69. The distinction between pastor and technician is not a distinction between the church's role and the state's role or between souls and bodies. In this case, it is an intra-ecclesial distinction regarding competencies within the church. Romero's view is that he is a pastor, and that it is not his job to specify exactly how a land reform must proceed. As he says elsewhere, "The language and attitude of the Church do not invade technical and political fields." But a refusal to invade is not the same as a refusal to engage or to guide. The distinction is intra-ecclesial because Romero assumes that it is the role of

his country should lead to lament and to repentance as well as to efforts, like the reform, to address the injustice. But while the path of repentance passes through such reform—along with other measures to address the disparities and to help facilitate common use—the path does not end there. Romero's purpose in the homily is therefore to locate the reform within this much more expansive moral and theological landscape within which the people of God in El Salvador are on pilgrimage.

God calls humankind to collaborate in the project of salvation centered in Christ, and Romero identifies this collaboration with "conversion toward God."[26] The gospel passage for the day is from Luke, in which John the Baptist cries out in the wilderness about repentance, and the need, in Isaiah's words, to prepare for the coming of the Lord—to straighten paths that are crooked, to smooth rough ways (Lk 3:3–5; Is 40:3–5). Conversion for Romero names how those who draw near to Christ must undergo preparation to be in his presence, a preparation that is characteristically a process, a path.

According to Romero, "conversion is personal, just as sin is personal." Conversion begins when persons "repent and seek the paths of justice."[27] But because of the kind of creatures humans are, sin cannot be contained in the sinner alone but necessarily ramifies outward, affecting structures, institutions, and landscapes, and causing all of God's good creation to groan. In El Salvador, this groaning can be perceived especially in the concentration of land and wealth, which is a clear sign for Romero that God's plan for the goods of the earth is being resisted. Acknowledgment of this reality, Romero thinks, should instill in Christ's followers a sense of complicity in sin and violence, to which the first and proper response is to embark upon the path that Romero calls conversion.

Conversion as Romero understands it does not substitute for the transformation of structures, institutions, and landscapes, but rather is the indispensable path toward true and lasting transformation of them. For those on this path see how sin ramifies outward, beyond the sinner,

---

baptized, lay Catholics to be involved in the determination of these specifics; see Romero, *Homilías*, 4:501; *Lumen Gentium*, nos. 30–38.

26. Romero, *Homilías*, 6:58.

27. Romero, *Homilías*, 6:60.

affecting structures, institutions, and landscapes. Conversion is therefore never only personal, as it also seeks social renewal. In chapter 1, we saw Romero say that it also tries "to expose the social mechanisms that marginalize workers and *campesinos*." It asks questions like, "Why are *campesinos* only able to earn wages during the harvests of coffee, sugar cane, and cotton? Why does our society need *campesinos* without work, poorly paid workers, and people without just wages?"[28] Christians must learn to ask such questions in order "to avoid being accomplices in this machinery that produces people who are poor, marginalized, destitute" and to work to dismantle it. Here, as elsewhere in his homilies, land reform prompts Romero to reflect upon the reform of people and societies more generally, citing the passage from Medellín about how a new continent will require new structures but above all new people.[29]

Because land concentration signals a failure to live in accordance with God's purpose for creation, conversion also inescapably involves learning to share "the good that God has given for all."[30] Sharing food, drink, shelter, clothing, and similar goods is the primary response to sin's damage to creation that God seeks to foster in creatures. Those with the world's goods must learn to ask themselves why they have wealth while so many of their neighbors do not. Questions like this, Romero says, evidence the work of God's grace; they are "the beginning of conversion."[31] If such questions are like the seed, sharing is the fruit.

As Romero takes up the gospel passage from Luke, the question posed by the crowds to John in the wilderness of Galilee—"What then should we do?" (Lk 3:10)—continues to resound in El Salvador in 1979. Throughout the homily, Romero repeatedly returns to John's first response to the crowds: "Whoever has two coats must share with anyone who has none; and whoever has food must do likewise" (3:11). And as Romero proceeds, he situates the struggle for land reform in his own time and place primarily in relation to this question and John's response. Preparing a straight and smooth path for the advent of the Lord and the coming of

28. Romero, *Homilías*, 6:63.
29. Romero, *Homilías*, 6:63.
30. Romero, *Homilías*, 6:61, 60.
31. Romero, *Homilías*, 6:61.

God's kingdom in the land of El Salvador, Romero argues, above all involves learning to share.

The theological grammar of creation as common gift informing social teaching helps us to appreciate the significance Romero discerns in John's words. Observe, for instance, how John is not saying that people should give away all their coats, but rather that they set out on the path to encounter Christ by keeping one of them and giving the others away. The point is not for people to neglect their own needs, but rather to discern their true needs—especially what they possess in excess of them. It is also to learn to see this excess primarily in relationship to those who lack bodily support. We have previously discussed this in terms of the formation of people whose lives are marked by the twofold movement of taking only what is necessary and giving their surfeit to others. To make the point in John's words, if a person has two coats, she should seek a person without one, and if she has more than enough food, she should go and do likewise.

What we are seeing is how the theological grammar of creation as common gift shapes Romero's understanding of conversion. Conversion for him centers upon people learning to regard their goods as common, which they acknowledge in a willingness to share with those in need, returning what they possess in excess to those to whom it rightfully belongs. The theological rationale informing Romero's view is that as people draw closer to Christ, the one who makes creation new, their lives will necessarily also reflect the common character of creation and how it holds together in and points toward him (see Col 1:15–17).

When people learn to share God's gifts, Romero says, solidarity results. People show solidarity when they refuse to accept that some "have been born to have everything and leave the rest with nothing, while those with nothing are unable to share what God has created for all."[32] Solidarity most basically involves people being united with one another, sharing interests, sympathies, or aspirations in common. As Romero sees it, an essential indication of its presence is the willingness of people to share their possessions and their lives with one another.

A society that learns to share in this way, Romero says, "is the kind

---

32. Romero, *Homilías*, 6:61.

of Christian society that God wants."[33] This is because learning to share not only prepares people to encounter Christ in their brothers and sisters in need, but also because it prepares them for their destiny. Sharing the gifts of creation in the present life is how people learn to live in anticipation of heavenly life. For in the heavenly land toward which they are on pilgrimage, everything that people possess and all that they are is ceaselessly at the service of God and neighbor. The gifts God has given humankind in Christ and in the Spirit—the gifts of God's own life—are likewise common gifts. As Romero puts it in the title of the homily, God gives these gifts for the salvation of all people.

Along these lines, Romero sometimes refers to earthly life as an *antecámara* or antechamber (from the Latin *ante camera* for "the room before"), a smaller room or vestibule that is an entryway into a main one. In one homily, for instance, Romero says, "As the Church hopes for heaven, it does not forget about this earth. It proclaims the need to work and to pay just salaries to workers [and we can also add: to support land reform], in order to make this earth … like an antechamber of that hope, that heaven."[34] In other words, people can prepare for the heavenly life they have in hope by working to make the lands where they live in this world into a clearer image of it. Romero thinks constitutive to this process is enacting land reform and other measures to foster justice in the distribution of land and property. Such measures offer glimpses, in the land of El Salvador, of the heavenly land they receive in Christ.

Romero's discussion of conversion in preparation for the advent of Christ and the coming of God's kingdom is the theological framework within which he situates his commentary upon the announcement of land reform. In the homily, Romero's principal point of reference is Catholic social teaching, which he draws upon to convey why the enactment of land reform is so imperative. "What is the position of the Church in this moment?" he asks, to which his response is a cascade of quotations.[35]

Romero quotes the passage from *Gaudium et Spes*, no. 71, examined

33. Romero, *Homilías*, 6:61.
34. Romero, *Homilías*, 1:459; see Vatican Council II, *Gaudium et Spes*, no. 43.
35. Romero, *Homilías*, 6:69–72.

in chapter 3 about "large or even extensive rural estates which are only slightly cultivated or lie completely idle for the sake of profit, while the majority of the people either are without land or have only very small fields," and about the legitimacy of expropriating such estates in certain circumstances. He then turns to this passage from John Paul II's address to *campesinos* in Oaxaca, Mexico, earlier in 1979, which itself draws on *Populorum Progressio*, nos. 22–24—the latter being the other key passage examined in chapter 3:

> The depressed rural world, the worker who with his sweat waters also his affliction, cannot wait any longer for full and effective recognition of his dignity, which is not inferior to that of any other social sector. He has the right to be respected and not to be deprived, with maneuvers that are sometimes tantamount to real spoliation, of the little that he has. He has the right to be rid of the barriers of exploitation, often made up of intolerable selfishness, against which his best efforts of advancement are shattered. He has the right to real help—which is not charity or crumbs of justice—in order that he may have access to the development that his dignity as a man and as a son of God deserves.
>
> Therefore, it is necessary to act promptly and in depth. It is necessary to carry out bold changes, which are deeply innovatory. It is necessary to undertake urgent reforms without waiting any longer [*Populorum Progressio*, no. 32].
>
> It cannot be forgotten that the measures to be taken must be adequate. The church does indeed defend the legitimate right to private property, but she also teaches no less clearly that there is always a social mortgage on all private property, in order that goods may serve the general purpose that God gave them. And if the common good requires it, there should be no hesitation even at expropriation, carried out in the due form [*Populorum Progressio*, nos. 22–24].[36]

Romero also cites and discusses many other passages from social teaching regarding land reform and its underlying theological rationale—for instance, from Medellín and John Paul's address at Puebla, as well as

---

36. John Paul II, *Address in Cuilapan, Mexico.*

statements from the Honduran and Guatemalan Episcopal Conferences.[37]

The constant reference to and citation of social teaching serve as reminders of the resistance Romero received from a powerful group of Salvadoran Catholics who opposed the church on these matters. This group regarded land reform as a particularly insidious act of thievery that had to be resisted at all costs. Moreover, their resistance took on greater urgency because the thieves were no longer operating in the shadows but under the cover of government.

This cascade of quotations also indicates the extent to which Romero and the archdiocese sought to base their support for and approach to land reform upon social teaching. As Romero says time and time again, the need for land reform to address conditions like those the Salvadoran people suffer is simply "the doctrine of the Church" and that the "position of the archdiocese" is nothing more than an attempt "to apply this general position of the Church."[38] Applying social teaching's call for land reform to El Salvador is among the main ways Romero works to incorporate his people's struggle for liberation into the great liberation of Christ—an indication of how social teaching for him participates in the proclamation of the gospel and how its message embodies an authentic form of liberation theology, to which someone like Grande bears witness.

The fundamental theological conviction articulated by these passages from social teaching is that creation is a gift God gives for all people in common, from which flows the notion that property has an essential and inescapable social function. This social function warrants expropriation of agricultural land in order to enable access to it by the landless and land-poor. The main criteria cited for such expropriation are: the size of the landholdings; their insufficient cultivation; and the presence of so many people who lack access to the land they need to farm. Although Romero does not make the connection explicitly, this understanding of

---

37. *Medellín*, "Justicia," 14; John Paul II, *Address at the Opening of the Third General Conference of the Latin American Bishops*; Conferencia Episcopal de Honduras, *Sobre el desarrollo del campesinado en Honduras*, Tegucigalpa, January 8, 1970; Conferencia Episcopal de Guatemala, *Unidos en la esperanza: La presencia de la Iglesia en la reconstrucción de Guatemala*, Quezaltenango, July 25, 1976.

38. Romero, *Homilías*, 6:69–72.

expropriation similarly expresses the logic of sharing God's gifts of creation—admittedly on a much larger, even societal scale and through the agency of the state. Just as John the Baptist proclaims that whoever has more than enough clothing and food must learn to share it in preparation for the coming of Christ, social teaching contends that the same applies to land and that the state can play a role in the process. Once again, we see how the politics of common use encompasses the interpersonal work of mercy as well as laws and policies like land reform in order to share what God has given to all people.

However, Romero does not see the state as the central actor in the politics of common use. In this regard, we saw in chapter 1 how Romero thinks land reform "from above," by way of the law and policy of the Salvadoran state, responds to what is already happening "from below" in the actions of ordinary people to make ends meet, for instance, by occupying and farming land titled to others. In addition to these spontaneous occupations, there is also an organized and widespread clamoring for such reform. *Campesinos*, rural workers, and the popular organizations, Romero observes, have not been waiting passively for the Salvadoran state to act but have long been advocating for justice in the distribution of land and trying to participate more fully in the economic and political life of their country. In announcing the latest land reform proposal, he therefore observes, the government "did not initiate the process" but has incorporated itself into a process long since initiated by the people of El Salvador.[39] Romero is effectively calling upon the state and the law to address this reality welling up from below.

This is also why the success of the reform for him depends upon the continued active participation of the beneficiaries themselves as well as the involvement of rural workers who have yet to organize.[40] The reform is in no way meant to supplant the work or agency of its beneficiaries. For its purpose, according to Romero, is to preserve, reestablish, and build up

---

39. Romero, *Homilías*, 6:73–74. Romero pleads with *campesinos* and agricultural workers not to be "passive before this decisive plan." Not only must they defend what is theirs and what has been historically denied them, but their engagement and participation in the process of land reform, Romero thinks, are crucial for its very viability.

40. Romero, *Homilías*, 6:76–77.

societies where they have been devastated so that people can make better provision for themselves and others as well as share more fully in the work of their hands and in the life of El Salvador. In short, the purpose of the land reform is much more than a better distribution of land: it is a better distribution of created goods more generally, so that there are also "doctors, schools, hospitals, electricity, and water" for *campesinos*.[41]

We have been examining Romero's emphasis upon sharing as preparation for the advent of the Lord. The underlying theological rationale is that receiving the gift of Christ rightly—the one who comes to make all things new—involves learning to receive the gift of creation rightly. New creation does not destroy but presupposes and perfects the old one.

Toward the conclusion of the homily, Romero directly addresses the "economically powerful" of El Salvador whose lands will be targeted by the reform. He pleads for collaboration rather than resistance, referencing reports that there is an influx of armaments into the country and that groups of mercenaries are forming—an allusion to the death squads linked to security forces and to landowners' associations.[42] "This is not," he tells them, "how one defends well-being."[43] In effect, Romero is urging them to come to terms with the violence in which their lives are enmeshed, particularly their brutal response to the prospect of land reform and related efforts to address the ordinary violence. Because they possess the land that belongs to all, peacemaking necessitates not only that they stop arming themselves and forming death squads, but also that they collaborate in the process of land reform and what it is trying to achieve.

Returning to the gospel passage for the week, Romero urges them to interpret the reform in relation to the words of John the Baptist: "Through the cries of the Salvadoran people, through this attempt at land reform … God is making a call to you this Sunday through the voice of John the Baptist, 'Whoever has two coats must share with anyone who

---

41. Romero, *Homilías*, 6:74, 76.

42. Romero, *Homilías*, 6:74–75. For more on death squads, see Ray Bonner, *Weakness and Deceit: U.S. Policy and El Salvador* (New York: New York Times Books, 1984), 330; Arnson, "Window on the Past," 88.

43. Romero, *Homilías*, 6:74–75.

has none; and whoever has food must do likewise' [Lk 3:11]."[44] God is asking them to share not only their clothing and food, but also their land and wealth, and even their lives.

Like all Christians, the economically powerful must also learn to share in preparation for the coming of the Lord, for this is the way of Christ. "Now is the time," Romero says, "to show yourselves to be generous Christians and love as Christ loved us."[45] That love, Romero continues, is beautifully described by Paul when he speaks of "the generous act of our Lord, Jesus Christ, that though he was rich, yet for your sakes he became poor, so that by his poverty you might become rich" (2 Cor 8:9).[46] In Christ, God gives God's own life as a common gift, for all people to share in its richness—a giving so complete that Christ willingly bears suffering and violence in order to give it. Conformity to this very same manner of giving is the destiny of all members of Christ's body. The path toward that conformity is the grace-filled imitation of the generous act of their Lord, which Romero interprets in terms of Puebla's message of the preferential option for the poor. What emerges as the homily proceeds is the Christological depth of Romero's understanding of this preferential option when read through Matthew 25:31-46. Romero's point is that Christ became poor not just in Christ's own time and place—in Jewish Palestine of the first century. Christ continues to be poor in El Salvador in 1979. In the eschatological parable of the sheep and the goats, Christ identifies so closely with the hunger, thirst, homelessness, nakedness, sickness, and imprisonment of others that he takes on their afflictions and they become his own. "Just as you did it to one of the least of these who are members of my family, you did it to me" (Mt 25:40) is the rule.[47]

Romero therefore contends that all Christians, rich and poor alike, must prepare for the coming of the Lord this advent season by encoun-

---

44. As an exemplification of such sharing, Romero recounts how, upon receiving the Nobel Peace Prize, Mother Teresa requested that the money for the celebration banquet instead be given to the poor of India. Romero asks his listeners to consider her "mind," for which it is an "insult" to spend in a single night what could feed so many people for a year; Romero, *Homilías*, 6:75.

45. Romero, *Homilías*, 6:75.

46. Romero, *Homilías*, 6:75.

47. Romero, *Homilías*, 6:76.

tering Christ where he continues to be present to his people, especially among those without land or work, who are the intended beneficiaries of the reform.[48] For as Romero sees it, to participate in the common life of God in Christ—to be a member of his ecclesial body—involves learning to share, in addition to food, drink, shelter, and clothing with others, life with them as well. In a formulation he frequently uses, Romero says the preferential option for the poor calls all Christians to assume the problems of the poor as if they were their own.[49] In a world suffering from sin and violence, mercy's work of feeding, slaking, welcoming, clothing, tending, and visiting illumines the mysterious contours of the common life God shares with humankind in Christ. Christ's ongoing appeal for mercy among the afflicted is how he builds up in the world a merciful body in his image. This is the basis of Romero's insistence that the preferential option for the poor does not foment class conflict, as his critics contend, but seeks to encounter and care for the Christ who is present in the midst of a violence that already exists and that excludes the many from what God has given for all.[50]

Romero's understanding of the preferential option for the poor has important ecclesial implications, to which he turns at the conclusion of the homily. The pursuit of land reform, which involves the participation of Salvadoran people in a more just distribution of land and wealth, Romero says, should lead the church to examine its own life. The church itself cannot evade the crowd's question to John the Baptist or John's response about sharing.[51] Drawing on Medellín, Romero says that all the church's members—not just the laity, but also the clergy and the religious—must recommit themselves to placing their goods and their lives at the service of others, especially the most needy, "sharing with them not only what is leftover but what is necessary." The church must put property, buildings, and the instruments of work "at the service of the human community."[52] The church itself, in the very visibility of its life in

48. Romero, *Homilías*, 6:75–76.
49. Romero, *Homilías*, 6:76.
50. Romero, *Homilías*, 6:75.
51. Romero, *Homilías*, 6:79.
52. Romero, *Homilías*, 6:79.

the wider world, still needs to be liberated from "the bonds of egotistical possession of temporal goods."[53]

Romero's remarks are brief but important because they reveal how reflection on land reform prompts him to reflect upon the church and the reform of its life. In other words, the struggle for a just distribution of land and wealth in El Salvador becomes an opportunity for Romero to reconsider what the church is and wants to be. Along these same lines—and again following Medellín—Romero speaks of "the poverty of the Church and of its members" as a "sign" of Christ's ongoing presence in the world among the afflicted.[54] Although Romero does not elaborate further, his concern is how, by reforming their use of property and possessions, church members can become a more luminous sign of what they truly are: the ecclesial body of the one who, though rich, became and continues to be poor for the sake of the salvation of all.

Once again, we see how the approach to land reform Romero receives from social teaching cannot be reduced to the state's expropriation and redistribution of land. Land reform signals the need for conversion, which is the heart of Christian life. It speaks to how people must learn to regard created goods as common, which entails using those goods to build up the societies of which they are members by addressing the social injustice that excludes so many from land and from social life. In this regard, Romero is also and especially concerned with the society that is the church. Land reform raises questions for him like, what kind of body is the church? What does it mean to be its member, and to participate in and build up its life in the world? How should its life to be characterized? We will return to the question of ecclesiology at length in chapter 5, but Romero's sense of the church's identity vis-à-vis the reform is important to underscore. To be sure, he thinks the gospel and social teaching helpfully illumine the reform and its theological significance. But Romero also wants the reform to teach the church about itself and its deepest identity —what it means for Christ to be formed in his members (Gal 4:19) so that they can grow up into the one who is their head (Eph 4:15).

53. Romero, *Homilías*, 6:79.
54. Romero, *Homilías*, 6:79.

Something the reform can teach the church about its identity is that, as Romero observes earlier in the homily, "the Church is born of sinners."[55] What he means is that the church's holiness derives solely from God and how Christ binds himself to a body of people so completely that Christ makes this body his own, which he does in order to incorporate its members into the common life of God. The path toward participation in this life is a process of ongoing and often painful conversion as Christ's ecclesial members learn to leave behind all that inhibits them from sharing more fully in it and being conformed to the generous act of their Lord. This means the holiness of the people of God on pilgrimage is imperfect. The church remains sinful and in need of conversion because its members are sinful and in need of conversion.[56] Because its members have not yet become who they are, the church is, to use Augustine's phrase, a *corpus permixtum* (mixed body), like a field of wheat and weeds growing together until the harvest at the end of the age (see Mt 13:24–30).

LAND REFORM, RURAL ORGANIZING, AND THE PERSECUTION OF THE CHURCH IN EL SALVADOR

At several points in the homily, Romero anticipates resistance to the land reform, alluding to armaments and death squads. Indeed, a conspicuous rise in repression accompanied the reform, with security forces, intelligence units, and death squads perpetrating much of it.[57] Because the JRG was incapable of stopping the violence, its authority and legitimacy eroded, enabling those behind the bloodshed to act with impunity.[58] The bloodletting escalated from the final months of 1979 until the beginning of civil war, with continuous monthly increases in arrests, disappearances, tortures, and homicides between 1979 and 1981.[59]

The violence of this time is complex, and understanding it would require attending to the internal conflicts between reformist and hardline

55. Romero, *Homilías*, 6:60.
56. Romero, *Homilías*, 6:60.
57. Stanley, *Protection Racket State*, 164–65.
58. Stanley, *Protection Racket State*, 168–69.
59. Commission on the Truth for El Salvador, *From Madness to Hope*; Socorro Jurídico Cristiano, "Informe No. 11, Año IX" (San Salvador: Arzobispado de San Salvador, 1984).

factions within the military, as well as to how the Salvadoran state was a constellation of competing actors who were involved in reforming and repressing in different ways. For our more modest purposes in this chapter, however, it is sufficient to note that the prospect of land reform led to an alliance between the oligarchy and sympathizers in the military bound by a commitment to stop the reform by any means necessary.[60] As one informant with close ties to both groups explains, "The acceleration of violence after January 1980 was predominantly a response to the prospect of [land reform]. With [some factions in] the military moving toward carrying out the reform, the right had to find a way to defend itself. So they put the D'Aubuisson group into action. The purpose of the violence was to stop the reforms by erasing the call for them."[61]

The demands on the part of the Salvadoran people both for land reform and for an end to the repression led to the October 1979 coup, which meant that the JRG's ability to restore governability to the country hinged upon its achievement of both. The strategy of the alliance between the oligarchy and military was therefore simple and straightforward: isolate, undermine, and destabilize the JRG by attacking its supporters and potential supporters, unleashing an unprecedented wave of repression against them.[62] The name "Roberto D'Aubuisson," which the informant also mentions, is synonymous with the death squads that tortured and killed thousands in the 1970s and 1980s. But he is perhaps best known as the mastermind behind the plot to kill Archbishop Óscar Romero.

U.S. Assistant Secretary of State Viron Vaky dubs this strategy of attempting to stop the land reform by erasing those who were calling for it "the *Matanza* approach"[63]—a reference to an event that has already come up at several points: the 1932 *campesino* uprising. While Romero was archbishop, D'Aubuisson and others discussed the *Matanza* approach publicly. Communism was a menace, they thought, that had infiltrated the church and the government, and dealing with it meant exterminat-

---

60. Stanley, *Protection Racket State*, 181, 188–92.
61. Quoted in Stanley, *Protection Racket State*, 190.
62. Stanley, *Protection Racket State*, 136–37, 153–59, 166–67, 177.
63. Quoted in Stanley, *Protection Racket State*, 168, 162.

ing hundreds of thousands of Salvadorans if necessary.[64] For the likes of D'Aubuisson, the clearest evidence of this menace was land reform, which attacked the very institution of private property. Therefore, one reason D'Aubuisson and his sympathizers resisted the land reform with such fury is that they interpreted the social unrest and the call for a more just distribution of land in light of what had happened in 1932.[65] The sociologist Paul Almeida describes 1932 as a kind of "condensed version" or "historical dress rehearsal" for the conflagration that would unfold beginning in the late 1970s with the JRG's land reform,[66] so a brief word about what happened is in order.

On January 22, 1932, thousands assaulted roughly one dozen municipalities throughout central and western El Salvador.[67] The insurrectionists were mostly descendants of the Nahuatal-Pibil peoples, who were bound by their experience as workers in the region's coffee *fincas*.[68] The targeted killings of landowners and creditors were likely tied to the property foreclosures and land loss affecting so many smallholders over the course of the preceding years, which we examined in chapter 1. In all, the uprising left about one hundred people dead, and it damaged various businesses and residences.[69] Insurrectionists briefly turned the world upside down, compelling local elites to do menial work like grind maize and make tortillas. They gave Emilio Redaeli—a large landowner, former mayor, and supplier of credit—a pauper's burial.[70] Participants also

64. Dermot Keogh, "The Myth of the Liberal Coup: The United States and the 15 October 1979 Coup in El Salvador," *Millennium: Journal of International Studies* 13 (1983): 183.

65. Since Anderson's seminal study, many have seen communism as central to the interpretation of the 1932 insurrection. According to this line of thought, the origins of 1932 reside in the organized left, especially the communist party; see Thomas P. Anderson, *Matanza: El Salvador's Communist Revolt of 1932* (Omaha: University of Nebraska Press, 1971). In contrast, revisionist accounts like Ching's want to locate the causes of the insurrection primarily in long-standing local conflicts and the organization of *campesino* communities themselves; see Ching, *Authoritarian El Salvador*, 296–304.

66. Almeida, *Waves of Protest*, 35.

67. Gould and Lauria-Santiago, *To Rise in Darkness*, 170.

68. Gould and Lauria-Santiago, *To Rise in Darkness*, 171; Ching, *Authoritarian El Salvador*, 319–21.

69. Gould and Lauria-Santiago, *To Rise in Darkness*, 149–51, 187–88; Ching, *Authoritarian El Salvador*, 1–2.

70. Gould and Lauria-Santiago, *To Rise in Darkness*, 197.

engaged in the systematic looting and redistribution of goods. In many of the towns, they focused on municipal buildings that housed archives, eliminating property records in anticipation of a future land reform.[71] In Juayúa, the leader Francisco Sánchez requested delivery of all the title deeds and began to draw up a program of reform himself.[72]

Two days after the insurrection began, troops under the command of General José Tomás Calderón traveled west by train and overwhelmed the insurrectionists, who mostly wielded machetes. The rebellion was quickly crushed, but the bloodletting continued. Over the ensuing month, the military systematically moved through the countryside. Witnesses recounted soldiers indiscriminately opening fire on peoples' huts, killing anyone inside. "They didn't ask for any declarations from anyone," Antonio Valiente recalls. "Whoever they saw, they shot."[73] Ramón Esquina remembers mass graves and soldiers heaving bodies into them like "bales of sugar cane."[74] There were mass executions in town squares.[75]

La Matanza was one of the most brutal and genocidal acts of state-sponsored terror in modern Latin American history.[76] As the Salvadoran revolutionary Miguel Mármol puts it, "After that damned year [1932] all of us are different, and I think that from then on El Salvador is a different country. El Salvador is today, before anything else, a creation of that barbarism."[77]

Among *La Matanza*'s many legacies is that, as Gould and Lauria-Santiago write, "officialist discourse elided, distorted, or falsified descriptions

71. Gould and Lauria-Santiago, *To Rise in Darkness*, 193; Ching, *Authoritarian El Salvador*, 290.

72. Gould and Lauria-Santiago, *To Rise in Darkness*, 180–82.

73. Gould and Lauria-Santiago, *To Rise in Darkness*, 240.

74. Gould and Lauria-Santiago, *To Rise in Darkness*, 184–86, 212.

75. Ching, *Authoritarian El Salvador*, 290.

76. It is commonplace to refer to what happened in terms of genocide, for the intention seems to have been "to destroy 'whole or in part' a race, nationality, religion or ethnicity," in the words of the United Nations Convention on the Prevention and Punishment of the Crime of Genocide. Gould and Lauria-Santiago describe the killings as fueled by an ingrained prejudice of the insurgents as backward, ignorant, lazy, and menacing *indios*. The insurrection, they write, "burst the dam holding back the accumulated hostility and hatred toward Indians on the part of the élite…. Very quickly *Indian, barbarian,* and *communist* became interchangeable epithets"; Gould and Lauria-Santiago, *To Rise in Darkness*, 226–39; 217–19.

77. Dalton, *Miguel Mármol*, 305.

of the killings in such a way that either perpetrators and victims were transposed, or at the very least, the distinction between them was made ambiguous."[78] "Bloodthirsty hordes," "vandals," and "raging savages" perpetrated the violence.[79] Soldiers and wealthy landowners responded with justice and courage even if meant *murieron justos por los pecadores* (the just died for the sinners), to use a formulation that continues to circulate among the survivors.[80] The "communism" that inspired the revolt was a virulent "disease"—a "social cancer"—affecting the body politic, and it had to be removed at any cost in order to stop the spread and restore health.[81] A pattern therefore begins to appear in Salvadoran history that is only exacerbated by the intensification of the Cold War in the 1970s and 1980s: the fight against communism—both perceived and actual— occasions and justifies bloodletting on a massive scale. As the historian Eric Ching describes it, "The [1932] rebellion enflamed elites' passions and made them more reactionary and resistant to change, hallmarks of their actions in subsequent decades."[82] This is apparent in the alliance between the military and oligarchy in response to the land reform in late 1979, especially in the embrace of the so-called *Matanza* approach to erase the reforms and those calling for them.[83]

The rise in repression accompanying the JRG's reform also relates to long-simmering conflicts surrounding the church's rural organizing efforts—efforts that were explicitly modeled on Catholic social teaching—and the growing and increasingly consolidated resistance to them. Romero inherits these conflicts upon becoming archbishop, and they are pivotal for understanding why the church came under attack, and ultimately, why he was killed.

We have seen Romero emphasize how, in addition to receiving just salaries, the landless and land-poor must be able to organize in order to make their living conditions more tolerable. Organizing accomplishes this by gathering those who have been scattered and by incorporat-

78. Gould and Lauria-Santiago, *To Rise in Darkness*, 234.
79. Gould and Lauria-Santiago, *To Rise in Darkness*, 235.
80. Gould and Lauria-Santiago, *To Rise in Darkness*, 210, 215, 238, 248.
81. Gould and Lauria-Santiago, *To Rise in Darkness*, 235–36.
82. Ching, *Authoritarian El Salvador*, 4.
83. Almeida, *Waves of Protest*, 35.

ing isolated individuals into social bodies. In chapter 3, we examined the significance of this process of gathering and incorporating in light of Catholic social teaching. Among other things, organizing helps workers to access the land and created goods they need in order to support themselves and others—to walk the path between work and property—and to address social injustice by participating in the movement of restoration themselves.

Yet in El Salvador, the very fact of rural organizing was extremely controversial. Another important legacy of *La Matanza* was the general ban on rural workers' organizations and associations by President General Martínez following the insurrection—a ban that was still in force when Romero became archbishop. Labor unions, associations of urban renters and students, autonomous political parties, organizations of agricultural laborers, and similar groups proliferated in the late 1920s during the presidency of Pío Romero Bosque (1827–1931).[84] Some of these groups forged close ties to preexisting indigenous-based Catholic fraternal orders called *cofradías*.[85] But in the aftermath of *La Matanza*, Martínez isolated rural workers by attacking any independent organizing by them.[86] The government declared all such organizations and associations illegal—not only radical ones like the Federación Regional de Trabajadores Salvadoreños (Regional Federation of Salvadoran Workers) and the Partido Comunista Salvadoreño (Communist Party of El Salvador)—but also mutual aid societies and workers' cooperatives. After 1932, any rural association or organization that wanted to reopen or form required a government license to do so.[87] To paraphrase Hittinger, the Salvadoran state permitted the existence of other social entities only by the concession of its own sovereignty, implicitly claiming to be the exemplary cause of the good.

84. Almeida, *Waves of Protest*, 35–53; Gould and Lauria-Santiago, "'They Call Us Thieves and Steal Our Wage,'" 226–29.

85. Almeida, *Waves of Protest*, 39–40, 50–53; Walter Guerra Calderón, *Asociaciones comunitarias en el área rural de El Salvador en la década 1960–1970: Análisis de las condiciones que enmarcan su desarrollo* (San José, Costa Rica: CSUCA, Programa Centroamericano de Ciencias Sociales, 1976), 257, 264–65.

86. Ching, *Authoritarian El Salvador*, 310.

87. Ching, *Authoritarian El Salvador*, 310, 345.

One response by the church was to establish and defend social entities other than the state, especially among rural workers. And with the church's assistance, such organizations and associations began to re-emerge and proliferate, especially by the 1960s and 1970s.[88] Despite the general ban on organizing among rural workers, El Salvador's 1950 constitution did permit the formation of cooperatives, a legal opening that enabled cooperatives of all kinds—savings and loan, purchasing, producer, and so on—to form. By the 1960s, the cooperative movement was widespread throughout El Salvador, with the church among the main organizers.[89] As a result, the church was beginning to have a new and expanding presence in the countryside.

The promotion of Catholic social teaching was a priority of Luis Chávez y González, Romero's predecessor as archbishop of San Salvador (1938–77).[90] To this end, he helped form the Secretariado Social Interdiocesano (Inter-Diocesan Social Secretariat, SSI) in 1961.[91] SSI's work, which was under the auspices of Fundación Promotora de Cooperativas (Foundation for the Promotion of Cooperatives, FUNPROCOOP), centered on the formation of and support for cooperatives among *campesinos.* FUNPROCOOP acquired legal recognition in 1968, and its influence spread rapidly.[92] By 1972, there were sixty-three such cooperatives operating in nearly one-fourth of the country's municipalities.[93]

Another sign of such organizing by the church was newsletters like

88. Juan Ramón Vega, *Las comunidades de base en América Central: Estudio sociológico* (San Salvador: Publicaciones del Arzobispado, 1994), 74, 76.

89. Almeida, *Waves of Protest*, 71, 75–77; Guerra Calderón, *Asociaciones comunitarias en el área rural de El Salvador*; Emilio Arturo Cuchillo, "El desarrollo cultural del campesino y la reforma agraria" (Ph.D. diss., Universidad de El Salvador, 1970), 214–26; "De la necesidad e importancia de las cooperativas," *Camino* 1, no. 3 (1961): 6–7.

90. See Luis Chávez y González, *Sobre la mejor y más justa distribución de los bienes* (San Salvador Arzobispado de San Salvador, 1961); Chávez y González, *La responsibilidad del laico en el ordenamiento de lo temporal* (San Salvador, 1966); Rosa Carmelita Samos Stibbs, *Estudio teológico de las cartas pastorales de Mons: Luis Chávez y González* (Universidad Francisco Marroquín, Facultad de Humanidades, Departamento de Teología, 1986).

91. Almeida, *Waves of Protest*, 76; Vega, *Las comunidades de base en América Central*; Guerra Calderón, *Asociaciones comunitarias en el área rural de El Salvador.*

92. Almeida, *Waves of Protest*, 75; Guerra Calderón, *Asociaciones comunitarias en el área rural de El Salvador.*

93. Almeida, *Waves of Protest*, 76; Guerra Calderón, *Asociaciones comunitarias en el área rural de El Salvador*, 224–25.

Camino. Started in 1961 by a Eucharistic adoration society, *Camino*'s motto was "toward the improvement of workers and *campesinos*." "What is one of the principal causes of this disunion we experience?" an article in one of the first issues of *Camino* asks, with the answer being the destitution of the many, which isolates and scatters the Salvadoran people. Cooperatives, the author contends, can contribute to ameliorating this situation by gathering people together and by "decentralizing the possession of goods so that they do not accumulate in the hands of the few and that they are distributed profusely among the people."[94] One immediate and concrete consequence of the formation and spread of savings and loan cooperatives was that *campesinos* began to be freed for the first time from predatory lending schemes.[95]

Camino is replete with articles about cooperatives and their structure and rationale, as well as the church's involvement in the process of organizing them.[96] Other major themes include the problem of land access, as well as the "permanent violation" of the freedom to form unions in El Salvador, as in much of the rest of Latin America.[97] Along these lines, articles detail the establishment of the Leo XIII Institute and its mandate to catechize workers and *campesinos* in Catholic social teaching.[98] Additionally, there are articles on land reform that commend the Brazilian bishops for their pioneering efforts in places like Río Grande do Sul,[99] as well as articles on convergences and divergences between the land reform proposals under public discussion and the church's social teaching.[100]

What is especially important for understanding the persecution of the church in El Salvador is that, as Jorge Cáceres Prendes argues, the legal protections afforded to cooperatives not only enabled their spread

94. "De la necesidad e importancia de las cooperativas," 6–7.

95. Vega, *Las comunidades de base en América Central*, 76.

96. *Camino*, San Salvador 1961, año 1, nos. 1–4.

97. "Permanentes violaciones a la libertad syndical en América Latina," *Camino* 1, no. 8 (1961): 6; "¿Por que se teme a los sindicatos?," *Camino* 1, no. 11 (1961): 6; "El campesino merece ayuda," *Camino* 1, no. 3 (1961): 6.

98. "Organizase curso de capacitación para obreros," *Camino* 1, no. 1 (1961): 3; "Inaugurase solemnemente Intituto de Capacitación Social Leon XIII," *Camino* 1, no. 3 (1961): 8.

99. "Apoyan la reforma agraria los obispos de Río Grande do Sul," *Camino* 1, no. 1 (1961): 3.

100. "Un programa promisor para América Latina," *Camino* 1, no. 10 (1961): 2.

throughout El Salvador, but also established an important social space for the proliferation of additional organizations and associations among rural workers, including *campesino* leagues, ecclesial base communities, literacy programs, and training centers.[101] As an outgrowth of these groups, *campesinos* increasingly began to organize around issues of land access and unionization, attempting to participate in opening the path between wage work and ownership of productive property like land.[102]

Among the groups formed in the 1960s, which later became a focal organization for protest in the 1970s, was the popular organization Federación Cristiana de Campesinos Salvadoreños (Christian Federation of Salvadoran Peasants, FECCAS).[103] Beginning in 1965, FECCAS started to hold annual conferences in which topics like land reform, minimum wage increases, improvement of working conditions on *haciendas*, reductions in land rental prices, and better legal protections for workers dominated the agenda. The archdiocese's Centro de Estudios Sociales y Promoción Popular (Center for Social Studies and Popular Promotion) worked with FECCAS and began publishing reports supporting land reform and legal protections for rural unions.[104] FECCAS spoke of "integral land reform," by which it meant something similar to what Romero meant by land reform: not simply a better distribution of land, but also a better distribution of social goods more generally, as well as the imperative for beneficiaries to participate fully in the process. FECCAS also pushed for

101. Jorge Cáceres Prendes, "Revolutionary Struggle and Church Commitment: The Case of El Salvador," *Social Compass* 30, no. 2–3 (1983): 261–98; Vega, *Las comunidades de base en América Central*, 95–96.

102. Vega, *Las comunidades de base en América Central*. See also Almeida, *Waves of Protest*, 86; Arístedes Augusto Larín, "Historia del movimiento sindical de El Salvador," *Universidad* 96, no. 4 (1971): 135–79.

103. FECCAS grew out of the Christian Democratic Party in the 1960s. Luis Chávez y González supported popular organizations like FECCAS and the *Unión de Trabajadores del Campo* (Rural Workers' Union, UTC) but had concerns about the clergy participating in them; Mario Lungo, *La lucha de las masas en El Salvador* (San Salvador: UCA Editores, 1987), 64. For more on the relationship between FECCAS and the cooperative movement, see Vega, *Las comunidades de base en América Central*, 119.

104. Almeida, *Waves of Protest*, 85; Guerra Calderón, *Asociaciones comunitarias en el área rural de El Salvador*, 236, 235–47; Vega, *Las comunidades de base en América Central*, 120; "Manifiesto de FECCAS/UTC a los Cristianos de El Salvador y Centro América," *Estudios Centroamericanos* 359 (1978).

the legalization of unions among rural workers and tried to leverage the legal protections afforded cooperatives as a toehold to do so.[105]

In the late 1960s, ecclesial base communities (*comunidades eclesiales de base*) likewise began to appear.[106] These communities arose within the marginal places of ecclesial life in El Salvador, and their membership consisted especially of the landless and land-poor. Ecclesial base communities typically began within parishes through the initiatives of priests and others in order to organize an ecclesial presence where it was lacking so that members could regularly gather to reflect on their life together in the light of the gospel.[107] Out of the ecclesial base community movement in El Salvador, extensive national and international networks developed that organized activities and training events related to illiteracy, cooperative formation, agricultural production on marginal land, nutrition, community organizing, and labor legislation.[108] Like the cooperatives, these base communities functioned as a fulcrum for further organizing, efforts that included *campesino* training centers such as Los Naranjos, with which Romero worked when he was bishop of the diocese of Santiago de María from 1974 to 1977.[109]

This proliferation of rural organizations and associations we have been sketching represents a widespread and multifaceted effort welling up to reconstitute societies in the spaces of their devastation. The formation of such groups was an attempt on the part of organizers to counter an exclusionary political-economic regime that was rapidly producing people without land and livelihood, dissolving social bonds, and leaving the many with little protection against ordinary violence. As Leo XIII argues in *Rerum Novarum*, without property or social membership in such groups, workers are exposed, and their isolation and vulnerability easily

---

105. Guerra Calderón, *Asociaciones comunitarias en el área rural de El Salvador*, 243–44.

106. Almeida, *Waves of Protest*, 85; Vega, *Las comunidades de base en América Central*, 95. See "Éxito de los cursos de comunidades de base," *Orientación*, September 19, 1971; "Curso de comunidades eclesiales de base," *Orientación*, August 29, 1971.

107. Vega, *Las comunidades de base en América Central*, 8–9, 16, 68, 156.

108. Almeida, *Waves of Protest*, 112; Vega, *Las comunidades de base en América Central*, 18, 95–96.

109. Díez and Macho, *En Santiago de Maria me topé con la miseria*; Almeida, *Waves of Protest*, 85; Vega, *Las comunidades de base en América Central*, 95–96; Tommie Sue Montgomery, *Revolution in El Salvador: From Civil Strife to Civil Peace* (Boulder, Colo.: Westview, 1995), 105.

become a site of exploitation and violence as their need forces them to accept unjust wages and criminal working conditions. In El Salvador, the organizers of such groups sought to counter a similar situation to the one described by Leo with a similar solution: by advocating for access to property in land and by trying to establish protective organizations and associations for workers. In so doing, organizers sought to help those affected gather together to address what Romero calls "the vital problems of subsistence, of land, of wages."

The proliferation of rural organizations and associations is also significant because it grows out of Catholic social teaching. As Romero writes in April 1968, Catholicism is flourishing in El Salvador, "especially in our immense rural sector where, through the tireless work of priests, organizations, lay apostolates, cooperatives, parochial schools, the radio, the press, etc., the faith is felt and reaches all people."[110] Of course, these rural organizing efforts were not applauded by all in El Salvador, and many among the oligarchy characterized these rural organizations and associations as illegal. As Pius XI writes in *Quadragesimo Anno*—with words that are applicable to these Salvadoran oligarchs—many powerful people, who are "plainly imbued by Liberalism," have openly opposed workers' associations and organizations, denying "with criminal injustice … the natural right to form associations to those who needed it most to defend themselves from ill treatment at the hands of the powerful."[111]

We will examine the Salvadoran oligarchy's adherence to the liberal economics or capitalism of which Pius speaks shortly. But in order to understand why those in the church who put themselves on the side of the impoverished were attacked, it is important to see that, by means of such organizations and associations, the position of the landless and the land-poor vis-à-vis their employers began to change, and the former began to be able to defend themselves more effectively before the latter. Many *campesinos* who participated in these groups depended upon seasonal wage labor in the coffee, cotton, and cane fields, and so they migrated each year

110. *Actividad de la Iglesia en El Salvador*, April 17, 1968, Archives of the Archdiocese of San Salvador, San Salvador, El Salvador.

111. Pius XI, *Quadragesimo Anno*, no. 30.

throughout El Salvador, following the harvests from farm to farm.[112] Juan Ramón Vega argues that tensions rose especially in the early 1970s when organized migrants began to pressure landlords to pay the minimum wage and to improve working conditions.[113] In Vega's account, the mere existence of workers' organizations and associations where they were previously absent was seen as subversion. "The crime," he writes, "was simply being organized."[114] In the face of the demands upon them, landowners retaliated by attacking leaders in order to decapitate these groups and scatter their members.[115] For Vega, the rise of the revolutionary left in El Salvador, whose constituency consisted of many former members of ecclesial base communities and other groups the church helped to organize, cannot be understood without taking into account the radicalizing effects of the repression of these rural organizations and associations.[116]

Scholars have rightly emphasized the significance of the Second Vatican Council and Medellín for the renewal of the church in Latin America and its embrace of the preferential option for the poor and outreach to *campesinos*.[117] While the Council and Medellín certainly encouraged and strengthened the organizing efforts of the church—along with its advocacy for land reform, just wages, and dignified working conditions—these efforts in El Salvador and elsewhere in Latin America preceded both ecclesial events and were grounded in pre-conciliar Catholic social teaching. In this regard, Vega's work also helps clarify why Romero would characterize the Second Vatican Council and its Latin Americanization at Medellín as contributing to the conscientization about social teaching and its implications. But Vega's work also makes clear why, as the 1970s wore on, one

---

112. Todd, *Beyond Displacement*, 27–29; Nora Hamilton and Norma Stoltz Chinchilla, "Central American Migration: A Framework for Analysis," in *Challenging Fronteras: Structuring Latina and Latino Lives in the U.S.* (New York: Routledge, 2014), 85–86.

113. Vega, *Las comunidades de base en América Central*, 97–98; Melvin Burke, "El sistema de plantación y la proletarización del trabajo agrícola en El Salvador," *Estudios Centroamericanos* 31, no. 335-336 (September–October 1976): 473-86.

114. Vega, *Las comunidades de base en América Central*, 96, 128, 156.

115. Vega, *Las comunidades de base en América Central*, 17, 89, 96, 121–28.

116. Vega, *Las comunidades de base en América Central*, 18; Almeida, *Waves of Protest*, 103, 115–16, 126–27.

117. Rubén Rosario Rodríguez has recently made this point in *Christian Martyrdom and Political Violence: A Comparative Theology* (New York: Cambridge University Press, 2017), 204.

implication of this conscientization was that those who identified themselves with this teaching began to suffer—and suffer greatly.

We have been considering the church's rural organizing efforts and the
conflicts surrounding them—conflicts that are crucial for understanding Romero's ministry and death. But why was there resistance from the
oligarchy on these particular matters? What reasons did this group's
members, most of whom were Catholic and so bound to the same social
teaching, give for their resistance? What led some oligarchs to join with
factions in the military to stop the land reform by unleashing the *Matanza* approach and brutally crushing those calling for it?

The Salvadoran oligarchy figures in much Romero scholarship as an
inscrutably evil force of unquenchable greed, frenetically amassing land
and wealth that it ruthlessly defends. Morozzo della Rocca's observation
that the oligarchy considered both El Salvador and the church as "a piece
of property" is typical in this regard.[118] Members of this group did tend to
espouse sole and despotic dominion in a Blackstonian sense, which is an
important reason why they regarded land reform as the blatant thievery
of what hard-working people had legitimately earned by the strength of
their own hands. At the same time, this characterization of the oligarchy,
despite its truth, can generate the false impression of a uniquely immoral
group from a foreign land—far removed from us—insofar as it overlooks
other arguments members of the oligarchy made in support of their po-
sitions.

A noteworthy example of such arguments can be found in the inaugu-
ral speech of Antonio Rodríguez Porth, the spokesperson for the entrepreneurial sector at the historic Congress on Land Reform in 1970, which
brought together representatives from across the Salvadoran political
spectrum. The legislative assembly organized the congress to address

118. Morozzo della Rocca, "La controvertida identidad de un obispo," 17, 32. A former
counselor of the nunciature to El Salvador reports that a member of a powerful Salvadoran
family once told him, "Monsignor, remember that we were the ones who built the Church in
El Salvador, and without us it would cease to exist"; Edward Idris Cassidy, "Romero visto de
cerca," in *Óscar Romero: Un obispo entre guerra fría y revolución* (Madrid: Editorial San Pablo
España, 2003), 151.

the crisis following El Salvador's war with Honduras in 1969. As briefly mentioned in chapter 3, the Honduran government's eviction of undocumented Salvadorans who had settled on Honduran land forced hundreds of thousands to return to their country, further aggravating the problem of land access.[119] Despite the invitation to participate in the congress, the whole entrepreneurial sector abruptly withdrew after the first day, an indication of their antipathy to the idea of land reform. But before withdrawing, Porth explained why the sector he represented thought that land reform would only worsen the agrarian crisis, and his speech epitomizes the thinking embraced by those who would resist land reform with brutality in the coming decades.

In his speech, Porth articulates a vision of technological development and progress that is a consequence of "the eternal values of liberty" and reason, against which "mystical revolutionary movements" have arisen that are "emotionally motivated."[120] Here and elsewhere, Porth suggests equivalence between support for land reform and communist-inspired revolutionary violence. Additionally, Porth portrays the state as a threatening, alien presence to private property. Land reform, he reasons, would be "impossible to achieve without coercive and arbitrary acts by the state, with grave consequences for the national economy." Salvadoran liberals like Porth characteristically appeal to *laissez-faire* economics as the basic justification for limiting the state's role to that of the defense of liberty, which they in turn associate with the freedom inherent in absolute property rights and enterprise. They oppose land reform, along with the formation of associations and organizations among rural workers, on the grounds that these are artificial and damaging interventions by the state in the smooth functioning of the economy. Against the view that the condition of the *campesinado* can be addressed by land reform, Porth therefore opposes "interventionism" of any kind.[121]

---

119. For more on the so-called Soccer War, see Durham, *Scarcity and Survival in Central America*; Thomas P. Anderson, *The War of the Dispossessed: Honduras and El Salvador, 1969* (Lincoln: University of Nebraska Press, 1981). For the response of the Catholic bishops, see Conferencia Episcopal de El Salvador, "Llamamiento del Episcopado Salvadoreño en nombre del país."

120. Asamblea Legislativa, *Memoria del primer congreso nacional de reforma agraria*, 26.

121. Asamblea Legislativa, *Memoria del primer congreso nacional de reforma agraria*, 28.

But crucially, Porth opposes land reform and other state "interventions" in the economy because he thinks they are an attack upon the common good. The reasoning is that state intervention damages the economy and therefore the common good. For liberals like Porth, the improvement of the condition of the *campesinado* in El Salvador "can only be achieved through the technification of agricultural production, which naturally would increase the productivity and the incomes of individual workers." Porth freely admits that the implementation of this vision of development and progress will lead to dispossession and dislocation. Nevertheless, the focus must be upon increasing production, to the exclusion of other social or economic consideration. "Turning agriculture into a veritable industry," he argues, is the only possible way forward.[122] In this regard, the defense of the existing property regime is absolutely essential, for otherwise production will falter and the economy along with it. Land reform is nothing short of an attack on the free enterprise system itself, along with the stable and secure property arrangements that enable its orderly functioning.

Porth works with a strikingly different conception of the common good than that of Catholic social teaching and proponents of it like Romero. For social teaching, the diffusion of the good happens through people doing good, which brings into existence new forms of participation in the common good. Because the common good can only be shared, people cannot promote it without promoting this coming together, this common sharing in it. For love of the common good seeks to preserve the good of the society as common, which means wanting to involve others in this sharing. What is more, according to this understanding of the common good, it is impossible to love any common good without loving this shareability. As we have seen, all this has significant implications for the use of property like land, especially the imperative to involve others in its use and to ensure access to what is theirs in justice.

In contrast, Porth's conception of the common good is that leaving landowners to raise crops for export and pursue their own private good—tearing down their barns and building even bigger ones to store the ex-

---

122. Asamblea Legislativa, *Memoria del primer congreso nacional de reforma agraria*, 28.

cess production—not only promotes the common good but is the only way to promote it. This is the common good understood as an aggregate of the private good of landowners, which, through them, becomes the good of all Salvadorans. Porth's view is that, given the right conditions, increased agricultural production fuels a growing economy, whose benefits eventually trickle down. This leads to Porth's conclusion that "the essential thing for combating misery" is to encourage the activity of free enterprise, because a growing economy alone can help the condition of the *campesinado*. "Interventions" by the state, such as land reform, only impede economic growth, generating a misery that "harms the weaker economic classes above all."[123] Opposing such measures, Porth thinks, is good—and not only for oligarchs like Porth, but for all Salvadorans.

The challenge of Porth's conception of the common good can therefore be posed as a question: What benefit could possibly come from attacking the foundation of the entrepreneurial sector, the engine of the Salvadoran economy and the generator of jobs? Ellacuría characterizes this view as the "oligarchic principle," according to which to advantage the most privileged of El Salvador is ipso facto to advantage all Salvadorans, and to promote their private good is to promote the common good.[124] Of course, Ellacuría's oligarchic principle is simply the logic of capitalism, according to which the common good is an inadvertent byproduct of self-interested action.[125] However, what is crucial to see is that, at least on Catholic social teaching's terms, Porth's conception of the common good is not really a *common good* at all, which can only be shared.

To be sure, Porth and the entrepreneurial sector frequently spoke of land reform as an act of theft, an unjust taking of the wealth they had secured by the power and might of their own hands. As Héctor Lindo-Fuentes and Eric Ching observe, "This appeal to the idea of wealth remaining with the people who created it would emerge as the most basic and fundamental line of rhetorical defense ... to oppose land reform and

---

123. Asamblea Legislativa, *Memoria del primer congreso nacional de reforma agraria*, 28.

124. Ignacio Ellacuría, "A sus órdenes, mi capital," *Estudios Centroamericanos* 31, no. 337 (November 1976): 639.

125. Friedrich A. Hayek uses the term "catallaxy" to refer to the spontaneous emergence of order in the absence of beneficence; Hayek, *Law, Legislation and Liberty*, vol. 2, *The Mirage of Social Justice* (Chicago: University of Chicago Press, 2012), 109–10, 115.

any other policy [the oligarchy] could portray as being redistributive."[126] Over the course of the 1970s, this group voiced its opposition to land reform not simply in public debate, but also through clandestine death squads and repression. But what also fuels the ferocity of its opposition was the view that land reform was no ordinary or innocuous act of theft, which could be dealt with through the normal channels. Rather, the "communists" advocating for it were steadily infiltrating the state, the church, and other sectors of Salvadoran society. Moreover, because land reform robbed land from its rightful owners—the entrepreneurial sector, El Salvador's economic engine and job generator—it uniquely imperiled the common good. Stopping it was therefore for the benefit of the whole country.

Consequently, as the calls for land reform expanded and intensified, so did the repression. By the mid-1970s, the repression reached new levels in response to the agrarian transformation project of President Molina.[127] The idea of the project was to begin by targeting 59,000 hectares of coastal land in Usulután-San Miguel before scaling up to the whole nation.[128] The initial zone included the Diocese of Santiago de María, where Romero was serving as bishop at the time. In response to the announcement of the agrarian transformation, Romero organized study circles and asked experts to give presentations about the project. One of them, Rubén Zamora, recalls that Romero was "always in the front row, taking notes like a very attentive student."[129]

The church publicly supported Molina's agrarian transformation project, as did the UCA.[130] But in the polarized atmosphere of the mid-1970s, this proved to be a lonely—and costly—position. Many who would have backed the project earlier in the decade now regarded it as counterrevo-

126. Lindo-Fuentes and Ching, *Modernizing Minds in El Salvador*, 67

127. For analysis of the entire agrarian transformation, see "De la guerra a la paz," *Estudios Centroamericanos* 31, no. 335–36 (1976).

128. Cardenal, *Historia de una esperanza: La vida de Rutilio Grande* (San Salvador: UCA Editores, 1985), 509–10; Bonilla Bonilla, *Tenencia de la tierra y reforma agraria en El Salvador*, 87.

129. Quoted in Morozzo della Rocca, *Primero Dios*, 146

130. Stephen Webre, *Jose Napoleon Duarte and the Christian Democratic Party in Salvadoran Politics 1960–1972* (Baton Rouge: Louisiana State University Press, 1979), 194; Teresa Whitfield, *Paying the Price: Ignacio Ellacuría and the Murdered Jesuits of El Salvador* (Philadelphia: Temple University Press, 1994), 67–69.

lutionary.[131] As historian Adolfo Bonilla Bonilla explains, by mid-decade "the left, especially the revolutionary left, … was interested in revolution; land reform was no longer a priority."[132] On the other side of the political spectrum, groups like the Frente Agrario de la Región Oriental (Agrarian Front of the Eastern Region, FARO) formed. FARO, the Asociación Nacional de la Empresa Privada (National Association of Private Enterprise, ANEP), and similar groups from the agricultural, industrial, commercial, and financial sectors, along with sympathizers in the military, formed a coalition that mounted an organized campaign against the project and successfully blocked its implementation.[133]

As Segundo Montes details, the fight over Molina's agrarian transformation project galvanized a new and especially hostile opposition to land reform among the oligarchy and factions in the military, which characterized it as a communist plot against property and mobilized to stop it by any means necessary. "This is how the dominant class became one," Montes contends, "organizing itself, fighting, and eventually defeating the project under the banner of defending unrestricted private property."[134] The coalition started a massive media campaign, flooding newspapers, radio, and television with opposition to the project, explicitly alluding to the possibility of an uprising similar to that of 1932.[135]

Because of its support of the project and its rural organizing, the church became one of the coalition's main targets.[136] Paid advertisements, articles, and news items openly accused the church of encouraging the robbery of property and the violation of the laws of the nation.[137] They characterized *campesina* organizations and associations like

131. Lindo-Fuentes and Ching, *Modernizing Minds in El Salvador*, 224; Knut Walter Franklin, "Ideales igualitarios y autodeterminación: 1961–1972," in *El Salvador: La república* (San Salvador: Fomento Cultural, Banco Agrícola, 2000), 546, 563.

132. Bonilla Bonilla, *Tenencia de la tierra y reforma agraria en El Salvador*, 88.

133. Montes, *El agro salvadoreño*, 153–55; Berryman, *Religious Roots of Rebellion*, 116–17.

134. Montes, *El agro salvadoreño*, 153.

135. Lindo-Fuentes and Ching, *Modernizing Minds in El Salvador*, 223.

136. Cardenal, *Historia de una esperanza*, 509; Vega, *Las comunidades de base en América Central*, 125; Report of the Latin American Bureau, *Violence and Fraud in El Salvador*, 19; Almeida, *Waves of Protest*, 93, 150–51.

137. *El Mundo*, December 8, 1976; "FARO siempre respectará la religion," *El Diario de Hoy*, May 30, 1977; "FARO contesta el comunicado de los curas," *Diario de Hoy*, December 21, 1976. For an overview, see *Persecución de la Iglesia en El Salvador*, 27–28, 34–35, 45.

FECCAS as "communist hordes" and "savage beasts," whose presence augured "a new and tragic chapter of the communist uprising of 1932" that was "right around the corner."[138] Backers in the church were "third world priests," foreign in origin, and abusers of the hospitality of the Salvadoran people.[139]

The situation deteriorated rapidly, with a dramatic increase in attacks upon the church, its membership, and its institutions. In 1976 alone, there were six successive bombings of the UCA, as well as a bombing of the publishing house of the archbishop.[140] Between January and February 1977, six priests and seminarians were deported, several of whom were tortured, and a bomb was planted in the car of another priest. February and March saw additional cases of arrests and torture of priests, as well as break-ins to their homes and deportations.[141] Less than a month after Romero became archbishop on February 22, 1977, Grande, who worked closely with ecclesial base communities, cooperatives, and groups like FECCAS, was killed. The repression of the Salvadoran people only continued to rise, with a massive escalation in detainment of political prisoners, disappearances, torture, targeted killings, and massacres.[142]

The stage was set for what would happen in 1979–80 in response to the land reform of the JRG. For if the *Matanza* approach meant stopping the reforms by erasing those calling for them, then this included voices like Romero's.

THE LAND OF THE SAVIOR

We have been examining the repression following the October 1979 coup and the announcement of land reform. In the end, the *Matanza* approach crippled the government, which proved powerless to stem the violence. With the resignation of the civilian members in January 1980, the first JRG disintegrated, and a new government formed. However, the killings,

138. "Hasta donde llegaremos?," *La Prensa Gráfica*, February 11, 1977.

139. The designation "Third World Priests" is from an Argentinian group known as the Priests for the Third World; see Christian Smith, *Emergence of Liberation Theology*, 137–39.

140. *Persecución de la Iglesia en El Salvador*, 16; Report of the Latin American Bureau, *Violence and Fraud in El Salvador*, 20.

141. *Persecución de la Iglesia en El Salvador*, 16.

142. *Persecución de la Iglesia en El Salvador*, 16–17; Almeida, *Waves of Protest*, 150–53.

disappearances, detentions, and torture only continued to rise. In 1980, approximately one thousand people died per month,[143] and people fled the terror in the countryside by the tens of thousands.[144] Romero's weekly litanies of the dead and disappeared in his homilies focused especially on *campesinos*, agricultural and urban workers, teachers, and students. While condemning the violence of the left, Romero often pointed out that it paled in comparison to that of the right.[145] The latter was part of what Romero characterized as "a general program of annihilation."[146] Those orchestrating it, he said, were "massacring the organized sector of our people for the mere fact of gathering in the streets to ask for justice and freedom."[147]

In the midst of this chaos and bloodshed, the land reform first announced in December 1979 hastily went into effect on March 6, 1980. With the end of the first JRG, the United States government and the American Institute for Free Labor Development (AIFLD) coordinated closely with the new government (the second JRG) to draw up a program that combined elements of the initial vision for reform with a counter-insurgency strategy modeled upon the Phoenix Program of the Vietnam War, which the United States and South Vietnam used against the Viet Cong.[148] In El Salvador, as in Vietnam, military operations and land reform were part of a unified strategy of rural pacification. Accordingly, with the implementation of the reform in March 1980, the Salvadoran

143. Socorro Jurídico Cristiano, *El Salvador: La situación de los derechos humanos, octubre 1979–julio 1981*; Cristiano, *El Salvador: Del genocidio de la junta militar a la esperanza de la lucha insurrecional* (San Salvador: Socorro Jurídico, 1981).

144. Romero, *Homilías*, 6:448.

145. Romero, *Homilías*, 6:378–79, 382.

146. Romero, *Homilías*, 6:382–83, 453, 355, 448.

147. Romero, *Homilías*, 6:243.

148. Philip Wheaton, *Agrarian Reform in El Salvador: A Program of Rural Pacification* (Washington, D.C.: EPICA Task Force, 1980); Roy Prosterman, "Land Reform in South Vietnam a Proposal for Turning the Tables on the Viet Cong," *Cornell Law Review* 53, no. 1 (1967); Colonel Andrew R. Finlayson, "Retrospective on Counterinsurgency Operations: The Tay Ninh Provincial Reconnaissance Unit and Its Role in the Phoenix Program, 1969–70," *Center for the Study of Intelligence Publications* 51, no. 2 (2007): 59–69. "In no way did I envision," said Rodrigo Guerra y Guerra, the principal author of the JRG's *Proclama*, "the kind of irrational land reform that began on 7 March 1980, two months after the members of the Junta Revolucionaria de Gobierno had resigned"; Guerra y Guerra, *Un golpe al amanecer*, 58–59.

government declared a state of emergency and censured the media as military units moved to occupy the whole country.[149] In his March 9 homily, Romero described the land reform actually being carried out as a "political-military action of the Armed Forces" that aimed at "a systematic militarization of the entire country through a series of militarized estates, which presents the possibility of the control and a systematization of the surveillance and repression directed against the popular forces."[150]

The stated rationale for military involvement was to ensure rapid and effective rollout of the reform and to prevent what had happened with Molina's agrarian transformation project earlier in the decade. But Romero was right that the occupation only intensified the repression, especially in areas of perceived opposition to the government.[151] Upon entering certain areas, troops burned fields and homes, clearing civilians before returning with helicopter gunships.[152] Cooperative members elected leaders who were summarily executed.[153] What became increasingly clear was that the land reform was functioning, among other things, as a tool to draw the opposition out into the open in order to eliminate it. As one representative of a federation of land reform cooperatives described the situation, "With the reforms, it made it easier and more legitimate to kill more people. If there is a reform, and people are still politically active, it must mean that they are leftists. Thus, the army could kill more freely."[154]

This descent into chaos and bloodshed is the context for Romero's final homilies, which were delivered during the season of Lent. These homilies offer a window into the way the rollout of the land reform was bathed with blood, and they reflect Romero's struggle to understand what exactly was happening with the reform. They also dwell at length upon

149. Wheaton, *Agrarian Reform in El Salvador*, 11.

150. Romero, *Homilías*, 6:385.

151. Montes, *El agro salvadoreño*, 299–300; Paige, *Coffee and Power*, 195–98; Americas Watch and American Civil Liberties Union, *Report on Human Rights in El Salvador* (New York: Random House, 1982); Wood, *Insurgent Collective Action and Civil War in El Salvador*, 106–8.

152. Wheaton, *Agrarian Reform in El Salvador*, 19.

153. Bonner, *Weakness and Deceit*, 1984, 199–200; Wheaton, *Agrarian Reform in El Salvador*, 17.

154. Quoted in Stanley, *Protection Racket State*, 195.

what it means to celebrate the Paschal mystery of Christ in El Salvador. In the homilies, Romero situates the pursuit of justice in the distribution of land and wealth in relation to that celebration.

During Lent, Christians prepare to celebrate the Paschal mystery of Christ. The season commemorates Jesus' forty days of solitude in the desert before his public ministry, during which time he endured temptation by Satan. Over the course of the Lenten season, the church and its members locate themselves in relation to these events, especially by way of prayer, fasting, and almsgiving. They therefore become, in an important sense, contemporaneous with Jesus' time of solitude in the desert. In Romero's words, "We, too, live in this time, which prepares us during the long pilgrimage … toward Easter and Pentecost.… If there is fasting, if there are penances, if there are prayers, it is because there is a positive goal: … Easter, resurrection."[155] In undertaking this Lenten pilgrimage, the people of God therefore also become contemporaneous with the Paschal mystery of Christ. "We do not celebrate a Christ who simply rises apart from ourselves," Romero says, "but who prepares us during the Lenten season to rise with him to a new life, to be the new people that our country so desperately needs."[156]

Romero's final Lenten homilies exhibit an important feature of his homiletical practice more generally: what Pfeil calls Romero's "thoroughly liturgical worldview," by which she means how Romero reads Salvadoran reality in relationship to the liturgy and the liturgy in relationship to Salvadoran reality.[157] As Romero says in an early homily, the liturgical year is the church's pilgrimage through salvation history. During Advent, Christmas, and Epiphany, the pilgrim church prepares to receive anew the God who becomes human. During Lent and Easter, it prepares to receive Jesus Christ's death on the cross and his resurrection on the third

155. Romero, *Homilías*, 6:275.
156. Romero, *Homilías*, 6:275.
157. Pfeil, "Óscar Romero's Theology of Transfiguration," 90; Morozzo della Rocca, *Primero Dios*, 292. As Anna L. Peterson shows, this worldview is deeply embedded in popular Catholicism in El Salvador, which, in her words, "places contemporary events in the light of sacred history." In this work, she is particularly interested in "political killings as re-enactments of the passion of Jesus and the deaths of later martyrs"; Peterson, *Martyrdom and the Politics of Religion: Progressive Catholicism in El Salvador's Civil War* (Albany: State University of New York Press, 1997), 10, 72–92.

day. And during Pentecost, it prepares to receive the descent of the Holy Spirit upon the disciples, the inauguration of the church in the time of its earthly pilgrimage. "Year after year," Romero continues, "the Church returns to the source of salvation history, presenting the *despliegue* (unfolding) of the redemptive mysteries of Christ."[158]

The liturgy is therefore no mere memory of a past event. Romero contrasts it with Salvadoran Independence Day, in which the people of El Salvador remember what happened on September 15 in 1821. Though continually recalled, the event remains in the past. The liturgy, however, differs because it makes the mysteries of Christ uniquely present. In celebrating these mysteries, the church remembers and participates in what happened in first-century Palestine and still continues to be contemporaneous to all times and places, for it lies at the heart of time and place itself. All reality gathers around the life, death, and resurrection of Jesus Christ. As Romero says in an Advent homily, "We are right now present to the mystery of Christ.… This very Sunday, we can enter into personal contact with Christ, who came over twenty centuries ago, but who continues to come to us through the mystery of the Church's liturgy."[159] Whenever and wherever these mysteries are celebrated, they draw the pilgrim church near to them.

According to Romero, the liturgical celebration of the mystery of Christ reveals to the people of God on pilgrimage their identity and purpose, inviting them to locate their lives in relation to him. Pfeil writes that for Romero, "the history of God's people and the history of salvation are not two different, parallel histories, but one narrative that culminates in the life, death, and resurrection of Jesus Christ."[160] In chapter 1, we saw how Romero thinks Puebla's message about property's social mortgage is the history of his people. Here we begin to see how he thinks Christ clarifies that message and the history of El Salvador, like all reality.

---

158. Romero, *Homilías*, 2:26.

159. Romero, *Homilías*, 2:26. In explaining the point, Romero quotes the Second Vatican Council's Constitution on the Sacred Liturgy, *Sacrosanctum Concilium*: "Recalling thus the mysteries of redemption, the Church opens to the faithful the riches of her Lord's powers and merits, so that these are in some way made present for all time, and the faithful are enabled to lay hold upon them and become filled with saving grace" (no. 102).

160. Pfeil, "Óscar Romero's Theology of Transfiguration," 110.

Another feature of these Lenten homilies closely related to Romero's liturgical worldview is his narration of the church in El Salvador in relationship to the people of Israel and their journey to the land God promises Abraham and his descendants (see Gen 12:7, 15:18–21). Like Israel, the church in El Salvador, Romero thinks, is still on pilgrimage; it has not left Israel's world. This is partially due to the Lenten season itself and how, as Romero observes, "the history of Israel is a fundamental element of Lenten catechesis."[161] The return to the situation of Israel during Lent reminds church members that they constantly fall away from the life offered them in Christ and that they are still in the midst of a long and difficult pilgrimage toward the land of promise.

But the church in El Salvador has not left Israel's world in an even more fundamental sense, which pertains to the very nature of the church itself. As Romero remarks in one of the homilies, "The history of Israel becomes, through the Church, the history of the Salvadoran people."[162] Or as he puts it in another homily, "God chose this people to be his from among all the peoples of the world," whose history in Christ becomes "the history of salvation for all peoples."[163] What do these statements mean? Most Salvadorans are baptized Catholics, yet Romero does not conflate the people of God and the people of El Salvador.[164] Neither is he suggesting that El Salvador subsumes the history of Israel, such that the nation becomes a light for the nations, a city upon a hill. Rather, Romero is pointing to how the church is a society that gathers all the peoples of the earth, including the people of El Salvador.[165] For in Christ, the Gentiles have been grafted onto Israel's story, like a wild olive shoot onto an ancient trunk (Rom 11:16–18). In this way, Israel's history, without ceasing to be its own, becomes a common gift, a blessing for all peoples (Gen 12:3, 22:18). Conversely, the story of other peoples can be read in relationship to Israel's story, in which they now share because of Christ.

One important implication of the foregoing is that Christ himself is

---

161. Romero, *Homilías*, 6:340. See Alexander Schmemann, *Great Lent* (New York: St. Vladimir's Seminary Press, 1974), 38–39.

162. Romero, *Homilías*, 6:370, 426.

163. Romero, *Homilías*, 6:340.

164. Romero, *Homilías*, 6:374, 426–27.

165. Romero, *Homilías*, 6:431–32.

for Romero the fulfillment of Israel's history, including God's promise of land to Israel. Over the course of Israel's history, the land God promises to Abraham and his descendants finds its unexpected fulfillment in Christ. As Romero says, "The Promised Land is not so much a geographical location as it is a society of saints and prophets that come to fruition in Mary, from whose womb the promise God makes to Abraham at last arrives." The promise of land has come in the very person of God, "the redeemer of Israel and of all peoples: Christ our Lord."[166] To paraphrase Augustine, Christ is humankind's great and profitable common land—or to use the scriptural idiom, the good and broad land flowing with milk and honey. What governs Romero's approach is the conviction that the advent of Christ changes everything, including God's promise of land. Over the course of Israel's life with God, the meaning of the promise undergoes transformation and, in Christ, ultimately finds its term.

For Romero, it follows from this that all people can now enter into the land of Christ and be nourished by it wherever they are. Romero sees El Salvador—the Land of the Savior—as one such land, despite Christianity's birth there in blood and fire and the pedagogy of death that has accompanied its transmission from the beginning. In an early homily, Romero comments on the prophet Isaiah's oracle of all nations and tongues streaming to Jerusalem. The prophet lists the names of distant lands where God's glory will be proclaimed: Tarshish, Put, Lud, Tubal, Javan, and all those other lands "that have not heard my fame or seen my glory" (Is 66:19). Romero envisions the people of El Salvador being gathered into those peoples streaming toward Jerusalem. "It is as if," he says, "one hears the concrete names of the Church that is now on pilgrimage [in El Salvador] ... Tenanchingo, San Sebastián de Ciudad Delgado, el Carmen and many other parishes and village communities ... which are the names of places being linked together, like pearls in the Kingdom of God."[167]

Even in El Salvador, the pilgrim people of God can enter into the Savior's land. Every celebration of the mass, Romero reminds them, is "an encounter with the promised land" because it is an encounter with Christ,

166. Romero, *Homilías*, 1:245.
167. Romero, *Homilías*, 1:272.

who sustains his people with himself as they travel toward him.[168] Romero can therefore describe God's call to each Christian in terms of God's call to Abraham: "Go, leave your life of sin, leave this comfortable situation of your money, your *haciendas*, all the ways in which you want to install yourself on earth, and … come towards the land that I will show you."[169]

The belief that God's promise of land to Israel finds its term in Christ is the theological heart of Romero's penultimate Sunday homily, "The Reconciliation of All Peoples in Christ, God's Plan of True Liberation." Romero delivered this homily on March 16, 1980, the fourth Sunday of Lent. Less than two weeks earlier, the government began to implement the long-awaited land reform, with the military occupying the country-side and *la locura* continuing to consume El Salvador. Together with the December 16, 1979, homily, this is Romero's most sustained engagement on the topic of land reform as he reflects upon the relationship between God's gift of the land to Israel and God's gift of Christ and what both have to do with the reconciliation he thinks El Salvador so desperately needs.

For Romero, the call to reconciliation unites the lectionary readings from Joshua 5:9–12, 2 Corinthians 5:17–21, and Luke 15:1–32. In explaining God's great "project of reconciliation," Romero frames Israel's entry into the land of promise as recounted in Joshua by first beginning with creation and God's formation of the people of Israel.[170] Creation is an act of love; God creates humankind, Romero says, to share in God's life, to be God's children. But as a consequence of sin, Adam and Eve are exiled from the garden where God originally places them. Romero's description of what has happened to them is essential to what follows: They have become landless (*desterrados*), he says.[171] Sin removes or separates (*des-*) them and their descendants from the land (*tierra*) of Eden and prevents their return (Gen 3:23). In the homily, landlessness functions for Romero as an image of sin and the damage it does to God's creation.

However, landlessness is not the end of the story but becomes a new

---

168. Romero, *Homilías*, 1:38, 40.
169. Romero, *Homilías*, 1:285.
170. Romero, *Homilías*, 6:391.
171. Romero, *Homilías*, 6:392.

beginning. A decisive moment in God's response to sin occurs when God brings Israel out of Egypt—the land of slavery—into the land promised to Abraham and his descendants (Gen 12:7). The restoration of land is a sign, Romero says, "of a return, of a search for reconciliation."[172] According to Romero, the whole history of Israel centers upon humankind's return to God, which Romero narrates principally in terms of the gift of land.[173] Of course, the land in question includes the land promised to Abraham and his descendants. But as we will see, what Romero is ultimately suggesting is that Christ himself is the land of promise incarnate and that sharing in his life is the destiny of all peoples as well as the way to their destiny.

Over the course of Lent, the church revisits God's project of reconciliation in Israel, and the first reading for this particular Sunday from the book of Joshua presents the Israelites first entering the land.[174] After having been liberated from bondage in Egypt and after sojourning in the wilderness, the people cross the Jordan River and encamp at Gilgal, on the plains of Jericho, where they celebrate the Passover, eating "of the produce of the land, unleavened cakes and parched grain" (Josh 5:11).[175] Romero views this description of Israel's entry into the land as a sign of God's work in the world to repair sin and to reconcile the world to God, alluding to events in El Salvador in relationship to it:

> At this moment in which the land of El Salvador is the object of such conflict, let us not forget that land is closely tied to God's blessings and promises. Israel now has its own land. "All this land I will give you" [Gen 13:15], God told the patriarchs, and after their enslavement, led by Moses and Joshua, here is the land. For this reason, they celebrate a great liturgy of thanksgiving: Israel's first Passover in the land, which calls to us to celebrate with equal gratitude, adoration, and appreciation the God who saves us, who has also brought us out of bondage. The God in whom we place our hope of liberation is the God of Israel.[176]

172. Romero, *Homilías*, 6:392.
173. Romero, *Homilías*, 6:392.
174. Romero, *Homilías*, 6:392.
175. Romero, *Homilías*, 6:392–93.
176. Romero, *Homilías*, 6:393, 311.

When read in relation to the other lectionary texts and against the backdrop of the implementation of the land reform, Israel's story begins to open up into new possibilities of meaning and application. In this case, it expands to include Romero's congregants and the whole people of God on pilgrimage in El Salvador, situating them and what is happening in their land in relation to Israel's entry into the land God gives them. Once again, we see how the church has not left Israel's world. Rather, it is as if its Salvadoran members are still lagging behind in the wilderness on the other side of the Jordan, looking upon the celebration on the plains of Gilgal from afar, awaiting their own entry into the land.

For Romero, the story of Israel underscores the "theological significance" of the relationship "between reconciliation and land," which is why he refers to the land reform as a "theological necessity."[177] What he means is that, although this new land is not Eden, it recalls Eden—and not only the loss of Eden, but also how God's project of reconciliation in an important sense involves the return to Eden. This is why God's restoration of land to Israel serves for Romero as a sign of God's ongoing work to repair sin and reconcile the world to God. It shows "Israel forgiven by God, returning to a land, now eating … the fruits of its own land, and the gift of land as a sign of the God who blesses."[178] Romero speaks in similar terms in his Louvain address about how the church has learned that "God maintains transcendental hope with signs of hope in history—even signs as apparently simple as those the prophet Isaiah proclaims when he says: 'They shall build houses and inhabit them; they shall plant vineyards and eat their fruit' (Isaiah 65:21)." Both Israel's entry into the land and the people of God in El Salvador's entry into theirs are part of God's reconciling work. While they are not that work's final fullness—the new heaven and the new earth—they are authentic signs of it.[179]

Romero regards God's gift of land to Israel as a particularly salient sign of reconciliation, but it also serves as a reminder of how far his own people are from such reconciliation. The land of El Salvador "groans," he says, because "the unjust hoard it and do not leave enough land for oth-

177. Romero, *Homilías*, 6:393.
178. Romero, *Homilías*, 6:393.
179. Romero, "La dimensión política de la fe desde la opción por los pobres," 190.

ers."[180] "A country's land cannot remain in few hands but must be given to all," he continues, "so that all can participate in the blessings of God."[181] The implication is that the path toward reconciliation in El Salvador involves addressing landlessness and enabling all Salvadorans to share in the land. All of this leads Romero to conclude, "There will not be true reconciliation between our people with God while there is no just distribution of land, while the goods of the land of El Salvador do not benefit and bring happiness to all Salvadorans."[182] Or as he puts it at the end of the homily, because reconciliation is so intimately tied to land, there can be no reconciliation until the economically powerful see that "they possess the land that belongs to all Salvadorans."[183]

Notice how reconciliation on Romero's terms is threefold. It includes restoration of right relationship between human beings and God. It also and at the same time includes restoration of right relationships between human beings who are estranged from one another. Finally, the restoration of both of these sets of relationships internally relates to restoration of right relationship to the created goods God gives people to foster right relationship with God and with one another. In other words, reconciliation with God and with one another cannot prescind from learning to share the land God gives them in common.[184] For this reason, any attempt at reconciliation that neglects the injustice embedded in the landscape merits the response of Jeremiah: "They have healed the wound of my people lightly, saying, 'Peace, peace,' where there is no peace" (Jer 6:14). In articulating reconciliation in these terms, Romero is simply following the pattern of the ministry of reconciliation described by Paul in 2 Corinthians 5:17–21, the second lectionary reading, in which God reconciles people to God through Christ, which not only enables the ministry of reconciliation with and for others, but also participates in a cosmic process whereby God is at work reconciling the whole world to Godself.[185]

---

180. Romero, *Homilías*, 6:393.

181. Romero, *Homilías*, 6:393.

182. Romero, *Homilías*, 6:393.

183. Romero, *Homilías*, 6:420.

184. Romero, *Homilías*, 6:392, 399, 401–2.

185. Richard B. Hays notes how Paul's articulation of new creation in Christ echoes Isaiah's vision in 65:17–19 of a new heavens and a new earth; Hays, *The Moral Vision of the New*

The path toward what Romero calls the "highest goods"[186]—the goods of grace, of God's own life in Christ and in the Spirit—inescapably involves learning to see and to use the gifts of God's creation as common.[187] A passage in the early Christian treatise the *Didache* elucidates Romero's reasoning. "Do not turn away from the needy," the author says, but "share everything … and do not say: 'It is private property.' If you are sharers in what is imperishable, how much more so in the things that perish?"[188] The question presumes that creation is a gift given by God for common use, but it also suggests that the acknowledgment of this commonality is intimately and mysteriously tied to sharing in God's common life in Christ. Receiving created goods as common gifts is the sine qua non for receiving the highest goods of all, because the latter are also common gifts, which God gives for the salvation of all people.

Yet Romero thinks too many Christians in El Salvador refuse to acknowledge that they receive their land and their harvests as gifts from God, which are meant to meet the needs of others besides themselves.[189] Instead, they hold themselves and their possessions over and against others, a parasitic posture that denies what creation most fundamentally is. They are therefore like the rich fool in Luke's parable, treating their possessions as absolutely and exclusively theirs, setting themselves up falsely as the organizing center of the world. Romero quotes from Augustine's prayer in book X of the *Confessions* to describe their sin: "You were within, but I outside, seeking there for you, and upon the shapely things you have made I rushed headlong, I, misshapen. You were with me,

---

Testament: Community, Cross, New Creation; A Contemporary Introduction to New Testament Ethics (San Francisco: HarperOne, 1996), 20.

186. Romero, *Homilías*, 6:390.

187. Romero, *Homilías*, 6:394.

188. *The Didache*, 4.5–8, in *The Didache, The Epistle of Barnabas, The Epistles and The Martyrdom of St. Polycarp, The Fragments of Papias, The Epistle to Diognetus*, trans. James Aloysius Kleist (Mahwah, N.J.: Paulist Press, 1948). This logic can also be found in scriptural passages like the second and fourth chapters in Acts, where it is as if the outpouring of the Spirit and the fullness of this sharing in God's life compels the acknowledgment among believers that nothing of what they possess is their own and that they should hold created goods in common (2:41–45; 4:31–32). This logic can also be found in the question posed by the author of 1 John: "How does God's love abide in anyone who has the world's goods and sees a brother or sister in need and yet refuses to help?" (3:17)

189. Romero, *Homilías*, 6:394.

but I was not with you. They held me back from you, those things which would have no being were they not in you."[190] As Romero explains, these wayward Christians see neither themselves nor other created things as God's gifts. They misconstrue their possessions because they misconstrue themselves and the world they inhabit, in which God gives them "their coffee farms, their estates, their ranches, their herds of cattle, all their possessions," not to be "instruments of exploitation" or to be used with "selfishness and injustice," but to make God visible in the world, and to incorporate all people into God's life.[191] Romero contrasts this with Israel's celebration of Passover on the plains of Jericho, which is a sign of what this revelation and the life it makes possible look like: "The Israelites harvested the grain; they praised the God who had given them the land and its harvests; and they shared with one another a true Passover feast…. Reconciliation instead of conflict."[192]

Although Israel's entry into the land and the Passover celebration on the plains of Jericho is an important sign of reconciliation, Romero is well aware that Israel's subsequent history is not one of perfect reconciliation with God, neighbor, and land. Even after this episode recounted in Joshua 5, Israel's life becomes a continual and complex process of turning from and struggling to return to the God from whom "they received their land and its harvests."[193] The people of Israel tend to forget that their possessions, like their lives, are gifts from God.

God's response to this turning away and forgetting is forgiveness. "This is the tenderness of God," Romero says, for God is "tireless in for-

---

190. Romero, *Homilías*, 6:394; quoting from Augustine, *The Confessions*, trans. Maria Boulding (New York: New City Press, 2001), X.27.

191. In elaborating upon the notion of land as an instrument of exploitation, Romero offers a detailed analysis of *Igreja e problemas da terra*, a pastoral letter by the Conferência Nacional dos Bispos do Brasil (National Conference of Bishops of Brazil). The document analyzes the land problem in Brazil by distinguishing between land for exploitation and land for work. The former prioritizes land as a tool to make money, without regard for human beings or their needs. The latter prioritizes human beings by ensuring all have access to land for the purpose of a livelihood and the provisioning food for themselves and others; Romero, *Homilías*, 6:395–97.

192. Romero, *Homilías*, 6:394–95.

193. Romero, *Homilías*, 6:394.

giving, tireless in loving."[194] As the March 16 homily moves toward its conclusion, God's tenderness becomes yet another sign for Romero— the definitive sign—of God's project of reconciliation, because Christ is the very incarnation of that reconciliation. God's tireless and forgiving love made flesh in Christ becomes the primary lens through which Romero reflects upon how God deals with the damage sin does and how God patiently and mercifully works to restore creation. Romero now examines God's ongoing life with Israel and the promise of land in light of Christ.

The gospel passage from the March 16 homily is Luke 15:1–32, the parable of the Prodigal Son. Romero calls it "the parable of Christian reconciliation" because for him the story concerns both brothers' need for reconciliation and above all their father's mercy.[195] The parable begins with the younger son asking for his share of the familial estate and his father complying with the request (Lk 15:11–13). After collecting the rest of his possessions, the son sets off to a "distant country" and promptly squanders his "property," losing himself in "dissolute living" (Lk 15:14).[196] He falls into such destitution that he envies the food fed to the pigs under his care and falls into such disrepute that "no one gave him anything" (Lk 15:15–16).

On Romero's reading, the story of the younger son is the story of sin. Therefore, it is an old story that continues to be repeated every day. "Each one of us," Romero says, "can see our own personal history in him."[197] God, like the father in the parable, wants to share God's life with those, who, like the younger son, would prefer to go off in search of life apart from God.[198] The younger son is for Romero a figure of all those who would regard their lives and their possessions as exclusively their own.[199] In this way, he is similar to the rich fool in Luke's parable. The illusion of such a life can be sustained for a time, Romero admits. As long as people

194. Romero, *Homilías*, 6:394.

195. Romero, *Homilías*, 6:397.

196. Though Romero does not comment upon it, the Greek word Luke uses for property is *ousian*, from *ousia*, which means "substance" or "being," implying a close connection between the son's squandering of his possessions and the squandering of his own substance or being.

197. Romero, *Homilías*, 6:397, 390.

198. Romero, *Homilías*, 6:397.

199. Romero, *Homilías*, 6:397.

have money, health, and friends, they can seem to be sufficient in their life apart from God. But, in one form or another, Romero believes, this sense of sufficiency will one day come to an end.[200]

Eventually, the younger son comes to his senses, and he decides to return to his homeland (Lk 15:17). His plan is to plead for forgiveness and to ask to be reinstated in his father's house—this time, not as a son but as a servant (Lk 15:18–19). But upon his approach, the son finds his father already waiting for him. The son does not need to say anything at all, because "while he was still far off, his father saw him and was filled with compassion; he ran and put his arms around him and kissed him" (Lk 15:20). A celebration immediately ensues. Romero reads the homecoming of the younger son as a sign of reconciliation. The son's journey homeward is the path of conversion incumbent upon all sinners, to which God's response is mercy. "When the son, whose life is marked by misery and by the abandonment of others remembers that there is no greater love than God's, he returns," Romero says. "And the son, who should find God resentful toward him or with the back turned, instead finds God turned toward him with arms outstretched, ready to celebrate his return."[201]

All people can find themselves in the figure of the younger son, but Romero thinks many in El Salvador can likewise find themselves in the figure of the older son.[202] The older son is out in the fields at the time of his brother's return. Upon hearing the sounds of music and dancing coming from the house, he becomes angry, refusing to enter and to participate in the festivities (Lk 15:25–28). He thinks that his father's response to his brother's return is a violation of justice. He has always been obedient to his father but has never been celebrated in this way (Lk 15:28–30). As far as the older brother is concerned, his younger brother's transgressions cannot be forgiven, and the home he has with his father cannot be shared.

In his complaints, as well as in his refusal to be with his brother, Romero finds echoes of the mutual recriminations of left and right in El

200. Romero, *Homilías*, 6:398.
201. Romero, *Homilías*, 6:397–98.
202. Romero, *Homilías*, 6:399.

Salvador, the intensifying polarization, and the recourse to violence.[203] Romero also finds pride in the older son's response, which is why Romero comments, "There is nothing more opposed to reconciliation than pride—those prideful people who think that they are clean and pure, who think they have the right to point to others as the cause of all the injustice, but who are unable to look within themselves and to acknowledge the part they have played in the chaos of our country."[204] El Salvador is full of people like the older brother who imagine themselves free from entanglements in injustice and who are characteristically shrill in their call for changes by others without seeing their own need to be made new in Christ. However, according to Romero, such a stance only exacerbates the violence by building up and reinforcing the barriers that must be broken down for true reconciliation to be possible.[205] In the end, the older brother finds himself in a similar position to his younger brother. He is alone outside the house, just like his younger brother was alone with the pigs. This feature of the parable conveys how the older brother is also in need of reconciliation, which is why, Romero observes, the father must go out to him in mercy as well.[206]

Although Romero does not make much of the connection in this homily, notice also how it is the celebration of the younger son and his inclusion in the sharing of the goods of the house—especially the prized possession of the fatted calf—that occasions the older brother's resentment and his refusal to enter (Lk 15:23, 30). In other words, the sharing of the goods of the home and the sharing of the life of the home are closely connected. Therefore, just as with the other lectionary readings for this Sunday, the reconciliation suggested by this parable of Christian reconciliation is threefold. The reconciliation it envisions involves the restoration of right relationship between the sons and their father, between the sons themselves, and finally with the goods of the home and the sharing of life they make possible.

Along these same lines, the father's response to the older son is cru-

---

203. Romero, *Homilías*, 6:399.
204. Romero, *Homilías*, 6:399.
205. Romero, *Homilías*, 6:398–99.
206. Romero, *Homilías*, 6:398–99.

cially important, not only for the meaning of the parable, but also for Romero's own understanding of the theological significance of land reform in El Salvador and its relationship to humankind's common destiny in Christ. "All that is mine is yours," the father says (Lk 15:31). Jesus describes the house of God—the house in which he will prepare a place for his followers—in almost the exact same terms in John's Gospel: "All I have is yours, and all you have is mine" (Jn 17:10; see 14:1-2, 20). The father must explicitly say to his elder son what his celebration of the younger son enacts: The life of this home is a common one, whose hallmark is a sharing from which no one is excluded. Even the younger son, who had sunk into destitution and disgrace, shares in its prized possession, the fatted calf. For in the life of this home, not only are prized possessions shared, but they are shared so that the home's inhabitants can share the highest good of all: the love that forgives sins and rejoices in the return of the lost.

Romero thinks this parable of reconciliation is ultimately about God's work in Christ. The conflict that prompts it, he observes, is the murmuring among the Pharisees and the scribes regarding how Jesus eats with sinners (Lk 15:1-2).[207] Understood in this way, the parable depicts Jesus Christ himself, with the father revealing the tireless and forgiving love of God, whose face is Christ. And this is why, as Romero repeatedly says, "There can be no reconciliation without clinging to Christ."[208] Sending the Son is how God reconciles the world to God; following Christ is how humankind learns to share in God's life and make its way toward the heavenly land it has been given by God in him.

Earlier we examined how and why Romero thinks the liturgy uniquely recalls the mystery of Christ and that, in the church's celebration of it, what happened in the land where Jesus lived, died, and rose continues to be present to all lands. But in our consideration of the December 16 homily, we also saw how Romero thinks Christ continues to be present in other ways as well, identifying so closely with those who hunger and

---

207. Romero, *Homilías*, 6:399.
208. Romero, *Homilías*, 6:399-400.

thirst or who are homeless, naked, sick, and imprisoned that he shares their afflictions. In concluding his reflections upon the readings for the fourth Sunday of Lent, Romero focuses especially upon this presence—Christ's presence among the needy and afflicted—and its import for reconciliation in El Salvador:

> Christ is the presence of God's reconciliation in the world…. God in Christ dwells very near to us. Christ has given us a guideline: "I was hungry and you gave me food." Where there are hungry people, Christ is near. "I was thirsty and you gave me something to drink." When someone arrives at your house asking you for water, there is Christ if you look with the eyes of faith. In the sick person in need of a visit, Christ tells you: "I was sick and you visited me." Or in prison. How many people today are scared to testify on behalf of the innocent! What terror has been sown among us such that even friends betray friends! If we could see Christ in the needy, the tortured, the imprisoned, and the murdered—in all those thrown to the curb with contempt like garbage—then we would discover Christ among the discarded, like a gold medallion that we would hold tenderly and kiss and not be ashamed.[209]

For Romero, Christ's ongoing association with those in need is bound to God's work of reconciliation in Christ. Romero is suggesting that the work of mercy is of infinite value—worth more than all the land and wealth a person possesses—because it is an encounter with Christ and the heavenly land he is. The image of the gold medallion evokes the Matthean parables that compare the kingdom of God to a treasure hidden in a field or to a pearl of great price (Mt 13:44-45). Seeing Christ in others and putting land, wealth, and other created goods at the service of their needs is the path of reconciliation, preserving its threefold form. Once more, the work of mercy offers a glimpse of how God renews creation and cultivates acknowledgment of its common destiny, which is revealed through Christ's ongoing presence among those in need of food, drink, clothing, shelter, care, and visitation. In pleading for mercy and in working to break down the barriers that land and wealth erect between people,

---

209. Romero, *Homilías*, 6:400.

Christ continues to build up his body in the world and reconcile all things to himself.

This passage also suggests that the violence of this time made people fear the work of mercy. People were scared to receive strangers, slake their thirst, tend to the sick, and visit the imprisoned. Indeed, the work of mercy involved great risks. Captain Álvaro Saravia, one of the men implicated in Romero's death, explains in a recent interview that the simple act of sharing tortillas with a stranger "would have been considered communist … in those days. Take him out, wreck his house and tell him 'sonofabitch, you're with the guerrillas.'"[210]

Not only feeding the hungry, but also comforting the afflicted and welcoming the stranger was dangerous work. By mid-March 1980, when Romero delivered this homily, the Archdiocese of San Salvador was in the midst of a massive refugee crisis as *campesinos* fled the repression in the countryside associated with the implementation of the land reform. Families abandoned their homes and slept in the mountains and forests, but they also came in droves to the archdiocese, where Romero sheltered them on church property. In the final weeks of his life, Romero was hard at work welcoming and caring for strangers, helping to establish makeshift refugee centers for the displaced in the San José de la Montaña Seminary, the Basilica of the Sacred Heart, and elsewhere.[211] But neither those in need of refuge nor those who were offering it could be assured of their safety. In his final homilies, Romero repeatedly defended the church's actions against charges that the refugee centers were sites of political indoctrination and military training.[212] In this case, as in many others, the merciful of El Salvador risked sharing in the suffering of those to whom they extended mercy.

In his March 16 homily, Romero clearly does not see Christ's association with those in need as a denial or a minimization of the other ways Christ continues to be with his people. Romero points to the church as

210. Carlos Dada, "Así matamos a Monseñor Romero," *El Faro*, March 22, 2010.

211. Romero, *Homilías*, 6:405, 414, 444–45; Roberto Cuéllar, "Monseñor Óscar Romero: Human Rights Apostle" (International Conference on Archbishop Óscar Romero, Notre Dame, Ind., 2014).

212. Romero, *Homilías*, 6:405, 444–45.

Christ's ecclesial body as well as Christ's promise at the end of Matthew's Gospel: "Remember, I am with you always, to the end of the age [28:20]." Christ is also present, Romero says, in the sacramental body that they are about to receive, where he continues to offer himself as nourishment for his people on pilgrimage.[213] For Romero, Christ's ongoing presence in his needy, ecclesial, and sacramental bodies are inextricably related to one another, for it is the same Christ who is present in each.

God's mercy in Christ is the foundation of their relationship. According to Romero, the church does not simply deliver a message about mercy; mercy is the basis of its existence as a body. The church exists only through God's work of mercy in Christ, which can be seen, among other ways, in the sacraments. That the church is Christ's ecclesial body means that its membership is the extension across time and space of Christ's merciful embrace of suffering humanity. But being part of Christ's ecclesial body also means that this embrace of suffering, which is perfect in Christ, is imperfect in his frail, fallible, and miserable members, who struggle to receive the mercy God offers them as they also struggle to be bearers of it themselves. "To try to discover this Christ," Romero therefore says in concluding his treatment of the lectionary texts the fourth Sunday of Lent, "is our great pastoral task, and if I refer here to the things of the earth or to politics it is for the purpose of guiding our reflection more closely to Christ."[214]

The effect of the March 16 homily as a whole is that the people of God on pilgrimage in El Salvador are surrounded on all sides by the gift of God's merciful presence in Christ. They live "saturated" with it, as Romero puts it in another of his homilies.[215] Moreover, the March 16 homily encourages us to see this saturation of God's presence in Christ in relation to the long story of God's dealings with sin, beginning with the landlessness of Adam, Eve, and their descendants, which for Romero is such a powerful and pertinent instance of it. Despite the refusal of God's gifts and the common life they are given to foster, and despite the death and violence unleashed into the world as a consequence of that refusal, God's

213. Romero, *Homilías*, 6:400.
214. Romero, *Homilías*, 6:400.
215. Romero, *Homilías*, 3:432–33.

characteristic response, Romero suggests, is not to withdraw but to come closer. The promises to Abraham, the exodus from Egypt, and the gift of land gather history in the direction of God's own coming in Christ. Even the rejection and crucifixion of the gift of Christ lead to further gifts of his presence in his needy, ecclesial, and sacramental bodies.

In the meantime, Romero's message to his people in his penultimate Sunday homily is that Christ continues to await their conversion, like the tireless and forgiving love of the father in the parable of the Prodigal Son. Christ's presence is a love that is always already there, ready to embrace those like the younger son who have fallen to their knees before creatures and who are trying to stand up and walk away, or those like the elder son who refuse to forgive sins and celebrate the return of the lost. But wherever people are, when they turn toward Christ they encounter the land toward which they travel, as well as the way to it. To find Christ is to discover that this land can only be shared. Working for a more just distribution of land in El Salvador, Romero thinks, affords his people an opportunity to anticipate its life.

Despite being surrounded on all sides by God's presence in Christ, the bloodletting unleashed upon the Salvadoran people by elements in the military and oligarchy continued. In his final two Sunday homilies, Romero repeatedly turns to the story of Cain and Abel, claiming that the question God poses to Cain after he kills his brother is the same one that God is presently asking of the Salvadoran people: "Where is Abel your brother?" All the blood being shed, Romero says, joins Abel's in crying out to God from the ground (Gen 4:9–10).[216] But in faith, Romero continues, Christians believe the cry is also that of Christ, for "whatever is done to the poor and the oppressed he receives as if done to himself [Mt 25:40]."[217]

Stopping the violence and finding shelter for those fleeing the repression became Romero's principal preoccupations during his final days. Regarding the land reform, Romero struggles to clarify his perceived am-

216. Romero, *Homilías*, 6:411, 453.
217. Romero, *Homilías*, 6:411.

bivalence to the reform and to explain the archdiocese's own understanding of the rapidly evolving situation. In addressing the perception that the church now seems to be against the reform it previously supported, Romero says in the March 16 homily, "Let it be very clear that, according to the bible, to the social doctrine of the Church, and to the very activity of the Church, the Church … supports 'the efforts of those in rural areas for an authentic land reform, that makes it possible for them to access land to cultivate.'"[218] "We are not against these reforms," Romero asserts at another point, for "the mystery of reconciliation with God and justice in the distribution of land belong to the revelation of God."[219] At the same time, Romero is adamant that "neither the land reform nor … the other promised measures can be productive if there is blood. We must not forget what God says to Cain: 'The blood-soaked ground can never be fertile.' Blood-soaked reforms can never be fruitful."[220]

According to Romero, then, the church opposes bloodshed, but not the land reform. Yet the implementation of the reform is only exacerbating the suffering of the Salvadoran people, contradicting the whole purpose of the reform and impelling the country closer to civil war and away from reconciliation.[221] The complexity and opacity of the situation raise a host of unresolved questions for Romero, which he continues to wrestle with until his death: What exactly is happening and why? Should the reforms proceed or must the violence end first? What is the best response to a situation in which efforts to address the injustice become complexly implicated in further injustice? In the end, Romero urges decoupling the reform from the repression. The bloodshed, he thinks, must cease before anything constructive can come of the land reform. "What is most needed at this moment," he insists, "is to halt the repression."[222]

But the repression did not end. Romero's homily on March 23, the fifth Sunday of Lent, was his last Sunday homily. At the outset, Romero observes that conditions in El Salvador provide their own form of Lent-

---

218. Romero, *Homilías*, 6:396. The quotation is from *Igreja e problemas da terra*.
219. Romero, *Homilías*, 6:411.
220. Romero, *Homilías*, 6:411. Romero is paraphrasing Gen 4:11–12.
221. Romero, *Homilías*, 6:412.
222. Romero, *Homilías*, 6:412, 419.

en preparation that reminds the pilgrim church that Easter is the celebration of Christ's victory over death and that "neither death nor all the signs of death" conquer those who are in Christ.[223] Yet since death continues to hold sway over earthly life, "it is first necessary to accompany Christ through Lent, through a Holy Week that is cross, sacrifice, martyrdom…. At present, our people are well prepared for this, because all that surrounds us proclaims the cross."[224] We therefore find ourselves, Romero observes later in the homily, "meditating on Christ's passion among a people that likewise carries a cross on its back."[225]

Near the end of the homily, Romero discusses the archdiocese's preparations for Holy Week—the location and times of the blessing of the palms, the route of the Palm Sunday procession, and the details surrounding the Chrism mass[226]—before turning to the events of the "tremendously tragic" past week.[227] He recounts what the archdiocese knows about the various military operations conducted in the countryside, the houses looted and burned, the *campesinos* killed, the damage done by a bomb blast at the Ministry of Agriculture, and the armed siege of the University of El Salvador, as well as the archdiocese's response to the violence.[228]

The homily famously concludes with Romero's appeal to members of the military involved in the repressive implementation of the land reform—an appeal that was likely Romero's death sentence because of the suggestion of insubordination. "You are killing your own *campesino* brothers and sisters," he tells them, "and faced with an order to kill that comes from human authority, God's law must prevail, which says: 'You shall not kill' [Ex 20:13; see Acts 5:29]. No soldier is obligated to obey an order contrary to God's law. No one has to obey an immoral law. It is time that you recovered your conscience and obeyed it rather than the order of sin."[229] Once again, Romero evokes God's words to Cain about Abel's

---

223. Romero, *Homilías*, 6:425.
224. Romero, *Homilías*, 6:425.
225. Romero, *Homilías*, 6:439.
226. Romero, *Homilías*, 6:438–40.
227. Romero, *Homilías*, 6:446.
228. Romero, *Homilías*, 6:446–51.
229. Romero, *Homilías*, 6:453.

blood crying out from ground, associating Abel's blood with the blood in the fields of El Salvador: "The reforms are worth nothing if they come stained with so much blood. In the name of God, in the name of this suffering people, whose laments rise to heaven each day more tumultuously, I beg you, I plead with you, I order you in the name of God: Stop the repression!"[230]

The next day, March 24, Romero was killed as he celebrated mass at the Chapel of the Hospital of the Divine Providence. A sniper stepped out of a red Volkswagen Passat, stood at the door of the chapel, and fired a single shot.[231]

Romero had just finished the homily moments before and had turned to take the corporal to begin the Eucharistic liturgy, the memorial of Christ's passion. The fragmentation bullet from the sniper's rifle entered Romero's chest, scattering inside and causing massive internal hemorrhaging. Romero slumped to the side of the altar and lay dying at the foot of the crucifix behind it, his blood pooling on the ground.[232]

230. Romero, *Homilías*, 6:453.

231. "Salvador Archbishop Assassinated by Sniper while Officiating at Mass," *New York Times*, March 25, 1980. There are discrepancies in the accounts of what happened. While some claim that the sniper fired from within the car, others say that he stepped out because the trajectory with which the bullet entered Romero would have been impossible had the sniper remained in the car. See Matt Eisenbrandt's discussion in *Assassination of a Saint: The Plot to Murder Óscar Romero and the Quest to Bring His Killers to Justice* (Oakland: University of California Press, 2017), 13, 182n44.

232. Those present quickly loaded Romero into the back of a pickup truck and rushed him to a local hospital, where he was declared dead soon after his arrival; Morozzo della Rocca, *Primero Dios*, 457–58.

Part 3

BODY OF CHRIST

−5−

THE WITNESS OF ÓSCAR ROMERO

The incarnation of God's solidarity with the poor (in every form) has
... a catastrophic logic: if he takes this seriously, it will bring him to
the cross.

> —Hans Urs von Balthasar, *The Glory of the Lord*

In the harassment, imprisonment, torture, disappearance and murder of destitute Salvadoran campesinos ... the Lord Jesus Christ has
been repeatedly crucified.

> —Óscar Romero, *Letter to Cardinal Baggio*

Chapter 4 located Romero's ministry and the conflicts that led to his
death within a much longer societal and ecclesial conversation about land
reform. We also saw how the church's advocacy for a more just distribution of land under Romero's leadership drew heavily upon Catholic social
teaching and its politics of common use, but also how that advocacy and
the rural organizing that was closely tied to it led to the persecution of
the church and the repression of the Salvadoran people.

However, it also became clear that not any and every part of the
church was attacked, but especially practitioners of the politics of common use. By applying the social teaching of the church, Romero and

253

many others faced suffering and death. In a recent pastoral letter, this is what José Luis Escobar Alas, the sitting archbishop of San Salvador, calls El Salvador's own *ruta martirial* (martyrial route), by which he means a path "soaked with the sanctity of all those men and women who gave their blood for the love of Christ personified in the face of the poor."[1] A striking feature of this letter, which is in part a Salvadoran martyrology, is how many of the martyrs Escobar Alas recalls advocated for land reform or worked with rural organizations and associations in some way—a reality that points to, as Gutiérrez puts it, "the density of the resistance that is necessary to overcome in transforming the 'anti-evangelical poverty' that reigns in the subcontinent."[2] In Romero—and in many others besides him—we see that the message of Puebla also became a story of martyrdom. That it became a story of martyrdom exemplifies the depth of the resistance to the politics of common use that is still present in the world, as well as the suffering and even death that its practitioners can face.

At the same time, it is important to recognize that this resistance to the politics of common use in El Salvador was not inevitable, and that events might have unfolded otherwise. The oligarchy might have responded to Romero by moving heaven and earth to address the agrarian crisis. The government might have successfully and smoothly rolled out its land reform without the oligarchy and military unleashing the *Matanza* approach. Alternatively, even in the midst of the mounting repression, Romero did not have to die a martyr. He might have succumbed to cancer, suffered a heart attack, or died in a car crash.

However, in relation to the story we have been telling in these pages, it is fitting that Romero did die a martyr. The notion of fittingness and theological arguments based upon it run deep in Christianity. They speak to the coherence—and even the beauty—of God's dealings with the world in becoming incarnate or in suffering and dying on a cross.[3] This chap-

---

1. See Escobar Alas, *Ustedes también darán testimonio*, 160.

2. Gutiérrez, *Beber en su propio pozo*, 154.

3. See Athanasius, *On the Incarnation of the Word* (Crestwood, N.Y.: St. Vladimir's Seminary Press, 1996), 10, 22, 26, 37, 41, 44; Anselm of Canterbury, *Why God Became Man*, in *The Major Works* (New York: Oxford University Press, 1998), 263, 285–86, 323, 339; Thomas Aquinas, *ST* III, q. 46, a. 4; Julian of Norwich, *Showings*, trans. Edmund Colledge, OSA, and James Walsh, SJ (Mahwah, N.J.: Paulist Press, 1978), chapters 1, 13, 40, 50.

ter makes a similar claim about Romero's martyrial route. In Romero's El Salvador, those who took the truth about God's creation as common gift seriously suffered greatly as a result, which shows how, under the conditions of sin and violence, the politics of common use tends toward the cross. Those like Romero who worked so that others had what was theirs in justice risked laying down their lives in charity. As Romero explains, "The greatest sign of the faith in a God of life is the testimony of those who are willing to give their lives. 'No one has greater love than this, to lay down one's life for one's friends' (Jn 15:13). And this is what we see daily in our country."[4] Romero's martyrdom was fitting because in laying down his own life in love for Christ personified in the face of the impoverished, Romero bore witness to God's work in the world in Christ.

Pope Francis addressed the fittingness of Romero's martyrdom in October 2015 when he said to a Salvadoran delegation that Romero's martyrdom did not simply occur at the moment of his death. Francis is referring to Romero's experience of suffering and persecution prior to his death, as well as to the defamation and slander he suffered (and continues to suffer) after it. Francis reports that, as a young priest in Argentina, he personally heard many unjustly criticize Romero. Romero was repeatedly "scourged with the hardest stone that exists in the world: the tongue." Francis then goes on to say, "*Es lindo verlo también así* (It is beautiful to see him like this): a man who continues to be a martyr … after giving his life, he continued to give it."[5] With these words, Francis is suggesting that in light of the life Romero lived, it is possible to discern beauty in his death, just as it is possible to discern beauty even amidst the damage to his reputation after death. Perhaps another way to put Francis's point is that the beauty of a life given in love is able to retain its shape despite all the suffering it endures. What is more, in a mysterious way, it is as if the persecution, the death, and the slander contribute to the splendor of the witness, because they only reveal the depth of the love that lives like Romero's image.[6]

4. Romero, "La dimensión política de la fe desde la opción por los pobres," 191.

5. Francis I, *Address of His Holiness Pope Francis to the Pilgrimage from El Salvador*, October 30, 2015.

6. Here, as elsewhere, this chapter is indebted to Natalie Carnes, *Image and Presence: A*

Romero's martyrdom also fittingly displays the relationship between justice and charity at the heart of this study—a relationship that illumines the grammar of creation. We have repeatedly seen that if God's purpose for creation is to be realized, the virtues of justice and charity must walk with one another. Justice guides because the belief that creation is a common gift concerns justice. But given how sin blocks the access of so many to what is theirs in justice, charity and its act of mercy are justice's crucial companions. Charity heals the damage sin does to creation, among other ways, by helping people to hold what is common in ways that preserve it as common out of love of God and neighbor— despite the often considerable cost of doing so. Charity strengthens and supports justice's work and, sometimes, even dies for it. In this way, the gift of charity conforms people to Christ, who restores creation, not from far off, but by coming near in order to share the fullness of God's life and by bearing the risk that love's vulnerability inescapably involves. For the one in whom all creation holds together brings peace and heals sin's damage precisely "through the blood of his cross" (Col 1:15–20).

By pursuing justice in charity, Romero and the countless others who have walked a similar martyrial route therefore witness to the way God's merciful work in Christ to restore creation is cruciform. Romero's insistence that the land of El Salvador belonged to all who lived there continued to cost him more and more—until it finally cost him everything. Charity accompanied justice not only in Romero's life, but also in his willingness to face death as he did. Therefore, we can say that while Romero worked for justice, the charity with which he bore witness to this justice became a revelation of Christ. In the end, Romero's life and death cohered so closely to God's relationship to the world in Christ that they became a luminous image of it, one in which God's creative and salvific work came into striking focus.

This is why our examination of Romero's participation in the reform of Salvadoran agriculture, in addition to clarifying the conflicts surrounding his martyrdom, also bears upon Romero's role in the drama of

---

Christological Reflection upon Iconoclasm and Iconophilia (Redwood City, Calif.: Stanford University Press, 2017).

salvation as a figure that represents and draws others into God's ongoing activity in the world in Christ and in the Spirit.[7] For in effect, Romero's own life became an answer to the question he posed in the funeral homily for Grande about what the church contributes to the universal struggle for liberation from so much misery. If, as Romero contends there, the church's prime contribution is to produce liberators who are inspired by the faith, motivated by love, oriented by social teaching, and who collaborate with Christ by bearing crosses, then Romero—like Grande—is an example of one. Attending to lives like his therefore helps "read" social teaching by concretizing the liberation it proclaims.[8]

This chapter returns to the question with which this work began: to what does Romero bear witness? The preceding pages have used notions of "witness" and "bearing witness" broadly. In this final chapter, the focus turns to a very specific form of witness: the witness of Romero as a martyr of the church. "Martyr" derives from the Greek *martus,* or "witness," and in this case it refers to those who suffer and die for having refused to renounce the Christian faith, bearing witness to Christ by imitating his passion.[9]

Roberto Casas Andrés has documented how popular traditions of recognizing and remembering Romero's martyrdom immediately arose in the wake of his death, despite the danger this involved.[10] Ten years later, Arturo Rivera y Damas, the archbishop of San Salvador at the time, opened a cause of beatification and canonization. Over the ensuing decades, the cause moved forward, though not without obstacles. The cause was delayed and then later stalled because of "prudential reasons"—the phrase frequently used in official statements.[11] It was also temporarily "blocked" by the Congregation for the Doctrine of the Faith because of

<hr>

7. Walatka, *Von Balthasar and the Option for the Poor,* 161–66.

8. See *Centesimus Annus,* no. 59.

9. For a good overview, see Servais Pinckaers, *The Spirituality of Martyrdom ... to the Limits of Love,* trans. Patrick Clark and Annie Hounsokou (Washington, D.C.: The Catholic University of America Press, 2016), 37–51.

10. Casas Andrés, *Dios pasó por El Salvador,* 193, 179–244.

11. The crux of the issue was Romero's posthumous remembrance and adoption as a symbol of the political left in El Salvador and elsewhere; see Benedict XVI, *Interview of His Holiness Benedict XVI during the Flight to Brazil,* May 9, 2007; Francis I, *In-Flight Press Conference of His Holiness Pope Francis from Korea to Rome,* August 18, 2014.

some questions concerning Romero's orthodoxy.[12] However, once Benedict XVI "unblocked" the cause in 2012, it moved forward rapidly, which continued after the election of Francis in 2013.[13]

Early in 2015, theologians at the Congregation for the Causes of Saints unanimously affirmed that Romero was murdered in hatred of the church's faith (*in odium fidei*)—the traditional criterion for martyrdom—and that Romero was indeed a martyr. That May—thirty-five years after he was killed—Romero was beatified in San Salvador, with hundreds of thousands gathered at a downtown landmark dedicated to the country's namesake patron: Plaza Salvador del Mundo (Savior of the World Plaza). Then, a little over three years later—on October 14, 2018—Romero was canonized in Rome alongside Pope Paul VI and five others, marking an end of the process of approval for Romero's cause for sainthood.

To what, then, does Romero bear witness? This chapter reflects theologically upon the claim that Romero is a Salvadoran Jesus Christ, which frequently occurs in the scholarship on Romero.[14] For instance, in a homily preached soon after Romero's death, Ignacio Ellacuría famously declared, "With Monsignor Romero, God passed through El Salvador."[15] By this, Ellacuría meant that God in Christ passed through El Salvador in the person of Romero. In his life and especially in his death, Romero was a manifestation of Christ. Christ's presence in Romero—what we might call Christ's martyrial presence—was analogous to Christ's presence in his needy, ecclesial, and sacramental bodies.

Ellacuría's claim, which Romero's beatification and canonization only substantiated, merits further theological reflection. At the end of chapter 4, we saw Romero console his people by telling them they are sur-

12. Romero's cause was studied by the Congregation of the Doctrine of the Faith beginning in 2000, which eventually concluded that the concerns over Romero's orthodoxy were unfounded. See "Un hombre de la Iglesia y del evangelio," *El Diario de Hoy*, March 22, 2005; Carlos Colorado, "Cronología de la causa de la beatificación, *Super Martyrio*, May 9, 2006."

13. Colorado, "Pope Francis and Óscar Romero," *Super Martyrio*, March 29, 2013; Colorado, "Romero in the Age of Francis," *Super Martyrio*, June 29, 2014; Clarke, *Óscar Romero: Love Must Win Out*, 3–6.

14. Peterson, *Martyrdom and the Politics of Religion*, 102.

15. Quoted in Jon Sobrino and Rolando Alvarado, eds., *Ignacio Ellacuría, aquella libertad esclarecida* (Santander: Editorial SAL TERRAE, 1999), 17; see also Casas Andrés, *Dios pasó por El Salvador*.

rounded by the gift of God's presence in Christ and that, despite the rejection of God's gifts and the violence the Salvadoran people experience, God remains near to them; they remain "saturated" with Christ's presence. This chapter follows these theological convictions by reflecting upon how the shape of Romero's own life and death light up Christ's abiding presence in the world—a presence that characteristically continues to give itself in the midst of mockery, beatings, and crucifixion because it is the presence of a love that has defeated them. Considering Romero's martyrdom involves considering the mystery of the crucifixion itself. For in attempting to stop the land reform by erasing those like Romero who were calling for it, Romero's killers unwittingly gave the world a Salvadoran Christ, through whose life God's purpose for creation and God's ongoing work to restore it are made known.

CIRCUMSTANCES OF ROMERO'S MARTYRDOM

The plot to kill Romero was known by its planners and operatives as *Operación Piña* (Operation Pineapple).[16] Because of the lack of investigation by the Salvadoran police in the immediate aftermath of Romero's assassination, as well as the killing or disappearance of key witnesses and the general obstructionism by authorities, much about the plot remains unknown.[17] Nevertheless, examining what is known offers a window into the world of those who opposed Romero—an opposition that reached the highest echelons of political and economic power in El Salvador and even the United States.

The man who killed Romero was a trained sniper who fired once before fleeing the scene. In a remarkable piece by the Salvadoran journalist Carlos Dada, "*Así Matamos a Monseñor Romero*" ("How We Killed Monsignor Romero"), Dada draws extensively on interviews with Captain Álva-

16. The meaning of *piña* (pineapple) in this connection is unclear. Ochoa reports that it is a reference to the bullet, which looked like a pineapple and was designed to fragment and expand upon entering Romero's chest. The Carmelite nuns who care for Romero's relics and home told me a similar story, adding that his attackers used this bullet to shred his heart, because Romero was the symbolic heart of the Salvadoran people. Others have suggested that the word as it actually appears in the plans is *PINA*, not *PIÑA*, an acronym rather than a reference to the fruit. See Ochoa, *Tiempos de Locura*, 294; Eisenbrandt, *Assassination of a Saint*, 180, n. 10.

17. Morozzo della Rocca, *Primero Dios*, 459–67.

ro Saravia, who was the only person to be held accountable by a court of law for the killing. In the piece, Saravia claims that the sniper came from the security detail of Mario Molina, the son of a former president of El Salvador. Saravia describes the sniper as a tall, slender, and bearded man, identifying him simply as a Salvadoran and a former national guardsman. To this day, his identity and whereabouts remain unknown.[18] Roberto Mathies Regalado, the owner of the local Volkswagen agency, donated the red Volkswagen Passat—the vehicle used to drive the sniper to the chapel—to Roberto D'Aubuisson, widely regarded as the mastermind behind *Operación Piña,* in order to support D'Aubuisson's anti-communist efforts.[19]

Saravia says the sniper was hired for one thousand Salvadoran *colones,* which at the time would have been approximately $200. The money allegedly came from a Salvadoran businessman named Eduardo Lemus O'Byrne, a former president of the ANEP, a federation of twenty-five associations that claimed to represent "the most productive sectors of the nation."[20] We encountered ANEP in chapter 4 when it withdrew from the Land Reform Congress in 1970 with the rest of the entrepreneurial sector and later spearheaded opposition to Molina's agrarian transformation project. According to Dada, it was O'Byrne's opposition to land reform in particular that led him to support D'Aubuisson.[21]

We also encountered D'Aubuisson in chapter 4. His "group," which had ties with the oligarchy and factions in the military, helped carry out the *Matanza* approach in response to the prospect of the JRG's land reform. D'Aubuisson's obituary in the *New York Times* describes him as a hero among the powerful of El Salvador, who regarded him as "a relentless crusader" against those "demanding land redistribution and political

18. Those others directly involved in the crime either remain in hiding or are deceased. The man who drove the sniper, Amado Garay, is a protected witness in the United States. According to Dada, apart from Garay, Saravia, and the sniper, the others have all died. "One was decapitated, one committed suicide, another disappeared, still another was killed at a highway checkpoint, and the fifth ended up torn to pieces"; Dada, "Así matamos a Monseñor Romero."

19. Dada, "Así matamos a Monseñor Romero."

20. ANEP, "Declarations on Land Reform and the Government's Response (July 1976)," in *The Central American Crisis Reader* (New York: Summit, 1987), 343.

21. Dada, "Así matamos a Monseñor Romero."

reforms."[22] In El Salvador, D'Aubuisson was also synonymous with the death squads that conducted extrajudicial killings and disappearances throughout the 1970s and 1980s. A former national guardsman and major in the Salvadoran army, D'Aubuisson helped found one group known as the Unión de Guerrera Blanca (White Warriors Union, UGB).[23] He also led another group known as the Brigada Anticomunista General Maximiliano Hernández Martínez (Maximiliano Hernández Martínez Anticommunist Brigade), named after the president who presided over *la Matanza* in 1932.[24] D'Aubuisson's extensive military experience included various tours in the United States, where he studied intelligence and security operations.[25] In the 1970s, he also trained in anti-communist counterinsurgency at the School of the Americas, which was then located at U.S. Army base Fort Gulick in the former Panama Canal Zone.

D'Aubuisson eventually became a successful Salvadoran politician in the 1980s, even founding the Alianza Republicana Nacionalista (National Republican Alliance, ARENA) in 1981, which ruled El Salvador from 1989 to 2009. ARENA and D'Aubuisson also had close ties to the Republican party in the United States,[26] and throughout his time in public office, D'Aubuisson continued to lead ARENA's opposition to land reform. He traveled to the United States, visited Congress and the State Department, held press conferences on Capitol Hill, and appeared on national news programs.[27] One visit was at the invitation of Jesse Helms, who was

22. Richard Severo, "Roberto D'Aubuisson, 48, Far-Rightist in Salvador," *New York Times*, February 21, 1992.

23. Severo, "Roberto D'Aubuisson, 48, Far-Rightist in Salvador"; Lauren Gilbert, "El Salvador's Death Squads: New Evidence from U.S. Documents" (Washington, D.C.: Center for International Policy, March 7, 1994); William M. LeoGrande, *Our Own Backyard: The United States in Central America, 1977–1992* (Chapel Hill: University of North Carolina Press, 2009), 49, 37–38. On the operation of the White Warrior Union in El Salvador, Brockman, *Romero*, 29, 65, 173, 175, 183, 197, 221.

24. Eisenbrandt, *Assassination of a Saint*, 107.

25. Severo, "Roberto D'Aubuisson, 48, Far-Rightist in Salvador."

26. Craig Pyes, "Salvadoran Rightists: The Deadly Patriots," *Albuquerque Journal*, December 1983; Jefferson Morley, "When Reaganites Backed D'Aubuisson, They Unleashed a Political Assassin: Washington's Right Was So Pleased with the Politician's Anti-Communism It Was Willing to Overlook His Abuse of Human Rights," *Los Angeles Times*, March 1, 1992; LeoGrande, *Our Own Backyard*, 159.

27. Morley, "When Reaganites Backed D'Aubuisson, They Unleashed a Political Assassin"; Philip Taubman, "Salvadoran Rightist Granted U.S. Visa," *New York Times*, December 4,

serving at the time on the Senate Foreign Relations Committee and who defended D'Aubuisson as "a free enterprise man and deeply religious."[28]

In El Salvador, D'Aubuisson was known for talking publicly and brazenly about the imperative to exterminate hundreds of thousands of Salvadorans in order to restore peace to the country.[29] "If we had to kill 30,000 in 1932," he is quoted as having said at a rally, evoking the legacy of *La Matanza*, "we'll kill 250,000 today."[30] He appeared on television and radio, announcing the names of alleged communists and communist sympathizers who later would often end up dead or disappeared. In February 1980, D'Aubuisson read a list of 200 people, and Archbishop Óscar Romero's name was on the list.[31]

Romero's death was a death foretold. From the beginning of his tenure as archbishop, there were threats against his life—mainly in the form of anonymous letters from groups like the UGB,[32] as well as phone calls at all hours.[33] The diary Romero began keeping in March 1978 often mentions these calls and letters, concerns from friends and acquaintances about his safety, and their advice to him about suitable precautions to take.[34] But in his final weeks and days, Romero increasingly sensed death's nearness. During a visit to Rome in January 1980, Romero told Monsignor Moreira Neves of the Congregation for Bishops that he thought he would be killed, but that he did not know if his killers would be from the political right or left.[35] Until late 1979, the threats came most-

<hr>

1984; "Salvadoran Rightist Leader Roberto D'Aubuisson Has Arrived in the U.S.," *United Press International*, June 27, 1984.

28. Eric Bates, "What You Need to Know about Jesse Helms," *Mother Jones*, June 1995, 68.

29. Loren Jenkins, "El Salvador," *Washington Post*, August 16, 1981.

30. Quoted in Berryman, *Stubborn Hope: Religion, Politics, and Revolution in Central America* (New York: New Press, 1995), 94.

31. Romero, *Homilías*, 6:267–68, 320; Morozzo della Rocca, *Primero Dios*, 448.

32. Romero, *Diario*, 188; Brockman, *Romero*, 197.

33. Morozzo della Rocca, *Primero Dios*, 448–49. There is a collection of these cards in the Archives of the Archdiocese of San Salvador.

34. Romero, *Diario*, 83, 148, 188, 297–98, 308; Morozzo della Rocca, *Primero Dios*, 450–51. In early March, a bomb was planted in the basilica of the Sacred Heart in San Salvador, where Romero was preaching at the time. It was apparently programed to detonate during mass but did not.

35. Morozzo della Rocca, *Primero Dios*, 449. See also Romero, *Homilías*, 5:530, where he attributes the threats against him both to the extreme left and right.

ly from those on the right, who considered him a communist subversive. However, after the October 1979 coup, he also began to receive threats from those on the left, who regarded his support of land reform as counterrevolutionary. Romero, they thought, was insufficiently radical, incompletely committed to the revolution.[36]

Throughout this whole time, Romero received many offers for shelter and protection—from the Salvadoran government, from the Vatican, and from friends and acquaintances.[37] But he refused them, explaining his rationale to government officials who offered him a bulletproof car. It would be a "counter-witness to ride in such safety while my people are so insecure."[38]

Although it was not always evident to others, Romero was afraid. A large avocado tree spread above the small house where he lived on the grounds of the Divine Providence Hospital. While sleeping, Romero would wake up startled when the ripe fruit thudded upon the roof, mistaking the falling fruit for a gunshot or a bomb. He began sleeping on a cot in the sacristy of the Divine Providence Chapel.[39] During the last week of February 1980, which was the first full week of Lent, Romero made his annual retreat in Los Planes de Renderos on the outskirts of San Salvador. There, too, he found it difficult to sleep, fearing the possibility of being shot through the window or the wall of his room. He opted to spend the night in the common area of the retreat house instead.[40]

In a journal entry from that same retreat, Romero admits he fears "violence to my person." "Others have advised me," he continues, "of serious threats precisely for this week. I fear for the weakness of my flesh, but I ask that the Lord give me serenity and perseverance." Later in the journal, he writes, "I find it difficult to accept a violent death." But he goes on to describe how his confessor, the Jesuit Segundo Azcue, helped

36. Romero, *Diario*, 297–98; Morozzo della Rocca, *Primero Dios*, 449. For more on the assassination plots on the Salvadoran left, see Colorado, "Romero and the Extreme Left," *Super Martyrio*, March 25, 2013; Roberto Valencia López, "Monseñor Romero y el Ejército Revolucionario del Pueblo," *Crónicas Guanacas*, March 24, 2013.

37. Morozzo della Rocca, *Primero Dios*, 450–51.

38. Morozzo della Rocca, *Primero Dios*, 452.

39. Morozzo della Rocca, *Primero Dios*, 450.

40. Morozzo della Rocca, *Primero Dios*, 450.

allay his fears and instill courage, helping him cultivate a disposition of willingness "to give my life for God whatever might be the end of my life." Romero continues, "The unknown circumstances will be lived through with God's grace. God assisted the martyrs, and if it is necessary, I will feel him very close to me as I offer my last breath."[41]

During the mass at which Romero was killed, the gospel passage upon which he was preaching was from John's Gospel, where Jesus says:

> The hour has come for the Son of Man to be glorified. Very truly, I tell you, unless a grain of wheat falls into the earth and dies, it remains just a single grain; but if it dies, it bears much fruit. Those who love their life lose it, and those who hate their life in this world will keep it for eternal life. Whoever serves me must follow me, and where I am, there will my servant be also. Whoever serves me, the Father will honor (12:23–26).

This passage in John's Gospel occurs at a point in which the "hour" of Jesus' glorification is imminent (Jn 2:4, 4:23, 5:25, 7:30). The glory is the glory of his crucifixion—the glory that emanates from the cross as he is lifted up upon it (Jn 12:32, 3:14, 8:28).

In his homily, Romero focuses upon the significance of these words for Jesus' followers and the courage they need to be faithful. "It is necessary not to love ourselves so much that we shelter ourselves from involvement in risks," Romero says. "Those who want to remove themselves from all danger will lose their lives. In contrast, those who offer themselves, for the love of Christ, in the service of others, will live like the grain of wheat does, the grain that dies…. If the grain bears fruit, it is because the grain dies, it lets itself be immolated (*inmolar*) into the earth. Only by being immolated does it bear fruit."[42]

Augustine speaks similarly in one of his homilies in terms of the Eucharist and its relation to Christ's death. Augustine explains the significance of the celebration of the Eucharist this way: in coming forward to receive Christ's body and blood, "it is the mystery meaning you that

41. Quoted in Delgado, *Óscar A. Romero*, 188, 190.
42. Romero, *Homilías*, 6:455.

has been placed on the Lord's table.... It is to what you are that you reply *Amen*.... What you hear, you see, is *The body of Christ*, and you answer, *Amen*. So be a member of the body of Christ, in order to make that *Amen* true.... Be what you can see, and receive what you are."[43]

For his part, Romero says to those present that by faith they believe that the bread becomes Christ's body and the wine becomes Christ's blood at the consecration. "So let this body immolated, this flesh sacrificed for all people feed us as well, so that we, too, can give our bodies and blood to the suffering and the pain, like Christ."[44] So that we, too, he might have said, become the mystery that means us.

Moments after speaking these words, Romero was shot. It is an arresting final image of Romero: his body broken by a bullet just as he was preparing to break the Eucharistic bread, which is the remembrance of Jesus' being broken for us and for our salvation.

OTHER CHRISTS

We have been considering the circumstances surrounding Romero's death. But to what does his death bear witness? What does it mean that the church has named Romero a martyr, confirming the *sensus fidelium* of all those who preserved his memory?

The gospels indicate that Jesus' disciples should expect to share in the fate of their Lord and carry their cross (Mt 10:24-25, 38-39; Mk 8:34-38; Lk 9:23-24; Jn 15:20), but the notion of being a witness as it emerges in the New Testament is quite broad. John the Baptist is not himself the Word, but he witnesses (*martureó*) to it (Jn 1:6-9). Although John eventually dies at Herod's hands, his witness is not explicitly associated with death. Similarly, in Acts, the risen Christ says to his followers that they are to be his "witnesses (*martyres*) in Jerusalem and in all Judea and Samaria and to the ends of the earth" (Acts 1:8). Their witness hinges upon their encounter with the risen Christ (Acts 1:22, 2:32, 3:15, 5:32, 10:41; Lk 24:48).

---

43. Augustine, *Essential Sermons*, trans. Edmund Hill, OP (New York: New City Press, 2007), Sermon 272.

44. Romero, *Homilías*, 6:458; 2:286-87. In another homily, Romero says the church is holy because of its head, but sinful because of its members. Members need God's grace to learn to offer themselves, along with the bread and the wine, to God, so as to become what they receive; Romero, *Homilías*, 2:81.

They are being called to give testimony to it by telling this good news to the nations. But, once again, this witness of Christ's followers does not primarily or exclusively signify their suffering and death.

However, even within the New Testament, there are instances in which bearing witness to Christ relates to the suffering and dying of those who testify on his behalf. Paul describes the stoning of Stephen as the shedding of "the blood of Stephen your witness (*martyros*)" (Acts 20:24). Similarly, the book of Revelation presents Jesus as the prototype of the martyrs (1:5, 3:14) where the witnesses are those "who had been slain for the word of God" (6:9, 17:6).

Over the ensuing centuries, bearing witness increasingly becomes associated with suffering and death. Writing in the third century, for instance, the theologian Origen claims in *Exhortation to Martyrdom*, "What was said of Abel, when he was slain by the wicked murderer Cain, is suitable for all whose blood is shed wickedly.... The verse 'The voice of your brother's blood is crying to me from the ground' (Gen 4:10) is said, as well, for each of the martyrs, the voice of whose blood cries to God from the ground."[45] According to Origen, those who face death for the faith give a particularly luminous witness to what it means for Christians to follow the path of their crucified Lord.[46]

But suffering and death alone do not make a martyr. Augustine formulated a principle that would be decisive for subsequent theological reflection upon martyrdom when he wrote in a letter to Festus, "It is not the punishment but the reason for suffering it that makes true martyrs."[47] Thomas Aquinas takes up this line of thought in specifying the reason for the suffering of the martyrs: "One suffers for Christ by suffering not only for the faith of Christ but for any just deed done for the love of Christ."[48]

---

45. Origen, *Exhortation to Martyrdom*, 50, in *Origen*, trans. Rowan A. Greer (Mahwah, N.J.: Paulist Press, 1979).

46. Pinckaers thinks the *Acts of Polycarp*, written in the middle of the second century, is the first use of *martus* and its derivatives in "the technical Christian sense"; Pinckaers, *Spirituality of Martyrdom*, 48.

47. Augustine, *Letters 1–99*. In The *Works of Saint Augustine*, vol. II, part 1, trans. Roland J. Teske (New York: New City Press, 2001), 89:2. Augustine is writing to Festus against the Donatists. His point is that although the Donatists claim to be suffering martyrdom, they are not because the reason for their suffering is not the faith of the church.

48. Aquinas, *Commentary on the Letter of Saint Paul to the Romans*, ed. J. Mortensen and

In other words, the martyr's suffering cannot be separated from the reason for it, and the reason is the love of Christ. What makes martyrs is that their lives exhibit this love, which leads to their acceptance of death. Martyrs do not die for abstract principles or causes; they die because of their love of Christ. The emphasis in the final Beatitude is explicitly personal: "Blessed are you when people revile you and persecute you and utter all kinds of evil against you falsely *heneken emou* (on my account)" (Mt 5:10–12). The suffering arises from the relationship. Martyrs bear witness to a person.

Because Christian martyrs bear witness to the person of Christ, their lives are especially conformed to and intimate with God's love as revealed in him. One of the earliest martyrs venerated by the church, the bishop Ignatius of Antioch, puts it well in a letter to Christians in Rome when he pleads, "Allow me to be an imitator of the passion of my Lord."[49] Ignatius wants to imitate the love that is willing to go to the cross because death cannot diminish or defeat it. As Candida Moss has argued, theological reflection upon martyrdom in early Christianity centered upon martyrdom as an imitation of Christ's love, with martyrs depicted as "other Christs."[50] Similarly, Anna L. Peterson's study of martyrdom and Christianity in El Salvador points to the centrality of *imitatio Christi* in the popular imagination, of suffering and death as repetitions of Jesus' passion. "Like the earliest Christians," she writes, "many Salvadorans in the 1970s and 1980s believed that the martyrs of their communities gave their lives … in [Christ's] image."[51]

This belief that martyrs are other Christs suggests a distinctive account of imitation, for martyrs' imitation of God's love as revealed in Christ is so intimate that their bodies become identifiable with his. This is why it is often said that martyrs do not simply suffer *for* Christ but *with* Christ. Martyrs participate in his passion, which is what makes them

E. Alarcón, trans. F. R. Larcher, Latin/English edition of *The Works of St. Thomas Aquinas* (Lander, Wyo.: Aquinas Institute for the Study of Sacred Doctrine, 2012), 37:241.

49. Ignatius of Antioch, "The Epistle to the Romans," in *Early Christian Writings*, ed. Andrew Louth, trans. Maxwell Staniforth (New York: Penguin, 1987), 6.

50. Candida R. Moss, *The Other Christs: Imitating Jesus in Ancient Christian Ideologies of Martyrdom* (New York: Oxford University Press, 2010).

51. Peterson, *Martyrdom and the Politics of Religion*, 13, 93–117.

other Christs—especially conspicuous images of their Lord. The love that led to Christ's suffering and death is discernable in their suffering and death.

Informing this belief about martyrdom is Paul's description of Christian life as a sharing in Christ's death and resurrection. Paul writes in 2 Corinthians that in their affliction and persecution, Christ's followers are "always carrying in the body the death of Jesus so that the life of Jesus may also be made visible" in them (4:10, 11–12; see also Rom 6:1–11; Phil 1:20, 29, 3:8–11; 1 Pt 2:21). Or as he writes in Colossians, "I am now rejoicing in my sufferings for your sake, and in my flesh I am completing what is lacking in Christ's afflictions for the sake of his body, that is, the Church" (Col 1:24). In these passages, Paul understands Christ's sufferings to be uniquely Christ's, yet they are Christ's in such a way that others like Paul can share in them. According to the gospels, Christ was crucified at the third hour of the day at a location near Jerusalem called Golgotha (Mt 27:33, 46; Mk 15:22, 34; Lk 23:33, 44; Jn 19:17), which was a time and place prior to Paul's ministry. Nevertheless, Christ's passion remains mysteriously present to Paul because it stands at the center of time and space as such.[52] Paul also suggests in these passages that access to Christ's passion has an important purpose, which is to make Christ's body visible in the bodies of his followers. Moreover, there are two bodies in view: an individual body and a social one. The Colossians passage in particular states that the revelation of the body of Christ in the body of Paul builds up the body of Christ that is the church.

We will return to this second, ecclesial body later. But first, more remains to be said about how Christ is made visible in the bodies of his individual followers like Romero. Once again, Thomas is helpful for understanding the significance of Romero's martyrdom and how Romero became an image of Christ. According to Thomas, charity is martyrdom's "primary impulse," its "first and most important moving force."[53] As

---

52. As Romero observes, Paul believes "suffering is already a communion with Christ who suffers, and death is a communion with the death that redeemed the world." Romero is commenting specifically on Phil 3:8–14, the second reading for that Sunday; Romero, *Homilías*, 6:437.

53. *ST* II-II, q. 124, a. 3, resp.; q. 124, a. 2, ad. 2.

Thomas puts it, while courage elicits martyrdom (*per modum virtutis elici- entis*), charity commands it (*per modum virtutis imperantis*).[54] It is love of God and neighbor that leads a person to accept martyrdom, which exem- plifies Jesus' words: "No one has greater love than this, to lay down one's life for one's friends (Jn 15:13)."[55] Martyrdom is for Thomas "the great- est proof of the perfection of charity" precisely because it manifests the "greater love" to which Jesus refers.[56]

In explaining the significance of this "greater love," Thomas observes that people tend to love their own lives above any other good they pos- sess, which he sees as evidenced in their natural aversion to death and pain.[57] Thomas marshals scriptural support, citing Satan's words to the Lord in Job: "All that people have they will give to save their lives. But stretch out your hand now and touch [Job's] bone and his flesh, and he will curse you to your face" (Job 2:4–5). According to Thomas, martyr- dom manifests the perfection of charity because martyrs willingly re- linquish all they possess, including their bones and flesh, for love of God and neighbor. They offer their greatest possession—life itself—without violent resistance to those who would unjustly rob them of it.[58] Moreover, they do so while praising rather than cursing God and while forgiving rather than condemning their killers. In this way, their offering witnesses to the love that extends to enemies (Mt 5:44, Lk 6:27) and that forgives its crucifiers (Lk 23:34, Acts 7:60).

According to Romero himself, few Christians are called to be mar- tyrs; martyrdom is a grace God grants only to some. Nevertheless, Rome- ro sees martyrdom as a latent possibility for all Christians, because to be a Christian means sharing in the life of the crucified and risen Christ. Martyrdom therefore orders even ordinary Christian existence. As Rome- ro explains, "To give one's life, to have the spirit of a martyr, is to give in one's duty, in silence, in prayer, in the honest fulfillment of one's respon- sibilities, in the silence of ordinary life, to go on giving one's life, little

---

54. *ST* II-II, q. 124, a. 2, ad. 2.
55. *ST* II-II, q. 124, a. 3, resp.; see q. 124, a. 2, obj. 2, ad. 2
56. *ST* II-II, q. 124, a. 3, resp.
57. *ST* II-II, q. 124, a. 3, resp.
58. *ST* II-II, q. 124, a. 4, resp.

by little."[59] As Romero sees it, taking up the cross is an inescapable and daily part of Christian discipleship. But Romero's words also suggest that giving one's life little by little is preparation for laying down one's life for one's friends. During the homily for Romero's beatification, Cardinal Angelo Amato made a similar point about Romero himself, saying his martyrdom "came after a long preparation (*tuvo una larga preparación*)."[60]

This notion of preparing for martyrdom relates to one of the central claims of this study—namely, that the work of justice is indispensable to such preparation. We have seen that justice and charity must walk together if God's purpose for creation is to be fulfilled and that justice helps to fulfill this purpose by opening others' access to what is theirs but that has been closed off to them because of sin. Viewed in this way, the work of giving to others what belongs to them in justice prepares its practitioners for the much more complex and difficult work of learning to give their lives in charity—even if most will go about giving their lives little by little, rather than all at once.[61] Justice helps people learn to follow Christ in love by teaching them to share the gift of their very selves, which is essential training for sharing in the life God offers in Christ, which is above all a common life.[62]

Augustine calls the work of justice the beginning of charity. If you are not ready to die for others, he counsels, then begin by giving your superfluous goods. For if you cannot learn to give what is superfluous to others, how can you ever learn to lay down your life? According to Augustine, tending to this beginning with "the word of God and the hope of future life" is how justice grows and flowers into "perfection."[63] Charity

59. Romero, *Homilías*, 1:89; 2:30, 66.

60. Cardinal Angelo Amato, *Homily for the Beatification of Martyr Monsignor Óscar Arnulfo Romero Galdámez*, San Salvador, May 23, 2015. Peterson describes how for popular Catholicism in El Salvador, the mass, the *vía crucis*, and other liturgical and para-liturgical events both model and prepare for martyrdom; Peterson, *Martyrdom and the Politics of Religion*, 81–82.

61. Romero, *Homilías*, 1:394–95; 2:266, 286–87, 330–91; 4:254; 5:272.

62. Charles De Koninck, "Primacy of the Common Good against the Personalists," in *The Writings of Charles De Koninck* (Notre Dame, Ind.: University of Notre Dame Press, 2009), 2:101.

63. Augustine, *Homilies on the First Epistle of John*. Translated by Boniface Ramsey. In *The Works of Saint Augustine*, vol. III, part 14 (New York: New City Press, 2008), 6:1; 5:12.

is like a seed—like a grain of wheat. But in order for the grain to be ready for sowing, it must first undergo a process of preparation. The seed head must harden and mature. Only then will it be ready when the time comes to fall into the earth and die, and in dying, bear fruit.[64]

Martyrs, then, display the perfection of charity for Augustine and for Thomas because of the supreme difficulty of accepting death for love of God and neighbor. Martyrs willingly lay down in love what is most difficult for people to part with, their most valuable "possession": their lives. This difficulty is yet another way martyrs like Romero image God's love as revealed in Christ. By enduring death for the sake of this love, martyrs make visible in the world what would otherwise remain hidden: a love they believe to be greater than even themselves, for the sake of which they willingly offer all that they have and are. In this way, martyrs bear witness to that love that underlies and transcends the loss of their lives.

Paul describes this love in Romans when he writes that "neither death, nor life, nor angels, nor principalities, nor things present, nor things to come, nor powers, nor height, nor depth, nor anything else in all of creation, will be able to separate us from the love of God in Christ Jesus our Lord" (Rom 8:38–39). For Paul, there are no barriers to sharing in this love. Not even suffering and death can deprive a person of its presence. In Christ, the love of God incarnate died—and it rose again on the third day. The attempt to erase this love from the face of the earth by crucifying it only ended up further disclosing its depths, revealing how this love orders the whole cosmos, and moves the sun and other stars. It is for this reason that the love of God made flesh in Christ cannot be overcome by suffering and death: it is stronger than they are, which is precisely what enables such love to retain its shape in the midst of the suffering and death. And this same love continues to show its strength and declare its victory across time and space by being especially present where it seems most absent. As Servais Pinckaers observes, "Christ opens to [martyrs] the way of life at [exactly] the point where others see only

---

64. Vatican Council II, *Lumen Gentium* (November 21, 1964), no. 42, addresses charity in similar terms. If the seed is to grow and bear fruit in the "highest witness of love," the seed must be tended.

torment and annihilation."[65] Christ opens the way of life at this point because neither torment nor annihilation can exclude the presence of the love that he is.

The resurrection of Christ therefore makes possible a path for others to follow—a path upon which Romero walked. In the words of Herbert McCabe, Christ's resurrection means "death is not just a matter of destruction, the end of life, but can be a revolution.... Resurrection is the revolution through death."[66] If death itself has become a site of liberation, then martyrs like Romero are its vanguard. The reason martyrs like Romero can follow Christ in laying down their lives is because, as Paul puts it, "Death has been swallowed up in victory." Though still present, death has lost its "sting" (1 Cor 15:26, 54–55).

According to Romero, one of the church's main contributions to the struggle for liberation is the gospel of Christ's death and resurrection, which produces people who willingly bear crosses because their lives are no longer determined by the fear of death. Such people, Romero thinks, reveal the true horizon of the struggle for liberation: the heavenly land God gives in Christ. The love that in Christ has broken death's dominion over human life is what produces this understanding of liberation and its cross-bearing liberators. Romero's own decision to face certain death rather than flee from it is difficult to grasp apart from this love. He speaks from his deep and abiding faith in it when he tells his listeners in one homily—those he calls his "intimidated, fearful, and fleeing" flock—"do not be afraid," because the path upon which they are traveling "does not end in a grave."[67]

So far, this chapter has examined the circumstances of Romero's death and reflected upon what it means to think about him as another Christ—a Salvadoran one—whose work of justice informed by charity reveals not only God's purpose for creation, but the one in whom all things hold together. However, in relation to Romero's martyrdom and the ferocity of the

---

65. Pinckaers, *Spirituality of Martyrdom*, 57; see also Hans Urs von Balthasar, *The Moment of Christian Witness* (San Francisco: Ignatius Press, 1994), 20.

66. McCabe, *Love, Law, and Language*, 133–34.

67. Romero, *Homilías*, 1:430.

resistance to the politics of common use, there is another issue that must be addressed: How does the particular martyrial path Romero walked meet the traditional criteria for martyrdom of being killed in hatred of the faith (*in odium fidei*)? For the agrarian crisis that occasioned Romero's death pitted Catholics against other Catholics, those who professed the same faith. This fact has led some to argue that Romero was killed not for *religious reasons* but for *political reasons*, and that his death was not a true martyrdom.[68] Jon Sobrino offers a different response to this same problematic. According to him, martyrdom has taken a new form in places like Latin America, where people die "not on account of their witness to faith [because these countries are predominantly Catholic] but because of the compassion that stems from their faith." Sobrino reasons that dying *in odium fidei* is therefore in a sense inapplicable to Latin America, where Catholics are dying at the hands of other Catholics.[69] The phrase Sobrino coins for such martyrs is "Jesuanic": martyrs who die like Jesus for justice.[70]

In contrast, Karl Rahner offers an alternative approach, which is especially generative because it forestalls an overly narrow understanding of the faith to which martyrs like Romero testify. In a seminal 1983 essay, Rahner argues for the need to "broaden" what he calls the "classical concept" of martyrdom.[71] According to Rahner, the heart of the classical concept is passive acceptance of death for the faith. But he contends that martyrdom involves not only passive acceptance of death but "active struggle for the Christian faith and its moral demands (including those affecting society as a whole)."[72] The underlying reason Rahner gives for

68. José Dueño, "Opposition to Óscar Romero's Canonization was 'Political,' Archbishop Paglia Says," *America*, April 17, 2017.

69. Sobrino, "Our World: Cruelty and Compassion," in *Concilium* (London: SCM, 2003), 16–17.

70. See Sobrino, *Jesus the Liberator: A Historical Theological Reading of Jesus of Nazareth* (Maryknoll, N.Y.: Orbis, 1994); Sobrino, "Los mártires Jesuánicos en el tercer mundo," *Revista Latinoamericana de Teología* 48 (1999); Sobrino, *Christ the Liberator: A View from the Victims* (Maryknoll, N.Y.: Orbis, 2001).

71. See Cunningham's discussion of "the new martyrs," in Lawrence S. Cunningham, *A Brief History of Saints* (Oxford: Blackwell, 2005), 115–19; Cunningham, "On Contemporary Martyrs: Some Recent Literature," *Theological Studies* 63 (2002): 374–81.

72. Rahner, "Dimensions of Martyrdom," 9.

the broadening is Christological. Active struggle better approximates how Christ's own death related to the life he lived.[73] Moreover, such broadening would better acknowledge as martyrs of Christ those like Romero. As Rahner asks in 1983—seven years before Romero's cause for beatification and canonization was even opened—"Why should not someone like Bishop Romero, who died while fighting for justice in a society—a struggle he waged out of the depths of his conviction as a Christian—why should he not be a martyr? Certainly, he was prepared for his death."[74] In the end, Rahner's plea amounts to finding a way forward by going backward, concluding his essay with an appeal to Thomas Aquinas's "more comprehensive concept of martyrdom."[75]

What is this more comprehensive concept, and how does it broaden the classical one? According to Thomas, martyrs bear witness bodily to the truth of the faith made known by Jesus Christ. Faith in Christ is constitutive of martyrdom, and martyrdom is a unique instance of how all Christians are called to testify to the truth of faith.[76] But faith alone (*sola fides*) is not the sole cause of martyrdom. Thomas cites Jesus' statement from the Beatitudes ("Blessed are they who suffer persecution for justice's sake" [Mt 5:10]) to indicate that other virtues besides faith—in this case, justice—can and do lead to martyrdom.[77]

What is the relationship of this justice to the faith? Thomas argues that a person testifies to the truth made known in Christ with words and with deeds and that a person's deeds can either affirm or deny the faith they profess with words.[78] Thomas draws on scripture to convey both how faith bears fruit in works of mercy ("I will show you my faith by my deeds" [Jas 2:18]) and how mercilessness contradicts the faith professed

---

73. Rahner, "Dimensions of Martyrdom," 10.

74. Rahner, "Dimensions of Martyrdom," 10.

75. Rahner, "Dimensions of Martyrdom," 11. Thomas L. Schubeck has taken up the task in an essay on Romero and the other Salvadoran martyrs, noting that "Thomas Aquinas … provided insights that contributed to the Church's enlarging the meaning of martyrdom in the twentieth century"; Thomas Schubeck, "Salvadoran Martyrs: A Love That Does Justice," *Horizons* 28 (2001): 11.

76. *ST* II-II, q. 124, a. 5, resp.

77. *ST* II-II, q. 124, a. 5, s.c.

78. See Leo the Great, *Sermons*, trans. Jane Patricia Freeland, CSJB, and Agnes Josephine Conway, SSJ (Washington, D.C.: The Catholic University of America Press, 1996), Sermon 9.2.

with words ("They profess to know God, but they deny him by their deeds" [Ti 1:16]). Although Thomas does not cite it, the context of the verse from James is instructive: "What good is it, my brothers and sisters, if you say you have faith but do not have works? Can faith save you? If a brother or sister is naked and lacks daily food, and one of you says to them, 'Go in peace; keep warm and eat your fill,' and yet you do not supply their bodily needs, what is the good of that? So faith by itself, if it has no works, is dead" (Jas 2:14–17). According to Thomas, faith alone is not the sole cause of martyrdom because of the essential relationship between the virtue of faith and justice. God gives faith to bear fruit in a life, and the good fruit borne in a life shows the faith, which leads Thomas to write, "All virtuous actions, insofar as they are referred to God, are professions of the faith."[79]

It follows from this that the work of justice and other virtuous actions can occasion persecution and even martyrdom. Thomas's example is the church's observance of the martyrdom of John the Baptist. Herod ordered John's death not because John refused to deny the faith he preached, but because John articulated the demands the faith made upon Herod's life regarding his adulterous relationship (Mt 14:1–12; Mk 6:14–29; Lv 18:16, 20:21). Herod's hatred of the faith John preached amounted to a hatred of these demands.[80] John therefore represents for Thomas how Christians can suffer persecution both for testifying to faith with words and for testifying to it with their deeds.[81]

This is the broadening of the classical concept of martyrdom that Rahner finds in Thomas.[82] Crucial to this broadening is how Thomas resists the whole idea of distinct kinds or tracks of martyrdom—those who are martyred for the faith and those who are martyred for justice—precisely because there is an inseparable relationship between the two. Faith is best seen in the fruit it bears in a life, and the hatred of faith's fruits like justice simply *is* hatred of the faith. As Reinhard Hütter explains, Thomas's account includes "the way of life in word and deed that

---

79. *ST* II-II, q. 124, a. 5, resp.
80. *ST* II-II, q. 124, a. 5, resp.
81. *ST* II-II, q. 124, a. 5, ad. 1.
82. However, differences remain between their respective accounts. For instance, Thomas does not speak as Rahner does of a polarity between passivity/death and activity/struggle.

gives rise to the hatred of virtue and truth."[83] Therefore, hatred of virtue and truth (*in odium virtutis et veritatis*) and hatred of the faith (*in odium fidei*) need not be construed oppositionally. "Martyrdom *pro virtute et veritate* does not replace, expand, or develop martyrdom *pro fide*; rather, the former is integral to the latter."[84] On these terms, to declare Romero a martyr means that his whole life stands as a testimony—in word and in deed—to the truth made known in Christ.

The idea that all virtuous actions can be professions of the faith, and therefore that any human good when directed to God can become a reason for martyrdom,[85] has important and expansive implications. Thomas's example is the refusal to lie,[86] which is apt, because the persecution of the church in El Salvador was in large part a consequence of truth-telling.[87] As Timothy Radcliffe writes, "Romero was murdered because every week he told the truth about the violence endured by the poorest: who had been arrested, who had disappeared, who had been assassinated, the threats made."[88] But as we have also seen at length, additional human goods that Romero directed to God included justice in the distribution of land and the ability of rural workers to organize for better wages and working conditions. The pursuit of these goods likewise became important reasons for Romero's martyrdom. Ultimately, he was killed because of this integrated testimony to the faith and its implications for human life.

Thomas's account of martyrdom also has implications for the description of Romero's persecutors and killers. For although they professed the Catholic faith with their words, they denied it with their deeds and therefore acted *in odium fidei*. They refused to relinquish the land that belonged to all Salvadorans, defending their possessions with brutal violence. When faced with so many brothers and sisters lacking basic bodily

83. Reinhard Hütter, "Testifying to the Truth *usque ad sanguinem—pro veritate mori*: The Contemporary Relevance of Thomas Aquinas's Integral Doctrine of Martyrdom," *Thomist* 78, no. 4 (2014): 500.

84. Hütter, "Testifying to the Truth *usque ad sanguinem—pro veritate mori*," 512.

85. *ST* II-II, q. 124, a. 5, ad. 3.

86. *ST* II-II, q. 124, a. 5, ad. 2.

87. See Romero, *Homilías*, 1:117; Romero, *Homilías*, 2:129, 214, 467, 481.

88. Timothy Radcliffe, "Vast, Hidden Violence on the Poor Could Destroy Our Society," *Tablet*, November 5, 2013.

support, they effectively responded to them by saying, "Go in peace; keep warm and eat your fill"—and then terrorized them when they did not. As James asks, "What is the good of that?" For such actions denote the absence of faith, not its presence.

MARTYRDOM AND THE CHURCH

We have been examining the significance of Romero as a martyr—a witness to God's love in Christ. Earlier we saw that for Paul, the suffering and affliction of Christ's followers present an image of Christ's body before the world, which in one sense is inescapably personal. In Colossians, Paul writes about the continuation of Christ's afflictions in his own flesh, and something similar can be said about Romero. It is *this* particular person—Óscar Arnulfo Romero y Galdámez—who is a martyr. The love that led to *his* slaying made him a Salvadoran Jesus Christ, a person in whose afflictions God's passage through El Salvador has been made known.

But in addition to this personal sense of martyrdom, there is also a social one. Christ's afflictions in Paul's flesh reveal and build up Christ's ecclesial body, the church. The traditional criterion of *in odium fidei* similarly indicates this ecclesial aspect of martyrdom. Martyrs are killed not for their private opinions but for their testimony to what the church holds to be true—the revelation of God in Christ, who gave his life in love for us and for our salvation. That the form of Christ's ecclesial body is love means that the ongoing life of this body depends upon the work of love by and among its members, which is why the church is sustained especially by the blood of martyrs, who have preeminently imitated the love of their Lord. For it is above all by love that Christ's followers are made known (Jn 13:35), and there is no greater love than that demonstrated by them (Jn 15:13).

Since the first centuries of Christianity, martyrs have therefore occupied a pivotal place in the church's life. The first Christians memorialized their *dies natalis*,[89] preserved and venerated their relics, and gathered and celebrated the liturgy at their graves.[90] "We can chart the rise to prom-

89. The day of birth into life eternal.
90. The second-century account of the martyrdom of Polycarp, the bishop of Smyrna,

inence of the Christian Church most faithfully," Peter Brown suggests, "by listening to the pagan reactions to the cult of the martyrs."[91] Among the primary pagan reactions to this cult was the unprecedented—and to them, abhorrent—communal form that included the dead within it and involved gathering and worshiping at graves. Julian the Apostate gives voice to the abhorrence: "You [Christians] keep adding many corpses newly dead to the corpse [Christ's] of long ago. You have filled the whole world with tombs and sepulchers."[92] According to Brown, the union of tomb and altar breached "the established map of the universe," "the immemorial boundary between the city of the living and the dead."[93] This redrawing of maps and breaching of boundaries directly follows from the belief that Christ's resurrection was a liberation from death's proprietary hold over human life, as a consequence of which death was no barrier to membership in the church.

With time, the union of tomb and altar became increasingly clear. The Council of Carthage (419) directed local bishops to destroy altars "in which no body nor relics of martyrs can be proved to have been laid up."[94] Later, the Second Council of Nicaea (787) decreed that churches must contain a martyr's relic to be consecrated and that churches consecrated without one must remedy the lack.[95] The current Code of Cannon Law preserves the tradition placing of relics under altars.[96] Over the centu-

---

attests to many of these features of the emerging cult of martyrs and its centrality to ecclesial life. After describing the struggle of those present to possess the remains of the martyred bishop of Smyrna and their anxiety "to claim our share in the hallowed relics," the scribe recounts what happened next: "So, after all, we did gather up his bones—more precious to us than jewels, and finer than pure gold—and we laid them to rest in a spot suitable for the purpose. There we shall assemble, as occasion allows, with glad rejoicings; and with the Lord's permission we shall celebrate the birthday of his martyrdom. It will serve both as a commemoration of all who have triumphed before, and as a training and a preparation for any whose crown may be still to come"; *Martyrdom of Polycarp*, in *Early Christian Writings: The Apostolic Fathers*, trans. Maxwell Staniforth (New York: Penguin, 1987), 17–18.

91. Peter Brown, *The Cult of the Saints: Its Rise and Function in Latin Christianity* (New York: University of Chicago Press, 2014), 6–7.

92. Brown, *Cult of the Saints*, 7.

93. Brown, *Cult of the Saints*, 4–5.

94. Council of Carthage, Canon 83, in Tanner, *Decrees of the Ecumenical Councils*.

95. Second Council of Nicaea, Canon 7, in Tanner, *Decrees of the Ecumenical Councils*.

96. Code of Canon Law, c. 1237, 2, in *The Code of Canon Law: Latin-English Edition* (Washington, D.C.: Canon Law Society of America, 1983).

ries, the church has therefore been built not only upon the succession of the apostles but also upon the bodies of the martyrs.[97]

Although the living and the dead share a common life in Christ's ecclesial body, the status of the martyrs as imitators of Christ's passion makes them privileged members of it—a privilege expressed in martyrs' ongoing work of love on behalf of the living. For Gregory of Nyssa, the martyrs are "unseen friends" with whom Christians in this life have fellowship and in whose grace they share.[98] Even though martyrs have arrived at the heavenly land, they are not cut off from those in the church still on pilgrimage in the lands of the living. Just as in life, so too in death, martyrs give themselves in love, building up Christ's ecclesial body and preparing its members for the life for which they are destined.[99]

The relationship between martyrs and the church is therefore an especially intimate one. Tertullian famously expresses this intimacy in his *Apology* when he tells magistrates who are persecuting Christians, "Go on kill us, torture us, condemn us, [and] grind us to dust.... The oftener we are mown down by you, the more in number we grow; the blood of Christians is seed."[100] Tertullian uses the seed imagery primarily to suggest the enlargement and expansion of the church's membership. In persecuting the church and killing its members, Tertullian suggests, the magistrates are only contributing to the church's growth. Romero himself speaks in similar terms in his homilies.[101] But our examination of martyrdom has suggested that the blood of the martyrs is seed in the even more basic sense of the wheat seed from John's Gospel—the seed that dies and, in dying, bears fruit.[102] The fruit that comes from scattering this seed is simply bearing witness to Christ's death and resurrection before the world, testifying to the love that founds the church and on whose basis

97. Erik Peterson, *Theological Tractates*, ed. Michael J. Hollerich (Stanford, Calif.: Stanford University Press, 2011), 151–56.

98. Gregory of Nyssa, "In Praise of Theodore, Holy and Great Martyr," in *One Path for All: Gregory of Nyssa on the Christian Life and Human Destiny*, by Rowan A. Greer (Eugene, Ore.: Cascade, 2015), 51, 195–98; Brown, *Cult of the Saints*, 50–68.

99. This paragraph draws on Greer, *One Path for All*, 195–201.

100. Tertullian, *Apology*, in *Ante-Nicene Fathers*, trans. Sydney Thelwall (Buffalo, N.Y.: Christian Literature., 1885), 3:50.

101. Romero, *Homilías*, 1:411; 2:166; and 3:212.

102. See Pinckaers, *Spirituality of Martyrdom*, xix–xx, 7.

it continues to exist—a love that willingly lays down its life for others.

Given the intimacy of the relationship between martyrs and the church, and given the criterion for martyrdom of *in odium fidei*, a difficult problem arises in the case of Romero's martyrdom that we have already touched upon briefly in this chapter. The problem can be posed in the form of a question: Who hates the faith in this case?

The resources of Thomas's account of martyrdom notwithstanding, this question remains especially pertinent and unsettling, not only because some of Romero's critics are still alive and prominent members of Salvadoran society, but also because many of them would doggedly resist the description that they hate the church's faith. Romero's critics saw themselves as faithful Catholics defending the church, whose most visible figurehead was leading it astray. In chapter 4, we examined the backlash against Molina's agrarian transformation project and how various groups denounced the church's support of it. In addition to the Agrarian Front of the Eastern Region and the National Association of Private Enterprise, these groups had names like the Association of Followers of Christ the King, the Association of Catholic Religious Women, and the Salvadoran Catholic Association.[103] The symbols in the insignia of Organización Democrática Nacionalista (National Democratic Organization, ORDEN), a paramilitary organization founded in 1961 that helped identify and eliminate purported communists, included a light representing the presence lamp next to the tabernacle, where the consecrated Eucharistic elements are reserved. The insignia's colors combined those of El Salvador and Vatican City.[104] D'Aubuisson's death squad—the UGB—spoke for all of these groups when it declared, "Our fight is not against the Church but against Jesuit terrorism."[105]

What all this means is that the church was deeply and complexly implicated in the violence that Romero sought to address and for which he suffered and died as a consequence. Regarding the persecution of the

103. See *El Mundo*, May 25, 27, and 30, 1977; *El Diario de Hoy*, May 26, 28, 29, 30, and 31, 1977. For an analysis of some of these attacks in the press, see Report of the Latin American Bureau, *Violence and Fraud in El Salvador*, 25; *Persecución de la Iglesia en El Salvador*, 14, 23–30.

104. José Inocencio Alas, *Iglesia, tierra y lucha campesina*, 133.

105. Quoted in Report of the Latin American Bureau, *Violence and Fraud in El Salvador*, 26.

church and the attack upon organized *campesinos* in the 1970s and 1980s, Vega observes:

> One did not hear [Catholic] voices in the dominant social stratum that at least offered themselves as arbitrators. Economic interests seemed to silence any attempt at justice, or at least a call to sanity when the army was sent to kill defenseless priests and *campesinos*. One did not hear the voice of capitalists who identified themselves as Catholic, or the intellectuals, or the medium business-owners, or the members of the military (despite the latter having among them a bishop and priests as chaplains).… [But all these Catholics] without a doubt prayed, baptized their children in the Catholic Church. Many even went to Catholic high schools and still regularly go to mass and receive the Eucharist.[106]

In considering Romero and the meaning of his martyrdom, we cannot evade the difficulty of the reality to which Vega points in this passage. Many of those who unleashed or condoned the repression were devout Catholics who did not regard their opponents as fellow brothers and sisters in Christ but rather as communists and communist sympathizers, who threatened the faith of the church. In their zeal to rid El Salvador of communism, these killers and those who supported them proved to be either unwilling or unable to distinguish between communism they opposed and the implementation of the church's social teaching.[107]

The gospels describe Jesus' followers as being sent out into the world as sheep among wolves (Mt 10:16; Lk 10:3). Given the natural vulnerability of sheep, it is unsurprising that there is danger and that the wolves would at times devour them. But the reality to which Vega is attending complicates the imagery considerably because it suggests the sheep cannot be straightforwardly identified with Christ's followers or the wolves with non-Christians. For in this case, the wolves are also within the visible precincts of the church. They look and sound like sheep, but their behavior reveals them to be wolves (Mt 7:15; Acts 20:29–30).

---

106. Vega, *Las comunidades de base en América Central*, 161.

107. For more on this, see Matthew Philipp Whelan, "The Business of War in Latin America," in *The Business of War: Theological-Ethical Reflections on the Military-Industrial Complex* (Eugene. Ore.: Cascade, forthcoming).

Many Catholics in Romero's El Salvador closely associated the faith—arguably even fused it—with defense of the nation and Western civilization against the threat of communism.[108] Such an understanding of the faith found sympathetic hearing among many priests and bishops. José Alberto "Chele" Medrano, one of the so-called fathers of the death squads, was a general who worked closely with counterinsurgency specialists from the United States to terrorize government opponents.[109] He also met regularly with priests—many of whom were army chaplains—to discuss what to do about the communist infiltration of the church.[110]

The Salvadoran bishops were notoriously divided during this time—at one point, even publicly issuing conflicting pastoral directives.[111] In a letter sent by various parishes in the Archdiocese of San Salvador to the Salvadoran bishops conference, the authors state their alarm that so many members of the church have been exposed to danger because of the bishops' disunity.[112] For his part, Romero acknowledges that unity is one of the distinctive marks of the church and that the public divisions within the church generate confusion among the faithful and imperil the church's mission in this land.[113]

Clearly, what we are encountering here is not simply a case of Catholics killing other Catholics in a culturally Catholic country, but also a fight among Catholics over the very identity of the church. As Romero describes the situation in his second pastoral letter, "In our country, there are an abundance of voices, on the radio and in the newspapers, claiming to judge what the Church is, distorting its true reality and mission."[114]

108. See *Persecución de la Iglesia en El Salvador*, 14.

109. José Napoleón Duarte refers to him as such; Allan Nairn, "Behind the Death Squads," *Progressive*, May 1984, 21.

110. José Inocencio Alas, *Iglesia, tierra y lucha campesina*, 131.

111. The divisions predated Romero's tenure as archbishop, but grew increasingly acute during it. Romero's fellow bishops charged him with being heterodox, mentally unstable, a puppet of the Jesuits, and so on; Morozzo della Rocca, *Primero Dios*, 362; Brockman, *Romero*, 132, 146, 168–70, 177–81, 189, 218; Whitfield, *Paying the Price*, 112. In an open letter from as recently as 2010, Msgr. Freddy Delgado gave voice to these views, arguing that Romero was manipulated by a "parallel magisterium" run by liberation theologians and Jesuits, who appealed to Romero's vanity, subservience, and cowardice; Delgado, "Mons. Óscar Arnulfo Romero: Imagen utilizada por el magisterio paralelo," *Farabunterra*, June 30, 2010.

112. Quoted in Morozzo della Rocca, *Primero Dios*, 356.

113. Romero, *Misión de la Iglesia en medio de la crisis del país*, 23.

114. Romero, *La Iglesia, cuerpo de Cristo en la historia*, 71.

In Romero's El Salvador, Christ's ecclesial body and its boundaries were themselves a site of contestation.

This is why narrating Romero primarily in terms of the church in El Salvador's heroic resistance to a neo-pagan state and its regime of absolute property, though tempting, evades the difficulty of reality before us. It lures us into forgetting that church members opposed the land reform and organized *Operación Piña*, just as they also terrorized those they regarded as communists rather than as fellow members of Christ's ecclesial body. In the United States, President Ronald Reagan in the 1980s justified an extraordinary expansion of support for the Salvadoran military by depicting El Salvador as the front line of a civilizational war with communism.[115] Against the opposition of the United States Conference of Catholic Bishops (USCCB) to these policies, many influential Catholic voices in the United States similarly encouraged fellow Catholics to view Latin America solely through the lens of anti-communism.[116] Doing so not only elided life-or-death distinctions between who were—and who were not—communists, as well as overlooking the reasons some might be accused of communism in this context; it also obscured the tradition of church teaching on property and land reform resourced by Romero and others throughout Latin America and the theological significance of the suffering that came as a consequence of their identification with it.

Attending closely to Romero's martyrdom and the complicity of the church's members in it raises unavoidable questions, like: What is the church, Christ's ecclesial body? What kind of body is it? What does it mean to be its member?

These questions were among Romero's constant preoccupations as archbishop. His episcopal motto was *sentir con la Iglesia*, from Ignatius of Loyola's *Spiritual Exercises*, a phrase that is often translated as "to think" or alternately "to feel with the Church." However, like the Latin *sentire*, the semantic range of the Spanish *sentir* is broader than thinking or feel-

115. Bonner, *Weakness and Deceit*, 234, 256.
116. Todd Scribner, *A Partisan Church: American Catholicism and the Rise of Neoconservative Catholics* (Washington, D.C.: The Catholic University of America Press, 2015), 137–92.

ing alone. Romero's own understanding of the phrase involves a process of ongoing discernment regarding the mystery of Christ's ecclesial body and its deepest identity.[117] As Romero himself says in a 1979 interview, the theology of *Spiritual Exercises* presents "a continuation of Christ in our history and in our Latin American reality lived from the Church, the Mystical Body of Christ.... A Church *sentida* not only as magisterium, but as people. People that puts its hope in the Church; people that is the same Church. A Christ incarnate in a Latin American Church of those who are poor, oppressed, and suffering. This is ecclesiology. The *sentir con la Iglesia* of St. Ignatius would be this *sentir con la Iglesia* incarnate in this people in need of liberation."[118]

During his three years as archbishop, Romero wrote four pastoral letters, all of which focused upon ecclesiology.[119] In one form or another, each elaborates upon a statement Romero makes in the fourth and final letter, "The Church's Mission amid the National Crisis": "This is the essential contribution that our Church should make to the life of the country: to be herself. This is what I call her own identity."[120] In this passage, Romero is responding to the question "What, then, is the contribution that the archdiocese ... offers to the process of liberation of our people?," which is the question he poses at Grande's funeral. Romero's response about the church being itself recalls Leo's argument in *Rerum Novarum* that the solution to the social question centers upon the mystery of the church itself. But Romero's response also suggests that the church is not yet what it is or should be—that its identity remains in some sense unfinished. How, then, does Romero think the church makes this contribution to the life of El Salvador? What is its identity, and how does the church learn to live into it?

117. See Rowan Williams, *Sentir con la Iglesia,* Westminster Abbey, March 28, 2010; Morozzo Della Rocca, *Primero Dios,* 279–349; Margaret Eletta Guider, OSF, "Sentir con la Iglesia: Archbishop Romero, an Ecclesial Mystic," in *Archbishop Romero: Martyr and Prophet for the New Millennium* (Scranton, Pa.: University of Scranton Press, 2006).

118. Pablo Lopez de Lara, *Ejercicios espirituales: En, desde, y para América Latina* (Torreón, Mexico: Casa Iñigo, 1980), 102.

119. The pastoral letters were, in order, *The Easter Church* (April 10, 1977); *The Church, The Body of Christ in History* (August 6, 1977); *The Church and Popular Political Organizations* (August 6, 1978); and finally, *The Church's Mission amid the National Crisis* (August 6, 1979).

120. Romero, *Misión de la Iglesia en medio de la crisis del país,* 31.

To begin to address these questions, it is helpful to return to June 1977, shortly after Romero had been installed as archbishop. Under his guidance, the SSI published a report entitled *Persecution of the Church in El Salvador* (*Persecution*) that begins, "The people of God in El Salvador, especially in the archdiocese, are living the communal experience of the Cross; they are living the Paschal mystery of death and resurrection."[121] Earlier we considered martyrs as other Christs, as participants in Christ's passion, which presumes Christ's sufferings can be shared, and that the purpose of such sharing is to make Christ visible and to build up his body in the world. The basis of this belief is that the crucifixion and resurrection of Jesus Christ stand at the center of reality. Christ's paradigmatic presence to a world still suffering from sin and its violence is his passion, which happened once and for all but which continues to gather all reality around it. *Persecution* assumes a fundamentally similar theological framework. Christ's sufferings, the document contends, are being made visible upon the body of a whole people. The people of God on pilgrimage in El Salvador have become an image of Christ's passion.

Part of what precipitated the release of *Persecution* was that in May 1977, the National Guard deployed to Aguilares to evict *campesina* families that had occupied farmland. The occupiers had been renters, but when they were refused contracts before the rains came in May, they started to farm the land anyway because they had nowhere else to go.[122] The National Guard named the eviction *Operación Rutilio* after Rutilio Grande, who was slain just months before. Troops searched and ransacked houses. They beat people and raped women, targeting especially those who had pictures of Grande in their houses or on their person. According to witnesses, the troops killed about fifty people and took away hundreds more, including three Jesuit priests, who were subsequently deported. In addition, troops entered the local parish church, El Señor de las Misericordias (The Lord of Mercies), took aim at the tabernacle, and opened fire, strew-

---

121. *Persecución de la Iglesia en El Salvador*, 1.

122. For details, see Romero, *Homilías*, 1:96–97, 115, 118, 128, 133, 135, 149–55; Cardenal, *Historia de una esperanza*, 596–99; Brockman, *Romero*, 31–32; Dean Brackley, "Rutilio and Romero: Martyrs for Our Time," in *Monsignor Romero: A Bishop for the Third Millennium* (Notre Dame, Ind.: University of Notre Dame Press, 2004), 79–100.

ing the consecrated hosts everywhere.[123] During the subsequent full-scale occupation of Aguilares, the military used the church as a barracks.

After several failed attempts, Romero was finally permitted to go to Aguilares to install a new pastor and rededicate the church. "It falls on me," he begins his homily upon his arrival, "to go to gather the bodies trampled upon, the corpses, everything the persecution of the Church is leaving behind." He tells those gathered that he comes to Aguilares for the church that has been profaned, whose tabernacle is riddled with bullets, "but above all else to gather up this people that have been humiliated and unnecessarily sacrificed." "We are truly with you, and we want to tell you," he continues, "that your suffering is the suffering of the Church."[124]

Romero draws on the first reading from the prophet Zechariah, where the Lord speaks about "pour[ing] out a spirit of compassion … on the house of David and the inhabitants of Jerusalem," so that they might weep and mourn, looking upon "the one whom they have pierced" (Zec 12:10–11). Romero says to those gathered, "You are the image of the God who was pierced…. This is the image of all peoples who, like those of Aguilares, are pierced through, who are affronted." Romero is recalling the Gospel of John's account of Jesus' death, which records how "one of the soldiers pierced his side with a spear" (Jn 19:34) before quoting the exact same verse from Zechariah: "They will look on the one whom they have pierced" (Jn 19:37; Zec 12:11). Romero's point is that the people of Aguilares image this piercing, this crucifixion. He interprets what they have endured in relation to the "mystery of the suffering" of Christ, in which all Christian life participates.[125]

Romero uses the language of martyrdom to describe what is happening in Aguilares and in El Salvador more generally. According to him, the church in El Salvador is full of martyrs who image the love that founds and sustains Christ's ecclesial body. They are a gift the church in this land is giving to the church in all lands.[126] In addition to gathering the

---

123. Aguilares was not the only instance; see Romero, *Homilías*, 1:115, 133.

124. Romero, *Homilías*, 1:149–50.

125. Romero, *Homilías*, 1:150–51.

126. Romero, *Homilías*, 1:152–55; 2:467; 3:204; 4:292; 5:354–55. However, Romero is careful to distinguish his judgment from the process whereby the church declares someone to be a martyr.

trampled bodies and corpses, Romero says he also goes to Aguilares to gather a witness—"a testimony"—that can be "presented to all parishes." Those Christians in Aguilares who have given their lives for the love of Christ are an "advanced party" of the church, displaying its deepest identity. They serve as a reminder that following Christ involves nothing short of "handing over our lives" and that martyrdom is a latent possibility for all who are incorporated into Christ's death by baptism (Rom 6:3).[127] But similar to *Persecution*, Romero's homily in Aguilares speaks not only of the presence of *martyrs*, but also of a whole *martyred people*.[128] The people of Aguilares have become a collective image of their Lord, who was pierced and crucified. As Romero later says in his Louvain address, "The true persecution has been directed against the impoverished, who are the body of Christ in history today. They are the crucified people; like Jesus, they are the persecuted servant of Yahweh. They are the ones who make up in their own bodies that which is lacking in Christ's passion."[129]

In *The Christian Imagination*, Willie James Jennings makes a point similar to Romero's. Jennings is examining the account of the royal chronicler of Prince Henry the Navigator, Gomes Eanes de Azuara (Zurara), on the occasion of the arrival of African slaves at the port of Lagos in 1444. Zurara's narrative attempts to emplot slaveholding and suffering within an *ordo salutis*, a tale in which slave bondage ultimately leads to salvation at the hands of benevolent Christian captors. However, Jennings shows how, in its very unfolding, Zurara's narrative exposes "a deep-

---

127. Romero, *Homilías*, 1:151–55; 4:392. Romero often attributes the prevalence of martyrdom in El Salvador to exclusive faith in the God revealed in Jesus Christ as opposed to faith in other gods; see Romero, *Homilías*, 4:392.

128. See Romero, *Homilías*, 2:90; 4:264.

129. Romero, *La dimensión política de la fe desde la opción por los pobres*, 188. The phrase "crucified peoples" appears throughout Romero's homilies; see Romero, *Homilías*, 2:302, 310; 4:427, 439. Since Romero, the tropes of martyrdom and crucifixion as descriptions of collective suffering have become a hallmark of Salvadoran theological reflection; see Ellacuría, "The Crucified People," in *Systematic Theology: Perspectives from Liberation Theology*, ed. Jon Sobrino and Ignacio Ellacuría (Maryknoll, N.Y.: Orbis, 1993); Sobrino, *Principle of Mercy: Taking the Crucified People from the Cross* (Maryknoll, N.Y.: Orbis, 2015); Sobrino, "The Crucified Peoples: Yahweh's Suffering Servant Today," in *Concilium—1492–1992: The Voice of the Victims* (London: SCM, 1990). For more on Catholicism in Latin America as a "religion of the vanquished," see Orlando Espín, "The God of the Vanquished: Foundations for a Latino Spirituality," *Listening: Journal of Religion and Culture* 27, no. 1 (Winter 1992): 11–31.

er point of coherence," which is none other than "the suffering Christ image, the paradigmatic image of suffering carried in the body of Jesus of Nazareth." Accordingly, Zurara unwittingly writes what Jennings describes as a "passion narrative," which ends up locating the slaves' suffering inside Christ's suffering. Although Zurara himself does not make the association explicit, "his language," Jennings writes, "cannot prevent it."[130] The image is conspicuous and inescapable for those with eyes to see and ears to hear.

Less than one hundred years later, Bartolomé de las Casas would make the association and underlying theological rationale explicit, drawing the gaze of the wider Christian world to this same Christological point of coherence.[131] "For I leave, in the Indies, Jesus Christ, our God, scourged and afflicted and buffeted and crucified," he writes in the *History of the Indies*, "not once but millions of times, on the part of all the Spanish."[132] The Spanish have been sent to the Americas to share the gospel. "The entire [papal] concession to the monarchs of Spain," Las Casas explains elsewhere, "its motivation, and the sovereignty they have over these lands and people, was and is for the life of the latter, and for the salvation and conversion of their souls."[133] Yet according to Las Casas, the vast majority of the Spanish and "those who call themselves Christians" in these lands,[134] who understand themselves to be carrying the gospel to its inhabitants, are in fact acting as Christ's contemporary executioners. Christ continues to suffer in this world in the suffering flesh of others, and in this case, it is a suffering being inflicted by Christians themselves,

130. Jennings, *Christian Imagination*, 20.

131. However, Jennings points to Las Casas's "inability to reckon with black flesh and African suffering in any theological substantial way"; Jennings, *Christian Imagination*, 100. For a more sympathetic approach to Las Casas, which canvasses in detail his views of slavery and his eventual repudiation of them, see Gutiérrez, *Las Casas*, 319–30.

132. Bartolomé de Las Casas, *Historia de las indias*, vol. 3, ed. A. Millares and L. Hanke (México, D.F.: Fondo de Cultura Económica, 1951), bk. 3, pg. 30.

133. Las Casas, "Carta a un personaje de la corte," in Las Casas, *Obras Escogidas: Opúsculos, cartas y memoriales*, ed. Juan Pérez de Tudela y Bueso (Madrid: BAE, 1958), 62a. This is also the rationale for the *encomienda*, a central institution of the colonies, which Las Casas critiques in *Octavo Remedio*, in Las Casas, *Tratados de 1552*.

134. This is Las Casas's phrase, which he uses repeatedly; see Las Casas, *An Account*, 29, 50, 61.

whom Las Casas depicts as ravenous wolves unleashed among sheep.[135] One of the most troubling features of this horror is that it is being perpetrated and condoned by those with substantive formation in the Christian faith. It is not an aberration on the margins of Christianity that can be easily discounted or dismissed. Rather, it is occurring in the very heart of the Christian world, drawing power and legitimacy from the Christian faith and its traditions, even as it betrays them—or as Las Casas would have it, as it scourges, afflicts, buffets, and crucifies Christ over and over again.[136]

Romero's words in Aguilares and their echoes in Zurara and Las Casas return us to the idea that all time and space mysteriously center upon Christ's death and resurrection and that the love they reveal discloses the heart of created reality. According to Romero, even the passion of the Salvadoran people in places like Aguilares witnesses to this love, which continues to show its power over suffering and death by its enduring proximity to those who are pierced through and affronted. That Romero goes to Aguilares in mercy similarly witnesses to it. For Romero, the suffering of this people is the suffering of Christ. It is therefore the suffering of Christ's ecclesial members, to which they must learn to tend.

In tending to Christ's suffering in the world, perhaps the key scriptural passage for Romero is the great eschatological parable at the end of Matthew's Gospel, in which Christ comes again in glory and separates the nations on the basis of mercy "to the least of these who are members of my family" (Mt 25:40, 31–46). "I was hungry and you gave me food, I was thirsty and you gave me something to drink, I was a stranger and you welcomed me, I was naked and you gave me clothing, I was sick and you took care of me, I was in prison and you visited me," Jesus says to those on his right (Mt 25:35–36). In this parable, Christ's passion continues in those in need of basic bodily support like food, drink, clothing, shelter, care, and visitation.

135. Las Casas frequently compares the Spaniards to tigers, lions, and wolves and the inhabitants of the Americas to sheep and lambs. While the language suggests Spanish brutality and indigenous innocence, it also carries scriptural resonances, not just of how Jesus speaks of his followers as sheep among wolves, but also of the larger Christological point about Christ's ongoing suffering in their flesh.

136. Jennings, *Christian Imagination*, 22.

Among the parable's many lessons is that the merciful encounter their Lord when they minister to the suffering and needy flesh of others. Inasmuch as they show mercy to the least of these, they show mercy to Christ (Mt 25:40). And although the merciful did not necessarily know that they were encountering Christ, Christ was nevertheless present, because he is always and especially near to those who suffer or are in need (Mt 25:37–39). In this way, Christ reveals their suffering and need to be an image of his own, an enduring sign of his identification with a suffering and needy humanity. He also and at the same time reveals this suffering and need to be a summons, an opening into life at the precise place there seems to be only closure and death, because he entreats the merciful to meet him there.

An important theme of this study has been the significance of the work of mercy for perceiving the way the world is, for disclosing the grammar of God's good creation. Staying with this passage from Matthew's Gospel, we can say the merciful inherit the kingdom prepared for them "from the foundation of the world" (Mt 25:34) because they acknowledge the world's foundation as a gift God gives in common. By habitually responding to the lack of basic bodily support and care afflicting humankind because of sin, the merciful show creation to be what it most fundamentally is: a gift God gives for common use. The work of mercy testifies to God's gift of the earth to feed, slake, clothe, shelter, and comfort all people. Fittingly, the merciful inherit the kingdom because their acknowledgment of creation as common gift prepares them for life with God, when all things will be common. In contrast, those who habitually refuse mercy's work, who recoil from the suffering flesh of others, or who even inflict suffering themselves, fail to acknowledge the truth about creation in their earthly lives (Mt 25:41–46). How, then, can they possibly be prepared for heavenly life? One reason Romero's homilies repeatedly return to this passage and its ecclesiological significance is that it reveals the gift character of the world and how the gift holds together in and points toward its giver, Christ.[137]

137. For a sampling, see Romero, *Homilías*, 1:33, 131, 180, 298, 386, 400, 407, 430; 2:256, 437; 3:152, 205, 272, 295, 430–33; 4:34, 216, 255, 320; 5:70, 190, 193, 272, 292, 328, 353, 388, 425; 6:107, 115, 400, 411.

Augustine likewise reflects extensively upon this passage, often elaborating upon how the one who will come again to judge the living and the dead remains present in the faces of the hungry, the thirsty, the stranger, the naked, the infirm, and the imprisoned. "Now though, as man, too, he has gone up rich to heaven, seated at the right hand of the Father," Augustine writes. "But still, as a poor man here, he's hungry, thirsty, in rags."[138] Of course, Christ's ongoing presence in suffering and needy flesh is a strange and mysterious presence, analogous to his ecclesial and sacramental presence. Christ has been raised from the dead and is now seated in glory at the right hand of God. Yet he continues to be present in the world where there is suffering and need. He is Lord, the one through whom all things were made and in whom all things hold together. Yet he remains destitute. In Augustine's words, "Though rich, he is in need even unto the end of the world."[139] The one who will one day judge the nations on the basis of mercy remains present until that time in all those in need of mercy. Augustine articulates the implications for Christ's followers in the form of an exhortation: "Here, then, let the hungry Christ be fed; let the thirsty Christ be given a drink; let the naked Christ be clothed; let the stranger Christ be sheltered; let the sick Christ be visited. The exigency of our journey makes this an obligation, for, on our journey through life, we must live where Christ is in need."[140]

A similar understanding of Christ's abiding presence structures Romero's whole argument in the Louvain address that the world of the poor and the ordinary violence inflicted upon them is the key to the Christian faith because it teaches church members about the *polis* to which they belong in Christ. The underlying theological rationale for this claim is that Christ's ecclesial members must not turn away from sin and the depths of its violence because Christ did not turn away from it—and

---

138. Augustine, *Sermons (94A–147A) on the Old Testament.* In *The Works of Saint Augustine*, vol. III, part 4, trans. Edmund Hill, OP (New Rochelle, N.Y.: New City Press, 1992), 123:4; Augustine, *Sermons (148–83) on the New Testament*, in *Works of Saint Augustine*, vol. III, part 5, 179:4.

139. Augustine, *Sermons on the Liturgical Seasons*, trans. Mary Sarah Muldowney, RSM, in *Fathers of the Church* (Washington, D.C.: The Catholic University of America Press, 1958), 239:6.

140. Augustine, *Sermons on the Liturgical Seasons*, 236:3.

he still does not turn away from it. Christ remains with those who suffer this violence and calls upon others to find him in the midst of it through the work of mercy. As Romero says, the church encounters the "contemporary sacrament of the suffering servant"[141]

> in *campesinos* without land or steady employment, without running water or electricity in their homes, without medical attention when mothers give birth, and without schools for their children grow older.... [In] workers without labor rights, who are fired from their jobs when they demand them and left to the cold calculations of the economy.... [In] the mothers and wives of the disappeared and political prisoners.... [In] shantytown dwellers, whose misery defies imagination, and who live the permanent insult of the nearby mansions.

Being moved and changed by the world of the poor and its ordinary violence, Romero argues, does not separate Christians from the faith but helps them to discover the faith and its political implications. And it is in this world, Romero says, which is especially close to Christ, that "the Church of my archdiocese has undertaken to incarnate itself."[142]

In concluding a reflection in one homily on Matthew 25:31–46 about seeing the face of Christ in *campesinos* in search of sustenance, in the harvesters, and in the torture of the prisons, Romero memorably says, "In these countries of ours, dear brothers and sisters, Christ is so profusely present among us that it would be a shame to have lived as saturated with that presence as we do—because we are saturated with impoverishment—and not to have known him; it would be a shame to have lived so many years ... in comfort, in wealth, in political well-being, and never to have preoccupied ourselves with that Christ who is at our doors or who met us on the streets."[143] Or as he states in another homily, "There is a rule for knowing if God is near or far from us ... all those who preoccupy

---

141. Paul VI speaks in similar terms at a mass during his visit to South America; see Paul VI, *Santa misa para los campesinos Colombianos*, Homilía del Santo Padre Paulo VI, August 23, 1968. For more on the significance of Paul VI's homily, see Bernard Bleyer, "Die Armen als Sakrament Christi Stimmen der Zeit," *Stimmen der Zeit* 226, no. 11 (2008): 734–46.

142. Romero, "La dimensión política de la fe desde la opción por los pobres," 186. See also Romero, *Homilías*, 2:258.

143. Romero, *Homilías*, 3:432–33.

themselves with the hungry, the naked, the poor, the disappeared, the tortured, the imprisoned—all those who draw near to suffering and needy flesh—have God near to them."[144] They have God near to them because they go out in mercy to those to whom Christ is always already near. They are like the Good Samaritan, who, as Gutiérrez observes, shows mercy not by remaining on his path but by leaving it in order to tend to the man stripped, beaten, and left for dead in a ditch.[145] "We, too, find ourselves," Romero says, "with a whole people lying wounded along many paths in our country,"[146] and "we have tried not to pass by, not to go around the wounded in the road, but to draw close."[147]

For Romero and the traditions upon which he is drawing, the work of mercy is humankind's way to God because it is God's way to humankind. "The one thing which really befits God's nature," writes Gregory of Nyssa, in articulating why God became incarnate, is "to come to the aid of those in need."[148] Human nature, he observes, was sick and needed health, had fallen and needed to be raised up, had lost life and needed restoration, was imprisoned and needed freedom, and was enslaved and needed liberation. "Were these trifling and unworthy reasons to impel God to come down and visit human nature, seeing humanity was in such a pitiful and wretched state?" Nyssen asks.[149] Augustine similarly wonders, "What greater mercy … could there be toward the miserable, than that which pulled the creator down from heaven?"[150]

For his part, Origen describes God's work of mercy in Christ in relation to a tradition of reading the parable of the Good Samaritan allegorically. According to this interpretation, the man going down the road from Jerusalem to Jericho is Adam; Jerusalem is paradise and Jericho the world; the robbers are the powers that oppose Christ; and the Good Samaritan is Christ. Moved by mercy, the Christ-Samaritan comes to the

144. Romero, *Homilías*, 2:257, 189, 510.
145. Gutiérrez, *Teología de la liberación*, 237–38.
146. Romero, *Homilías*, 2:381.
147. Romero, "La dimensión política de la fe desde la opción por los pobres," 186.
148. Gregory of Nyssa, *Address on Religious Instruction*, in *Christology of the Later Fathers*, ed. Edward R. Hardy, Library of Christian Classics (Louisville, Ky.: Westminster John Knox Press, 1954), 266.
149. Gregory of Nyssa, *Address on Religious Instruction*, 290–91.
150. Augustine, *Sermons on the Liturgical Seasons*, 207:1.

aid of humankind, which has been stripped, beaten, and left half-dead in a ditch by sin. The Christ-Samaritan tends to humankind's wounds and bears it upon his body to an inn—the church—for care (Lk 10:25–37).[151] Peter Lombard invokes this same tradition of interpreting the parable when he begins book IV of the *Sentences*: "For the Samaritan, assuming responsibility for the wounded man, applied the bindings of the sacraments to care for him."[152]

Along similar lines, John Chrysostom patterns God's work of mercy upon Matthew 25:31–46. According to Chrysostom, Christ invites a hungry and thirsty humankind to a table where he nourishes and slakes it with himself. He welcomes all those who have been estranged from God into the church, which opens up to them the doors of heavenly life. He clothes those who enter with the garments of salvation, tending to the sin-sick by healing them and raising them to new life with him. For in the incarnation, Christ's visitation of humankind imprisoned by sin offers liberation from the bondage of death.[153]

When Romero says that the fundamental contribution of the church to El Salvador is to be itself, he simply means that its members must become the mystery they are: Christ's ecclesial body, the extension across time and space of God's merciful embrace of human suffering and need, including their own. Christ continues to feed his members with his sacramental body so they can be strengthened to give themselves in imitation of the one they receive, learning to find him and serve him in his suffering and needy body.

Romero thinks that Christ's suffering and needy body has often been

---

151. Origen, *Homilies on Luke*, ed. and trans. J. T. Lienhard, SJ, Fathers of the Church 94 (Washington, D.C.: The Catholic University of America Press, 1996), 34:3. For more on Origen's reading of the parable—a reading Origen does not attribute to himself but to his "elders"—and the favor it found within the Christian tradition as "a full statement of our collective history," "an epitome of the whole mystery of our redemption," see de Lubac, *Catholicism*, 204–5. To my mind, the most remarkable rendering of the parable can be found in Passus XIX of William Langland, *Piers Plowman: A New Annotated Edition of the C-Text*, ed. Derek Pearsall (Exeter: University of Exeter Press, 2008).

152. Peter Lombard, *The Sentences: On the Doctrine of Signs* (Toronto: Pontifical Institute of Mediaeval Studies, 2010), dist. 1, chap. 1. The theme of Christ as the Good Samaritan runs throughout the *Sentences*.

153. John Chrysostom, *Homilies on Matthew*, ed. Philip Schaff, Nicene and Post-Nicene Fathers 10 (Buffalo, N.Y.: Christian Literature, 1888), 45:3.

neglected—even by the church—because learning to perceive it necessarily entails turning toward the world of the impoverished and bearing the associated risks. But Christ's suffering and needy body, as well as Christ's ecclesial and Eucharistic bodies, are internally ordered to one another, for it is the same Christ who is present in all of them.[154] One of Romero's guiding theological intuitions is that Christ's bodies cannot be separated from one another without misconstruing the mysterious kinds of presence they bear and the form of life they are all given by God to build up. Christ's ecclesial body must be with and tend to Christ's suffering and needy body simply because it is the Lord—the head of the church—who identifies with those who are suffering and in need.

Christ's presence among those who are suffering and in need is a permanent sign of the love that cannot be overcome by affliction or death. This is the love that became incarnate in Christ, that founded and sustains Christ's ecclesial body, and that continues to give itself in the sacraments, especially in Christ's Eucharistic body. Romero's martyrdom likewise bears witness to it. Romero gave all that he had and was out of the belief that God would be close to him as he offered his last breath, and that nothing, not even a violent death, could separate him from the love of God in Christ Jesus. By living in this way, Romero became a Salvadoran Jesus Christ. God passed through El Salvador in him, as well as in the lives of so many others who have walked a similar martyrial path.

We have been reflecting upon the relationship between martyrs and the church, especially how martyrs bear bodily witness to Christ and the love that founds and sustains his ecclesial body. Yet Romero's claim that the essential contribution of the church to El Salvador is to be itself suggests that the identity of the people of God on pilgrimage remains incomplete and that many of the church's own members fall short of the mystery they are. The resistance to the politics of common use, which led to persecution and martyrdom of some members at the hands of others, only serves to underline this incompleteness.

154. See Gary Anderson, *Charity: The Place of the Poor in the Biblical Tradition* (New Haven, Conn.: Yale University Press, 2013).

Romero's statement about the church and its unfinished character can be helpfully clarified by a comment John XXIII makes in a radio address just before the Second Vatican Council begins. In the address, John hopes that one fruit of the conciliar renewal will be to present the church "as she is and as she wants to be—as the Church of all people and especially the Church of the poor."[155] This formulation resonates with Romero's, similarly implying that the church's identity is in some sense unfinished and that its members are not yet what they are. In this case, the church both is and is not yet the church of the poor.

In what way is the church already the church of the poor? Approximately two years after John's address, *Lumen Gentium*, the Dogmatic Constitution on the Church, offers an answer:

> Just as Christ carried out the work of redemption in poverty and persecution, so the Church is called to follow the same route that it might communicate the fruits of salvation. Jesus Christ, "though he was in the form of God ... emptied himself, taking the form of a slave" [Phil 2:6–7]; and "though he was rich, yet for your sake he became poor" [2 Cor 8:9].... Christ was sent by the Father "to bring good news to the poor" [Lk 4:18] ... "to seek and save the lost" [Lk 19:10]. Similarly, the church encompasses with love all who are afflicted with human suffering and in the poor and afflicted sees the image of its poor and suffering founder. It does all it can to relieve their need and in them strives to serve Christ.[156]

155. John XXIII, "Pope's Address to the World a Month before the Council Opened," in *Council Daybook*, ed. Floyd Anderson (Washington, D.C.: National Catholic Welfare Conference, 1965). The phrase "Church of the poor" became the banner of a group known as "The Group of the Church of the Poor," which met over the years of the Council. For more about the group and its influence upon the Council, see Giuseppe Alberigo and Joseph A. Komonchak, eds., *History of the Second Vatican Council*, vol. 2, *Formation of the Council's Identity: First Period and Intersession, October 1962–September 1963* (Maryknoll, N.Y.: Orbis, 1997), 200–203; Alberigo and Komonchak, eds., *History of the Second Vatican Council*, vol. 3, *The Mature Council: Second Period and Intersession, October 1963–September 1964* (Maryknoll, N.Y.: Orbis, 2000), 164–66; Alberigo and Komonchak, eds., *History of the Second Vatican Council*, vol. 4, *Church as Communion: Third Period and Intersession, September 1964–September 1965* (Maryknoll, N.Y.: Orbis, 2003), 382–86. See also Group of Bishops, "Thirteen Commitments," *Concilium* 104 (1977): 109–11.

156. Vatican Council II, *Lumen Gentium*, no. 8. In his intervention in the debates about the first draft of what became *Lumen Gentium*, Cardinal Giacomo Lercaro argues that the idea of the church of the poor should be "the synthesizing idea, the point that gives light and coherence to all the subjects thus far discussed, of all the work that we must undertake." Specifically, he urges the Council toward a deeper understanding of the relation

Lumen Gentium does not use the phrase "the Church of the poor," but the Dogmatic Constitution affirms its meaning as John and Romero understand it.[157] The church is already the church of the poor with respect to its founder and head. According to *Lumen Gentium*, the church is the body of the one who empties himself in love, who becomes poor, who brings good news to the impoverished and release to captives, and who seeks and saves the lost. Medellín similarly states, "Christ our Savior, not only loved the poor, but 'being rich became poor' [2 Cor 8:9], lived in poverty, focused his mission on proclaiming the poor of his liberation and founded his Church as a sign of poverty among people."[158] Jesus Christ's identity and work along these lines did not end with his death and resurrection, but extends even into the present, paradigmatically in his ongoing association with the poor and afflicted who bear his image and whom the church is called to serve in mercy.

Impoverishment therefore pertains to the church's innermost identity. Because the church is the body of the one who became and remains poor, the church is and will continue to be the church of the poor until Christ comes again in glory. "We will never be ashamed of saying 'the Church of the poor,'" Romero therefore declares, "because Christ wanted to put his *cátedra* (seat) of redemption among them."[159]

For Romero, as for *Lumen Gentium* and Medellín, the underlying theo-

---

between Christ's ecclesial and Eucharistic presence, on the one hand, and Christ's suffering and needy presence as described in Mt 25:31–46, on the other. Together, these presences, he argued, are "truths of the mystery of Christ in the Church." While the relationship between Christ's ecclesial and Eucharistic presence has received substantial theological reflection, their relationship to Christ's suffering and needy presence has not. Yet the poor, as Giacomo Lercaro put it, are "the great sacrament, I say, in Christ and in the Church (*sacramentum magnum, dico, in Christo et in ecclesia*)"; quoted in Alberigo and Komonchak, *History of the Second Vatican Council*, 2:202, 345–46. On this point, see also Bleyer, "Die Armen als Sakrament Christi Stimmen der Zeit," 736; Paul Gauthier, *Les Pauvres, Jésus et L'Église*, Chrétienté Nouvelle (Paris: Éditions Universitaires, 1963), 63.

157. See also *Gaudium et Spes*, nos. 1, 27, 88; *Ad Gentes* (December 7, 1965), nos. 5, 12; *Presbyterorum Ordinis* (December 7, 1965), no. 6; *Optatam Totius* (October 28, 1965), no. 8; *Christus Dominus* (October 28, 1965), no. 13; *Perfectae Caritatis* (October 28, 1965), no. 13; *Apostolicam Actuositatem* (November 18, 1965), no. 8. For a more extended treatment of this topic, which focuses upon *Lumen Gentium*, no. 8, see Marie-Dominique Chenu, "Vatican II and the Church of the Poor," *Concilium* 104, no. 4 (1977): 56–61.

158. Medellín, "Pobreza de la Iglesia," 5.

159. Romero, *Homilías*, 4:110.

logical rationale for this poverty is Christological and soteriological. The church is poor because it is Christ's body. For this reason, *Gaudium et Spes* begins by announcing, "The joys and the hopes, the griefs and the anxieties of the people of this age, especially those who are poor or in any way afflicted, these are the joys and hopes, the griefs and the anxieties of the followers of Christ."[160] Christ's followers share especially in the joys, hopes, griefs, and anxieties of the poor and afflicted because Christ shares especially them. Christ continues to be mercifully present where the effects of sin and its violence are most pronounced and where his creatures seem most abandoned. That he continues to call from there for mercy is how he restores the world to its created form. Christ makes all things new by cultivating the mercy he is among his creatures, the practice of which shapes them into his own likeness.[161]

We have been examining how the church is poor because it is the ecclesial body of the one who became poor. But in the radio address, John says he hopes the Council will present the church not only as it is, but also as it wants to be. Like Romero's statement from the fourth pastoral letter, this suggests a gap or an interval between the *is* and the *wants to be*, between the church's identity and the fulfillment of its identity.

In what sense does the church want to be the church of the poor? Although the joys, hopes, griefs, and anxieties of the poor and afflicted belong to the followers of Christ because they are Christ's, clearly not all members of Christ's ecclesial body believe this, much less live as though it were true. Insofar as they do not look for Christ where he says he will meet them, they fail to discern the body of which he is the head and they are the members. In other words, they also suffer from the misery of sin and are in need of God's mercy. For they fail to see the world as it truly is: how through goodness, God gives the earth and its harvests for common use; how God calls upon human creatures to participate in the giving of

---

160. Vatican Council II, *Gaudium et Spes*, no. 1.

161. As Gregory of Nyssa writes in his homily "On Good Works," "Mercy and good deeds are works God loves; they divinize those who practice them and impress [or stamp] them into the likeness of goodness, that they may become the image of the Primordial Being, pure, who surpasses all intelligence"; Gregory of Nyssa, "On Good Works," in *The Hungry Are Dying: Beggars and Bishops in Roman Cappadocia*, trans. Susan Holman (New York: Oxford University Press, 2001), 197.

these gifts; how sin and its violence impede God's purpose for creation and darken perception of it; and finally, how these gifts—like all things—have been created through Christ and for Christ and hold together only in Christ. All this is why, every time they gather, Christ's ecclesial members confess that they suffer from the misery of sin in their thoughts and in their words, in what they have done and in what they have failed to do. Such misery is why they plead that God look not on their sins but on the faith of the whole church. And it is why, when they approach the altar to receive Christ, they do so with the words of the Roman centurion on their lips, unworthy as they are that Christ should enter under their roof (Mt 8:8; Lk 7:6).

While some of Christ's ecclesial members show the church what it means to be itself—and martyrs like Romero are preeminent in this regard—most do not. As Puebla frankly admits, "Not all of us in the Church in Latin America are sufficiently committed to the poor; we are not always concerned about them or in solidarity with them. Serving them demands constant conversion and purification on the part of all Christians in order to achieve an ever fuller identification with the poor Christ and with all who are poor."[162] According to Puebla's diagnosis, the presence of so many in need of basic bodily support implicates the church and its membership. It points to the church's failure to be what it is by neglecting the head of its body and his identification with all those in need of mercy. The response to this failure and neglect should be lament and repentance and, above all, conversion. As Romero himself comments upon this passage, "Not only do bishops, priests, and religious communities lack [sufficient commitment to, concern about, and solidarity with the poor], but Christians in general lack it. The path the Church signals for a way out of the crisis we face … is to be converted and to find Christ in the place where he says he is: 'Truly I tell you, just as you did it to one of the least of these who are members of my family, you did it to me' (Mt 25:40)."[163] For Puebla, as for Romero, conversion involves finding Christ by sharing what God has given for common use. The bishops at Puebla therefore exhort the church's members to reflect upon what they have and are in relation to this impoverishment so

162. *Puebla*, 4.1.1140.
163. Romero, *Homilías*, 5:190, 69.

as to identify more faithfully with the mercy of their Lord and, in so doing, become a more luminous sign of the mystery they are. For the cultivation of mercy that comes from Christ's being in need until the end of the world is how he feeds, slakes, welcomes, clothes, and lifts up a people into the life God shares in him.

Just as Romero's critics accused him of being a communist for his support of land reform, he was similarly accused for speaking about the church of the poor. In this phrase, Romero's detractors could only hear a call to class conflict and church division. They thought he was failing to proclaim the Good News to all people by excluding the wealthy and, consequently, that he was dividing the church between the rich and the poor.[164] Of course, Romero thinks these accusations are false and unsubstantiated, and he often seeks to dispel them.[165] According to him, the ecclesiology of the church of the poor is not about demographics or constituency and certainly not about instigating conflict or division in the church's life. Rather, Romero insists that there is only one church, whose life already suffers from conflict and division. In preaching and teaching about the church of the poor, Romero is trying to attend to these conflicts and divisions that are deeply lodged in the church's life, like invasive weeds that have infested a field, and to show the salvific tools God gives in Christ and in the Spirit to uproot them.

Romero attributes an important source of the conflict and division to the proclivity of church members to worship creatures rather than the Creator, to bow down before gods other than the one revealed in Jesus Christ. While the idols in question are legion, Romero is especially concerned with the idol of wealth and private property, which is insatiable in its thirst for blood.[166] The worship of this idol, he thinks, is the root cause of El Salvador's various forms of violence, and many are being martyred for their refusal to prostrate themselves before it.[167] Nevertheless, Rome-

---

164. For a compendium and analysis of these criticisms from Romero's early days as archbishop—criticisms that only intensified over the years—see *Persecución de la Iglesia en El Salvador.*

165. See, for instance, Romero, *Homilías,* 1:175–76, 313; 3:88, 152, 295, 297, 303, 336, 362; 4:28–29, 110, 225, 320, 344; 5:70, 523; 6:287.

166. Romero, *Misión de la Iglesia en medio de la crisis del país,* 42–51.

167. Romero, *Misión de la Iglesia en medio de la crisis del país,* 45.

ro regards these idolaters as wayward members of the same church, and he always acts as if it is his responsibility to help them find the path of conversion. Those in thrall to this idol are imprisoned and in need of the liberation that only Christ brings. They need to be freed from the sin that enslaves the human heart and that encloses the self and its possessions from others. Consequently, in preaching and teaching about the church of the poor, Romero finds himself in the precarious position of trying to set free those who are attacking him for preaching this very same message.[168] But the church of the poor, Romero is convinced, is gospel—good news—for the whole church, including those who are prepared to use violence to defend their possessions.[169] The message of the church's poverty must also reach them, because learning to share what they have and are for the love of God and neighbor is the great liberation Christ brings. It is how they lose their life in order to find it.

For this reason, Romero never tires of saying that Christ's followers must attend to suffering and needy flesh wherever they find it, especially to those in need of food, drink, shelter, clothing, care, and visitation. Such suffering and need are the consequence of sin, and mercy is the salve God applies in Christ and gracefully works to cultivate in creatures. Romero therefore repeats like a refrain, you must learn to feel "the need, the anguish" of others.[170] You must preoccupy yourselves with it as if it were *suya* (your own),[171] *un asunto propio* (your own issue),[172] *su propia causa* (your own cause).[173] You must relate to those experiencing it as if they were *su propia familia* (your own family)[174] or *amistades* (friends).[175] For we are *la misma carne* (the same flesh), with the same origin and destiny.[176] Learning to share the suffering and need of others is how you discover it to be Christ's, and also that the grace you receive to share in it

168. Romero, *Misión de la Iglesia en medio de la crisis del país*, 24–25.
169. Romero, *Homilías*, 5:272.
170. Romero, *Homilías*, 3:336.
171. Romero, *Homilías*, 6:283.
172. Romero, *Homilías*, 4:255.
173. Romero, *Homilías*, 5:272, 70.
174. Romero, *Homilías*, 5:110.
175. Romero, *Homilías*, 6:138.
176. Romero, *Homilías*, 2:256.

comes from him, which he gives in order for Christ to be formed in you and for you to share in the heavenly life he brings.[177]

What the foregoing suggests is that the failure of the church to be itself is no inconsequential feature of the people of God on pilgrimage in the world. The church is, after all, a body founded on God's merciful work on behalf of the wounded, which is humankind as a whole. The presence of sin within the church, like weeds that have taken root and are sprouting up everywhere, cannot be evaded or dismissed. Learning to be itself is therefore a task that is ceaselessly before the church, which is in need of continual reformation to be what it is and to anticipate the land toward which its members pilgrim. This is yet another reason it is misleading to narrate the church's resistance under Romero to a brutally repressive regime and its supporters in binary terms, as if its members were not also among them, as if the church were not also deeply implicated in the established disorder Romero sought to confront. Such a narration misconstrues the kind of body the church is by imagining its boundaries to be straightforward, visible, and delimitable—as if the sheep were already separated from the goats; as if the wheat were already stored safely in the barn, apart from the weeds bundled for burning. But the mixture—and all the difficulties that come with it—remain until the Lord comes again in glory, until the harvest of the merciful at the end of the age.

"The Church is not a field of pure wheat," Romero says in a homily on the parable of the wheat and the tares. Rather, the church is a field in which weeds have sprouted up among the wheat God has sown. Both grow together, side by side (Mt 13:24–30).[178] In the parable, against the suggestion that the weeds be immediately removed and burned, the landowner counsels patience, lest the wheat be uprooted along with the weeds (Mt 13:29). Romero's reflection of the parable suggests additional reasons for patience. Not only do wheat and weeds grow together, but also, when one is actually in the midst of the field, it is often difficult to distinguish

---

177. Romero, *Homilías*, 4:255; 5:272.

178. Romero, *Homilías*, 3:118–19. This does not mean that God is not at work within the church. As Romero puts it, "If there is a Church that wants to boast that all of its members are saints, it will not be the true Church." The proliferation of weeds should therefore come as no surprise.

between the two. In what human life, Romero asks, cannot both wheat and weeds be found growing together, to a greater or lesser degree?

There are still more reasons for patience. As Romero observes, the land being cultivated by God is no ordinary land. In it, weeds need not necessarily remain weeds forever. How many there are in El Salvador, Romero says, "who have their hands stained with blood and with violence! How many there are who are weeds!" Yet, he continues, "God is waiting for them. Do not uproot them, Christ says. Wait for them. So, we wait." God "calls to them, wants to forgive them, wants to save them." Patience is required, because in the field that is the church on pilgrimage, even "weeds can become wheat."[179]

Needless to say, such a stance, which imitates God in waiting and refusing to uproot, and which hopes for the conversion of enemies and even prays for and forgives persecutors, places those who embrace it in a position of extreme vulnerability, with little in the way of protection against the wolves of the world. But it is a stance that witnesses to the love in which all things hold together and have their being; the love that causes the sun to rise on the evil and the good; that sends rain on the just and the unjust; and that establishes a land where grains of wheat can grow, harden into maturity, and bear much fruit.

179. Romero, *Homilías*, 3:117–19. This raises an important question about the regret that courses through Dada's interview with Captain Álvaro Saravia. The interview reads as if Saravia is in the processes of coming to himself, like the prodigal son (Lk 15:17). Among the interview's most remarkable features is Saravia's empathy for those he once killed without hesitation. Now his life apparently depends upon *campesino* neighbors. The house where he lives is on loan. Another family provides him tortillas. "If that's being a communist," he says, "it's communist. It would have been considered communist … in those days"; Dada, "Así matamos a Monseñor Romero."

Romero's comments also relate to a story told by Maria Luisa D'Aubuisson de Martínez, the extraordinary sister of Roberto D'Aubuisson. Maria Luisa took a very different path than her brother. As a young woman, she became involved in the Juventud Obrera Católica (Catholic Worker Youth), a group that sought to promote the church's social teaching. Her husband, Edín Martínez, was the president of the Fundación Monseñor Romero (Monsignor Romero Foundation) until recently, when he passed away. Maria Luisa frequently visited D'Aubuisson as he succumbed to throat cancer in 1991, sitting at his bedside and reading him the Bible as he lay dying. She recounts pleading with him to ask forgiveness, reporting that at one point he opened his eyes, drew her close to him, and wept, because the cancer had left him unable to speak; Mike Lanchin, "Romero Remembered," *National Catholic Reporter*, March 17, 2000; Christian Guevara, "De la guerra a la paz: María Luisa D'Aubuisson Arrieta," *El Faro*, February 5, 2016; Personal communication with Edín Martínez.

EPILOGUE

Do we truly realize that something is wrong in a world where there are so many farmworkers without land, so many families without a home, so many laborers without rights, so many persons whose dignity is not respected?

—Pope Francis, *Address at the Second World Meeting of Popular Movements*

"Don't call me a saint," Dorothy Day once quipped. "I don't want to be dismissed that easily."[1] Her words evoke a sentimental piety that sanitizes saints of their radicality and softens the collective memory of their scandalous work of incarnating the gospel in the world. When I was in San Salvador the week before Romero's beatification, I heard throughout the city people voicing a similar worry.[2] Will Romero's canonization blunt the radicality of his witness? Will it evade the difficulties that came to light when the gospel grew feet in El Salvador?[3] Martyrs and saints like Romero are gifts God gives for the church and for the world. But as with any gift, there is always the danger that its reception will go awry. I also saw in San Salvador that there were still others who did not want this gift, who saw Romero as "too political" to be named a saint. Would the church forget his politics to make his cause more palatable?

1. Quoted in James Martin, SJ, "Don't Call Me a Saint?" *America*, November 14, 2012.
2. Colorado, "Romero: Whose Beatification Is It, Anyway?," *Super Martyrio*, May 11, 2015.
3. See Kelly, *When the Gospel Grows Feet.*

That danger is of particular concern in Romero's case—and for that matter, Day's, as well. In *The Long Loneliness*, Day recalls a question that haunted her as a child: "Why was so much work done in remedying social evils instead of avoiding them in the first place? … Where were the saints to try to change the social order, not just to minister to the slaves, but to do away with slavery?"[4] Romero is in many ways an answer to Day's question, an example of the kind of saint she thought the church needed. For the message of Romero's sanctity contains important lessons, not only for the path of personal piety and for church reform, but also for social and economic transformation. In one of his *Easy Essays*, Peter Maurin, co-founder with Day of the Catholic Worker, describes "the dynamite" inherent in the church's message and how Catholic scholars have "wrapped it up/in nice phraseology,/placed it in an hermetic container/and sat on the lid."[5] Romero shows us what blowing the lid off the container looks like and the social dynamism that results. For that reason, he is, as Cardinal Rosa Chávez has characterized him, *un santo incómodo* (an uncomfortable saint).[6]

The politics of common use remains an underappreciated and still very pertinent aspect of Romero's legacy. Romero by no means invents this politics. It has deep roots in Catholic social teaching and its sources, and it can be found elsewhere as well. But Romero remains among the best exemplifications of its concrete form and application and the inherent risks involved in bearing witnessing to the belief that God's creation is a common gift.

One important place where we see Romero's legacy today is with the World Meeting of Popular Movements (WMPM) and what it represents in the life of the church. This is an initiative on the part of Pope Fran-cis to establish an "encounter" between leadership in the church and *los movimientos populares* (popular movements) from around the world that have been established by people whose access to land, housing, and work is insecure or denied altogether. As we have seen, Romero defended the

4. Dorothy Day, *The Long Loneliness* (New York: Harper and Brothers, 1952), 45.
5. Peter Maurin, "Blowing the Dynamite," in *Easy Essays* (Eugene, Ore.: Wipf and Stock, 2010), 3.
6. Cardinal Rosa Chávez, "Es un santo incómodo," *Alpha y Omega*, September 20, 2018.

existence of similar groups and the justice of the demands being made by them.[7] The first of the WMPM took place in October 2014, which con-vened representatives of over one hundred such groups, thirty bishops and other church representatives, and staff members of various other church groups and nongovernmental organizations.[8] Subsequently, there have been additional worldwide meetings: in Bolivia in 2015, in Rome again in 2016, and then via video conference in 2021. We have also entered a period of regional meetings.

The WMPM seeks to address what Francis calls in *Evangelii Gaudium* the "economy of exclusion and inequality" by bringing together, as he puts it in his first address, those who "suffer [this] exclusion and inequality in the flesh."[9] Participants lack land: they are landless farmers and smallholders, sharecroppers, day laborers, and seasonal farm workers. They lack housing: they are slum or street dwellers, squatters, occupiers of abandoned housing, and invaders of new settlements. And they lack work: they are day laborers and domestic help, junk dealers, waste pickers, urban recyclers, street vendors, and sidewalk artisans.[10] Many of the participants are therefore part of what is known as the "informal economy" with its associated lack of legal protection and precariousness of livelihood. Because this economy exists "outside" the economy as that term and its accounting are typically understood, to encounter its members one must "leave the 'center' of the economic system and go to the peripheries and enter the slums, the dumps, the open-air markets, and the clandestine workshops," as the Argentine activist and scholar Juan Grabois puts it.[11]

Perhaps the most significant feature of WMPM, then, is simply its existence: Francis has invited the peripheries to the ecclesial center. Like Romero, Francis has endeavored to call the church's attention to forms of

---

7. See Romero, *Iglesia y organizaciones políticas populares.*

8. Michael Czerny and Paulo Foglizzo, "La forza degli esclusi: L'incontro mondiale dei movimenti popolari in Vaticano," *Aggiornamenti Sociali*, January 2015.

9. Francis I, *Address of His Holiness Pope Francis to the Participants in the World Meeting of Popular Movements*, October 28, 2014.

10. Czerny and Foglizzo, "La forza degli esclusi."

11. Juan Grabois, "Trabajo informal, trabajo precario y economía popular," *América Latina en movimiento*, October 16, 2014.

violence that are difficult to perceive and therefore defend against and that have continued to be hidden, even from the gaze of the church.

Appropriately, the foundational themes of the WMPM are *Tierra, Techo, Trabajo* (Land, Lodging, Labor)—what Francis refers to as *las tres T's* (the three *T's*)—which reflect the politics of common use as we have been examining it. As Francis explains in his first address, "This meeting of ours represents a concrete desire … a desire for what should be within everyone's reach, namely land, housing and work. However, it is sad to see that nowadays land, housing and work are ever more distant for the majority." In discussing the theme of land, he refers to the elimination of peasant farmers due to the prevalence of land- and water-grabbing and deforestation. Noting that some of the participants are demanding land reform, Francis tells them they have an ally in social teaching, and he affirms the participants' struggle "for the dignity of the rural family, for water, for life, and so that everyone can benefit from the fruits of the earth."[12] In his second address, Francis wonders, in the words of the epigraph, "Do we truly realize that something is wrong in a world where there are so many farmworkers without land, so many families without a home, so many laborers without rights, so many persons whose dignity is not respected?"[13] Among the problems with such a world is that it goes against the grain of the reality. It contradicts the belief that "creation is a gift … given to us by God so that we might care for it and use it, always gratefully and always respectfully, for the benefit of everyone."[14]

Throughout these addresses, we also find that for Francis, as for Romero, the theological grammar of creation as common gift yields a view of justice according to which material goods belong to those who need them simply because they are members of the community of humankind to which God gives the gift. As Francis explains, "Working for a just distribution of the fruits of the earth and human labor is … a moral obligation…. It is about giving to the poor and to peoples what is theirs by

12. Francis I, *Address of His Holiness Pope Francis to the Participants in the World Meeting of Popular Movements*.

13. Francis I, *Participation at the Second World Meeting of Popular Movements Address of the Holy Father*, July 9, 2015.

14. Francis I, *Address of His Holiness Pope Francis to the Participants in the World Meeting of Popular Movements*.

right. The universal destination of goods is not a figure of speech [but] a reality prior to private property."[15] To be precise, it is not simply a reality *prior* to private property but it also shapes *what we understand property to be*—what is ours and what is not—along with how we use the world God gives us. This is why, in a different context, Francis remarks, "Remember well, whenever food is thrown away it is as if it is stolen from the table of the poor, from the hungry!"[16]

This account of justice, which arises from the claim that creation is a common gift, also leads Francis, like Romero, to employ the language of rights. "By 'rights' we mean that *campesinos* should have land, and that workers must be able to organize and to be paid just salaries," we saw Romero say in the homily upon his return from Puebla. "Land, housing and work, what you struggle for," Francis similarly says throughout these addresses, "are sacred rights," the defense of which, he argues, is deeply and inextricably implicated in the proclamation of the gospel. Yet for Francis, as for Romero, such rights are a source of controversy. "It is strange but if I talk about this," Francis says, "some say the Pope is a communist." But to make such claims about land, housing, and work, he continues, "is nothing unusual; it is the social teaching of the Church."[17]

The accusation of communism during Latin America's Cold War was often deadly, and Romero's witness points to how the politics of common use can take a cruciform shape. In the case of Romero, we saw this primarily in terms of his work to facilitate a more just distribution of land in El Salvador. But for many people today, the cruciformity of this politics also relates to defending existing—though threatened—access to land, water, grazing, fishing grounds, and forests. Pressures on farmland related to

15. Francis I, *Participation at the Second World Meeting of Popular Movements Address of the Holy Father*. See also his comments about Jesus' picking grain on the Sabbath in *Address of His Holiness Pope Francis to Participants in the Third World Meeting of Popular Movements*, November, 6, 2016.

16. Francis I, *Udienza Generale*, June 5, 2013. The spontaneous remark only appears in the Italian: "*Ricordiamo bene, però, che il cibo che si butta via è come se venisse rubato dalla mensa di chi è povero, di chi ha fame!*" See also *Evangelii Gaudium*, no. 57; Francis I, Encyclical Letter *Laudato Si'* (May 24, 2015), no. 50.

17. Francis I, *Address of His Holiness Pope Francis to the Participants in the World Meeting of Popular Movements*. For a sampling of this controversy, see "*Quo Vadis, Domine?* Reverent and Filial Message to His Holiness Pope Francis from Prince Bertrand of Orleans-Braganza," February 13, 2014.

population growth, erosion, and soil depletion continue to be exacerbated by export-driven agricultural policies that favor large-scale landholdings for the production of food, energy, and cash crops.[18] As demand for land increases, governments, private companies, and others find ways to acquire land, often with little regard for those who presently live on it. People and communities that resist such encroachment risk their lives.

Recent years have been the worst on record for the killing and criminalization of land and environmental defenders,[19] which has increasingly produced those Willis Jenkins describes as "environmental martyrs," such as Sister Dorothy Stang, who was gunned down for her efforts to protect rural farmers and prevent deforestation in Brazil.[20] Another victim of this violence was Berta Cáceres, an indigenous Lenca woman from Honduras, who organized opposition to an internationally financed dam project that would have dispossessed her people from their ancestral lands. She was also a participant in the initial WMPM. In 2016, armed intruders murdered her in her home, a slaying that increasingly seems to have been planned by Honduran military intelligence specialists, some of whom had ties to the School of the Americas, where Roberto D'Aubuisson trained.[21] Pope Francis acknowledged Cáceres's death and the cruciformity of the politics of common use when he said in his third address, "I know that many of you lay your own lives on the line. I know—and I want to say this—that some are not here today because they did lay down their lives.... But there is no greater love than to give one's life. That is what Jesus teaches us."[22]

Much more remains to be said about the WMPM and the reality to which it directs us than can be conveyed here. But by way of conclusion,

18. Olivier De Schutter, *Access to Land and the Right to Food*, Report presented to the 65th General Assembly of the United Nations, August 11, 2010.

19. Global Witness, *Deadly Environment: The Dramatic Rise in Killings of Environmental and Land Defenders* (London: Global Witness, 2014); *How Many More?* (London: Global Witness, 2015); *On Dangerous Ground: The Killing and Criminalization of Land and Environmental Defenders Worldwide* (London: Global Witness, 2016).

20. Willis Jenkins, *Ecologies of Grace: Environmental Ethics and Christian Theology* (New York: Oxford University Press, 2008), 242–43.

21. Nina Lakhani, "Berta Cáceres Court Papers Show Murder Suspects' Links to U.S.-Trained Elite Troops," *Guardian*, February 28, 2017.

22. Francis I, *Address of His Holiness Pope Francis to Participants in the Third World Meeting of Popular Movements*.

it is important to say something about the politics of common use as it pertains to another prominent theme running through these addresses and through Francis's pontificate more generally: ecology. "Our common home," Francis says in the second address, "is being pillaged, laid waste, and harmed with impunity.... People and their movements are called to cry out, to mobilize, and to demand—peacefully, but firmly—that appropriate and urgently needed measures be taken." In his final Sunday homily, Romero memorably declares, "In the name of God ... I beg you, I plead with you, I order you, in the name of God, stop the repression." Echoing these famous words, Francis similarly pleads, "I ask you, in the name of God, to defend Mother Earth."[23]

This work has argued that the theological grammar of creation as common gift shapes Romero's advocacy for land reform. The WMPM exemplifies how this theological grammar and the account of justice arising from it continue to offer important guidance for enabling people's access to the land, lodging, and labor that they need to survive and to flourish. But in these addresses, Francis extends and deepens reflection upon the politics of common use by underscoring its unavoidable ecological implications. "An economic system centered upon the deity of money," Francis observes in the first address, leads to a "throw-away culture" in which the excluded "are discarded, are 'leftovers.'" People without access to land, labor, and lodging are the result. But such a system, he continues, also "plunder[s] nature to sustain consumption at the frenetic level it needs."[24] Throughout his pontificate, Francis has pointed to the intimate relationship between the use this system makes of people and the use it makes of the earth itself—the devastation it does to whatever is fragile. The "invisible thread" that binds this devastation is a system that "has imposed the mentality of profit at any price, with no concern for social exclusion or the destruction of nature."[25]

Romero did not explicitly articulate the ecological commitments im-

23. Francis I, *Participation at the Second World Meeting of Popular Movements Address of the Holy Father.*

24. Francis I, *Address of His Holiness Pope Francis to the Participants in the World Meeting of Popular Movements.*

25. Francis I, *Participation at the Second World Meeting of Popular Movements Address of the Holy Father.*

plied by his convictions about creation. But concern for the care of our common home is a logical development of the politics of common use that guided him. The gift-character of creation demands that human use of the earth and its fruits must always acknowledge the commons to which God gives the gift, which is the whole of humankind. From this conviction flows the justice that hungers and thirsts for people to have what they need. But the common destination of created goods also and crucially entails that God gives the gift to meet the needs of people both in the present time and across all times. There is an inescapable temporal unfolding to commonality of the gift, which means the politics of common use necessarily implies a justice that is also ecological. If Romero did not always make this relationship explicit, Francis does.

At the canonization mass for Romero, Francis wore Romero's cincture, and in doing so, identified himself and his papacy with Romero. It was the same cincture Romero had on when he was martyred, which was still stained with his blood. Among the many questions this gesture and its symbolism raise for practitioners of the politics of common use today are: What habits of use acknowledge the commonality of the gift, so that those who follow us on this fragile earth will also be able to enjoy what God has given? And more pointedly, what sacrifices are necessary to bear witness to it?

BIBLIOGRAPHY

Indispensable websites for the study of Romero are: http://www.romeroes
.com, the official website (in Spanish) for the beatification and canonization
of Romero, run by the Office of Canonization of the Archdiocese of San Salvador; http://www.romerotrust.org.uk, run by the Romero Trust, which promotes
knowledge and awareness of the life and work of Romero and which contains
a wealth of primary and secondary literature by and about Romero in English
and in Spanish; and http://polycarpi.blogspot.com and http://eminens-doctrina
.blogspot.com, the best blogs about Romero, with well-informed news and commentary in English, Spanish, and Italian.

Agamben, Giorgio. *The Highest Poverty: Monastic Rules and Form-of-Life*. Translated
    by Adam Kotsko. Stanford, Calif.: Stanford University Press, 2013.
Alas, José Inocencio. *Iglesia, tierra y lucha campesina: Suchitoto, El Salvador, 1968–
    1977*. San Salvador: Asoc. de Frailes Franciscanos OFM de C.A., 2003.
Alberigo, Giuseppe, and Joseph A. Komonchak, eds. *History of the Second Vatican
    Council*. Vol. 2, *Formation of the Council's Identity: First Period and Intersession,
    October 1962–September 1963*. Maryknoll, N.Y.: Orbis, 1997.
———, eds. *History of the Second Vatican Council*. Vol. 3, *The Mature Council: Second
    Period and Intersession, October 1963–September 1964*. Maryknoll, N.Y.: Orbis,
    2000.
———, eds. *History of the Second Vatican Council*. Vol. 4, *Church as Communion: Third
    Period and Intersession, September 1964–September 1965*. Maryknoll, N.Y.: Orbis,
    2003.
Almeida, Paul. *Waves of Protest: Popular Struggle in El Salvador, 1925–2005*. Minneap-
    olis: University of Minnesota Press, 2008.
Ambrose of Milan. *On Naboth*. In *Ambrose*, edited by Boniface Ramsey. New York:
    Routledge, 1997.

Americas Watch and American Civil Liberties Union. *Report on Human Rights in El Salvador*. New York: Random House, 1982.

Amnistía Internacional. *El espectro de los "escuadrones de la muerte."* London: 1996.

Anderson, Gary. *Charity: The Place of the Poor in the Biblical Tradition*. New Haven, Conn.: Yale University Press, 2013.

Anderson, Thomas P. *Matanza: El Salvador's Communist Revolt of 1932*. Omaha: University of Nebraska Press, 1971.

———. *The War of the Dispossessed: Honduras and El Salvador, 1969*. Lincoln: University of Nebraska Press, 1981.

Andrés, Roberto Casas. *Dios pasó por El Salvador: La relevancia teológica de las tradiciones narrativas de los mártires salvadoreños*. Bilbao: Desclée de Brouwer, 2009.

ANEP. "Declarations on Land Reform and the Government's Response (July 1976)." In *The Central American Crisis Reader*, edited by Robert S. Leiken and Barry Rubin, 342–44. New York: Summit, 1987.

Anselm of Canterbury. *Why God Became Man*. In *The Major Works*, edited by Brian Davies and G. R. Evans, 260–356. New York: Oxford University Press, 1998.

Apostolic Vicariate of Darien, Panama. *Tierra de todos, tierra de paz*. Darien, December 8, 1988.

"Apoyan la reforma agraria los obispos de Río Grande do Sul." *Camino* 1, no. 1 (1961).

Aquinas, Thomas. *Summa Theologiae*. 61 vols. Various translators. Blackfriars Edition. New York: Cambridge University Press, 2006.

———. *Commentary on the Letter of Saint Paul to the Romans*. Edited by J. Mortensen and E. Alarcón. Translated by F. R. Larcher. Latin/English Edition of *The Works of St. Thomas Aquinas*. Vol. 37. Lander, Wyo.: Aquinas Institute for the Study of Sacred Doctrine, 2012.

Aristotle. *Nicomachean Ethics*. Translated by Martin Ostwald. Upper Saddle River, N.J.: Prentice Hall, 1962.

———. *The Politics*. Translated by T. A. Sinclair. New York: Penguin, 1981.

Arnson, Cynthia J. "Window on the Past: A Declassified History of Death Squads in El Salvador." In *Death Squads in Global Perspective: Murder with Deniability*, edited by B. Campbell and A. Brenner, 85–124. New York: Palgrave Macmillan, 2002.

Asamblea Legislativa. *Memoria del primer congreso nacional de reforma agraria*. San Salvador: Publicaciones de la Asamblea Legislativa, 1970.

Astill, Grenville. *The Countryside of Medieval England*. Cambridge, Mass.: Blackwell, 1992.

Athanasius. *The Life of Antony*. Translated by Robert C. Gregg. Classics of Western Spirituality. Mahwah, N.J.: Paulist Press, 1980.

———. *On the Incarnation of the Word*. Translated by John Behr. Crestwood, N.Y.: St. Vladimir's Seminary Press, 1996.

Augustine. *Sermons on the Liturgical Seasons*. Translated by Mary Sarah Muldowney, RSM. Fathers of the Church 38. Washington, D.C.: The Catholic University of America Press, 1958.

———. *Sermons (148–83) on the New Testament*. In *The Works of Saint Augustine*, vol. III, part 5, translated by Edmund Hill, OP. New York: New City Press, 1992.

———. *Sermons (94A–147A) on the Old Testament*. In *The Works of Saint Augustine*, vol. III, part 4, translated by Edmund Hill, OP. New York: New City Press, 1992.

———. *Sermons 341–400 on Various Themes*. In *The Works of Saint Augustine*, vol. III, part 10, translated by Edmund Hill, OP. New York: New City Press, 1995.

———. *The City of God against the Pagans*. Edited by R. W. Dyson. New York: Cambridge University Press, 1998.

———. *The Confessions*. In *The Works of Saint Augustine*, vol. 1, part 1, translated by Maria Boulding. New York: New City Press, 2001.

———. *Letters 1–99*. In *The Works of Saint Augustine*, vol. II, part 1, translated by Roland J. Teske. New York: New City Press, 2001.

———. *Essential Sermons*. In the *Works of Saint Augustine*, translated by Edmund Hill, OP. New York: New City Press, 2007.

———. *Homilies on the First Epistle of John*. In *The Works of Saint Augustine*, vol. III, part 14, translated by Boniface Ramsey. New York: New City Press, 2008.

Ault, Warren Ortman. *Open-Field Farming in Medieval England*. London: Allen and Unwin, 1972.

Avila, Charles. *Ownership: Early Christian Teaching*. Maryknoll, N.Y.: Orbis, 1983.

Baloyra, Enrique A. *El Salvador in Transition*. Chapel Hill: University of North Carolina Press, 1982.

Barrera, Albino. *Modern Catholic Social Documents and Political Economy*. Washington, D.C.: Georgetown University Press, 2001.

———. *Economic Compulsion and Christian Ethics*. New York: Cambridge University Press, 2007.

Barros Souza, Marcelo de, and José Luis Caravias. *Teología de la tierra*. Madrid: Ediciones Paulinas, 1988.

Basil the Great. "I Will Tear Down My Barns." In *On Social Justice*, translated by C. Paul Schroeder, 59–71. Crestwood, N.Y.: St. Vladimir's Seminary Press, 2009.

———. *The Rule of St. Basil*. Translated by Anna Silvas. Collegeville, Minn.: Liturgical Press, 2013.

Belloc, Hilaire. *The Servile State*. Boston: Le Roy Phillips, 1913.

———. *An Essay on the Restoration of Property*. Norfolk, Va.: IHS, 2012.

Benedict XVI. *Caritas in Veritate*. Encyclical Letter. June 29, 2009.

Benjamin, Walter. *Illuminations*. New York: Schocken, 1969.

Berry, Wendell. *Sex, Economy, Freedom and Community: Eight Essays*. New York: Pantheon, 1993.

———. "Private Property and the Common Wealth." In *Another Turn of the Crank: Essays*, by Wendell Berry, 46–63. Berkeley, Calif.: Counterpoint, 2011.

Berryman, Phillip. *The Religious Roots of Rebellion: Christians in Central America*. Maryknoll, N.Y.: Orbis, 1986.

———. *Stubborn Hope: Religion, Politics, and Revolution in Central America*. New York: New Press, 1995.

Bingemer, Maria Clara. *Latin American Theology: Roots and Branches*. Maryknoll, N.Y.: Orbis, 2016.

Blackstone, William. *Commentaries on the Laws of England* [1765]. Vol. 2. Chicago: University of Chicago Press, 1979.

Blancarte, Roberto. "Romero, mártir de la guerra fria." In *Óscar Romero: Un obispo entre guerra fría y revolución,* edited by Roberto Morozzo della Rocca, 217–39. Madrid: Editorial San Pablo España, 2013.

Bleyer, Bernard. "Die Armen als Sakrament Christi Stimmen der Zeit." *Stimmen der Zeit* 226, no. 11 (2008): 734–46.

Bonilla Bonilla, Adolfo. *Ideas económicas en la Centroamérica ilustrada, 1793–1838.* San Salvador: FLASCO Programa El Salvador, 1999.

———. *Tenencia de la tierra y reforma agraria en El Salvador: Un análisis histórico.* San Salvador: Centro Nacional de Investigaciones en Ciencias Sociales y Humanidades, 2013.

Bonner, Ray. *Weakness and Deceit: U.S. Policy and El Salvador.* New York: New York Times Books, 1984.

Brackley, Dean. "Rutilio and Romero: Martyrs for Our Time." In *Monsignor Romero: A Bishop for the Third Millennium,* edited by Robert S. Pelton, CSC, 79–100. Notre Dame, Ind.: University of Notre Dame Press, 2004.

Breckman, Warren. *Marx, the Young Hegelians, and the Origins of Radical Social Theory: Dethroning the Self.* New York: Cambridge University Press, 2001.

Brockett, Charles D. *Land, Power, and Poverty: Agrarian Transformation and Political Conflict in Central America.* Boulder, Colo.: Westview, 1998.

Brockman, James R. *Romero: A Life.* Maryknoll, N.Y.: Orbis, 2005.

Brown, Peter. *The Cult of the Saints: Its Rise and Function in Latin Christianity.* Chicago: University of Chicago Press, 2014.

Browning, David. *El Salvador: Landscape and Society.* New York: Oxford University Press, 1971.

Brunk, Samuel. *The Posthumous Career of Emiliano Zapata: Myth, Memory, and Mexico's Twentieth Century.* Austin: University of Texas Press, 2008.

Bulmer-Thomas, Victor. *The Political Economy of Central America since 1920.* New York: Cambridge University Press, 1987.

Burke, Kevin F. "Archbishop Óscar Romero: Peacemaker in the Tradition of Catholic Social Thought." *Journal for Peace and Justice Studies* 13, no. 2 (2003): 105–24.

Burke, Melvin. "El sistema de plantación y la proletarización del trabajo agrícola en El Salvador." *Estudios Centro-Americanos* 31, nos. 335–36 (September–October 1976): 473–86.

Cabarrús, Carlos Rafael. *Genesis de una revolución: Análisis del surgimiento y desarrollo de la organización campesina en El Salvador.* México, D.F: Centro de Investigaciones y Estudios Superiores en Antropologia Social, 1983.

Cáceres Prendes, Jorge. "Revolutionary Struggle and Church Commitment: The Case of El Salvador." *Social Compass* 30, no. 2–3 (1983): 261–98.

Calvez, Jean-Yves, and Jacques Perrin. *The Church and Social Justice: The Social Teaching of the Popes from Leo XIII to Pius XII (1878–1958).* Chicago: Henry Regnery, 1961.

Cardenal, Rodolfo. *Historia de una esperanza: La vida de Rutilio Grande.* San Salvador: UCA Editores, 1985.

———. *Rutilio Grande: Mártir de la evangelización rural en El Salvador.* San Salvador: UCA Editores, 2015.

Cardenal, Rodolfo, Ignacio Martín-Baró, and Jon Sobrino, eds. *La voz de los sin voz: La palabra viva de Monseñor Romero*. San Salvador: UCA Editores, 1986.

Carnes, Natalie. *Image and Presence: A Christological Reflection upon Iconoclasm and Iconophilia*. Redwood City, Calif.: Stanford University Press, 2017.

Carranza, Salvador, Miguel Cavada Diez, and Jon Sobrino. *XXV Aniversario de Rutilio Grande: Sus homilías*. San Salvador: Centro Monseñor Romero, UCA, 2002.

Cassidy, Edward Idris. "Romero visto de cerca." In *Óscar Romero: Un obispo entre guerra fría y revolución*, edited by Roberto Morozzo della Rocca, 149–54. Madrid: Editorial San Pablo España, 2003.

Cavanaugh, William. "Dying for the Eucharist or Being Killed by It? Romero's Challenge to First-World Christians." *Theology Today* 58, no. 2 (2001): 177–89.

———. "Killing for the Telephone Company: Why the Nation-State Is Not the Keeper of the Common Good." *Modern Theology* 20, no. 2 (2004): 243–74.

———. "Dispersed Political Authority: Subsidiarity and Globalization in *Caritas in Veritate*." In *Jesus Christ: The New Face of Social Progress*, edited by Peter J. Casarella, 89–106. Grand Rapids, Mich.: W. B. Eerdmans, 2015.

Chanta Martínez, René Antonio. "Antimasonería y antiliberalismo en el pensamiento de Óscar Arnulfo Romero 1962–1965." *REHMLAC* 3, no. 1 (2001):121–41.

Chávez y González, Luis. *Sobre la mejor y más justa distribución de los bienes*. San Salvador: Arzobispado de San Salvador, 1961.

———. *La responsibilidad del laico en el ordenamiento de lo temporal*. San Salvador: Arzobispado de San Salvador, 1966.

Chenu, Marie-Dominique. "Vatican II and the Church of the Poor." *Concilium* 104, no. 4 (1977): 56–61.

Chesterton, G. K. *What's Wrong with the World*. New York: Dodd, Mead, 1912.

———. *The Outline of Sanity*. New York: Dodd, Mead, 1927.

Ching, Erik. *Authoritarian El Salvador: Politics and the Origins of the Military Regimes, 1880–1940*. Notre Dame, Ind.: University of Notre Dame Press, 2014.

Clarke, Kevin. *Oscar Romero: Love Must Win Out*. Collegeville, Minn.: Liturgical Press, 2014.

Clement of Alexandria. *Paedagogus*. Boston: Brill, 2002.

Code of Canon Law: Latin-English Edition. Washington, D.C.: Canon Law Society of America, 1983.

Colón-Emeric, Edgardo. *Óscar Romero's Theological Vision: Liberation and the Transfiguration of the Poor*. Notre Dame, Ind.: University of Notre Dame Press, 2018.

Commission on the Truth for El Salvador. *From Madness to Hope: The 12-Year War in El Salvador; Report of the Commission on the Truth for El Salvador*. New York: United Nations, 1993.

Compendium of the Social Doctrine of the Church. Washington, D.C.: United States Conference of Catholic Bishops, 2004.

Conferencia Episcopal de Costa Rica. *Madre tierra: Carta pastoral sobre la situación de los campesinos y indígenas*. San José, August 2, 1994.

Conferencia Episcopal de El Salvador. "Llamamiento del Episcopado Salvadoreño en nombre del país." *Estudios Centroamericanos* (1969): 254–55.

Conferencia Episcopal de Guatemala. *Unidos en la esperanza: La presencia de la Iglesia en la reconstrucción de Guatemala.* Quezaltenango, July 25, 1976.

———. *El clamor por la tierra.* Guatemala de la Asunción, February 29, 1988.

Conferencia Episcopal de Honduras. *Documentos oficiales de la Conferencia Episcopal de Honduras: 1968–1978.* Tegucigalpa: Conferencia Episcopal de Honduras, 1970.

———. *Sobre el desarrollo del campesinado en Honduras.* Tegucigalpa, January 8, 1970

———. *Mensaje sobre algunos temas de interés nacional.* Tegucigalpa, August 28, 1995.

Conferencia Episcopal de Paraguay. *La tierra, don de Dios para todos.* Asunción, June 12, 1983.

Conferencia General del Episcopado Latinoamericano. *Río de Janeiro, Medellín, Puebla, Santo Domingo: Documentos pastorales.* Chile: San Pablo, 1993.

Conferência Nacional dos Bispos do Brasil. *Igreja e problemas da terra.* Itaici: Conferência Nacional dos Bispos do Brasil, February 14, 1980.

———. *Manifesto pela terra e pela vita a CPT e a reforma agrária hoje.* Goiânia, August 1, 1995.

———. *Pro-memória da Presidência e Comissão Episcopal de Pastoral da CNBB sobre as consequências do Decreto n. 1775 de 8 de Janeiro de 1996.* Brasília, February 29, 1996.

———. *Exigências Cristãs para a paz social.* Itaici, April 24, 1996.

Corr, Anders. *No Trespassing: Squatting, Rent Strikes, and Land Struggles Worldwide.* Cambridge, Mass.: South End, 1999.

Cortés y Larraz, Pedro. *Descripción geográfico-moral de la diócesis de Goathemala,* A.G.I, Audiencia de Guatemala, leg. 940, fol. 35 (2001) [1770].

Crandall, Russell. *The Salvador Option: The United States in El Salvador, 1977–1992.* New York: Cambridge University Press, 2016.

Cuchillo, Emilio Arturo. "El desarrollo cultural del campesino y la reforma agraria." Ph.D. diss., Universidad de El Salvador, 1970.

Cuéllar, Roberto. "Monseñor Óscar Romero: Human Rights Apostle." In *Monsignor Romero: A Bishop for the Third Millennium,* edited by Robert S. Pelton, CSC, 35–46. Notre Dame, Ind.: University of Notre Dame Press, 2004.

Cunningham, Lawrence S. "On Contemporary Martyrs: Some Recent Literature." *Theological Studies* 63 (2002): 374–81.

———. *A Brief History of Saints.* Oxford: Blackwell, 2005.

"Curso de comunidades eclesiales de base." *Orientación,* August 29, 1971.

Cyprian of Carthage. *Works and Almsgiving.* In *Treatises,* translated by Roy J. Deferrari, 225–53. Fathers of the Church 36. New York: Fathers of the Church, 1958.

Czerny, Michael, and Paulo Foglizzo. "La forza degli esclusi: L'incontro mondiale dei movimenti popolari in Vaticano." *Aggiornamenti Sociali,* January 2015.

Dada, Carlos. "Así matamos a Monseñor Romero." *El Faro,* March 22, 2010

Dahlman, Carl J. *The Open Field System and Beyond: A Property Rights Analysis of an Economic Institution.* New York: Cambridge University Press, 2008.

Dahrendorf, Ralf. *Society and Democracy in Germany.* Garden City, N.Y.: Anchor, 1992.

Dalton, Roque. *Miguel Marmol.* New York: Curbstone, 1995.

Davies, Katherine, and Toby Garfitt, eds. *God's Mirror: Renewal and Engagement in*

French Catholic Intellectual Culture in the Mid-Twentieth Century. New York: Fordham University Press, 2014.

Day, Dorothy. *The Long Loneliness.* New York: Harper and Brothers, 1952.

de Ávila, F. Bastos. "Igreja e propriedade: Fundamentação doutrinal." In *A Igreja e a propriedade da terra no Brasil: Comentarios ao document da CNBB: Igreja e problemas da terra, Itaici, 1980,* edited by Matias Lenz, 57–88. São Paulo: Edições Loyola, 1980.

de Janvry, Alain, Elizabeth Sadoulet, and Linda Wilcox Young. "Land and Labour in Latin American Agriculture from the 1950s to the 1980s." *Journal of Peasant Studies* 16, no. 3 (1989): 396–424.

De Koninck, Charles. "Primacy of the Common Good against the Personalists." In *The Writings of Charles de Koninck,* vol. 2, edited and translated by Ralph McInerny, 63–108. Notre Dame, Ind.: University of Notre Dame Press, 2009.

"De la guerra a la paz." *Estudios Centroamericanos* 31, no. 335–36 (1976).

"De la necesidad e importancia de las cooperativas." *Camino* 1, no. 3 (1961).

de Lara, Pablo Lopez. *Ejercicios espirituales: En, desde, y para América Latina.* Torreón, Mexico, D.F.: Casa Iñigo, 1980.

de Lubac, Henri. *Catholicism: Christ and the Common Destiny of Man.* San Francisco: Ignatius, 1988.

Delgado, Jesús. *Óscar A. Romero.* San Salvador: UCA Editores, 1990.

———. "Romero, un joven aspirante a la santidad." *Orientación,* March 25, 2007.

———. "La cultura de Romero." In *Óscar Romero: Un obispo entre guerra fría y revolución,* edited by Roberto Morozzo della Rocca, 47–64. Madrid: Editorial San Pablo España, 2013.

Dempsey, Bernard W. *The Functional Economy: The Bases of Economic Organization.* Englewood Cliffs, N.J.: Prentice-Hall, 1958.

De Schutter, Olivier. *Access to Land and the Right to Food.* Report presented to the 65th General Assembly of the United Nations, August 11, 2010.

Diamond, Cora. "The Difficulty of Reality and the Difficulty of Philosophy." In *Philosophy and Animal Life,* 43–90. New York: Columbia University Press, 2008.

Didion, Joan. *Salvador.* New York: Vintage, 1994.

Denaux, Guillermo. "Desde Guatemala: Carta de Padre Denaux y Bernardo Survil." *Orientación,* March 27, 1977.

Diario Oficial. "Ley de extinción de comunidades." Vol. 10, no. 49 (February 26, 1881).

———. "Ley de la extinción de ejidos." Vol. 12, no. 62 (March 2, 1882).

The Didache, The Epistle of Barnabas, The Epistles and The Martyrdom of St. Polycarp, The Fragments of Papias, The Epistle to Diognetus. Translated by James Aloysius Kleist. Mahwah, N.J.: Paulist Press, 1948.

Díez, Zacarías, and Juan Macho. *"En Santiago de Maria me topé con la miseria": Dos años de la vida de Mons. Romero (1975–1976).* Costa Rica, 1994.

Dinan, Andrew. "Manual Labor in the Life and Thought of St. Basil the Great." *Logos: A Journal of Catholic Thought and Culture* 12, no. 4 (2009): 133–57.

Dorr, Donal. *Option for the Poor: A Hundred Hears of Vatican Social Teaching.* Maryknoll, N.Y.: Orbis, 1983.

Dunkerley, James. *Power in the Isthmus*. New York: Verso, 1989.

———. *Political Suicide in Latin America: And Other Essays*. London: Verso, 1992.

———. "El Salvador Since 1930." In *The Cambridge History of Latin America*, edited by Leslie Bethell, 251–82. New York: Cambridge University Press, 1990.

Durham, William. *Scarcity and Survival in Central America: Ecological Origins of the Soccer War*. Stanford, Calif.: Stanford University Press, 1979.

Ederer, Rupert J. *Pope Pius XII on the Economic Order*. Lanham, Md.: Scarecrow, 2011.

Eisenbrandt, Matt. *Assassination of a Saint: The Plot to Murder Óscar Romero and the Quest to Bring His Killers to Justice*. Oakland: University of California Press, 2017.

"El campesino merece ayuda." *Camino* 1, no. 3 (1961).

"El cooperativismo: Una realización obrera." *Orientación*, San Salvador, December 29, 1969.

Ellacuría, Ignacio. "Apuntes sobre la violencia en El Salvador." Ignacio Ellacuría Archives, Universidad Centroamericana, Box 13, Folder 30.4. San Salvador, El Salvador, n.d.

———. "A sus órdenes, mi capital." *Estudios Centroamericanos* 31, no. 337 (November 1976): 637–43.

———. *Veinte años de historia en El Salvador (1969–1989): Escritos políticos*. Vol. 1. San Salvador: UCA Editores, 1992.

———. "The Crucified People." In *Systematic Theology: Perspectives from Liberation Theology*, edited by Jon Sobrino and Ignacio Ellacuría, 257–78. Maryknoll, N.Y.: Orbis, 1993.

Ellacuría, Ignacio, and Jon Sobrino, eds. *Mysterium liberationis: Conceptos fundamentales de la Teología de la Liberación*. 2 vols. San Salvador: UCA Editores, 1993.

Ely, James W. *The Guardian of Every Other Right: A Constitutional History of Property Rights*. New York: Oxford University Press, 2007.

Erdozaín, Plácido. *Monseñor Romero, mártir de la Iglesia popular*. San José, Costa Rica: Departamento Ecuménico de Investigaciones, 1980.

Escobar Alas, José Luis. *Veo en la ciudad violencia y discordia*. San Salvador: Arzobispado de San Salvador, 2016.

———. *Ustedes también darán testimonio, porque han estado conmigo desde el principio*. San Salvador: Arzobispado de San Salvador, 2017.

Espín, Orlando. "The God of the Vanquished: Foundations for a Latino Spirituality." *Listening: Journal of Religion and Culture* 27, no. 1 (Winter 1992): 11–31.

"Éxito de los cursose de comunidades de base." *Orientación*, September 19, 1971.

Ferree, William J. *Introduction to Social Justice*. Arlington, Va.: Center for Economic and Social Justice, 1997.

Finlayson, Colonel Andrew R. "Retrospective on Counterinsurgency Operations: The Tay Ninh Provincial Reconnaissance Unit and Its Role in the Phoenix Program, 1969–70." *Center for the Study of Intelligence Publications* 51, no. 2 (2007): 59–69.

Fisher, Douglas. *The Industrial Revolution: A Macroeconomic Interpretation*. New York: Springer, 2016.

Flee to the Fields: The Faith and Works of the Catholic Land Movement—A Symposium. London: Heath Cranton, 1934.

Forché, Carolyn. *The Country Between Us.* New York: Harper and Row, 1981.

———. *What You Have Heard Is True.* New York: Penguin Press, 2019.

Francis I. *Udienza Generale.* June 5, 2013.

———. *Evangelii Gaudium.* Apostolic Exhortation. Washington, D.C.: United States Conference of Catholic Bishops, November 24, 2013.

———. *Address of His Holiness Pope Francis to the Participants in the World Meeting of Popular Movements.* October 28, 2014.

———. *Laudato Si'.* Encyclical Letter. May 24, 2015.

———. *Participation at the Second World Meeting of Popular Movements Address of the Holy Father.* July 9, 2015.

———. *Address of His Holiness Pope Francis to the Pilgrimage from El Salvador.* October 30, 2015.

———. *Address of His Holiness Pope Francis to Participants in the Third World Meeting of Popular Movements,* November, 6, 2016.

Franklin, Knut Walter. "Ideales igualitarios y autodeterminación: 1961–1972." In *El Salvador: La república,* edited by Álvaro Magaña Granados, 468–99. San Salvador: Fomento Cultural, Banco Agrícola, 2000.

Franks, Christopher A. *He Became Poor: The Poverty of Christ and Aquinas's Economic Teachings.* Grand Rapids, Mich.: William B Eerdmans, 2009.

Friede, J. "Proceso de formación de la propiedad territorial en la América inter-tropical." *Jahrbuch für Geschichte von Staat, Wirtschaft und Gesellschaft Lateinamerikas* 2 (1965): 75–87.

Freire, Paulo. *Pedagogy of the Oppressed.* Translated by Myra Bergman Ramos. New York: Bloomsbury, 2000.

Garnsey, Peter. *Thinking about Property: From Antiquity to the Age of Revolution.* New York: Cambridge University Press, 2007.

Gaus, Gerald F. "Property, Rights, and Freedom." *Social Philosophy and Policy* 11, no. 2 (1994): 209–40.

Gauthier, Paul. *Les Pauvres, Jésus et L'Église.* Chrétienté Nouvelle. Paris: Éditions Universitaires, 1963.

Gilbert, Lauren. "El Salvador's Death Squads: New Evidence from U.S. Documents." Washington, D.C.: Center for International Policy, March 7, 1994.

Gill, Lesley. *The School of the Americas: Military Training and Political Violence in the Americas.* Durham, N.C.: Duke University Press, 2004.

Gonner, E. C. K. *Common Land and Inclosure.* Abingdon on Thames: Taylor and Francis, 1912.

Gould, Jeffrey L., and Aldo Lauria-Santiago. "'They Call Us Thieves and Steal Our Wage': Toward a Reinterpretation of the Salvadoran Rural Mobilization, 1929–1931." *Hispanic American Historical Review* 84, no. 2 (May 2004): 191–237.

———. *To Rise in Darkness: Revolution, Repression, and Memory in El Salvador, 1920–1932.* Durham, N.C.: Duke University Press, 2008.

Graham, Mark E. *Sustainable Agriculture: A Christian Ethic of Gratitude.* Eugene, Ore.: Wipf and Stock, 2009.

Greenan, Thomas. "La opción por los pobres en las homilías de Monseñor Romero y de San Juan Crisóstomo: Análisis de las convergencias y de las peculiaridades en los presupuestos teológicos y en las orientaciones morales." Ph.D. diss., Universidad Pontificia Comillas, 2003.

Greer, Rowan A. *One Path for All: Gregory of Nyssa on the Christian Life and Human Destiny*. Eugene, Ore.: Cascade, 2015.

Gregory of Nyssa. *Address on Religious Instruction*. In *Christology of the Later Fathers*, edited by Edward R. Hardy, 268–326. Louisville, Ky.: Westminster John Knox Press, 1954.

———. "On Good Works." In *The Hungry Are Dying: Beggars and Bishops in Roman Cappadocia*, by Susan Holman, 193–99. New York: Oxford University Press, 2001.

Grenier, Yvon. *The Emergence of Insurgency El Salvador: Ideology and Political Will*. Pittsburgh, Pa.: University of Pittsburgh Press, 1998.

Group of Bishops. "Thirteen Commitments." *Concilium* 104 (1977): 109–11.

Guerra Calderón, Walter. *Asociaciones comunitarias en el area rural de El Salvador en la década 1960–1970: Análisis de las condiciones que enmarcan su desarrollo*. San José, Costa Rica: CSUCA, Programa Centroamericano de Ciencias Sociales, 1976.

Guerra y Guerra, Rodrigo. *Un golpe al amanecer: La verdadera historia de la Proclama del 15 de octubre 1979*. San Salvador: Índole Editores, 2009.

Guider, Margaret Eletta, OSF. "Sentir con la Iglesia: Archbishop Romero, an Ecclesial Mystic." In *Archbishop Romero: Martyr and Prophet for the New Millennium*, edited by Robert Pelton, CSC, 73–89. Scranton, Pa.: University of Scranton Press, 2006.

Guidos Véjar, Rafael. "La crisis política en El Salvador (1976–1979)." *Estudios Centroamericanos* 19 (July–August 1979): 507–26.

Gutiérrez, Gustavo. *Los pobres y la liberación en Puebla*. Bogotá: Indo-American Press, 1979.

———. *Teología de la liberación: Perspectivas*. Salamanca: Ediciones Sígueme, 1984.

———. *Las Casas: In Search of the Poor of Jesus Christ*. Maryknoll: Orbis, 1993.

———. "New Things Today: A Rereading of *Rerum Novarum*." In *The Density of the Present: Selected Writings*, translated by Margaret Wilde, 39–56. Maryknoll, N.Y.: Orbis, 1999.

———. *Beber en su propio pozo: En el itinerario espiritual de un pueblo*. Salamanca: Ediciones Sigueme, 2007.

———. "The Option for the Poor Arises from Faith in Christ." *Theological Studies* 70, no. 2 (2009): 317–26.

Habiger, Matthew. *Papal Teaching on Private Property (1891–1981)*. Lanham, Md.: University Press of America, 1990.

Hamilton, Nora, and Norma Stoltz Chinchilla. "Central American Migration: A Framework for Analysis." In *Challenging Fronteras: Structuring Latina and Latino Lives in the U.S.*, edited by Mary Romero, Pierrette Hondagneu-Sotelo, and Vilma Ortiz, 81–100. New York: Routledge, 2014.

Hammond, J. L., and Barbara Hammond. *The Village Labourer, 1760–1832: A Study of the Government of England before the Reform Bill*. London: Longman Green, 1911.

Hart, John. *The Spirit of the Earth: A Theology of the Land*. Mahwah, N.J.: Paulist Press, 1984.

Hassett, John J., and Hugh Lacey. *Towards a Society That Serves Its People: The Intellectual Contribution of El Salvador's Murdered Jesuits*. Washington, D.C.: Georgetown University Press, 1991.

Hayek, Friedrich A. *Law, Legislation and Liberty*. Vol. 2, *The Mirage of Social Justice*. Chicago: University of Chicago Press, 2012.

Hays, Richard B. *The Moral Vision of the New Testament: Community, Cross, New Creation: A Contemporary Introduction to New Testament Ethics*. San Francisco: HarperOne, 1996.

Hebblethwaite, Peter. "Liberation Theology and the Roman Catholic Church." In *The Cambridge Companion to Liberation Theology*, edited by Christopher Rowland, 179–98. New York: Cambridge University Press, 2007.

Hennelly, Alfred T., ed. *Liberation Theology: A Documentary History*. Maryknoll: Orbis, 1990.

Hittinger, Russell. "Social Roles and Ruling Virtues in Catholic Social Doctrine." *Annales Theologici* 16 (2002): 385–408.

———. "Leo XIII (1810–1903)." In *The Teachings of Modern Roman Catholicism on Law, Politics, and Human Nature*, edited by John Witte Jr. and Frank S. Alexander, 39–75. New York: Columbia University Press, 2007.

———. "The Coherence of the Four Basic Principles of Catholic Social Doctrine: An Interpretation." In *Pursuing the Common Good: How Solidarity and Subsidiarity Can Work Together*, Proceedings of the 14th Plenary Session, 2–6 May 2008, edited by Margaret S. Archer and Pierpaolo Donati, 75–123. Vatican City: Pontifical Academy of Social Sciences, 2008.

———. "Toward an Adequate Anthropology: Social Aspects of *Imago Dei* in Catholic Theology." In *Imago Dei: Human Dignity in Ecumenical Perspective*, edited by Thomas Albert Howard, 39–78. Washington, D.C.: The Catholic University of America Press, 2013.

Hobsbawm, Eric. *The Age of Extremes: A History of the World, 1914–1991*. New York: Vintage, 1994.

Holman, Susan R. *The Hungry Are Dying: Beggars and Bishops in Roman Cappadocia*. Oxford Studies in Historical Theology. New York: Oxford University Press, 2001.

Hopcroft, Rosemary Lynn. *Regions, Institutions, and Agrarian Change in European History*. Ann Arbor: University of Michigan Press, 1999.

Hütter, Reinhard. "Testifying to the Truth *usque ad sanguinem-pro veritate mori*: The Contemporary Relevance of Thomas Aquinas's Integral Doctrine of Martyrdom." *Thomist* 78, no. 4 (2014): 483–517.

Hyde, Lewis. *Common as Air: Revolution, Art, and Ownership*. New York: Farrar, Strauss and Giroux, 2012.

Ignatieff, Michael. *The Needs of Strangers*. New York: Penguin, 1986.

Ignatius of Antioch. "The Epistle to the Romans." In *Early Christian Writings*, edited by Andrew Louth, translated by Maxwell Staniforth, 83–89. New York: Penguin, 1987.

Ignatius of Loyola. *The Spiritual Exercises of St. Ignatius.* Chicago: Loyola Press, 2010.

"Inaugurase solemnemente Intituto de Capacitación Social Leon XIII." *Camino* 1, no. 3 (1961).

Jenkins, Willis. *Ecologies of Grace: Environmental Ethics and Christian Theology.* New York: Oxford University Press, 2008.

Jennings, Willie James. *The Christian Imagination: Theology and the Origins of Race.* New Haven Conn.: Yale University Press, 2011.

John Chrysostom. *Homilies on Matthew.* Edited by Philip Schaff. Nicene and Post-Nicene Fathers 10. Buffalo, N.Y.: Christian Literature, 1888.

John Paul II. *Address at the Opening of the Third General Conference of the Latin American Bishops*, Puebla, Mexico, January 28, 1979.

———. *Address in Cuilapan, Mexico*, January 29, 1979.

———. *Puebla: A Pilgrimage of Faith.* Boston: St. Paul Editions, 1979.

———. *Redemptor Hominis.* Encyclical Letter. March 4, 1979.

———. *Laborem Exercens.* Encyclical Letter. September 14, 1981.

———. *Sollicitudo Rei Socialis.* Encyclical Letter. December 30, 1987.

———. *Centesimus Annus.* Encyclical Letter. May 1, 1991.

———. *Veritatis Splendor.* Encyclical Letter. August 6, 1993.

John XXIII. *Mater et Magistra.* Encyclical Letter. May 15, 1961.

———. "Radio-Television Message." In *Acta Apostolicae Sedis*, vol. 54, September 11, 1962.

———. *Pacem in Terris.* Encyclical Letter. April 11, 1963.

———. "Pope's Address to the World a Month before the Council Opened." In *Council Daybook*, edited by Floyd Anderson, 18–21. Washington, D.C.: National Catholic Welfare Conference, 1965.

Julian of Norwich. *Showings.* Translated by Edmund Colledge, OSA, and James Walsh, SJ. Mahwah, N.J.: Paulist Press, 1978.

Kelly, Thomas M. *When the Gospel Grows Feet: Rutilio Grande, SJ, and the Church of El Salvador.* Collegeville, Minn.: Michael Glazier, 2013.

Kemp, Tom. *Industrialization in Nineteenth-Century Europe.* New York: Routledge, 1997.

Keogh, Dermot. "The Myth of the Liberal Coup: The United States and the 15 October 1979 Coup in El Salvador." *Millennium: Journal of International Studies* 13 (1983): 153–83.

LaFeber, Walter. *Inevitable Revolutions: The United States in Central America.* New York: W. W. Norton, 1984.

La Iglesia en El Salvador. San Salvador: UCA Editores, 1982.

Lamperti, John W. *Enrique Alvarez Córdova.* Jefferson, N.C: McFarland, 2006.

Langholm, Odd. *Economics in the Medieval Schools: Wealth, Exchange, Value, Money and Usury according to the Paris Theological Tradition 1200–1350.* New York: Brill Academic, 1992.

———. *The Legacy of Scholasticism in Economic Thought: Antecedents of Choice and Power.* New York: Cambridge University Press, 2006.

Langland, William. *Piers Plowman: A New Annotated Edition of the C-Text.* Edited by Derek Pearsall. Exeter: University of Exeter Press, 2008.

Lantigua, David. "The Image of God, Christian Rights Talk, and the School of Salamanca." *Journal of Law and Religion* 31, no. 1 (2016): 19–41.

Larín, Arístedes Augusto. "Historia del movimiento sindical de El Salvador." *Universidad* 96, no. 4 (1971): 135–79.

Las Casas, Bartolomé de. *Historia de Las Indias.* Vol. 3. Edited by A. Millares and L. Hanke. México, D.F.: Fondo de Cultura Económica, 1951.

———. *Obras Escogidas: Opúsculos, cartas y memoriales.* Edited by Juan Pérez de Tudela y Bueso. Madrid: BAE, 1958.

———. *Octavo Remedio.* In *Tratados de 1552: Impresos por Las Casas en Sevilla.* Obras Completas, vol. 10. Madrid: Alianza, 1988.

———. *An Account, Much Abbreviated, of the Destruction of the Indies with Related Texts.* Translated by Andrew Hurley. Indianapolis: Hackett, 2003.

Laurentin, René. *Liberation, Development, and Salvation.* Maryknoll, N.Y.: Orbis, 1972.

Lauria-Santiago, Aldo. *An Agrarian Republic: Commercial Agriculture and the Politics of Peasant Communities in El Salvador, 1823–1914.* Pittsburgh: University of Pittsburgh Press, 1999.

———. "The Culture and Politics of State Terror and Repression in El Salvador." In *When States Kill: Latin America, the U.S. and Technologies of Terror,* edited by Cecelia Menjívar and Néstor Rodriguez, 85–114. Austin: University of Texas Press, 2005.

Lee, Michael. *Revolutionary Saint: The Theological Legacy of Óscar Romero.* Maryknoll, N.Y.: Orbis, 2018.

Leo the Great. *Sermons.* Translated by Jane Patricia Freeland, CSJB, and Agnes Josephine Conway, SSJ. Washington, D.C.: The Catholic University of America Press, 1996.

Leo XIII. *Sapientiae Christianae.* Encyclical Letter. January 10, 1890.

———. *Rerum Novarum.* Encyclical Letter. May 15, 1891.

———. *Au Milieu.* Encyclical Letter. February 16, 1892.

LeoGrande, William M. *Our Own Backyard: The United States in Central America, 1977–1992.* Chapel Hill, N.C.: University of North Carolina Press, 2009.

Lindo-Fuentes, Hector. *Weak Foundations: The Economy of El Salvador in the Nineteenth Century 1821–1898.* Berkeley: University of California Press, 1991.

Lindo-Fuentes, Héctor, and Erik Ching. *Modernizing Minds in El Salvador: Education Reform and the Cold War, 1960–1980.* Albuquerque: University of New Mexico Press, 2012.

Lockhart, James, and Stuart B. Schwartz. *Early Latin America: A History of Colonial Spanish America and Brazil.* New York: Cambridge University Press, 1983.

Lombard, Peter. *The Sentences: On the Doctrine of Signs.* Toronto: Pontifical Institute of Mediaeval Studies, 2010.

Long, A. A. "Stoic Philosophers on Persons, Property-Ownership, and Community." In *Aristotle and After.* Edited by Richard Sorabji, 13–32. London: Bulletin of the Institute of Classical Studies, 1997.

Lungo, Mario. *La lucha de las masas en El Salvador.* San Salvador: UCA Editores, 1987.

MacIntyre, Alasdair. *After Virtue: A Study in Moral Theory.* Notre Dame, Ind.: University of Notre Dame Press, 2007.

Maier, Martin. *Monseñor Romero: Maestro de espiritualidad.* San Salvador: UCA Editores, 2005.

Mäkinen, Virpi. "Rights and Duties in Late Scholastic Discussion on Extreme Necessity." In *Transformations in Medieval and Early-Modern Rights Discourse,* edited by Virpi Mäkinen and Heikki Pihlajamäki, 37–62. New Synthese Historical Library 56. Dordrecht: Springer, 2006.

"Manifiesto de FECCAS/UTC a los cristianos de El Salvador y Centro América." *Estudios Centroamericanos* 359 (September 1978).

Maritain, Jacques. *Man and the State.* Chicago: University of Chicago Press, 1951.

Márquez Ochoa, Armando. *No basta la justicia, es necesario el amor: Compendio de la catequesis social de Mons. Romero.* San Salvador: Comunidades eclesiales de base de El Salvador, 2007.

Martyrdom of Polycarp. In *Early Christian Writings: The Apostolic Fathers,* edited by Andrew Louth, translated by Maxwell Staniforth. New York: Penguin, 1987.

Marx, Karl. *Capital.* Vol. 1. New York: Penguin, 1976.

Marx, Karl, and Friedrich Engels. *The Communist Manifesto.* New York: Penguin, 2004.

Matz, Brian. "The Principle of Detachment from Private Property in Basil of Caesarea's Homily 6 and Its Context." In *Reading Patristic Texts on Social Ethics: Issues and Challenges for the Twenty-First Century,* edited by Johan Leemans, Brian J. Matz, and Johan Verstraeten, 161–84. Washington, D.C.: The Catholic University of America Press, 2011.

Maurin, Peter. "Blowing the Dynamite." In *Easy Essays,* by Peter Maurin, 3. Eugene, Ore.: Wipf and Stock, 2010.

May, Roy H. *The Poor of the Land: A Christian Case for Land Reform.* Maryknoll, N.Y.: Orbis, 1991.

Mazoyer, Marcel, and Laurence Roudart. *A History of World Agriculture: From the Neolithic Age to the Current Crisis.* New York: Monthly Review, 2006.

McCabe, Herbert. *Love, Law, and Language.* New York: Continuum, 2003.

McLean, George F., and John Kromkowski. *Cultural Heritage and Contemporary Change.* Vol. 5, *Urbanization and Values.* Washington, D.C.: Council for Research in Values and Philosophy, 1991.

McManus, Philip, and Gerald Schlabach, eds. *Relentless Persistence: Nonviolent Action in Latin America.* Philadelphia: New Society, 1991.

Mejía, Carlos F. *La doctrina social en la Iglesia universal y en la Iglesia particular de San Salvador.* San Salvador: Imprenta Criterio, 2006.

Menjívar, Rafael. *Acumulación originaria y desarrollo capitalista en El Salvador.* San Salvador: Editorial Universitaria Centroamérica, 1980.

Moggach, Douglas, and Paul Leduc Browne. *The Social Question and the Democratic Revolution: Marx and the Legacy of 1848.* Ottawa: University of Ottawa Press, 2000.

Montes, Segundo. *El agro salvadoreño: 1973–1980.* San Salvador: UCA Editores, 1986.

Montesinos, Antonio. "Advent Sermon." In *A History of Christianity in Asia, Africa, and Latin America, 1450–1990: A Documentary Sourcebook,* edited by Klaus Koschorke, Frieder Ludwig, and Mariano Delgado, 286–87. Grand Rapids, Mich.: William B. Eerdmans, 2007.

Montgomery, Tommie Sue. *Revolution in El Salvador: From Civil Strife to Civil Peace.* Boulder, Colo.: Westview, 1995.

Morozzo della Rocca, Roberto. *Primero Dios: Vida de Monseñor Romero.* Buenos Aires: Edhasa, 2010.

———. "La controvertida identidad de un obispo." In *Óscar Romero: Un obispo entre guerra fría y revolución,* edited by Roberto Morozzo della Rocca, 13–46. Madrid: Editorial San Pablo España, 2013.

———. *Msr. Oscar Romero.* Translated by Chrystèle Francillon. Paris: Éditions Desclée de Brouwer, 2015.

Moss, Candida R. *The Other Christs: Imitating Jesus in Ancient Christian Ideologies of Martyrdom.* New York: Oxford University Press, 2010.

Mrowczynski-Van Allen, Artur. *Between the Icon and the Idol: The Human Person and the Modern State in Russian Literature and Thought—Chaadayev, Soloviev, Grossman.* Translated by Matthew Philipp Whelan. Theopolitical Visions. Eugene, Ore.: Cascade, 2013.

Naughton, Michael. *The Good Stewards: Practical Applications of the Papal Social Vision of Work.* Lanham, Md.: University Press of America, 1992.

Neeson, J. M. *Commoners: Common Right, Enclosure and Social Change in England, 1700–1820.* New York: Cambridge University Press, 1996.

O'Boyle, Edward J. "Blessed John Paul II on Social Mortgage: Origins, Questions, and Norms." *Logos: A Journal of Catholic Thought and Culture* 17, no. 2 (2014): 118–35.

Ochoa, Armando Márquez. *No basta la justicia, es necesario el amor: Compendio de la catequesis social de Mons. Romero.* San Salvador: Comunidades Eclesiales de Base de El Salvador, 2007.

Ochoa, Rafael Menjívar. *Tiempos de locura, El Salvador 1979–1981.* San Salvador: FLASCO-Programa, 2006.

"Organizase curso de capacitación para obreros." *Camino* 1, no. 1 (1961).

Origen. *Exhortation to Martyrdom.* In *Origen,* translated by Rowan A. Greer, 41–79. Mahwah, N.J.: Paulist Press, 1979.

———. *Homilies on Luke.* Edited and translated by J. T. Lienhard, SJ. Fathers of the Church 94. Washington, D.C.: The Catholic University of America Press, 1996.

Ostrom, Elinor. *Governing the Commons: The Evolution of Institutions for Collective Action.* New York: Cambridge University Press, 1990.

Ots Capdequí, José M. *El régimen de la tierra en la América Española durante el período colonial.* Ciudad Trujillo: Universidad de Santo Domingo-Editora Montalvo, 1946.

Overton, Mark. *Agricultural Revolution in England: The Transformation of the Agrarian Economy, 1500–1850.* New York: Cambridge University Press, 1996.

Paglia, Vincenzo. "Sentir con la Iglesia." In *Óscar Romero: Un obispo entre guerra fría y revolución*, edited by Roberto Morozzo della Rocca, 119–29. Madrid: Editorial San Pablo España, 2013.

Paige, Jeffery M. *Coffee and Power: Revolution and the Rise of Democracy in Central America*. Cambridge, Mass.: Harvard University Press, 1998.

Paul VI. *Populorum Progressio*. Encyclical Letter. March 26, 1967.

———. *Santa misa para los campesinos Colombianos*. Homilía del Santo Padre Paulo VI. August 23, 1968.

———. *Octogesima Adveniens*. Encyclical Letter. May 14, 1971.

———. *Evangelii Nuntiandi*. Apostolic Exhortation. December 8, 1975.

Paulhus, Normand J. "Social Catholicism and the Fribourg Union." *Selected Papers from the Annual Meeting of the Society of Christian Ethics* (1980): 63–88.

———. *The Theological and Political Ideals of the Fribourg Union*. University Microfilms, 1986.

Pearce, Jenny. *Promised Land: Peasant Rebellion in Chalatenango, El Salvador*. London: Latin America Bureau, 1986.

Pelton, Robert S., CSC, ed. *Monsignor Romero: A Bishop for the Third Millennium*. Notre Dame, Ind.: University of Notre Dame Press, 2004.

———. *Archbishop Romero: Martyr and Prophet for the New Millennium*. Scranton, Pa.: University of Scranton Press, 2006.

———. *Archbishop Romero and Spiritual Leadership in the Modern World*. Lanham, Md.: Lexington, 2015.

Peñalver, Eduardo M., and Sonia Katyal. *Property Outlaws: How Squatters, Pirates, and Protesters Improve the Law of Ownership*. New Haven, Conn.: Yale University Press, 2010.

"Permanentes violaciones a la libertad syndical en América Latina." *Camino* 1, no. 8 (1961).

Persecución de la Iglesia en El Salvador. San Salvador: Publicaciones del Secretariado Social Interdiocesano, 1977.

Pesch, Heinrich. *Heinrich Pesch on Solidarist Economics: Excerpts from the Lehrbuch der Nationalökonomie*. Translated by Rupert J. Ederer. New York: University Press of America, 1998.

Peterson, Anna L. *Martyrdom and the Politics of Religion: Progressive Catholicism in El Salvador's Civil War*. Albany: State University of New York Press, 1997.

Peterson, Erik. *Theological Tractates*. Edited by Michael J. Hollerich. Stanford, Calif.: Stanford University Press, 2011.

Pfeil, Margaret R. "Óscar Romero's Theology of Transfiguration." *Theological Studies* 72 (2011): 87–115.

Pinckaers, Servais. *The Spirituality of Martyrdom . . . to the Limits of Love*. Translated by Patrick Clark and Annie Hounsokou. Washington, D.C.: The Catholic University of America Press, 2016.

Pironio. Eduardo. *Escritos Pastorales*. Madrid: BAC, 1973.

Pius X. *Il Fermo Proposito*. Encyclical Letter. June 11, 1905.

Pius XI. *Quadragesimo Anno*. Encyclical Letter. May 15, 1931.

———. *Non Abbiamo Bisogno*. Encyclical Letter. June 29, 1931.

———. *Mit Brennender Sorge*. Encyclical Letter. March 14, 1937.

————. *Divini Redemptoris*. Encyclical Letter. March 19, 1937.

Pius XII. *Sertum Laetitiae*. Encyclical Letter. November 1, 1939.

————. *Summi Pontificatus*. Encyclical Letter. October 20, 1939.

————. *Discourse of His Holiness Pius XII to Commemorate the 50th Anniversary of the Encyclical "Rerum Novarum" of Pope Leo XIII on the Social Question."* In *Acta Apostolicae Sedis*, vol. 33, June 1, 1941.

————. *Radiomessaggio di Sua Santità Pio XII alla vigilia del Santo Natale*. December 24, 1942.

————. *Radiomensaje en el V aniversario del comienzo de la guerra*. September 1, 1944.

————. *Radiomessaggio di Sua Santità Pio XII nel V anniversario dall'inizio della guerra mondiale*. September 1, 1944.

————. *Radiomensaje del Santo Padre Pío XII a los trabajadores de España*. In *Acta Apostolicae Sedis*, vol. 43, March 11, 1951.

————. *Adscriptis Sodalitati Catholicae Ex Operariis Italicis: Ob Commendationem Litterarum Encyclicarum "Rerum Novarum" Coadunatis*. In *Acta Apostolicae Sedis*, vol. 45, May 14, 1953.

————. "The Basis and Importance of a Healthy Agricultural Class." *Speech delivered by His Holiness to the Delegates at the Convention of the Address to the National Farmers' League of Italy in Rome*. November 15, 1946. In R. J. Ederer, *Pope Pius XII on the Economic Order*. Lanham, Md.: Scarecrow, 2011.

————. "The Church and Labor." *Address to Workers in Rome*. June 13, 1943. In R. J. Ederer, *Pope Pius XII on the Economic Order*. Lanham, Md.: Scarecrow, 2011.

————. "'Economic and Cultural Self-Help on the Part of the Rural Community': A Letter to the Organization of Irish Agricultural People," July 14, 1954. In R. J. Ederer, *Pope Pius XII on the Economic Order*. Lanham, Md.: Scarecrow, 2011.

————. "The Farmer's Status as a Pressing Problem of Social Order." *Letter to the Leaders of the Social Week of Canada*. August 31, 1947. In R. J. Ederer, *Pope Pius XII on the Economic Order*. Lanham, Md.: Scarecrow, 2011.

————. "A Farmer's Three Duties." *Address to the Confederations of Italian Tenant Farmers*. April 11, 1956. In R. J. Ederer, *Pope Pius XII on the Economic Order*. Lanham, Md.: Scarecrow, 2011.

————. "Farming: Model of Human Effort." *Discourse to the Italian Catholic Federation of Farmers*. May 18, 1955. In R. J. Ederer, *Pope Pius XII on the Economic Order*. Lanham, Md.: Scarecrow, 2011.

————. "Human Claims on Economic Expansion." *Letter to the President of French Social Week*. July 10, 1956. In R. J. Ederer, *Pope Pius XII on the Economic Order*. Lanham, Md.: Scarecrow, 2011.

————. "The Problem of Fair Distribution." *A Letter Addressed to Semaine Sociale of Dijon, France*. July 7, 1952. In R. J. Ederer, *Pope Pius XII on the Economic Order*. Lanham, Md.: Scarecrow, 2011.

————. "The Problems of Rural Life." *An Address to the Social Week of Italy*. September 18, 1957. In R. J. Ederer, *Pope Pius XII on the Economic Order*. Lanham, Md.: Scarecrow, 2011.

————. "Problems in the World of Agriculture." *Address Before the First International Congress for the Problems of Agriculture*. July 2, 1951. In R. J. Ederer, *Pope Pius XII on the Economic Order*. Lanham, Md.: Scarecrow, 2011.

———. "Production for Human Needs." *Address for the Catholic International Congress of Social Study*. June 3, 1950. In R. J. Ederer, *Pope Pius XII on the Economic Order*. Lanham, Md.: Scarecrow, 2011.

———. "The Question of Agricultural Reform." *Papal Letter Transmitted by J. B. Montini to the 22nd Social Week at Naples*. September 15, 1947. In R. J. Ederer, *Pope Pius XII on the Economic Order*. Lanham, Md.: Scarecrow, 2011.

———. "The Value of Agricultural Science for the World Economy." *Address to the Ninth International Congress of Agricultural Industries*. May 29, 1952. In R. J. Ederer, *Pope Pius XII on the Economic Order*. Lanham, Md.: Scarecrow, 2011.

———. "The Vocational Tasks and the Cultural Mission of the Farmer." *Address to the Italian Farmers' Association*. April 16, 1958. In R. J. Ederer, *Pope Pius XII on the Economic Order*. Lanham, Md.: Scarecrow, 2011.

Polanyi, Karl. *The Great Transformation: The Political and Economic Origins of Our Time*. Boston: Beacon, 2001.

Pontifical Council for Justice and Peace. *Toward a Better Distribution of Land: The Challenge of Agrarian Reform*. Rome: Libreria Editrice Vaticana, 1997.

"¿Por que se teme a los sindicatos?" *Camino* 1, no. 11 (1961).

Posada, Marcelo Germán, and Mario López. "El Salvador 1950–1970: Latifundios, integración y crisis." *Revista de Historia de América* 115 (1993): 37–62.

Prosterman, Roy. "Land Reform in South Vietnam: A Proposal for Turning the Tables on the Viet Cong." *Cornell Law Review* 53, no. 1 (1967): 26–44.

Prosterman, Roy, and Jeffery M. Riedinger. *Land Reform and Democratic Development*. Baltimore: Johns Hopkins University Press, 1987.

Purdy, Jedediah. *The Meaning of Property: Freedom, Community, and the Legal Imagination*. New Haven, Conn.: Yale University Press, 2011.

Rahner, Karl. "Dimensions of Martyrdom: A Plea for Broadening a Classical Concept." *Concilium* 163 (1983): 9–11.

Report of the Latin American Bureau. *Violence and Fraud in El Salvador*. London: Latin American Bureau, 1977.

Rivera Navarrete, Claudia Marlene. "La denuncia profética de la riqueza: Resonancia de la patrística en la teología Latinoamericana de la liberación." Master's thesis, Universidad Centroamericana, 2015.

Robbins, Lionel. *The Theory of Economic Policy in English Classical Political Economy*. London: Macmillan, 1961.

Rodríguez, Rubén Rosario. *Christian Martyrdom and Political Violence: A Comparative Theology*. New York: Cambridge University Press, 2017.

Romero, Óscar A. "La *Rerum Novarum* perene y urgente." *El Chaparrastique*, May 26, 1961.

———. "Los campesinos no son parias." *Orientación*, July 4, 1971.

———. "Soluciones humanas." *Orientación*, October 24, 1971.

———. "¿Cuál patria?" *El Chaparrastique*, September 8, 1972.

———. "Educación liberadora." *Diario de Oriente*, May 30, 1973.

———. "Reformas estructurales y salvación." *Orientación*, October 28, 1973.

———. "Parcelaciones rurales, un gran enemigo de reforma agraria." *Orientación*, March 31, 1974.

———. "Hacia una mejor política agraria." *Diario de Oriente*. October 11, 1974.

———. "La dimensión política de la fe desde la opción por los pobres." In *La voz de los sin voz: La palabra viva de Monseñor Romero*, edited by Rodolfo Cardenal, Ignacio Martín-Baró, and Jon Sobrino. San Salvador: UCA Editores, 1980.

———. *Iglesia y organizaciones políticas populares: Tercera carta pastoral*. In *La voz de los sin voz: La palabra viva de Monseñor Romero*, edited by Rodolfo Cardenal, Ignacio Martín-Baró, and Jon Sobrino. San Salvador: UCA Editores, 1980.

———. *La Iglesia, cuerpo de Cristo en la historia: Segunda carta pastoral*. In *La voz de los sin voz: La palabra viva de Monseñor Romero*, edited by Rodolfo Cardenal, Ignacio Martín-Baró, and Jon Sobrino. San Salvador: UCA Editores, 1980.

———. *Misión de la Iglesia en medio de la crisis del país: Cuarta carta pastoral*. In *La voz de los sin voz: La palabra viva de Monseñor Romero*, edited by Rodolfo Cardenal, Ignacio Martín-Baró, and Jon Sobrino. San Salvador: UCA Editores, 1980.

———. *Su Diario*. San Salvador: Imprenta Criterio, 2000.

———. *Sus cartas personales, pensamientos, y consejos*. San Salvador: Imprenta Criterio, 2004.

———. *Homilías Monseñor Óscar A. Romero*. 6 vols. Edited by Miguel Cavada Diez. San Salvador: UCA Editores, 2005–9.

Rosset, Peter, Raj Patel, and Michael Courville, eds. *Promised Land: Competing Visions of Agrarian Reform*. Oakland, Calif.: Food First, 2006.

Rourke, Thomas R. *The Roots of Pope Francis's Social and Political Thought: From Argentina to the Vatican*. New York: Rowman and Littlefield, 2016.

Rowley, Trevor. *The Origins of Open-Field Agriculture*. London: Croom Helm, 1981.

Ruíz Granadino, Santiago. "Modernización agrícola en El Salvador." *Estudios Sociales Centroamericanos* 22 (1979): 71–95.

Ryan, John Augustine, and Raymond Augustine McGowan. *A Catechism of the Social Question*. Mahwah, N.J.: Paulist Press, 1921.

Samers, Michael. *Migration*. New York: Routledge, 2010.

Samos Stibbs, Rosa Carmelita. *Estudio teológico de las cartas pastorales de Mons: Luis Chávez y González*. Universidad Francisco Marroquín, Facultad de Humanidades, Departamento de Teología, 1986.

Sánchez, Peter M. *Priest under Fire: Padre David Rodríguez, the Catholic Church, and El Salvador's Revolutionary Movement*. Gainesville: University Press of Florida, 2015.

Satterthwaite, Ridgeway. "*Campesino* Agriculture and *Hacienda* Modernization in Coastal El Salvador, 1949–1969." Ph.D. diss., University of Wisconsin, 1971.

Scannone, Juan Carlos. "La teología de la liberación: Caracterización, corrientes, etapas." *Stromata* 38 (1982): 3–40.

Schmemann, Alexander. *Great Lent*. New York: St. Vladimir's Seminary Press, 1974.

Schubeck, Thomas. "Salvadoran Martyrs: A Love That Does Justice." *Horizons* 28 (2001): 7–21.

Scott, James C. *Seeing Like a State: Why Certain Schemes to Improve the Human Condition Have Failed*. New Haven, Conn.: Yale University Press, 1988.

Scott, Tom. *The Peasantries of Europe: From the Fourteenth to the Eighteenth Centuries*. London: Longman, 1998.

Scribner, Todd. *A Partisan Church: American Catholicism and the Rise of Neoconservative Catholics*. Washington, D.C.: The Catholic University of America Press, 2015.

Secretaria de Comunicación Social del Arzobispado. "Boletín Informativo Internacional No. 55." San Salvador, January 1979.

———. "Boletín Informativo Internacional No. 56." San Salvador, January 1979.

Sewell, William H., Jr. *Work and Revolution in France: The Language of Labor from the Old Regime to 1848*. New York: Cambridge University Press, 1980.

Shadle, Matthew A. "Cavanaugh on the Church and the Modern State: An Appraisal." *Horizons* 37, no. 2 (2010): 246–270.

Shannon, Thomas A. "Commentary on *Rerum Novarum: The Condition of Modern Labor*." In *Catholic Social Teaching: Commentaries and Interpretations*, edited by Kenneth R. Himes, 127–50. Washington, D.C.: Georgetown University Press, 2005.

Silko, Leslie Marmon. *Almanac of the Dead*. New York: Simon and Schuster, 1991.

Smith, Adam. *The Wealth of Nations*. New York: Bantam Classics, 2003.

Smith, Christian. *The Emergence of Liberation Theology: Radical Religion and Social Movement Theory*. Chicago: University of Chicago Press, 1991.

———. *Christ the Liberator: A View from the Victims*. Maryknoll, N.Y.: Orbis, 2001.

Sobrino, Jon. *Romero: Martyr for Liberation*. London: Catholic Institute for International Relations, 1986.

———. "The Crucified Peoples: Yahweh's Suffering Servant Today." In *1492–1992: The Voice of the Victims*, edited by Leonardo Boff and Virgil Elizondo. *Concilium* 5 (1990): 120–29.

———. *Monseñor Romero*. San Salvador: UCA Editores, 1993.

———. *Jesus the Liberator: A Historical Theological Reading of Jesus of Nazareth*. Maryknoll, N.Y.: Orbis, 1994.

"Los mártires Jesuánicos en el tercer mundo." *Revista Latinoamericana de Teología* 48 (1999): 241–46.

———. "Our World: Cruelty and Compassion." In *Rethinking Martyrdom*, edited by Teresa Okure, Jon Sobrino, and Felix Wilfred. *Concilium* 1 (2003): 15–23.

———. *Witnesses to the Kingdom: The Martyrs of El Salvador and the Crucified Peoples*. Maryknoll: Orbis, 2003.

———. *Principle of Mercy: Taking the Crucified People from the Cross*. Maryknoll, N.Y.: Orbis, 2015.

Sobrino, Jon, and Rolando Alvarado, eds. *Ignacio Ellacuría, aquella libertad esclarecida*. Santander: Editorial Sal Terrae, 1999.

Socorro Jurídico Cristiano. *El Salvador: Del genocidio de la junta militar a la esperanza de la lucha insurreccional*. San Salvador: Socorro Jurídico, 1981.

———. *El Salvador: La situación de los derechos humanos, octubre 1979–julio 1981*. Mexico City: Socorro Jurídico Cristiano, 1981.

———. "Informe No. 11, Año IX." San Salvador: Arzobispado de San Salvador, 1984.

Spieker, Manfred. "The Universal Destination of Goods: The Ethics of Property in the Theory of a Christian Society." *Journal of Markets and Morality* 8, no. 2 (2005): 333–54.

Stanley, William. *The Protection Racket State: Elite Politics, Military Extortion, and Civil War in El Salvador.* Philadelphia: Temple University Press, 1996.

Stolzenberg, Nomi. "Facts on the Ground." In *Property and Community,* edited by Gregory S. Alexander and Eduardo Peñalver, 107–39. New York: Oxford University Press, 2010.

Tanner, Norman P., ed. *Decrees of the Ecumenical Councils: Nicaea I to Lateran V.* Vol. 1. Washington, D.C.: Sheed and Ward, 1990.

Tertullian. *Apology.* In *Ante-Nicene Fathers,* vol. 3. Translated by Sydney Thelwall. Buffalo, N.Y.: Christian Literature, 1885.

Thompson, E. P. *The Making of the English Working Class.* New York: Vintage, 1963.

Thompson, Paul B. *The Spirit of Soil: Agriculture and Environmental Ethics.* New York: Routledge, 1994.

Tierney, Brian. *The Idea of Natural Rights: Studies on Natural Rights, Natural Law, and Church Law.* Atlanta: Scholars Press, 1997.

Todd, Molly. *Beyond Displacement: Campesinos, Refugees, and Collective Action in the Salvadoran Civil War.* Madison: University of Wisconsin Press, 2010.

Tornielli, Andrea, and Giacomo Galeazzi. *This Economy Kills: Pope Francis on Capitalism and Social Justice.* Collegeville, Minn.: Liturgical Press, 2015.

Torres, Abelardo. *Tierras y colonización.* San Salvador: Instituto de Estudios Económicos, 1961.

"Un programa promisor para América Latina." *Camino* 1, no. 10 (1961).

Urioste, Ricardo. *Monseñor Romero mártir por el magisterio eclesiástico.* San Salvador: Fundación Monseñor Romero, 2012.

Useros, Manuel, and María López Vigil. *La vida por el pueblo: Cristianos de comunidades populares en América Latina.* Madrid: Editorial Popular, 1981.

Vatican Council II. *Sacrosanctum Concilium.* December 4, 1963.

———. *Lumen Gentium.* November 21, 1964.

———. *Unitatis Redintegratio.* November 21, 1964.

———. *Christus Dominus.* October 28, 1965.

———. *Optatam Totius.* October 28, 1965.

———. *Perfectae Caritatis.* October 28, 1965.

———. *Apostolicam Actuositatem.* November 18, 1965.

———. *Ad Gentes.* December 7, 1965.

———. *Gaudium et Spes.* December 7, 1965.

———. *Presbyterorum Ordinis.* December 7, 1965.

Vega, Juan Ramón. *Las comunidades de base en América Central: Estudio sociológico.* San Salvador: Publicaciones del Arzobispado, 1994.

von Balthasar, Hans Urs. *The Moment of Christian Witness.* San Francisco: Ignatius Press, 1994.

von Ketteler, Wilhelm Emmanuel. *The Social Teachings of Wilhelm Emmanuel von Ketteler.* Translated by Rupert J. Ederer. Washington, D.C.: University Press of America, 1981.

von Mises, Ludwig. *Economic Policy: Thoughts for Today and Tomorrow.* Auburn, Ala.: Ludwig von Mises Institute, 2006.

Walatka, Todd. *Von Balthasar and the Option for the Poor: Theodramatics in the Light of Liberation Theology*. Washington, D.C.: The Catholic University of America Press, 2017.

Webre, Stephen. *Jose Napoleon Duarte and the Christian Democratic Party in Salvadoran Politics 1960–1972*. Baton Rouge: Louisiana State University Press, 1979.

Weeks, David. "European Antecedents of Land Tenure and Agrarian Organization of Hispanic America." *Journal of Land and Public Utility Economics* 23, no. 1 (February 1947): 60–65.

Wheaton, Philip. *Agrarian Reform in El Salvador: A Program of Rural Pacification*. Washington, D.C.: EPICA Task Force, 1980.

Whelan, Matthew Philipp. "Land, Economy, and the Measure of Christ: The Catholic Agrarianism of Vincent McNabb, O.P." *Nova et Vetera* 10, no. 1 (2012): 253–77.

———. "The Grammar of Creation: Agriculture in the Thought of Pope Benedict XVI." In *Environmental Justice and Climate Change,* edited by Jame Schaeffer and Tobias Winright, 103–23. New York: Lexington, 2013.

———. "Jesus Is the Jubilee: A Theological Reflection on the Pontifical Council for Justice and Peace's *Toward a Better Distribution of Land.*" *Journal of Moral Theology* 6, no. 2 (2017): 204–29.

———. "You Possess the Land That Belongs to ALL Salvadorans: Archbishop Óscar Romero and Ordinary Violence." *Modern Theology* 35, no. 4 (2019): 638–62.

———. "The Business of War in Latin America." In *The Business of War: Theological and Ethical Reflections on the Military-Industrial Complex,* edited by James McCarty, Matthew Tapie, and Justin Barringer. Eugene, Ore.: Cascade, forthcoming.

Whitfield, Teresa. *Paying the Price: Ignacio Ellacuría and the Murdered Jesuits of El Salvador*. Philadelphia: Temple University Press, 1994.

Will, Emily Wade. *Archbishop Óscar Romero: The Making of a Martyr*. Eugene, Ore.: Resource, 2016.

Williams, Robert G. *Export Agriculture and the Crisis in Central America*. Chapel Hill: University of North Carolina Press, 1986.

Wilson, Everett Alan. "The Crisis of National Integration in El Salvador, 1919–1935." Ph.D. diss., Stanford University, 1970.

Wood, Elisabeth Jean. *Insurgent Collective Action and Civil War in El Salvador*. New York: Cambridge University Press, 2003.

Woodward, Kenneth L. *Making Saints: How the Catholic Church Determines Who Becomes a Saint, Who Doesn't, and Why*. New York: Simon and Schuster, 1996.

World Handbook of Political and Social Indicators: Cross-National Attributes and Rates of Change. Vol. 1. Edited by Charles L. Taylor and David A. Jodice. New Haven, Conn.: Yale University Press, 1983.

Wright, Scott. *Óscar Romero and the Communion of the Saints: A Biography*. Maryknoll: Orbis, 2009.

Yoder, John Howard. "Fuller Definition of 'Violence.'" Goshen Biblical Seminary, March 28, 1973.

Blood in the Fields: Óscar Romero, Catholic Social Teaching, and Land Reform
was designed in Inka with Impact and Hypatia Sans display type and composed
by Kachergis Book Design of Pittsboro, North Carolina. It was printed on
55-pound Natural Offset and bound by Maple Press of York, Pennsylvania.